BUILDING ZION

ARCHITECTURE, LANDSCAPE, AND AMERICAN CULTURE SERIES
Katherine Solomonson and Abigail A. Van Slyck, Series Editors

Medicine by Design: The Architect and the Modern Hospital, 1893–1943
Annmarie Adams

Building Zion: The Material World of Mormon Settlement
Thomas Carter

Little White Houses: How the Postwar Home Constructed Race in America
Dianne Harris

Manhood Factories: YMCA Architecture and the Making of Modern Urban Culture
Paula Lupkin

Fallout Shelter: Designing for Civil Defense in the Cold War
David Monteyne

Designing the Creative Child: Playthings and Places in Midcentury America
Amy F. Ogata

Women and the Everyday City: Public Space in San Francisco, 1890–1915
Jessica Ellen Sewell

194X: Architecture, Planning, and Consumer Culture on the American Home Front
Andrew M. Shanken

A Manufactured Wilderness: Summer Camps and the Shaping of American Youth, 1890–1960
Abigail A. Van Slyck

The Architecture of Madness: Insane Asylums in the United States
Carla Yanni

BUILDING ZION

The Material World of Mormon Settlement

THOMAS CARTER

ARCHITECTURE, LANDSCAPE, AND AMERICAN CULTURE SERIES

University of Minnesota Press
Minneapolis
London

The University of Minnesota Press gratefully acknowledges financial assistance provided for the publication of this book from the University Research Committee at the University of Utah and the Charles Redd Center for Western Studies at Brigham Young University.

Published by the University of Minnesota Press
111 Third Avenue South, Suite 290
Minneapolis, MN 55401–2520
http://www.upress.umn.edu

LIBRARY OF CONGRESS CATALOGING-IN-PUBLICATION DATA
Carter, Thomas.
Building Zion : the material world of Mormon settlement / Thomas Carter.
(Architecture, landscape and American culture series)
Includes bibliographical references and index.
ISBN 978-0-8166-8956-9 (hc) — ISBN 978-0-8166-8957-6 (pb)
1. Mormon architecture—West (U.S.). 2. Cultural landscapes—West (U.S.). 3. Zion (Mormon Church). I. Title.
NA725.C37 2015 720.88'289378—dc23
2014032696

Printed in Canada on acid-free paper

21 20 19 18 17 16 15 10 9 8 7 6 5 4 3 2 1

For Jan

Pr [Heber C.] Kimball arose and . . . spoke of the facilities of this Valley. Said he liked this place also said if the people or Saints would be faithful in all their callings and to those who control in this Church and Kingdom, they will have power to make it a fruitful Valley; showed how to obtain the blessings of the earth that is by faith and works.

—Manti Ward General Minutes, April 28, 1853

CONTENTS

Preface xi

Note on Illustrations xv

INTRODUCTION
A Landscape of Difference xvii

1 FAITH AND WORKS
A Historical Framework 1

2 THE SETTLEMENT MATRIX
Towns and Temples 23

3 ACCORDING TO NEED
Family Stewardships and the Distribution of Resources 64

4 FRONTIER FASHION
Domestic Architecture and Individual Display 93

5 POLYGAMY AND PATRIARCHY
Women in the Landscape 134

6 BUSINESS AS USUAL
The Americanization of the Mormon Main Street 175

7 MEETINGHOUSES
The Search for Mormon Identity 209

8 MANSION ON THE HILL
The Temple as Ritual Space 240

CONCLUSION
The Enduring Zion 274

Acknowledgments 285

Notes 289

Index 323

PREFACE

> What I find encouraging are signs that at last some historians are beginning to look at artifacts as sources of ideas about a whole range of topics that are just now coming into prominence.
>
> —*Cary Carson, "Doing History with Material Culture," in* Material Culture and the Study of American Life

MANY YEARS AGO I was asked to give a lecture on nineteenth-century Mormon housing at the annual Fife Folklore Conference in Logan, Utah. As a graduate student at Indiana University's Folklore Institute, I had just started a dissertation on Mormon architecture in Nauvoo, Illinois, so this opportunity to speak more generally seemed a good way to collect my thoughts. My conclusion that day went like this:

> While miners and Oregon-bound pioneers spread out over the land, the force of religious conviction and strong leadership impelled the LDS movement ever inward. In other areas of the West, the Eastern [American] social structure broke down, even if only momentarily, and produced a heterogeneous housing style. Compared to the architectural hodgepodge of a mining town or ranch community, the Mormon landscape, in its controlled continuity with the East, stands in striking contrast. Removing ourselves, standing back to take a broader look, we see order juxtaposed with chaos, a well-behaved family–agrarian landscape [set] in relief against a hell-for-leather, male-dominated, boomtown backdrop. The Mormon experience [in the West] is unique, and the domestic architecture shows it. Not because all the houses look the same—though they do present a unified front in terms of appearance—but because they are here at all. Once the group was safely nursed along the trail and settled down in the Great Basin, the eastern emphasis on housing conformity merely reinstated itself. Church prescription of house types, official and unofficial, was unnecessary. These people were not western adventurers. They were solid citizens who, accustomed to certain amenities of life, naturally hoped to continue their previous lifestyle. The Mormon landscape is in the West, but not of it.[1]

For those in the audience expecting something more sensational, such as the unveiling of a uniquely Mormon approach to housing, the idea that all I could say on the topic was that it was pretty normal did not sit well. The fact is, though, thirty years and what seems like a lifetime of looking at old Mormon buildings later, I am led to the same conclusion: the domestic architecture of

Mormons in Utah is best understood as the western extension of mainstream American architectural styles and practices. As we shall see, continuities can be as telling as deviations, but they do not stir people's emotions in quite the same way. With the obvious exception of several large dormitory-like dwellings built by leaders of the Church of Jesus Christ of Latter-day Saints for their multiple wives, one would be hard pressed to single out a Mormon house (even ones built for polygamous families) in an architectural lineup. When fashions changed in the "States," the Mormons simply changed along with them and often not all that belatedly.

That there is more to the Mormon architectural story must be obvious, otherwise there would be no need for this book. When I discovered that little fieldwork-based research existed on Mormon housing in Utah, the focus of my dissertation shifted from Illinois to the Great Basin, and after a survey of possible study areas, I settled on the Sanpete Valley of east-central Utah. This area was not only rich in historic Mormon architecture but also small enough to be documented in detail. From the outset I knew that the little square houses I was learning about so thoroughly were embedded in an incredibly complex social world that contained many other buildings, including stores, meetinghouses, and, most important, temples. After rigorously studying the residential architecture, I faced the question of how the temples, some of the most culturally "other" buildings in the United States, fit into the puzzle that was the Mormon nineteenth-century landscape. The temples with their spires and secret rituals stood apart from the predictably American-style housing (Figure P.1), but how could the normative quality of the housing be reconciled with the radical "this isn't Kansas anymore" posture of the temples? How could these two seemingly contradictory architectures coexist? This question drove the project forward.

I started this book at the beginning of my teaching career, and I am finishing it in my academic twilight years. Had I completed it earlier, however, I believe I would have missed much of what is important. My central thesis is that rather than competing with each other, or stemming from deep inconsistencies or contradictions within the culture, the two sides of the Mormon landscape, "the temple and the house" (to borrow Lord Raglan's ancient duality),[2] were creatively combined to give the Latter-day Saints two elements essential for their survival: from the temples came an *otherness* that staked out a distinctive and decidedly Mormon religious identity, and from the houses (and other normative aspects of the landscape) came an *orthodoxy* that allowed them to fit rather seamlessly into mainstream American culture.

Telling the story of how they achieved this bifurcated structure is the point of this book, but the basic process, as I understand it, was not that hard. First, the sacred rituals of the church were closeted within the walls of

Figure P.1. The temple in Manti, Utah, close to completion (circa 1888), with typical houses in the foreground. Photograph by George Edward Anderson. Courtesy of the Church History Library, Church of Jesus Christ of Latter-day Saints.

the temples, and then the temples were moved out of the town center. Clear distinctions were drawn between the sacred (and secret) *other* from the profane (and public) *norm,* an arrangement that allowed the Saints to maintain an alternative stance (necessary to attract converts) while embracing core values (necessary to keep them). I often joke with friends about how the Saints cleverly "lowered the bar" so that being a Mormon in the nineteenth century was not too difficult (say, in comparison to being Amish or a Shaker, which required renouncing the comforts of a bourgeois lifestyle). Polygamy, the practice by Mormon men of marrying multiple wives, would remain a flash point until it was all but abolished in 1890, but in regard to Mormonism's accommodation with American culture, the landscape led the way.

What follows is the story of how the Sanpete Valley Saints laid out their towns, built their buildings, and made a home for their new religion. As much as possible, the goal is to blend straightforward chronology and the recounting of relevant names and dates with a deeper concern for the inner workings of the collective mind (what the French call *mentalité*) of the place. I tried to be open to new theories and points of view, and to include a wide range of landscape elements, while searching for the subtle genius that made the place understandable to its nineteenth-century inhabitants. A landscape history approach to the Mormon past is new, since town plans and building types are not traditional documents of historical writing. My hope is that this perspective presents fresh ideas and offers another way of looking at the history of this intriguing American subculture.

At one time I thought that a landscape properly studied would speak for itself, that the historian's role was primarily that of mouthpiece, a device through which the people of the past could speak directly to present-day readers. Of course, the more I listened to what was being said the more I recognized I was hearing my own voice. It is important to emphasize that the narrative is mine—this is my story of a people and the material world they built. Along the way, I got to know them well. I spent long hours in the spaces they occupied; I read their journals and diaries; I heard them speak in the minutes of church meetings; I know where they were born, how big their families were, what they did for a living, how much they were worth on the tax rolls, when they died, and where they are buried. Through fieldwork, I met and talked with their children and their children's children. Doing vernacular landscape history is like being a door-to-door salesman: you knock on doors and try to explain in less than a minute what you're selling (which is your project), hoping folks will let you in to measure their buildings. This familiarity brought a great deal of empathy but little definitive knowledge of what these past people were thinking or feeling as they created their version of the City of Zion. Such reflection rarely makes it into print, nor is it explicit in the landscape, so historians must fill in this aspect of their lives, inferring motives and deciphering meanings from evidence left behind, which here includes temples and houses as well as words.

My not being a Mormon made my task more challenging, but not because my access to important buildings or documents was restricted as an "outsider." Just the opposite was true. The Latter-day Saints I talked with over the course of the project were courteous and helpful, even a bit amused by my attempts to write their history. My trouble as a non-Mormon (a "Gentile" in local parlance) stemmed from knowing practically nothing about the group or its beliefs when I began my study. Starting from scratch on such a complicated topic proved rather intimidating. Both sides of my family came west in the late 1840s and early 1850s as Mormons, but they quickly left the church. What caused my people to part ways with their people is a long story, but it happened so long ago that no one in my family bothered to speak of it. As a child growing up in Salt Lake City, I was just another Gentile and never thought for a moment that one day I would be reading the Book of Mormon. My involvement in the field of Mormon studies surprised my parents, and certainly it was not a path I intentionally chose. I was drawn to the buildings, and they ultimately led me to this book.

Yet the Zion-making proposition is intriguing. How many people have the opportunity to invent a new world? This is precisely what these Mormon pioneers did, and I increasingly found this world-building idea compelling, wondering if we moderns could learn from their trials and tribulations. This book owes much to an abiding curiosity about the social world the Latter-day Saints constructed in the Intermountain West during the second half of the nineteenth century. If this was their ideal society, what did it look like? How did it work? The story has been told before, but perhaps never in this way.

NOTE ON ILLUSTRATIONS

THE MAJORITY OF DRAWINGS in this book are based on original fieldwork conducted in the Sanpete Valley of Utah during a period of ten years, from 1978 to 1988. An assortment of colleagues, friends, and students assisted me in this work. University of Utah graduate student Cory Jensen transformed many of the field sheets into measured pencil-on-vellum drawings and helped conceptualize several of the diagrams. In all but a few instances, James Gosney, now a graduate student in the University of Delaware's preservation studies program, inked the final drawings. His artistic touch and eye for detail immeasurably improve the book.

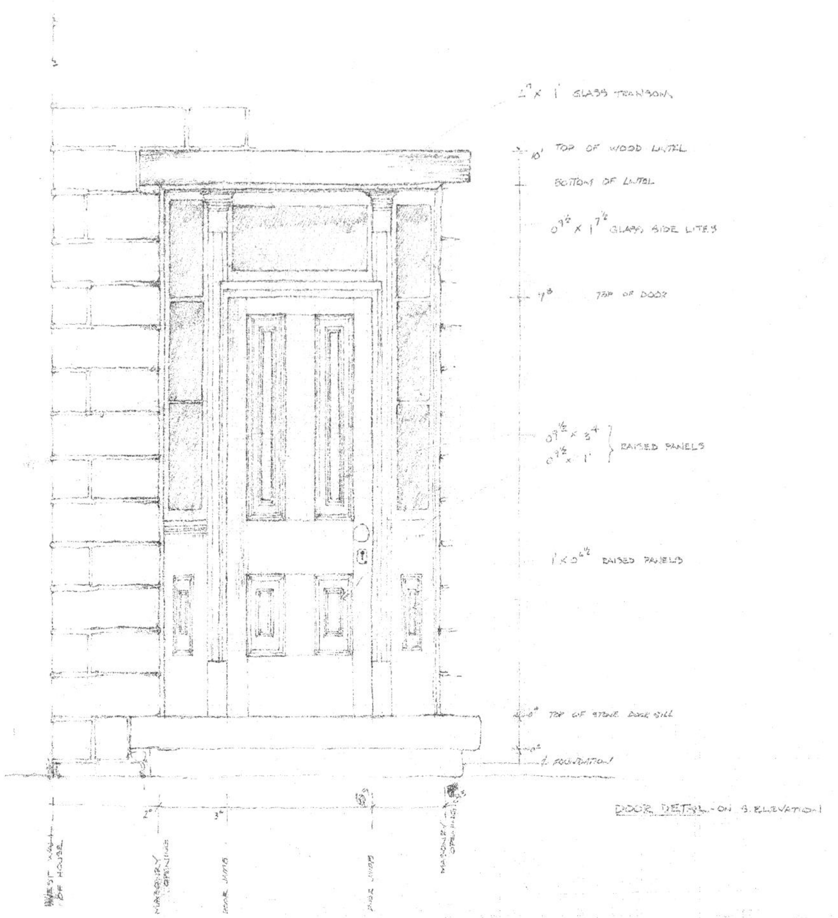

Vernacular architectural research depends on the in situ drawing of historic buildings. The documentation process begins with measured field sketches like this one by graduate student Jack Brady, completed on July 7, 1993. It gives the front door dimensions for the Henry Parsons family house, 304 West, 200 North, Manti, Utah, circa 1860. Cory Jensen and James Gosney later turned these kinds of pencil sketches into the finished inked drawings printed in this book.

The key to reading the plan drawings is as follows: first period is indicated by open space; second period, by cross-hatching; and third period, by stippling. All other later additions are noted by single lines.

Except where credited otherwise, the photographs are mine.

Seven photographs by George Edward Anderson in the book show reversed writing at the bottom of the image. Anderson labeled his glass plate negatives on the back, and that writing is appearing here; the images have been properly reproduced.

All field sheets, final drawings, and photographs are deposited in the Western Regional Architecture Program files in the Special Collections section of the University of Utah's Marriott Library. They have been reprinted here with permission.

INTRODUCTION
A LANDSCAPE OF DIFFERENCE

> A revolution that does not produce a new space has not realized its full potential; indeed it has failed in that it has not changed life itself.
>
> —*Henri Lefebvre,* The Production of Space

On April 25, 1877, LDS Church president Brigham Young and a small band of followers climbed the hill above the town of Manti, Utah, to dedicate the site for a new Mormon temple. A cold wind blew rain from the northwest; the audience waited, huddling for warmth. Young's voice soon rose against the darkening sky:

> We dedicate this ground on which we now are, which has been surveyed for Temple purposes, we dedicate the spur of the mountain of which it is a part, and we dedicate the mountain itself and the valley round about to the name and service of the Lord. We dedicate also the land occupied by our brethren for farming purposes, for gardens and orchards. Cause that the same may be blessed, that it may bring forth in abundance for the sustenance and comfort of the people. We also dedicate unto thee the habitations of thy people, that they may be the sanctuaries of peace and happiness. But especially do we dedicate unto thee this ground, on the Southeast corner of which we now kneel, for the purpose of building a Temple unto thy most holy name, and we ask that it may be made holy, that the rock and the soil and every part and portion of it may be sanctified for this purpose.[1]

As Young's prayer ended, the storm deepened and the crowd dispersed. His words lingered on, drifting across the freshly plowed fields, down the tree-lined streets of the growing city, and into houses filled with Saints eager to take on this new building project. For the Mormon faithful, the Lord's plan was clear. Their mission, and the reason they had left their homes in the eastern United States, the British Isles, and Scandinavia, was to establish a Kingdom of God in the mountain valleys of the Great Basin West. The cornerstone of the Kingdom was the City of Zion, a community whose literal realization, they believed, would bring about the Second Coming of Christ and usher in the eagerly awaited millennium. Temples like the one at Manti were key elements in the City of Zion, but they were, as Brigham Young's dedicatory prayer makes clear, only pieces in a larger material construct that joined all aspects of the built environment—towns, farms, houses, stores, meetinghouses, and temples—into a collective whole, a human landscape shaped on religious principles (Figure I.1).

Building Zion tells the story of the making of the human landscape that was the City of Zion in the Sanpete Valley of central Utah (Figure I.2). The timeline for the narrative begins in 1849, with the founding of the first Mormon settlement at Manti in the southernmost part of the valley, and ends with the completion of the monumental temple above that city in 1888, an event that effectively signaled the closing of the initial or "Kingdom Building" phase of the valley's history. Although a peripheral colony, located 120 miles south and east of the "core" Mormon settlements in and around Salt Lake City, the Sanpete Valley, containing ten principal towns (Figure I.3)—Manti (1849), Ephraim (1853), Spring City (1853), Mount Pleasant (1859), Fairview (1859), Moroni (1859), Fountain Green (1859), Wales (1861), Sterling (1865), and Chester (1870)—makes a worthy subject for investigation. It was settled early, the second Mormon colony outside Salt Lake City; it lay beyond the sphere of non-Mormon or Gentile influence, making it a relatively "pure" example of the Zion-making process; it contained all the major components of the Mormon landscape, including a temple; and finally, it retained much of its original architectural character into the 1970s when the major portion of the field research for this book was completed (Figure I.4).

A book about the material world of early Mormonism is long overdue. While the towns, temples, and meetinghouses have received their fair share of attention from urban and architectural historians,[2] and cultural geographers

Figure I.1. Manti City, Utah, from the southwest, circa 1888. Photograph by George Edward Anderson. Reprinted by permission from Utah State Historical Society; all rights reserved.

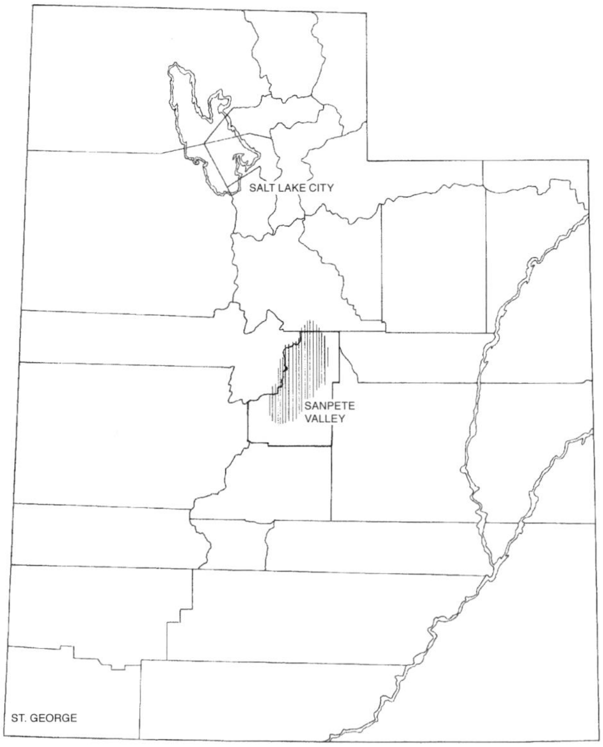

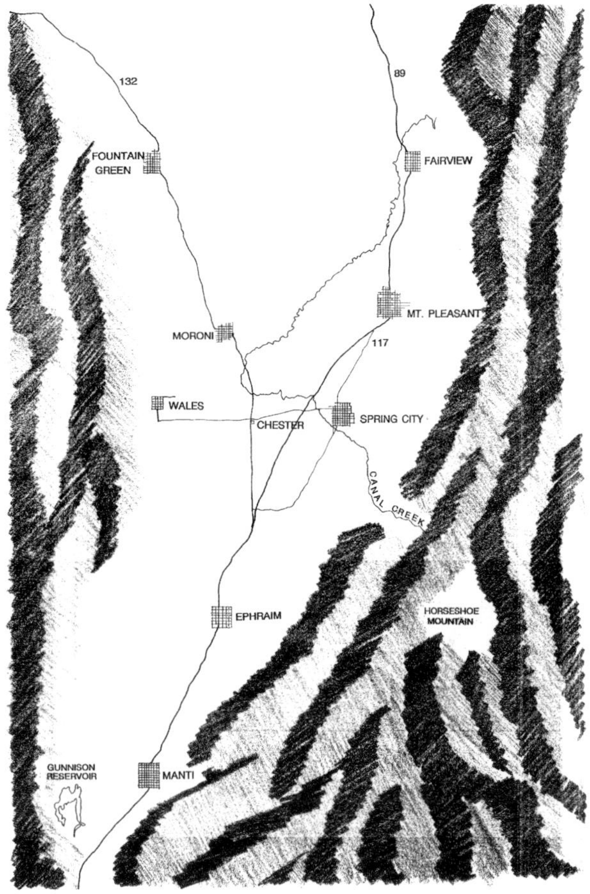

Figure 1.2 ***(left).*** The shaded area in this map of Utah shows the location of the Sanpete Valley study area.

Figure 1.3 ***(above).*** This map of the Sanpete Valley highlights its principal towns and sheltering mountain ranges. The Wasatch Plateau lies to the east and rises to a height of nearly eleven thousand feet; the lower Sanpitch Range is on the west, to the left in the drawing. Map by Julie Osborne.

long ago identified a set of building types and settlement features that could be used to map the contours of a Mormon western culture region (Figure 1.5),[3] no one has approached the built environment of the City of Zion in a comprehensive fashion, treating it as a functioning system of social, economic, and cultural relations. One reason for this failure is the immense size of the Mormon-settled area in the Great Basin West, which includes not only all of Utah but also parts of Colorado, Arizona, Idaho, and Nevada (Figure 1.6). In all, there are over three hundred early Mormon settlements, each with its own set of historic resources. Given the magnitude of the undertaking, it is little wonder that few have been willing to tackle it, and it is why this book confines itself to one small part to see the landscape, not as a collection of specific towns and buildings, but as a socially constructed world where the whole is more than the sum of its parts.[4]

Judging from their writings, the Saints seem to have seen things this way. God tells the prophet Joseph Smith to "keep my commandments, and seek to *bring forth and establish the cause of Zion*";[5] Article Ten in the LDS Church's Articles of Faith reads: "We believe in the literal gathering of Israel and in the restoration of the Ten Tribes; that *Zion will be built upon this [the American]*

Figure I.4. View of Manti City from the south, circa 1978.

continent";[6] Apostle Orson Pratt reminds the faithful in a sermon that they were a "people who shall have their abiding place in the mountains, and *who shall build a city that shall be called Zion*";[7] and Danish farmer Hans Jensen Hals in his daybook describes putting up his house and harvesting his crops, concluding that he was "happy to do good for the *upbuilding of the Kingdom [Zion] in Manti*" (emphases added).[8] Zion making, not building individual temples, meetinghouses, or houses, stood at the center of the Mormon restoration project. When ancient Christian principles once again had a home on earth, then and only then would Christ return and bestow his blessings on mankind. Build it and He will come was the idea.

But what got built? What was the City of Zion like as an actual place? Answering these and related questions is the goal of this book. The intention is to present a detailed account of the Zion-making process as it played out in one representative area of the Mormon-settled West. The human landscape fashioned by the Sanpete Valley Latter-day Saints followed a pattern of experimentation and invention that was generally typical of Mormon western settlements, both big and small, and thus gives us a reliable read on the City of Zion as a going concern. It is important to remember that no overarching blueprint existed within the LDS Church for laying out towns or designing

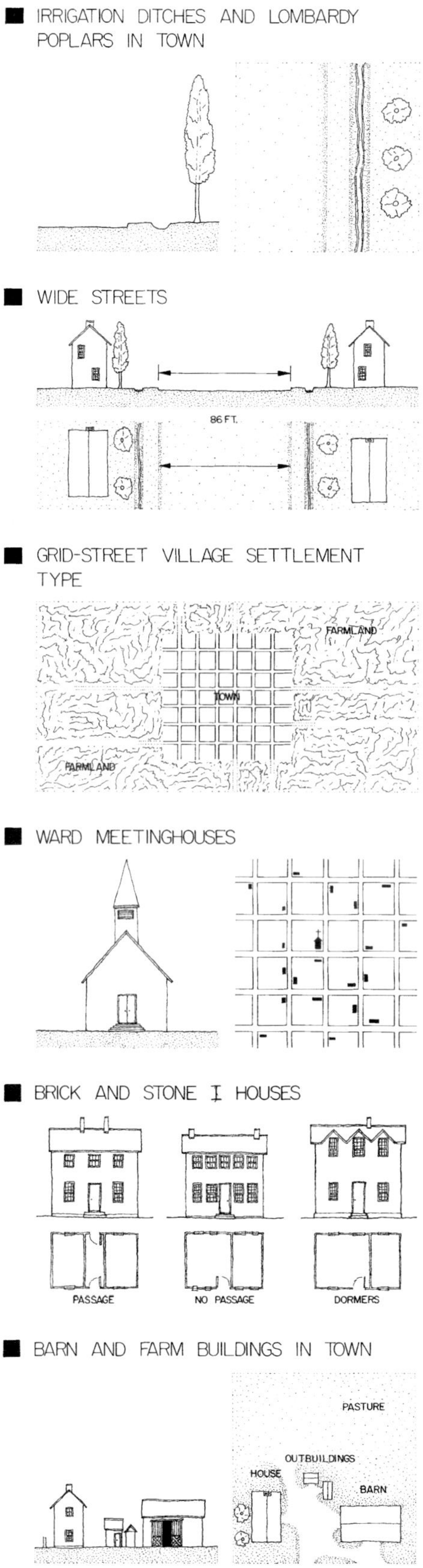

Figure I.5. Landscape elements in the Mormon culture region. These are the principal landscape features used in identifying Mormon settlements in the Great Basin.

Figure I.6. The Mormon-settled "culture region" in the western United States (after D. W. Meinig, "The Mormon Culture Region").

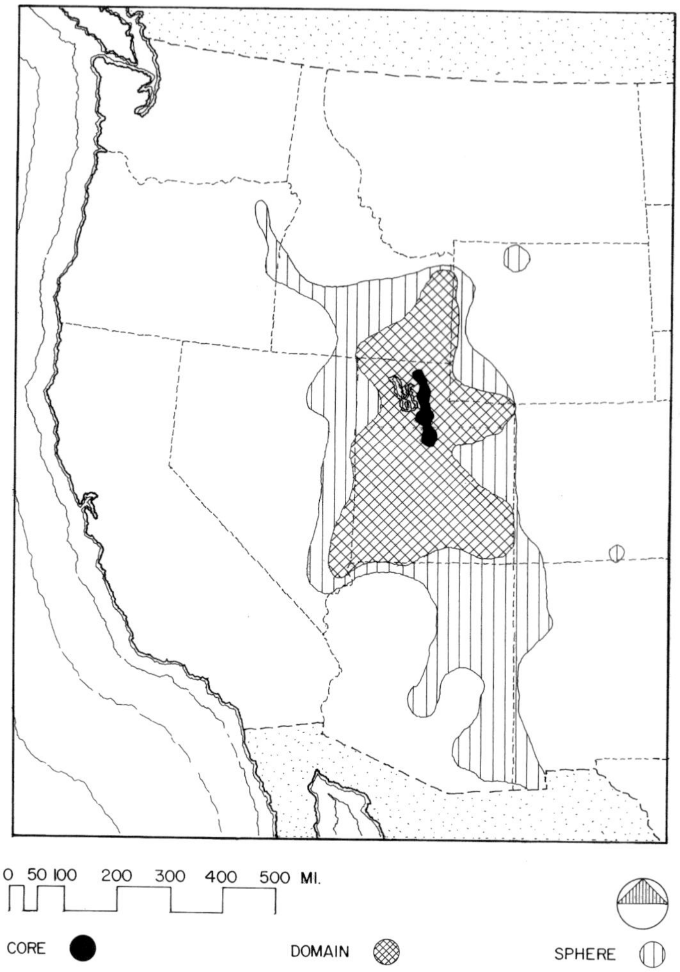

buildings. In the early 1830s, the prophet Joseph Smith developed a plat for the City of Zion for the Mormon settlements in Missouri, but the plan was never fully implemented, nor was it later adopted in Illinois or Utah. Smith's successor, Brigham Young, never felt obligated to speak of it or supply a replacement document.[9] In fact, the more closely one looks at the Zion-making process, the clearer it becomes that the whole enterprise depended on a rather loose though widely agreed upon acceptance of planning principles such as having nucleated village-type towns, centrally placed meetinghouses, and houses built of permanent materials like brick or stone, but beyond that, the proposition seems to have been rather wide open, with the Saints in each community working independently (albeit with ample advice and counseling from Young) on what was largely a trial-and-error basis. The result was a Mormon landscape style that displayed a degree of diversity (within the structure of gridded town) and came into being slowly, achieving a degree of stability only during the 1870s and early 1880s.[10]

The book begins and ends with chapters on history; chapter 1 places the local landscape within the larger framework of nineteenth-century Mormon thought, while the conclusion suggests ways this story contributes to a better understanding of Mormonism's formative years in the American West. In between are chapters on the principal components of the Sanpete Valley landscape. In chapter 2, the focus is on the history of towns and town planning; chapter 3 looks at the distribution of resources, particularly land and water, and the composition of individual family homestead lots; in chapter 4 it is houses that are of concern and the way these buildings conveyed ideas of gentility and class status; chapter 5 extends the domestic architecture discussion to houses constructed for polygamous families while exploring generally the place of women within LDS society; chapter 6 not only takes in the various buildings found along main street, from church tithing offices to privately owned stores to public buildings like schools and city hall, but also shows how the landscape became divided into distinct sacred and secular zones; chapter 7 concentrates on the meetinghouses and how architectural style was employed in the service of group affiliation and identity; and in chapter 8 the discussion moves to what must be considered the Sanpete Zion makers' crowning achievement, the temple on the hill above Manti. The temple not only is the largest and most impressive building in the valley, it also serves as a kind of summary statement, a building in which the various symbolic trajectories meet to form a single stream of social and cultural meaning.

Landscape History

The Sanpete incarnation of the City of Zion landscape may be viewed as an assortment of roads, fields, towns, and buildings, but if we want to use it as a vehicle for doing history then we must also accept it as the product of ideas people had about how their social world would be constituted. Mircea Eliade, in his book *The Sacred and the Profane,* notes that "establishment in a particular place, organizing it, inhabiting it, are acts that presuppose an existential choice—the choice of the universe one is prepared to assume by 'creating' [that place]."[11] Nineteenth-century Mormons faced such a choice: in building up their City of Zion in the sparsely populated Great Basin, they had the opportunity to create a symbolic universe of their own design, not only one that reflected in its physical form their core beliefs about what an ideal religious community should be but also one that put these beliefs on display as the tangible reality of everyday life. In this sense, Zion was both a metaphysical proposition about human salvation and a literal place where this proposition would be built and tested. It is the fundamental connection between these two entities, the conceptual Zion and the material Zion, that must be of greatest concern.[12]

Effective social life depends upon the knowledge people have of the symbolic world they inhabit. Such knowledge comes from a number of sources: oral tradition, formal education, scripture, and to an extent not always appreciated, one's experience of the built environment. The human landscape—the human-produced environment—functions didactically to externalize the ideas, values, and beliefs of the group.[13] It becomes a metaphor, a "way of conceiving of one thing [the Mormon concept of the ideal community] in terms of another [the physical reality of the community itself], and its primary function is understanding."[14] A person's ability to comprehend such a symbolic system, to read the landscape metaphorically, is part of an ongoing process of objectification, or symbolization, which involves, as architectural historian Dell Upton has pointed out, the simultaneous acts of "constructing and construing." The social reality is *constructed,* he opines, as a system of signs that must constantly be interpreted or *construed* by its makers and users. It is how people interpret the landscape, or more precisely, how they subjectively invest it with meaning, and not the landscape itself that allows communication.[15]

Inserting ourselves into past symbolic processes is not easy, but it is doable if we are willing to privilege in our analysis the act of production over its products. Material culture study (landscape history is a subfield) is based on a relatively simple cause-and-effect formula whereby the effect, the end product, is known, but the causes, the ideas that lay behind it, must be discovered.[16] In a number of essays, folklorist Henry Glassie has shown that artifacts of all kinds, from the grandest to the most common, result from choices people make about their form, construction, and use (and reuse). Such choices are structured, Glassie explains, both by what makers know how to do (competence) and what they are able to do, given the constraints imposed upon them by their immediate context (performance). From a repertoire of possibilities, particular elements are selected that most satisfactorily meet the community's building needs. By viewing the landscape in this way, not as a static object, but as the dynamic outcome of a series of mental operations, it is possible for us to see people "constructing and construing," placing value in the things they are designing and building. Choices are made from a set of alternatives, and when people favor one solution over another, a particular value is expressed. In this way, the analyst follows the process that led to the object's creation and use: we walk through the decisions that confronted past designers and experience again, albeit vicariously, the things they found workable and desirable—expressive of an emerging Mormon identity.[17]

For the purposes of this study, I view landscape production taking place simultaneously at two levels, one social and the other cultural. The first is more transparent and exists at the observable level of sign. People communicate most readily through the production and use of explicit signs that function to organize the group along class, racial, ethnic, religious, and gender lines, to mention a few of the many possible structuring categories. Here interpretation links objects directly and empirically to concepts. For example, in many societies building *size* announces financial success, and since the wealthy usually have the biggest houses, the architectural landscape syllogistically reinforces the idea that bigger is more expensive and therefore better; building *location*—where a particular building is situated within a community—also communicates status, for proximity to centers of power and the sources of power is often considered strategic; building *types* such as houses, stores, schools, and churches are associated with specific residential, commercial, educational, or religious functions, and speak to a need within the group for readily distinguishable "marked" spaces; and finally, building *styles,* through their formal and aesthetic attributes, convey important information about group identity, affiliation, and difference. Again, these landscape features are the valued-added manifestation of ideas and reveal a great deal about what their makers and subsequent users felt was appropriate. The social landscape—folklorist Bernard Herman calls it "social topography"—of a place is easily understood if rarely noticed, since it is often lost in the routines of everyday life.[18]

A second kind of interpretation occurs when explicit signs are linked to deeper and more abstract exegetical concepts that reside at the cultural level of the human mind. Culture may be defined as the underlying values, beliefs, and ideologies of a particular social group. It informs all social actions, guiding behavior, determining choices, and providing meaning, for symbolization at the deeper cultural plane integrates the disparate meanings of observable social realities into stories that lend credence to the perceived world. Every society, from the most primitive to the most modern, has these validating stories, which are expressed, when they are verbalized at all, in the form of myth. Myth is a potentially misleading word, since it is so often equated with "falsehood" or "superstition." Yet when used anthropologically to refer to the etiological or "origin" stories that help people explain where they come from, what their beliefs and values are, and how they should behave, the word has great power. It is through myth, as Upton again reminds us, that people "fuse their surroundings into a meaningful whole."[19]

An example from the Sanpete Valley illustrates how this interpretive process works. We begin with a set of late nineteenth-century buildings found on Ephraim's main street (Figure 1.7). At the social level of sign, the architecture speaks explicitly about function (even without the applied signage):

Figure I.7. Commercial storefronts as sign and symbol: the east side of Main Street, Ephraim, Utah, circa 1890. Reprinted by permission of Utah State Historical Society; all rights reserved.

the square-front designs are typical of commercial establishments throughout the country, and we know by looking at them that these are stores of one kind or another and not, say, houses. At the same time, implicit in the buildings are other, profounder meanings: they are privately owned and operated (separate buildings for individual owners); transactions occur (goods and services are bought and sold); business supports capitalism (as an economic system); and the objective is profit (the pursuit of happiness). All this leads to a supporting mythology of the free market—society is best served by private enterprise, which is grounded in both personal freedom (the opportunity to advance one's condition) and consumerism (the acquisition and display of material things). Because such objects are so commonplace, it is easy to take them for granted and overlook the role they play in publicizing and promoting the ideological systems that make the communities around them work.

A Landscape of Difference

This study unfolds, then, as a series of landscape investigations framed broadly around the question of choice. While it is impossible to fully reconstruct the thought process behind the various town plans and building types, Mormonism's identity as a new religion tells us a great deal. A young church has certain needs, the most salient of which involves finding a way to distinguish itself, to make itself unique. Historian John Gager, in his book *Kingdom and Community,* points out that in "established religions under stable conditions, the main emphasis [within the group] will be on the aspect of world-maintenance, i.e., the processes whereby a given social world is maintained and legitimated for those who inhabit it. But in treating new religions," he continues, "the emphasis will fall on world-construction, i.e., the processes whereby a new world is brought into being and seeks to establish itself in competition with numerous other worlds."[20] For Mormonism to survive and prosper, it had to offer potential converts a new way of being in the world; otherwise why would they bother to join? To do this, as Gager suggests, an alternative program had to be advanced, both metaphysically in terms of theology and physically in the form of a community where people would live the principles of the new order. Of the alternate Mormon theology more will be said later, but it is important here, in laying out a method for analyzing the landscape evidence, to stress the inherently oppositional nature of Zion as an alternative community. Brigham Young put it to the Saints quite simply: "We can make Zion, or we can make Babylon."[21]

Viewing Zion making in places like the Sanpete Valley as a struggle between competing ideologies, one American and the other Mormon, is not, then, a far-fetched or forced proposition. The trouble has been, however, that historians have customarily portrayed the conflict in strictly oppositional terms, with American culture embodying a set of specific values—individualism, free-enterprise capitalism, democratic governance, and the separation of church and state—vigorously contested by the Latter-day Saints, who advocated a social world built on cooperation, socialism, authoritarian governance, and the melding of church and state. From this polarity springs perhaps the most widely known form of explanation in Mormon history—what might be called the "Americanization of Utah for Statehood" thesis.[22] In it the Latter-day Saints are cast as cultural holdouts fighting to maintain their subaltern identity in the face of intense U.S. government pressure to conform to American norms. A number of coercive antipolygamy laws in the 1870s and 1880s, coupled with the coming of the Transcontinental Railroad in 1869–70, an event that effectively ended Mormon isolation, led to what historian Leonard Arrington calls the "great capitulation."[23] Arrington posits that because of these events

> the church no longer offered a geographic and institutional alternative to Babylon. Faith became increasingly separated from community policy, and religion from society. Individualism, speculation, and inequality—once thought to be characteristics of Babylon—were woven into the fabric of Mormon life.[24]

In sacrificing the principles of Zion, according to this view, the Saints were transformed into good (though now also presumably sinful) Americans. The way was paved for Utah's statehood in 1896, a symbolic act of both abdication and acceptance.

Undoubtedly things were tense between the Mormons and their American adversaries, but it is wrong to paint such a contrasting "either/or" portrait.

Arrington himself, in describing the origins of Mormon economic thought, acknowledges its complexity, naming it a blending of a Puritan-based corporate work ethic with the strong individualism of Jacksonian democracy.[25] While seemingly contradictory, these two impulses, one directed toward the well-being of the group and the other toward the individual, appear early on in the development of the church, and much of Mormonism's early history involves negotiating a workable synthesis of these antithetical ideologies. The key words here are "workable synthesis," for if we pay close attention to the social level of landscape production we will see not only the choices the Sanpete Saints made between possible alternatives (Figure I.8) but also how these choices creatively conflated group and individual interests. Central in this action were Mormonism's essential myths: *millennialism, continuing revelation,* and *agency.* These cultural stories are introduced in chapter 1 along with a road map for reading their relative importance through time. It is true that federal action and laws would be needed to break down theocratic church–state institutions and effect the cessation of church-sanctioned plural marriages. And certainly, too, the railroad's presence drew Utah closer to eastern ideas and merchandise. In terms of everyday life, however, the Saints appear to have been quite capable of Americanizing themselves, working not so much against the mainstream as within it, trying on their own to find a way of slipping into the flow while at the same time preserving a sense of their own identity.

Navigating such turbulent water is, of course, an age-old problem, and historically—particularly in Western society—the individual and the material have most often trumped the collective and spiritual. So the fact that the Latter-day Saints faced such a challenge is not surprising. What is unusual and what makes their history so compelling is, first, the innovative nature of

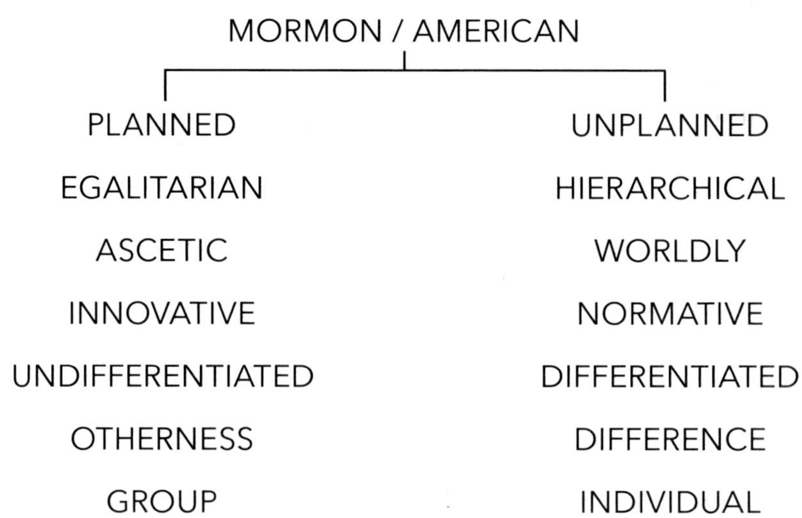

Figure I.8. The decisions faced by nineteenth-century Sanpete Valley Zion makers as a series of "structural oppositions" between Mormon otherness and the American norm. Most choices lay between the extremes. The value of this model is that it underscores the "tendencies" within the community toward a particular type of behavior at a given time.

their solution, one that melded Mormon (corporate) and American (individual) values, and second, that the landscape figured so prominently in bringing it to fruition.[26]

What this means for the study of the Sanpete Valley landscape (and by extension other parts of the far-flung Mormon western empire) is that instead of seeing the City of Zion as an *other* world, a place established in direct opposition to American values (and doomed to destruction), we must accept it as a landscape of *difference,* a social world with strong sacred and secular components that effectively united the new and extraordinary (giving it an identity) with the old and familiar (giving it a chance to survive).[27] Through a series of experimentations and adaptations, the Saints found ways of being both Mormons and Americans. That concessions were made is obvious: over the course of its early history, the church abandoned its initial radical posture, becoming ever more moderate in its social constructions. It is significant, however, that these accommodations never involved outright capitulation nor were they a "post-Manifesto" phenomenon (coming after the 1890 proclamation officially abandoning polygamy). Rather they came as part of the group's natural progression toward viability, shedding part of its strident Mormonness to become another American religious community.

Looking back, two dates are pivotal. The first is 1841, when the Law of Tithing replaced the initial Law of Consecration and Stewardship. In adopting the "lesser law" of tithing, church leaders effectively abandoned communalism and social leveling and reinstituted private enterprise as the cornerstone of the City of Zion society. Theirs, however, was not just any kind of private enterprise, but rather one that mixed Puritan and Yankee virtues. The best name for it is *republican,* a political and social philosophy current in the United States during the late eighteenth and early nineteenth centuries. In addition to its strong antimanufacturing position (associated with Thomas Jefferson's idyllic dream of an agrarian state), republicanism also placed individuals in the service of society, encumbering personal freedom, that is, with a sense of public responsibility and a devotion to the good of the whole. More will be said of this Mormon–republican connection in the concluding chapter. It is enough at this point to say that the union was well under way before the Latter-day Saints arrived in Utah, and it became the basis for the social world constructed there.[28]

The second key date is 1871, when the decision was made to move the temples from the town center to locations just outside town, effectively dismantling what had been a single homogeneous religious world revolving around the temple (all things sacred) and replacing it with a differentiated one with clearly ascribed sacred (temple) and secular (the town and all in it) zones. This was a defining moment in LDS Church history and a date that figures prominently in this book, since it fundamentally changed the way the Utah landscape was organized and understood. In the following pages it will become evident that this move affected some aspects of the landscape more than others. Public components, for instance, such as towns, main street buildings, and meetinghouses, experienced the greatest change, while the private side, mainly the houses (monogamous and polygamous) and city lots, was largely immune, since from the outset there was little to distinguish it from eastern American practices.

Why these changes? Again, it has been easy to blame the Gentiles, the intolerant outsiders, who brought pressure on the Saints to cease their un-American ways, or the railroad, completed in 1869 and extended to Salt Lake City in 1870, which reintroduced the Saints to the material bounty of American capitalist culture. That these were important factors in shaping Mormon actions (and reactions) cannot be disputed, but the point I want to make here is that internal factors cannot be ignored either. For example, the distancing of the Saints from their communistic origins occurred early and stemmed not so much from external forces as it did from a deep-seated aversion to noncapitalistic modes of production (putting it mildly—the Mormons were reluctant revolutionaries). One could argue, too, that the railroad's arrival, although it brought the world closer (especially when it came to consumer goods and fashions), merely facilitated behaviors already under way in Mormon communities rather than causing them.

I believe the best way to account for the changing face of Zion is through the principal Mormon mythologies. It is not unreasonable to think of this early phase of Mormon history (from the church's inception in 1830 to the ending of polygamy in 1890) as a slow transition from the first, the millennial story with its message of the immediacy of the End Times, to the third, the one about personal agency that elevated the role of the individual in all aspects of church life, both sacred and secular. The shift is from a corporate mentality, where a collective group effort is required to prepare the earth for the imminent Second Coming, to the less frantic and more personal one of agency that defers the apocalypse and leaves it to the Saints working on their own to achieve salvation and exaltation. After 1871 and the relocation of the temples, the change becomes more noticeable in the landscape, but when we look at the totality of what got built, it is clear that the diminishing of the first and the ascendency of the third influenced the kind of decisions being made (and may in fact have inspired the one concerning temple placement). It also should be said that the whole cultural process was made possible (and palatable) by the presence of the second myth about continuing revelation. It was this story that lent church members the internal flexibility they needed to accept change.

What follows, then, is a history of a religious landscape gleaned largely from its material evidence. If this seems like a strange place to look for answers about early Mormonism, then we should listen to Saints like LDS Church apostle Orson Hyde. Hyde made his home in Spring City and anticipated the theoretical position taken in this book when he told a gathering of the Saints in 1863 that "public improvements [and by this he was referring to the erection of buildings and the construction of roads] are the index to the hearts of the people."[29] To update him, we might add "minds," public improvements are the index into the *hearts and minds* of the people, but we have to hand it to Hyde, for he recognized long ago what many historians are only now beginning to grasp, that the landscape is powerfully bonded to worldview. In the Sanpete Valley it is possible to see a set of very specific Mormon concepts, both social and cultural, being projected outwardly through the symbolization process as the objective reality of everyday life in Zion. The material world built and used by the Sanpete Latter-day Saints reflected and facilitated Mormon belief and value systems, while at the same time, through the imaginative myths that supported it, it provided Zion with an ideological foundation, conceptually defining what it meant to be a Mormon in the nineteenth century.

1 FAITH AND WORKS
A HISTORICAL FRAMEWORK

> When [we] talk about spiritual things and temporal things we talk about a distinction without a difference.
>
> —*John Taylor, LDS Church President, Sanpete Quarterly Conference, May 20, 1883*

THE MORMON FAMILIES who made their way to the Sanpete Valley after 1849 were a well-traveled and diverse lot. The core group, which included most of the valley's early leaders, came from New England and had been part of the Mormon Church since its founding in Upstate New York during the late 1820s and early 1830s. These converts, like thousands of their friends and neighbors, had left homes in the Northeast for a better life on the opening western frontier. For them, the West at this point meant western New York State, where the availability of land coupled with the completion of the Erie Canal in 1825 had created opportunities for those hoping to improve their circumstances. It was here, too, in the rolling countryside between Albany and Buffalo, that they heard and embraced the "restored" gospel preached by the prophet Joseph Smith Jr., becoming the first members of his Church of Christ, later renamed the Church of Jesus Christ of Latter-day Saints, or simply the Mormon Church, after its principal scripture, the Book of Mormon.[1]

The Smith family, including Joseph Sr., his wife, Lucy, and their eight children, joined the out-migration from New England in 1816. The Smiths moved from their home in Sharon, Vermont, and settled in Palmyra, New York, just east of Rochester. As did the other transplants, they brought with them a tradition of religious skepticism, a questioning of ecclesiastical authority that ignited a series of intense spiritual revivals from which this part of New York State received its name the "Burned Over District," so powerful here were the flames of religious enthusiasm. It was from this milieu that the Smiths' third son, Joseph Jr., emerged as a prophet of God. As a seeker of religious truth, the youthful Joseph prayed for divine guidance in finding the right church to join. In response came what Mormons call the "First Vision." In it Christ told Joseph to shun all existing religions, for the people of the world had "turned aside from the Gospel" and the time of judgment when He would return to "visit them according to their ungodliness" was quickly coming. Further prayer by Smith led to visitations by an angel named Moroni, who gave the soon-to-be prophet a history compiled by his father, Mormon, telling of the flight to the Americas of small groups of Israelites, the civilization they established there, their visitation by Christ following His resurrection, and the internal warfare that ultimately led to their destruction and disappearance.[2]

These early revelations were crucial in Mormonism's initial formulation. On one hand, by proclaiming the apostasy of contemporary Christian churches, the way was paved for the creation of a new religious order whose mission, as Joseph Smith soon found out, was to restore Christ's true church to earth in the last days. On the other, they brought forth the Book of Mormon, a text that not only physically substantiated his claims to divine communion but also contained a prophecy of his own role as leader of the restoration, destined to occur in the New World. The earth lay in a state of sin, and it was Joseph's appointed task to set things straight before it was too late.[3]

Fundamental to the restoration was the establishment of Zion, the earthly abode of God's chosen people. Through revelations came a number of general guidelines—Zion was a place: God tells the Saints to "seek to bring forth and establish my Zion" (1829); an urban place: "And it shall be called the 'New Jerusalem,' a land of peace, a city of refuge, a place of safety for the saints" (1831); and finally an urban place inhabited by the righteous: "let Zion rejoice, for this is Zion—THE PURE IN HEART" (1833)[4]—but nowhere was the City of Zion and the larger landscape that would accompany it clearly prescribed. It would be left to Joseph Smith and his immediate successor, Brigham Young, in their multifaceted roles as prophets, church presidents, city planners, and chief architects, to piece together a coherent plan for its implementation. In this Zion-making work, they were not alone, for many capable assistants with ample experience in laying out towns and putting up buildings surrounded them. Nor were they lacking in spiritual inspiration, for even without a divinely sanctioned plan, church leaders came to the task armed with several key beliefs, drawn from Mormon scripture, around which their city would crystallize.

The first was millennialism, the apocalyptic imperative that provided the underlying raison d'être for the City of Zion project; second was the doctrine of continuing revelation, a belief in the ongoing nature of heavenly intervention that made Mormons uncommonly amenable to the idea of change; the third key belief was a fundamental commitment to human agency, an active, human-centered cosmology wherein individuals became responsible for their own salvation. These faith-based assumptions about the way the world worked gave the westward-moving Saints a set of mythic stories to live and build by, and it is through them that our study of the City of Zion landscape must proceed.

An End Times Landscape

Historian Grant Underwood has rightly argued that the Mormon conceptualization of Zion must be seen as but one part of a larger millennial worldview embraced by the early Latter-day Saints. He describes nineteenth-century Mormon millennialism as a creative reworking of Judeo-Christian eschatology. At its core was an unswerving belief in the imminent apocalypse, the Day of Judgment when God steps in and purifies the earth in a "great reversal" of fortune—the wicked majority is swept away, and the long-suffering but righteous few are elevated to their rightful position of eminence. Unlike most other millennial churches and sects, Mormon scripture did not specify the time of the event, though it was widely believed in the early days that the "winding-up time" would come in 1890.[5]

Tied to a belief in the End Times was the millennium, which in the Judeo-Christian tradition referred to a thousand-year reign of Christ on earth. The millennium is generally perceived as an idyllic, paradisiacal period of existence during which righteousness triumphs over evil and there is universal peace, prosperity, and abundance. For some, Christ would appear only *after* the millennium had run its course. They believed that the millennial had begun and its clock had started ticking with the founding of the Catholic Church, an institution whose role it was to create conditions of paradise throughout the world. For this group, called by scholars *postmillenarians,* the idea of an earthly millennium was largely symbolic, equated with the "spiritual kingdom" of the soul. In another camp were those who placed the advent of the millennium right after Christ's return. For these *premillennialists,* the earthly sojourn of Christ would begin with the Second Coming and the event was taken quite literally: the Son of God would reappear and then reside with his chosen people in a Kingdom of God. After a preliminary judgment of the wicked, the righteous would be resurrected to live at the side of Christ on earth, and it was only at the conclusion of the millennium, on a final day of reckoning, that the wicked would be banished to hell.[6]

Nineteenth-century Mormons generally adhered to premillennialist principles, a position that not only defined their eschatology but also set them at odds with the postmillennialists, who, they believed, had fallen away from the apocalyptic message of early Christianity. When the Saints spoke of Christ's "True Church," they were specifically referring to the primitive apostolic order that existed prior to the institutional rise of Catholicism in the second and third centuries. Believing they held "the same principles, the same doctrines, the same organization of the Church, the same authority that was in the Church in ancient days,"[7] the Latter-day Saints saw themselves principally as a restoration movement charged with bringing back a form of Christianity lost during centuries of first popish and later Protestant apostasy.

In truth, Mormonism is much more. Historian Jan Shipps has shown that Mormon doctrine, while being rooted in early Christian practice, also contains both Hebraic and New World components and must be viewed not as a simple restoration of apostolic primitivism but rather as a "new religious tradition."[8] In Mormonism, Shipps explains, Old Testament features such as Solomonic temples and the plural marriage customs of Abraham, Isaac, and Jacob are combined with New Testament teachings about the atonement of Jesus, baptism, and apostolic governance, and all are placed within a distinctively new "Mormon" belief system that stresses the multiplicity of gods, eternal families, and priesthood ordinations, to name a few of its defining elements.[9] What this means for students of the Mormon landscape is that we must see the "New Jerusalem" not as a city with biblical antecedents but as the product of a contemporary synergy, the coming together of disparate ideas, some old and taken from the scriptures, some typical of nineteenth-century America, and others entirely new revelations suited to specifically Mormon institutions. The goal was to create a community for God's chosen people and a habitation for Christ during the millennium. This work, as we shall see, involved invention as much as it did restoration.

One thing was certain: if there was going to be a City of Zion, the Saints would have to build it. One of the most striking aspects of early Mormon millenarianism was its emphasis on action. For the Latter-day Saints, it was not enough to wait around, expecting the miraculous appearance of Zion at the time of the Second Coming. Quite the reverse was true; Christ would make his entrance only when the Saints themselves had perfected the earth and made it ready for His reign. Speaking in Salt Lake City in 1857, Brigham Young admonished those new arrivals who "gather here with the spirit of Zion resting upon them, expecting to find Zion in its glory, whereas their own doctrine should teach them that they are coming to *make Zion*."[10] Young knew that by rejecting the American Babylon and all its trappings, the Mormons were compelled to fashion a new social order to replace the discarded old one and thereby establish "the moral, social, and political conditions necessary before Christ's return could occur."[11] The Zion-making project revolved around three simultaneous moves: announcing the "restoration" to the world, gathering the chosen out of Babylon, and constructing the New Jerusalem. All commenced immediately after the founding of the church in 1830.[12]

The first missionaries were dispatched to the Western Reserve of New England in northeastern Ohio, and there they succeeded in converting a large group of disaffected Campbellites (followers of Alexander Campbell's primitivist Disciples of Christ Church) near the town of Kirtland, on the southern shore of Lake Erie. A desire to consolidate church membership led Smith to shift his headquarters from Upstate New York to Kirtland in 1831, though he warned that the place would serve as home to the Saints only "for a little season"[13] while he awaited God's naming of the permanent location for the New Jerusalem. The answer came soon in a revelation in June of that year: Missouri, and more specifically the land around the town of Independence in Jackson County, was designated as the gathering place for the Saints, the "land of promise, and the place for the city of Zion."[14] It was further revealed to Smith that Jackson County lay close to the original Garden of Eden, and here Christ would return at the time of the Second Coming. The Saints now had their marching orders, and the trek to Missouri began.

Beginning in the fall of 1831, Mormon agents purchased large tracts of land in both Independence and the surrounding Jackson County countryside, setting up several communities for the hundreds of Saints moving in from Ohio. Hostilities with the non-Mormon population, who feared Mormon political and economic power, began almost immediately. The situation turned violent in the summer of 1833. After a series of skirmishes, the Saints retreated north from Jackson County, relocating in the more sparsely occupied Caldwell County. Again, towns were platted, this time at Far West and Adam-ondi-Ahman, and again, Mormon–Gentile friction ensued. Tempers flared and in 1838 open warfare broke out. It was a short battle, with the Missourians, backed by the state's political establishment, capturing Far West and taking Joseph Smith and other prominent LDS Church leaders into custody. They would be released after a four-month imprisonment, but the Mormon experiment in Eden was over; the main body of Saints moved east that winter, into Illinois, establishing yet another iteration of Zion, this time on the banks of the Mississippi River.[15]

After the Missouri debacle, instead of dispersing—"scattering like sheep" was how Brigham Young phrased it—the dedicated and resilient Saints regrouped and began again their Kingdom-building program.[16] In the early summer of 1839, Smith purchased rights to the town of Commerce, north of Quincy, Illinois, and renamed it "Nauvoo," which he said meant "beauty and repose" in Hebrew. The repose part was apparently ignored, for by the early 1840s, the Saints had laid out their new city, established productive farms in the surrounding town lands, constructed hundreds and hundreds of houses, and started building a temple. With a population of over five thousand, Nauvoo quickly emerged as one of the principal cities on the upper Mississippi (in population size it rivaled Chicago), but success brought trouble; the old conflicts that had plagued the Saints in Missouri once more surfaced. As a unified voting bloc, the Mormons held considerable political leverage, and this, coupled with their exclusionist economic solidarity and Smith's grandiose dreams of a separate Mormon state, placed them at odds with Illinois Gentiles, who saw their presence as a real threat. A tense standoff ensued, with Mormon and Gentile militias armed and ready to fight. All that was needed was a flash point, and this came, curiously, from inside the Mormon community itself over the issue of "celestial marriage."[17]

Undoubtedly the most incendiary practice introduced during the Nauvoo years, and the one most closely associated with Mormonism generally, is polygamy, the taking by Mormon men of more than one wife. Joseph Smith initiated the principle of "celestial marriage," "patriarchal marriage," or simply "the principle" as it was often called, in the early 1840s. There are indications that he intended it to be adopted earlier, but circumstances, mostly a fear of how church members would react, deferred the announcement. When it came, it came secretly, with Joseph privately informing the inner circle of leaders concerning their new marriage responsibilities. Many questioned the practice but were told that the introduction of polygamy was but one part of the general restoration "of all things" pertaining to the "ancient" church. Since the patriarchs of old—men like Abraham, Isaac, and Jacob—had multiple wives, then so should the Latter-day Saints.[18]

They were also made aware that "the principle" was integral to a view of the afterlife that was emerging at the time. LDS Church doctrine holds that salvation is merely the first step toward "exaltation," the highest degree of heavenly glory. One of the requirements for exaltation is celestial marriage, the union of men and women for both "time and eternity." In heaven, families are reunited, and Mormon men who have had more than one wife, whether because of remarrying after a spousal death or divorce, or by having more than one wife through polygamy, will be blessed in the afterlife as great patriarchs ruling over an expanded posterity. Polygamy was one way for Mormon men to carry earthly status into the future.[19]

In Nauvoo, even though the acceptance of patriarchal marriage was never officially announced (an open proclamation would not come until 1852), it was widely enjoined by Smith and other church leaders. Rumors of what was perceived as Mormon lasciviousness abounded within both the Gentile and non-polygamous Mormon populations. Something as sensational as the taking of plural wives, however, could not be kept under wraps for long, and as word got out the news fractured the church, with many members vehemently opposed to such a radical and for them immoral assault on monogamy. An opposition group formed and established a newspaper named (appropriately) the *Nauvoo Expositor,* which denounced the practice. Smith, acting with the support of the city council, responded by closing down the paper and destroying the press, a reactionary act that gave the Gentiles the incentive to crack down on the prophet and his followers. Smith was arrested and jailed in nearby Carthage, where on the night of June 27, 1844, he was murdered by a non-Mormon mob. Following Smith's martyrdom, Brigham Young, who had presided over the Quorum of the Twelve Apostles, seized the reins of church leadership.[20] It was Young who made the decision in 1845 to abandon Nauvoo and begin the westward exodus to the sanctuary of the Great Salt Lake Valley. The Latter-day Israelites were on the move again.[21]

It should be said that through these early, troubled years, the church missionary program went ahead full steam. Gathering the "chosen" out of Babylon remained key to preparing the earth for a second Advent, and after being baptized into the church, all converts were admonished to "come out of the wicked world, from Babylon." No one would be safe from the destructive forces of the apocalypse, Joseph Smith warned, "for after today [the latter days] cometh the burning—this is speaking after the manner of the Lord—for verily I say, tomorrow all the proud and they that do wickedly shall be as stubble; and I will burn them up, for I am the Lord of Hosts; and I will not spare any that remain in Babylon."[22] Because time was short, the intention was never to convert the entire world's population. Rather, the call was to spread the word of the restoration as widely as possible so that an "elect" few could escape and gather to Zion, which would serve as a place of refuge during the coming storm.[23]

Initial proselytizing efforts were limited to the northeastern United States, and through the early 1830s the church displayed a strong New England cultural bias. This homogeneity did not last, for the move to Missouri added to the rolls many converts from the Midwest and South, and then, in 1837, at a time when Mormon fortunes were at perhaps their lowest ebb, Smith sent his most trusted lieutenants to England to open a British Mission. The Mormon Gospel was warmly embraced in England, particularly among the urban populations around London, in the West Midlands, in Lancashire, and later in South Wales; by 1890 nearly fifty-five thousand British Saints had converted and moved to Zion. Beginning in the early 1840s and peaking in the mid-1850s, the arrival of these British converts sustained the church through its two major rebuilding periods following the expulsions from Missouri in 1838 and Illinois in 1846.[24]

The same thing may be said about the decision by Brigham Young in 1850 to establish a Scandinavian Mission. In the years between 1853, when the first contingent of Nordic immigrants arrived in Salt Lake City, and about 1890, when the stream of new LDS converts dried up, Denmark, Sweden, and Norway contributed some twenty-three thousand immigrants to the Mormon population in Utah. These immigrants, like the British Saints before them, arrived at a fortuitous time, providing church leaders with both the numbers and skills to implement successfully a policy of expansion throughout the Great Basin country during the 1860s and 1870s.[25]

An Evolving Landscape

One of the main problems in Mormon landscape studies (and Mormon history generally) is a tendency among scholars to fixate on the City of Zion as a static construct, something set in place during the 1830s as the LDS Church came into existence, and then remaining intact through the settlement years in Utah. Following this line of reasoning, Zion was conceived as a religious utopia—"And the Lord called his people Zion, because they were of one heart and one mind, and dwelt in righteousness; and there were no poor among them"[26]—and when deviations occurred (as they did early and often), they are explained either as a failure on the part of the Saints to live up to their calling or as a capitulation to pressures from governments at every level to drop what were perceived as un-American practices—the "they made us do it" argument.[27] Aspects of both positions are valid, certainly. Backsliding and selfishness were a regular part of life for the Saints, as were the increasingly bitter relations with politicians in Missouri, Illinois, and Washington, D.C., principally over church authority and polygamy, but these views ignore the remarkable ability the Saints had of finding, on their own, a way of being in the world that worked for them in real life. They were religious people, but they were also people with a strong capitalistic spirit, and for the Zion-making project to succeed, the New Jerusalem had to serve both the spiritual and the entrepreneurial sides of the Mormon psyche. The millennial fervor of the 1830s gave way over time to pragmatism, a move that in the end allowed the resilient Saints to solve many of their earthly problems, including the major one about reconciling sacred with profane existence.

If it seems strange to imagine Zion being different things at different times, just remember that nearly everything about the church was in flux during these decades. Whether adding new practices like temple endowments (secret rituals) and celestial marriage (polygamy), or relocating the restoration's center from Ohio to Missouri to Illinois to Utah, or erecting new kinds of buildings like endowment houses and temples, the Saints had to adapt. Some of these changes came as a reaction to persecution, and others can be traced to the inherently experimental nature of inventing a new social world, but remarkably, the majority of Saints took these transmutations as a natural part of God's plan, a flexibility drawn from their belief in the doctrine of continuing revelation.

Mormonism is largely based on the premise that the God of old continues to speak through modern-day prophets, answering questions and providing solutions to current problems. After all, "God, who is the same yesterday, today, and tomorrow, would not reveal His will in the past without being willing to reveal it today."[28] For the Saints the Bible is the word of God, but it is not the last word, and changes in doctrine and even reversals of previously revealed doctrine are considered both normal and even expected occurrences. Pliancy, fortified with a healthy dose of pragmatism, became a hallmark of what historian Leonard Arrington deemed the "Mormon Ethic," a worldview that "profited from implementation of the principle of continuing revelation, which facilitated change and adjustment, made possible an instrumental approach to social and economic problems, and stimulated a social inventiveness that is rare in the history of religion."[29]

Like the church it served, the City of Zion must be viewed as a work in progress, a constantly evolving social world. This is not to say that it lacked direction or purpose, for changes in the way Zion was imagined and executed closely tracked the pattern of change in the religion itself, and followed what religious studies professor Douglas Davies calls a shift from a "Protestant-millenarian Mormonism [to a] symbolic temple Mormonism."[30] For Davies, the church began as a variant of mainstream Protestantism, emphasizing such things as baptism, repentance, salvation, and regular Sunday worship. Then it slowly morphed into a new type of Christianity dominated by secret temple-based rituals and the individual's quest for celestial advancement in the afterlife.[31] The emergence of the new temple-ritual Mormonism began during the Nauvoo period. Up to this point, the focus of attention within the church had been on salvation, the saving of human souls. But in a series of revelations from the early 1840s, Joseph Smith laid out a bold new plan making it possible for Latter-day Saints not only to be saved and stand in the presence of God but also to attain a higher degree of heavenly glory whereby they could achieve godhood in their own right. As already indicated, the ultimate Mormon state of salvation was *exaltation,* and it came only to those who had demonstrated worthiness on earth.[32]

The idea of conquering death is to some extent present in all religions, but visions of the afterlife vary greatly from one denomination to the next. For Mormons, beginning in the Nauvoo years, salvation was increasingly viewed as but one in a series of episodes starting with preexistence, where humans-to-be are created as "spirit children of God the Father." Birth brings a second stage, which is human life on earth, and finally, after death, salvation, and resurrection, comes eternal life in the hereafter. In the Mormon cosmological scheme, heaven is multitiered and hierarchical—there are three levels of eternity: the first, the *telestial,* is synonymous with evil and home to those who rejected the gospel of Christ; the second, the *terrestrial,* is designated for those who have been misled into believing other creeds or remain unwilling to accept the teachings of the restored church; and ultimately the *celestial* level is reserved for those who have embraced the gospel and have lived in faithful obedience to the church and its teachings. In the celestial realm, the crowning distinction of exaltation is given to those who have held the priesthood, performed their ritual ordinances, including their endowments, and have entered into the sacred union of celestial marriage. It should be pointed out, because it has serious implications for understanding the Zion-making process, that exaltation is received in heaven but earned on earth, the product of a person's works, for in Mormonism "each individual gains a reward [in heaven] according to achievement on earth."[33]

Not surprisingly, the coming of temple-ritual Mormonism necessitated changes in City of Zion thinking. For one thing, someone had to figure out what a temple would look like, how it would function, and where it would be located—no small order in and of itself, since there was no clear precedent for such a building. But there were two bigger problems: the first involved finding a way to make room for both sacred and profane existence within the church community; while the second focused on reconciling the church's new emphasis on individual exaltation with an older community-based Protestant sensibility. At stake was the question of Mormon identity itself: in a changing world, how would the Saints construct their "Mormonness"?

Answering this question in terms of the landscape requires paying close attention to modes of cultural definition. One of the principal ways groups, whether ethnically, racially, or religiously motivated, define themselves is through the generation and maintenance of boundaries that separate them from others. Such boundaries are necessarily social and are formed through the identification and display of distinctive traits and qualities that bind the group together while at the same time marking it off as different. Applying this train of thought to Mormonism, Shipps notes that "without boundaries to set them apart, without 'Gentiles' to stand over and against, a chosen people cannot exist; their very identity depends on their perception of specialness; and that specialness, in turn, depends on their being separate in some way from that part of the population that is not special."[34]

Calling themselves out as a chosen people required the Mormons to set up recognizable boundaries between their New Jerusalem and the outside world of Babylon. The first sixty years of Mormon landscape history is the story of how this boundary shifted from the outer edge of the community (from the "body" of the church) to the actual Saints themselves (to the "body" of the individual church member). One way to think of this change is in terms of the community's internal cohesion. In religious societies, as Eliade and others have shown, the inscription of a sacred point, a holy place that is viewed as "wholly different" from the surrounding profane world, establishes a fixed center for the symbolic universe. This center serves as an *axis mundi,* functioning not only as a point of interface between earth and heaven but also quite literally as the axis around which all life revolves. The spatial world becomes knowable to its faithful inhabitants in systemic terms: a sacred center locks all elements of the landscape into a unified orbit, providing both internal cohesion and external boundaries. In this way, group identity is defined in relation to the center, and the dividing line between the sacred and the profane (the "us" versus "them" threshold) lies outside the gravitational field, at the edge of the community.[35]

Contrast this type of unity with a society, either religious or secular, that functions without a clearly inscribed sacred center. Here the power of the axis mundi fails, its strength sapped by the presence of competing spaces, both sacred and profane. In such a contested realm, the systemic unity created by the center gives way to a less cohesive structure that demands differentiation: signs (both literal and figurative) must be placed within the landscape so that inhabitants can successfully negotiate their way through the social topography. For example, when the center is strong and the whole community is considered sacred, a spatial homogeneity results, since there is no need for internal differentiation of elements. But in a contested landscape, the opposite is true: spaces within the landscape, both sacred and profane, must be separated out according to their functions and then clearly marked so they can be easily read—churches have steeples; courthouses, bell towers; and houses, picket fences. Furthermore, with the sacred core compromised, the unity of the group weakens and community boundaries can no longer be kept intact. Rather, they must be erected in more personal ways. The result is a landscape where cultural identity is constructed and maintained by individuals, not the group.[36]

The evolution of the City of Zion landscape is best understood in terms of a move from sacred and undifferentiated to a sacred/secular and differentiated space. What began in the 1830s as a theoretical proposition for an ideal community formed around an ascribed sacred center in Jackson County (Figure 1.1) slowly became, first, a place with no center (Nauvoo), then a place with a new sacred center (Salt Lake City), and then, beginning in the 1870s with the building of regional temples in Utah, a multicentered one consisting of Salt Lake City, St. George, Logan, and Manti, with Jackson County still exerting its distant presence (Figure 1.2). As the conceptualization of Zion changed, so too did the built environment: a group-oriented (corporate) style with a strong center and homogeneous architecture was replaced by a new, more person-driven (individualized) style that had multiple sacred points, relatively equal sacred and profane spatial zones, and a highly differentiated

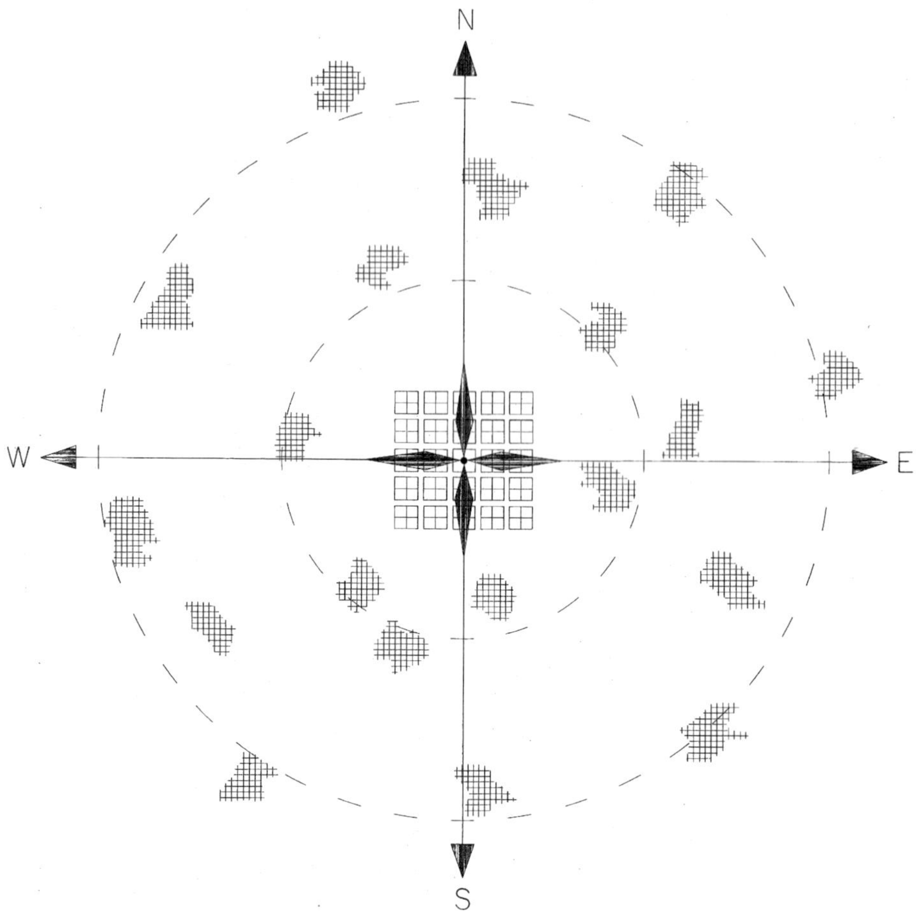

Figure 1.1. The three essential elements of the unified or "theoretical" Zion: centrality (the presence of a sacred center), cardinality (all parts linked orthogonally to the sacred center), and inductance (a religious force field emanating from the sacred center).

approach to building design. From the vantage point of landscape style, four incarnations of the historical Zion may be identified.

The Theoretical Zion, 1830–1841

The perfect world exists if it remains unrealized, and this can be said for the earliest manifestation of the City of Zion, the one that surfaced immediately after the founding of the church. Anthropologist Steve Olsen has used Mormon scripture and church leaders' writings to show how an LDS "ideology of place" coalesced around the ceremonial qualities of *centrality,* whereby the world revolved around the sacred center in Jackson County, Missouri; *cardinality,* by which the various (and often scattered) parts of the Kingdom were linked orthogonally to the sacred center; and *inductance,* which refers to the ability of one aspect of culture, in this case the religious order (grounded in centrality and cardinality) to sympathetically "energize" all aspects of the society. As Olsen describes it, "Zion's ideal urban society would be permeated

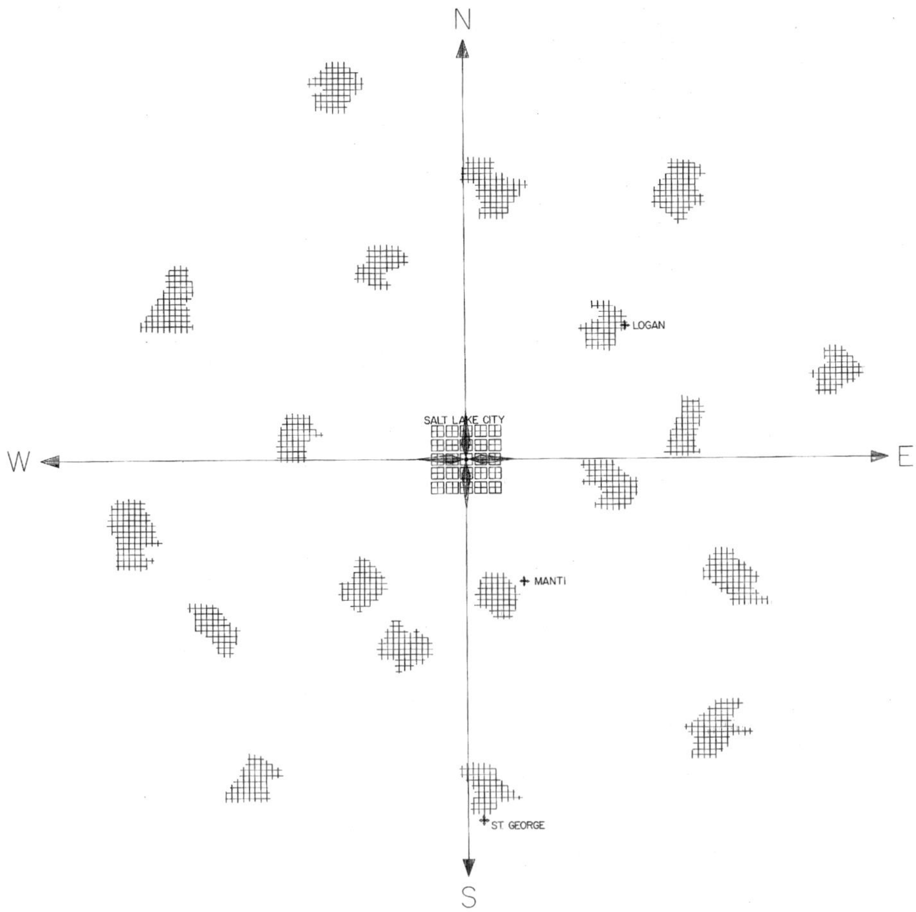

Figure 1.2. By the Utah Period, Zion had lost its idealized form and had assumed a less cohesive structure organized loosely around several center places (Salt Lake City and Jackson County, Missouri) and a number of sacred points (the temples at Salt Lake City, St. George, Logan, and Manti).

by religion. Religion, not the government, would ensure domestic tranquility. Religion, not the military, would provide for a common defense. Religion, not the market, would promote the general welfare."[37]

In its ideal form, Zion was a true sacred landscape: a strong axis mundi integrated all elements—towns, roads, fields, and buildings—into a single coherent system. Explicit internal signs of difference and otherness were unnecessary because such things as a radical theology and an anticapitalistic commitment to social leveling (all property was to be donated to the church and then redistributed according to need) were enough to define the group and separate it from its Gentile neighbors. If this early version of Zion remained largely theoretical—an unrealized plan for an ideal world—it was not for lack of trying. Repeated attempts by Smith to implement his original plan for the City of Zion in a series of Missouri settlements were spoiled by both reactionary neighbors and a general aversion among the Saints to the prospect of wealth redistribution. When they reached Nauvoo, a different approach to building Zion would be attempted.

The Experimental Zion, 1841–1847

The flight from Missouri to Illinois ushered in a second and largely experimental stage in Zion's development. Here, at Nauvoo, with the ideal shattered and the Edenic center abandoned, the Saints began rethinking the basic structure of their New Jerusalem. As already pointed out, new ritual practices were introduced at this time that demanded both a new type of building (the temple) and a new plan for creating spaces for both sacred and secular activities within the community. A temple had been constructed in Kirtland, and one contemplated for Missouri, but both these buildings, while having two ranges of pulpits for the restored priesthoods, retained the open, congregational function of typical American churches. At Nauvoo, however, Smith began the process of inventing the true temple as a closed sacred place reserved for secret rituals. As it acquired ritual capabilities, the temple as a uniquely Mormon building type began to exert a presence of its own within the landscape as a sanctified space that seriously challenged the one left behind in Jackson County.

As construction on the temple proceeded, so did work on a rival project, the Nauvoo House, a hotel to be built by the church to house visiting dignitaries, though a profit-making motive was also evident. The Nauvoo House was located "on the flat," an area along the river that Smith promoted as the city's chief commercial district. The prophet's plan apparently was to isolate the temple, which stood "on the hill" above the river, from the hotel–business part of the city and thus effectively separate sacred and secular zones. Trouble began, however, when some business-minded Saints failed to cooperate and started developing commercial properties "on the hill" around the temple. A city with two "centers" resulted, an arrangement that lacked the cohesion necessary to establish either internal unity or external boundaries, but it served to highlight a problem that the Saints in Utah would eventually have to solve, namely, how to reconcile a need for sacred space with a concomitant need for space to accommodate secular activities.[38]

The Experiential Zion, 1847–1870

The third phase of Zion making can be found in Utah and the adjoining areas of the Great Basin during the pioneer years of Mormon western settlement. What is fascinating about this period in LDS landscape history is that in many ways it represents a throwback to the older, millenarian Zion visualized for Missouri and comes closest to achieving Joseph Smith's plan for the ideal Zion. No temple was completed during this phase, though a site for it was dedicated on Temple Square in Salt Lake City in 1847, thus giving the Mormon West a sanctified sacred center. Jackson County may have been the symbolic center of the restoration, but for all intents and purposes Salt Lake City became the de facto spiritual, cultural, and economic center of the church, complete with a set of orbiting satellite settlements that included those in the Sanpete Valley.

In addition to a strong sense of symbolic centrality and orthogonal integration, the social world that emerged in the Mormon western empire was energized, Shipps shows, by the experience of making the trek to Zion, a feat that, in the Mormon mind, recapitulated the Exodus story of the Old Testament. One's Mormonness was established through the act of traveling to and living in a manifest Zion.[39] Lost in "sacred time," the Utah Saints could forget about the sacred/secular rift that had concerned them in Nauvoo; Mormon cities and towns in the West could have separate religious and commercial (where capitalism flourished) zones, but the centripetal force of the center, its power enhanced by the Saints' belief in the imminent millennium, precluded the need for long-range planning.

Such strong internal unity meant that the boundaries of the Kingdom could be loosely drawn along territorial lines, and the awareness of specialness was almost innate; without a "them" there was little need to aggressively define "us." It is little wonder that temple construction in Salt Lake City was deferred during this period, since there was no pressing need for the Saints to display an extroverted otherness. Although an attempt was made to strike a rebellious pose in the designs for the first two Salt Lake tabernacles, the most dramatic expression of Mormon separateness at this time was the announcement in 1852 of polygamy as a central tenet of the church. While the public proclamation was greeted with some grumbling, no mass defection ensued, and during the first two or three decades in Utah, Mormon society in effect became polygamous, with roughly 30 percent of the population actively participating in the principle and nearly all members touched in some ways by its prevalence.[40]

The intrusion of the world into Mormondom began in earnest in the late 1860s. The First Transcontinental Railroad would be completed in 1869, and federal efforts to stamp out polygamy took a serious turn in the following decades, with a series of antipolygamy laws passed by an increasingly aggressive U.S. Congress. It would take another thirty years for the Saints to back down on polygamy, but by the late 1860s, the accommodation process was well under way in the landscape, ushering in the final phase in Zion's development.

The Enduring Zion, 1870–1890

The fourth and final rendering of Zion began to appear around 1870 and was embodied in a landscape increasingly divided into discrete sacred and secular zones. As the experiential Zion began to break down, a dramatic reshaping of the landscape followed. Perhaps such an idyllic condition was destined to be short lived, but it was rather quickly undermined by an exponential growth in the second-generation Mormon population, a widening of economic interests among the Saints, and the specter of Gentile intrusion in the form of the Transcontinental Railroad. At the core of this change was a distancing of the group from the original millennial vision, the idea that the building of Zion would bring about the Second Coming, and replacing it with a newfound pragmatism. The Saints would set aside their End Times expectations and settle in for the long haul, building a community that could survive within the framework of the larger American society. In effect, this era marked the end of the true City of Zion and the beginning of what might be called simply the Mormon city, a place that retained a strong religious identity but nevertheless remained overtly secular in its basic structure. Gone was the immediacy of the apocalypse, and in its place came a workaday routine—the workable city.[41]

What we will see is that by the early 1870s, the process of landscape desacralization was well under way. Where before the burden of establishing Latter-day otherness fell upon the shoulders of the City of Zion as a whole—the sacred world of Mormonism—it was now being transferred solely to the temple, or better, temples, since before the end of the century there would be four such buildings in the Mormon West, in St. George (dedicated in 1877), Logan (1884), Manti (1888), and Salt Lake City (1893). To avoid the tensions that plagued a similar attempt at creating distinct sacred and secular zones within Nauvoo, beginning with St. George in 1871 the temples were removed from the center of town and located a respectable distance from the central commercial district, with the chosen site being a piece of high ground or hill outside the city. The building of regional temples met the ritual needs of the membership in outlying areas, but it also meant that the church was abandoning its commitment to preserving a "centered" social world. Instead, it accepted the reality of a more complex condition where there were two symbolic centers, in Salt Lake City and Jackson County, but also a set of secondary sacred spaces in the form of the St. George, Manti, and Logan temples. The perfect union of church and state dissolved, and in an increasingly secular landscape, the performance of Mormon otherness became the responsibility of the individual Latter-day Saint.

It seems natural to say that what happened to the Mormon landscape beginning in the 1870s was part of an "Americanization" process, because in fact it was: the built environment of the Mormon West was reshaped in a way that made it more workable within the American cultural system. The danger of this explanation, however, is that it implies submission, an abandonment of the old Zionist principles, and this is wrong. The Mormon landscape that emerged in the second half of the nineteenth century was still Mormon, but its demonstrable Mormonness came not from it in its entirety but rather from the fact that it had both monumental edifices, the temples, and a secular polity that simultaneously stressed group and individual works. In short, the Mormon landscape became an American landscape of difference, not of otherness, meaning that it became a variation on rather than a departure from the normative tradition.

In many ways, Salt Lake City stands out as an anomaly in this new world, because there the temple site was established long before the switch to off-center temples had been made. Still, the move toward landscape secularization was everywhere felt in the Great Basin Kingdom, a land that would remain distinctive, but not dangerously so.

A Landscape of Works

The Saints' struggle to achieve the right balance between group and individual priorities constitutes one of the primary themes in Mormon landscape history. In the end, a form of individualism won out, not only because it was the American way and what good Americans upheld, but also because the idea of agency, the ability of each human being to take personal responsibility for his or her own salvation and exaltation, lay deeply embedded in Mormon theology. So powerful is this belief in human action that it must be considered one of, if not the most essential myths of Mormonism, and it takes the form of what might be called the gospel of works—the link between a person's achievements on earth and his or her ultimate position in the afterlife. Again, it is a developing principle; it was part of the religion from the beginning but gained in strength as millennialism waned and the church moved into the temple-ritual phase of its development (Figure 1.3).

For Mormons, grace was bestowed through the atonement and free for all to attain. But as Mormon theologian James Talmage made clear in his *A Study of the Articles of Faith,* "[Redemption] is . . . conditioned on individual effort . . . [for] there is a judgment ordained for all, and all will be judged 'according to their works.'"[42] In the Mormon mind, human agency, the ability to control one's own destiny, is critical, and while faith—an abiding "trust in the being, purposes, and word of God"—remains indispensable, by itself it is not enough.[43] Brigham Young perhaps expressed it best when he reminded a group of Saints gathered at Manti in 1853 that "faith [will] do you no good unless your works follow or are with it."[44]

An emphasis on works, while placing people in charge of their destiny, presents some problems, among which is that in stressing the importance of works, the question automatically arises about how a person knows when he

Figure 1.3. Public works, most often in the form of tithed labor, figured prominently in the everyday lives of the Sanpete Saints. In this anonymous photograph from 1885, a crew of workmen poses before the nearly finished Manti South Ward Meeting House. Reprinted by permission of Utah State Historical Society; all rights reserved.

or she has performed "enough" works to warrant God's grace. The Saints are left with a dissonance between a call for "works" and a standard against which works may be measured for the reward of, first, salvation and, later, exaltation. To quote Douglas Davies again, "There are some dedicated Latter-day Saints who do wonder whether they can ever do enough to ensure that they will gain the highest exaltation."[45] The answer, presumably, was that everyone should just work harder, for there was always more that could be done. Yet the prospects were daunting and led one newspaper editor in Manti to quip, "Some think that the building of a city wall is 'a big job,' but each one will do a 'bigger job' before he puts the capstone on the walls of his own Kingdom."[46] Such an open-ended, Sisyphean proposition was not a completely promising thought, and it is no wonder the Mormon Saints looked for some kind of sign—an assurance—that their works were in fact working.

In looking for signs, the Mormons were walking a path laid out by their Puritan forebears, though with clear distinctions. Puritan theology emphasized the Doctrine of Predestination, which contends that human salvation is preordained by the will of God and "Man cannot work it [grace] in himself by his own efforts, no matter how hard he tries."[47] A strong faith, coupled with discipline—those who could not achieve grace through works could surely demonstrate depravity by *not* working—was all the Puritans had to prove their election. So they looked for signs, which is not to say they believed that accumulation and wealth were proof of grace, but rather, turning it around, that failure in business affairs and poverty clearly signaled the opposite.[48]

It was a backdoor kind of equation, with an absence of earthly achievements adding up to the same as having them in the eyes of God. The Mormons simply straightened it out, adopting a variant of the Protestant doctrine of "works righteousness" whereby works and their results, from performing rituals in the temple to helping the poor to profiting from enterprise and building a big house, were fundamental to securing both salvation and exaltation. The lineage between Puritans and Mormons, at least in terms of works, was recalled by Welcome Chapman, president of the church's Manti branch, who in an 1860 sermon reminded the Saints that "we should be rewarded according to our works," while at the same time he "condemned Predestination Doctrine as advance[d] by some here."[49]

That signs of grace could be both received and recognized by the faithful is given validity in a sermon Brigham Young delivered in 1855 at Salt Lake City. Young explained that "at the same time when I exhort the brethren to have faith, I really had rather that they would have good works; I don't care half so much about their faith as I do about their works. *Faith is not so obvious a principle, but in good works you see a manifestation, an evidence, a proof that there is something good about the person who is in the habit of doing them.*"[50] But what were such evidences? No official guidelines were issued, but within the church rested a general acceptance of "reciprocity": receiving is commensurate with one's works, and assurances of grace in the form of earthly rewards for good works were eagerly looked for and named "blessings," for they were signs that God had indeed blessed the recipient.

The concept of providential blessings is not overtly doctrinal in the church, but it operates fully within the Latter-day Saint folk consciousness. Examples are abundant from the Sanpete Valley. Manti bishop John Lowery told his congregation he was confident in the settlement's prospects "as long as we continue in good works and keep the commandments of God so long will the valley of the mountains be blessed and watered and continue to produce better and better until the Saints are satisfied."[51] Similarly, Manti resident Freeborn DeMill rose in church meeting and spoke of "the necessity of doing our duties with pure motives . . . [for] we should all be 'rewarded according to our works' [for] we had to make our [own] happiness."[52] Manti mayor Dan Jones warned of the need "of all [Saints] approximating to higher attainment and said it was by merit that every one would attain to the blessings of God that are held out to every one."[53] In the other towns it was the same; for example, Fairview resident L. S. Brady said he "wished the brethren would be watchfull and prayerfull, and believed that men will only receive what blessings they have merited . . ."[54] The next speaker, Henry Sanderson, put it more bluntly: "The Lord helpes them that helpes themselves."[55]

Blessings could come in many forms: healthy and ample families, sufficient rainfall, abundant harvest, success in business ventures, a new city hall, the money to build or buy a new house—practically any kind of good fortune would qualify. The essential ingredient was industry. LDS apostle Ezra T. Benson, visiting the Sanpete colony in 1853, remarked that "we reached Manti City and truly our hearts felt to rejoice and to praise the Lord, when we behold what improvements our brethren had made and how our Father had blessed the labors of their hands."[56] A nice town, a fine house, a large family, and a productive farm were all viewed as blessings bestowed by the Lord in return for faith and good works. Philip Klingensmith of Manti may have said it best when he called attention to "the blessings that are injoyed under such circumstances, especially the blessing of perperty [property] in this life" (Figure 1.4).[57]

Always, in seeking blessings, the Saints were walking a fine line between assurance and avarice. Hard work led to God's favor, and this favor in turn produced prosperity and even riches. But affluence for its own sake, and what was considered ostentatious materialism were frowned upon. Apostle Orson Hyde, in 1861, reminded the Sanpete Saints about "the folly of Grasping after Riches; that we should leave these things to the Lord: the Obedient and faithful would ultimately win."[58] The key idea, however, was winning. In a wonderfully simple expression of the Mormon Ethic, Bishop Jones of Fairview

Figure 1.4. Private works paved the way to exaltation, a state of grace made manifest through such blessings as a large family and a fashionable house. This photograph from around 1880 shows Jens Christian and Karen Nielson Jensen standing with their son John Henry (to the left of the gate) and an unidentified visitor in front of the house they built in Ephraim for their six children. Photograph courtesy of Cory Jensen.

in 1861 said, "He [the bishop] thought the man there [that] accomplishes the most, is the man there [that] is doing the best."[59]

And if they were rewarded for their good works, the Saints would be punished for not doing them. Apostle E. T. Benson, again in Manti, spoke of good works in opposition to the evils of such activities as land speculation: "said that this land we now inhabit has been given us by the God of Heaven, said that he that speculated out of his brethren by selling land would not be prospered."[60] James Jones reported from his Fairview Ward that Brigham Young had spoken in Manti, the president saying that "we should wake up to our duties, gave the idea that the Lord wanted to bless this people, but could not because we are not ready to receive these blessings and recommended improvements of all kinds, so [such] as lay out gardens, plant trees and flowers."[61] Bishop Jones again, in 1862, "spoke to some length upon the principle of union and warned the brethren against going into speculation on the expence of their fellow being[s] that the Lord would withhold his blessings from all such."[62]

During the nineteenth century, works within the Mormon Church took three forms (Figure 1.5). First, there was the public work associated with active participation in various kinds of community involvement, ranging from assisting the poor to working on various church and public building projects. Spiritual work comprised a second component in a person's "works" and consisted primarily of maintaining moral virtue, participating in priesthood activities, entering into celestial marriage, and most importantly after 1840, performing sacred rites in the temples. And finally, there were personal works, which involved striving to improve one's own temporal circumstances, whether it was a nicely manicured city lot or a substantial and well-appointed

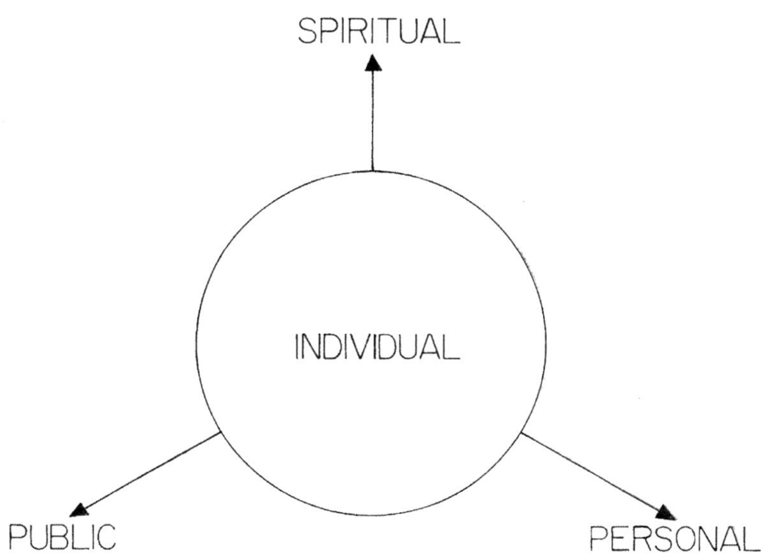

Figure 1.5. The City of Zion was built on the backs of individuals whose spiritual (religious), public (community), and personal (private) works helped turn the Mormon vision of a heavenly community into material reality.

house. If the triad rings a bell, it is because it bears a remarkable similarity to an older and largely discredited American republican ethos. There were differences, of course, but a symbolic universe built upon works, both for individual profit and the benefit of the group, was not completely new. Falling back on tradition, Mormons sought spiritual and social order amid the rising turmoil of antebellum America.[63]

The Gospel of Works played a crucial role in the establishment of the social world of Zion. It cannot be overemphasized that Mormon society from the outset retained its American materialism. Church leaders like Joseph Smith and Brigham Young could preach about the evils of "worldliness," but in everyday practice their words went unheeded, even by themselves. Possessing fine objects of all kinds was one of the most visible manifestations of God's blessings, and in all aspects of LDS material culture the conspicuous display of wealth through the possession of large houses, fancy furniture, and fine clothing was deemed appropriate, even admired, for it advertised a family's status both on earth and in the afterlife.[64] The best evidence of the "works righteousness" equation lies in the built environment itself, for we may see in the cities, houses, and other buildings a decision being made in favor of accumulation and display over abstinence and asceticism. But it can also be seen in other kinds of actions, like the choosing of church leaders.

The preferred qualification for positions of authority was a man's (and the most important church leaders were all male) worldly accomplishments—and his blessings of wealth and good fortune. In a Manti meeting of 1855, one speaker, J. D. [Chase], talked of "appointing men to office for their ability and not their good feeling."[65] The message is subtle, almost subliminal. For example, during the 1860s the bishop of Fairview resigned, and Orson Hyde, who presided over the Sanpete Valley colonies, was called to choose a replacement. Hyde first asked if the Fairview brethren would sustain him in his right to choose a new bishop, a motion that carried unanimously. He then proceeded to say that "Andrew Peterson has the bigest wheat that I have seen and I will nominate him to take charge."[66] Peterson became the new bishop, and although Apostle Hyde never explained his logic, the message was probably clear enough to the brethren: having some "evidences" was a good thing. The human landscape crafted by the Saints in places like the Sanpete Valley was ultimately a celebration of human agency as much as it was a call to earthly action.

Making Zion, or better yet, "making up Zion," became a central component of the Mormon restoration project, and as we shall see in the following chapters devoted to specific elements in the human landscape of Zion, it was a task that increasingly rested on the shoulders of the individual Saints.

2 THE SETTLEMENT MATRIX
TOWNS AND TEMPLES

> Come, capitalists, this county abounds with wealth. Would not the rich emigrants be doing good by coming here and helping the county of Sanpete to enrich a whole people and they enrich themselves[?]
>
> —*David Candland, Manti City,* Deseret News, *June 10, 1863*

Even as the first Mormons entered the Salt Lake Valley in 1847, a program for consolidating their dearly bought freedom began. The building of Zion subsumed a combined policy of self-sufficiency *and* land occupation. By promoting home industry, cooperation, and abstinence, church leaders felt they could keep interaction with the outside world to a minimum, and by physically occupying as much of the Great Basin as possible through an organized system of colonization, they could ensure Latter-day Saint hegemony in the area. The ultimate goal was to prevent Gentiles from gaining a foothold within the borders of Zion and once again thwarting the Kingdom-building process. Thus as one part of a sweeping plan to occupy and settle the Great Basin, a small party of Saints left Salt Lake City in the fall of 1849 for the Sanpete Valley in what is now central Utah.[1]

The journey took them south, past the newly planted Mormon colony at Provo, to Salt Creek Canyon, which they traversed in a southeasterly direction into the upper end of the Sanpete Valley. Standing above Unita Springs (later the town of Fountain Green), the valley unfolded before them as a V-shaped basin roughly forty miles long and varying in width from about twenty miles in the north to less than two in the "narrows" at its southern end (Figure 2.1). To the west they could see the San Pitch Mountains, which ranged from 6,000 to 8,000 feet in elevation, while on the east loomed the more impressive Wasatch Plateau, rising to between 8,000 and 11,000 feet. Life for agriculturalists here would not be easy: the valley's 5,500-foot average elevation made for a short growing season and what water there was—the annual precipitation rate is around eight to fourteen inches—came mostly in the form of snow at the higher elevations. Even though one pioneer described the trip as "journeying . . . through an unbroken wilderness, with the stupendous Wasatch Mountains frowning down on every side,"[2] the high

Figure 2.1. In 2012 architectural historian Peter Goss took this photograph of the Sanpete Valley looking toward the southeast. The view approximates that of the first Mormon settlers as they entered the valley in November 1849.

mountains made farming here possible, for as the winter snowpack melted in the spring and early summer it filled streams (and later Mormon irrigation ditches) with the water needed to sustain the economy of Zion. All the mountain-fed streams emptied into the north-south-running Sanpitch River, and it was this watercourse that the pioneer company followed as it headed for its appointed destination in the southern end of the valley. They called the place "Sanpete" because this was how they pronounced the name of the Piute band living there, the Sanpitch (peech) Indians.[3]

Like their counterparts in other Mormon colonies, the Sanpete Zion makers adopted the town as the primary instrument of settlement (Figure 2.2). The idea of an "urban" frontier, where the establishment of towns and cities coincided with or even preceded the arrival of a farming population, is not unique to the Mormon West. Historian John Reps has shown in a number of excellent studies that urban communities of various kinds and sizes were ubiquitous in frontier America and more often than not served as catalysts for settlement rather than resulting from it. A typical scenario, according to Reps, would have an individual or group claim a town site, lay out a grid, sell lots to businesses and professionals, and then have the surrounding countryside fill up with farm families.[4] In the case of the Mormons, the church rather than individual investors acted as the principal land agent, and LDS leaders located and surveyed town sites before dividing the land (at no initial cost) among the membership.[5] What made the Mormon settlement system so unusual was the way the towns were constituted. Rather than functioning as a commercial center within a landscape of dispersed single-family farms (Figure 2.3), the LDS town worked like an older medieval village where all the people lived together and commuted to their farms and other work places in the surrounding town lands (Figure 2.4).[6] During the often lengthy daily journey to and from their fields, Mormon farmers would perhaps recall the words of their first prophet: "Let everyman live in the city, for this is the city of Zion."[7]

The village gave the Saints everything they needed. Not only did it set them off as a chosen people by providing a clear alternative to the dispersed type of living found in mainstream America, its nucleated structure fostered a strong sense of group solidarity. Like many in their day, the Saints believed that a properly arranged physical environment helped shape a person's behavior. Quite simply, they felt that those who lived together would be more unified in their actions than those who lived scattered about on individual farms. Physical proximity to church buildings too made attending ecclesiastical

Figure 2.2. At 11,928 feet, Mount Nebo is the tallest mountain in the Wasatch Range. It stands at the north end of the Sanpete Valley and is visible in the background of this photograph by George Edward Anderson from the late 1880s. The town of Moroni is in the foreground, while Salt Creek Pass, the route used by the original Mormon settlers, shows below the towering mountain. George Edward Anderson Photographs, MSS P-1, L. Tom Perry Special Collections, Brigham Young University. Anderson labeled his glass plate negatives on the back; note the reversed writing at the bottom of the image.

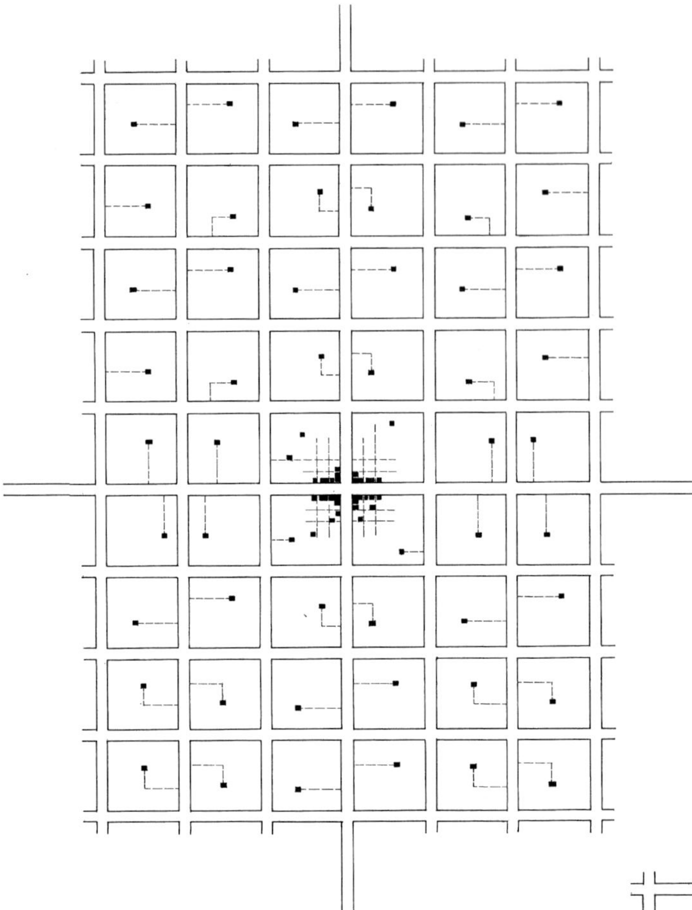

Figure 2.3. Typical American agricultural settlement pattern with a grid-street town surrounded by dispersed and individually owned and operated farms. Drawing by Eric Harker and James Gosney (after Lowry Nelson, *The Mormon Village*).

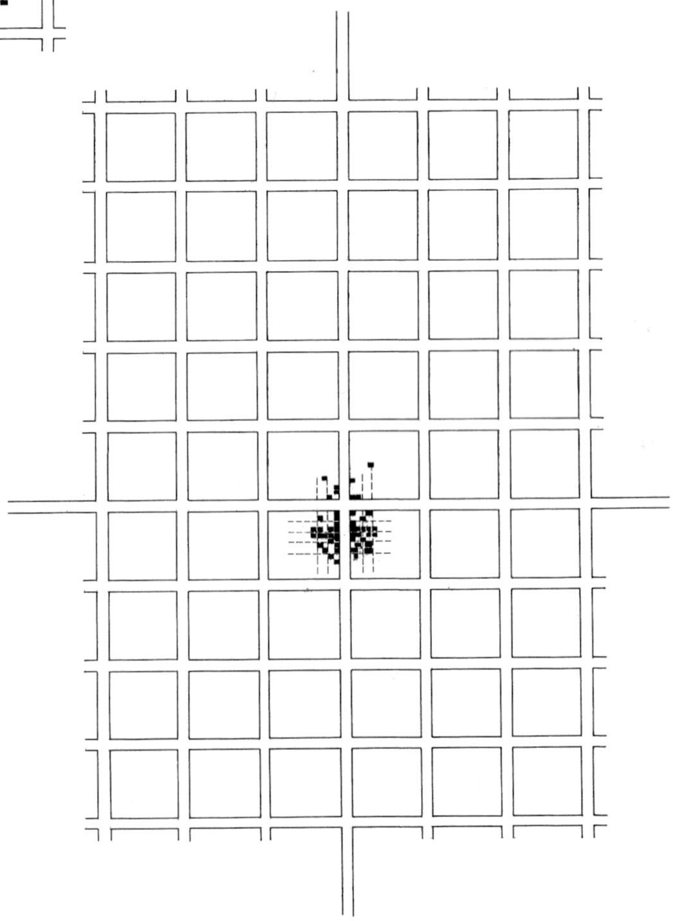

Figure 2.4. Typical Mormon settlement pattern where the gridiron town contains farmers' residences and is surrounded by individually owned and operated farms. Drawing by Eric Harker and James Gosney (after Lowry Nelson, *The Mormon Village*).

meetings and community social functions easier and thus helped forge a common spirit in the membership. Moreover, it should not be overlooked that the lack of privacy in such a compact living situation ensured an extra degree of social control, for the village came with a built-in surveillance system—the watchful eyes of next-door neighbors. The fact that these neighbors were more often than not also church-appointed teachers and leaders added another safeguard against backsliding.[8]

The City Foursquare

Speaking to a Salt Lake City crowd in 1873, Apostle Orson Pratt confessed, "The nature of the city of Zion is nowhere fully described," but, he said, "God by revelation will inspire his servants and will dictate to them the order of the buildings of that city—the number and width of the streets, the kind of houses, the character of the Temple that is to be built therein, the kind of rock, timber and the various materials that will have to be brought from a distance to enter into the composition of that beautiful city."[9] In fact, revelations containing specific instructions for building the City of Zion were few, God choosing instead to work, as Pratt explained, first through Joseph Smith, who oversaw the initial phase of LDS Zion making in Ohio, Missouri, and Illinois, and later his successor Brigham Young, the man chiefly responsible for orchestrating the Mormon occupation and settlement of the Great Basin West. The objective was to build a community where the faithful could openly live their religion while working to perfect themselves and the earth in anticipation of the millennium's arrival—the prophetic New Jerusalem had to be turned into the real City of Zion.

The first indication of what the Mormon community would resemble is found in an 1833 sketch sent by Smith to the Saints laying out new towns in Missouri (Figure 2.5). Starting with a basic gridiron street pattern, the prophet drew up a symmetrical city consisting of blocks measuring 660 feet to a side and containing ten acres each. Streets were a uniform width of 132 feet. A band of larger rectangular blocks ran through the middle, with three in the center reserved for special church functions: one for the bishop's "store-houses," and two containing twelve temples each for the Mormon priesthoods. In keeping with the live-away-from-your-work village ethos, a specially designated area outside the city was set aside for barns and stables and beyond that the whole thing ringed with farm- and pasturelands.[10] Within a short time, Smith revised his plan, increasing the size of the city, reducing the number and size of the central blocks (two rather than three), and making all the blocks equal in size to achieve a uniform grid.[11] The essential features of the plan, its symmetrical grid, village social structure, and centrally

Figure 2.5. This diagrammatic reworking of Joseph Smith's original plat of the City of Zion calls out its key ingredients: a symmetrical gridiron plan; three centrally located public squares, two reserved for temples (numbering twenty-four) and one for church storehouses; blocks with house lots placed at right angles to ensure separation between houses; a large area at the edge for barns, stables, and corrals; and farmland surrounding the community.

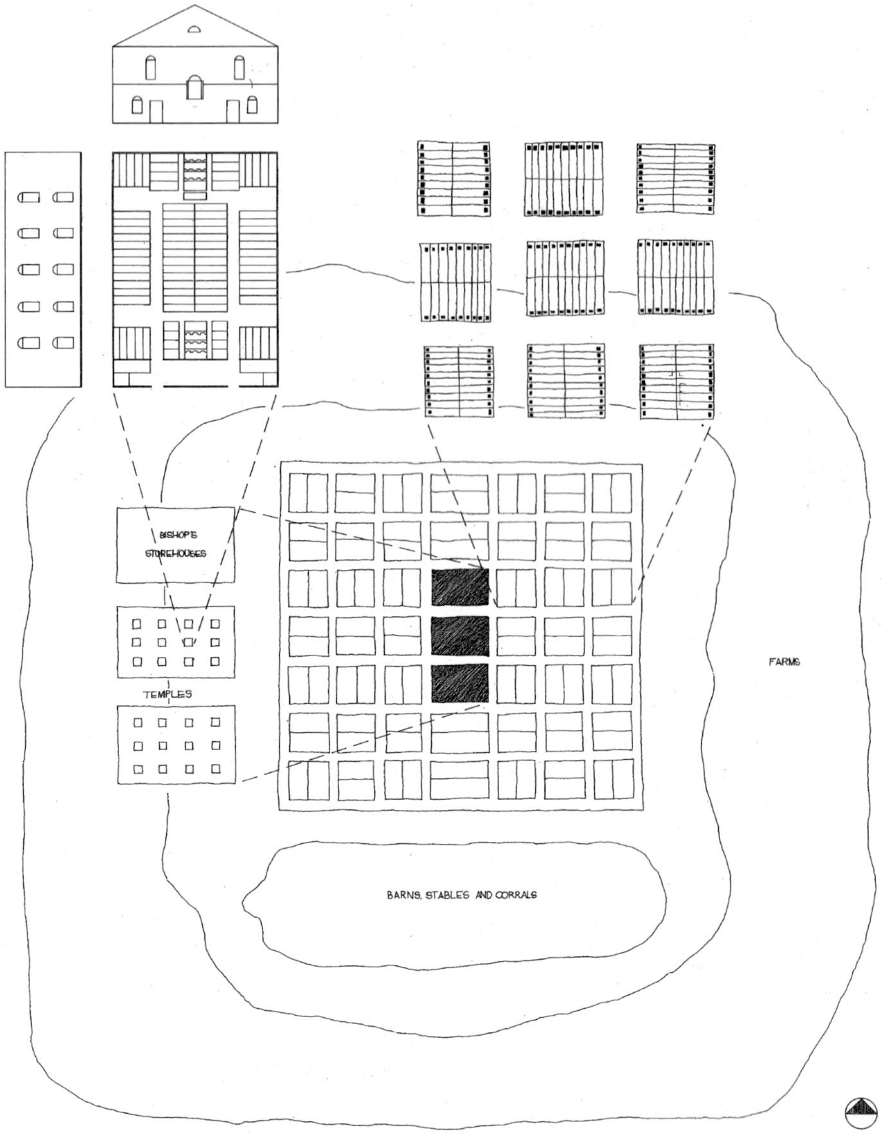

placed temple, were retained, however, and became the conceptual underpinning for most subsequent Mormon settlement.[12]

One noteworthy aspect of Smith's City of Zion was its low population density, a quality that lent it a decidedly suburban feel. The prophet stipulated that no lot "contain more than one house, and that to be built twenty-five feet back from the street, leaving a small yard in front to be planted in a grove, according to the taste of the builder; the rest of the lot for gardens."[13] Furthermore, the individual lots were to be arranged perpendicular to each other, so that houses faced away from each other in an apparent attempt to counter the congested feeling found in most urban areas. Nor was the city supposed to grow beyond a certain size; Smith thought that when the population reached between fifteen thousand and twenty thousand people a new one should be started "to fill up the world in these last days."[14] In theory the directive worked this way: Mormon leaders, especially in the West, stuck to the pattern of establishing a large number of small towns rather than a few larger cities. The exception early on was Salt Lake City: as the population grew, instead of hiving off to form a new town, the Saints simply added a series of additions to the original plat, making it one of the largest cities in the Trans-Mississippi West by 1890.[15]

While it is customary to speak of Mormon towns as "villages," the label is misleading. For one thing, many LDS communities were far larger than the name implies, and they also lacked the organic irregularity normally associated with the village settlement type. One of the distinguishing features of villages is their disheveled appearance, since historically they were unplanned, growing naturally through time around an open public space or religious building as a series of layered accretions. The result was a jumbled array of narrow winding streets coupled with houses packed tightly on top of one another in a composite arrangement shaped by centuries of constant addition and subtraction. The village form dominated the landscape of medieval Europe and appears today in non-Western countries where traditional life patterns continue.[16] In North America, some villages were constructed during the colonial period, particularly in New England and New Amsterdam, where they remain visible in the oldest sections of cities like Boston and New York (Figure 2.6).[17] It was also the favored settlement type for utopian religious groups like the Shakers, Harmonists, and Inspirationists.[18]

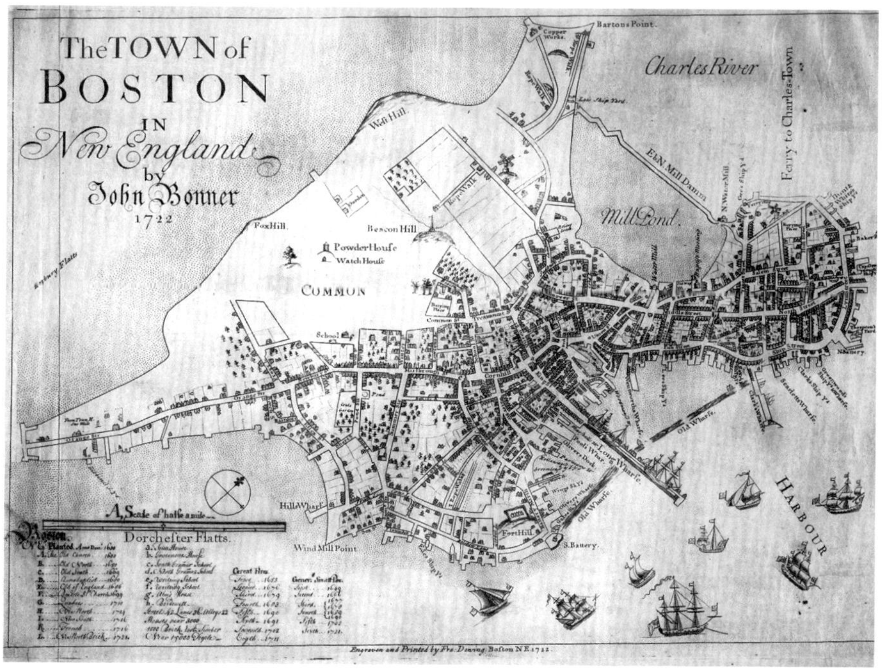

Figure 2.6. Medieval village pattern, plan of Boston, Massachusetts, 1722. I. N. Phelps Stokes Collection, Miriam and Ira D. Wallach Division of Art, Prints, and Photographs, New York Public Library, Astor, Lenox, and Tilden Foundations.

Except for the compaction created by having people live together rather than apart, Mormon towns bear little resemblance to traditional villages. They are orderly and planned, have wide and evenly spaced streets, their individually owned houses are located on separate lots, and actually from a distance appear much like most other American towns of the time. The urban landscape with which Mormon leaders were most familiar was dominated by the gridiron-plan city, and it was this design that they adopted as their own, though they used it as a village. Grids, of course, are ubiquitous worldwide. In the Western tradition they are most often identified with Greece and Rome, and then later Renaissance Europe, when the classical grid found new life as the poster child of modernity. In rebuilding older medieval cities or building new ones in the colonies, European planners from the fifteenth century on found the geometry of the grid, with its harmonious aesthetic balance and rational scientific precision, an ideal expression of humanistic values. What better way to demonstrate the power of the intellect than to impose an artificial order on the irregularities of nature?[19]

The grid's great proponent in North America was William Penn, who employed it in his 1683 plan for the city of Philadelphia (Figure 2.7).[20] The Philadelphia plan struck a responsive chord in the new land, satisfying both colonial and then later American demands for what historian Richard Bushman calls a culture of "refinement."[21] By the early years of the nineteenth century, members of the emerging bourgeois class were increasingly preoccupied with the acquisition and display of particular modes of behavior and kinds of objects associated with the civilized "genteel" culture of the old aristocracy. The idea was that possessions made the man, so to speak, and the status of both people and their communities could be judged by the way they carried and presented themselves, and this equation did not go unnoticed by the Saints. Speaking in Salt Lake City in 1868, Young noted that "a truly civilized person is one who is a real gentleman or lady; in language and manners he is truly refined, and gives way to no practice that is unhallowed or uncomely. This is what we are after, and trying to attain to."[22] In this world of appearances, the gridiron city, part of the reapplication of classical principles that historians often label "neoclassicism," was much admired as a symbol of progressive, refined thinking, and it is not surprising that, as Bushman notes "every settlement with any aspiration began with a plan of straight streets forming regular geometrical blocks."[23]

The basic plan for the "beautiful" City of Zion, then, consisted of four principal elements: (1) a symmetrical gridiron street pattern; (2) a low-density layout of individually owned building lots; (3) a temple square (or temple squares) located in the center of town; and (4) a nucleated "village" social structure. Each resulted from specific ideas Smith, Young, and other Mormon

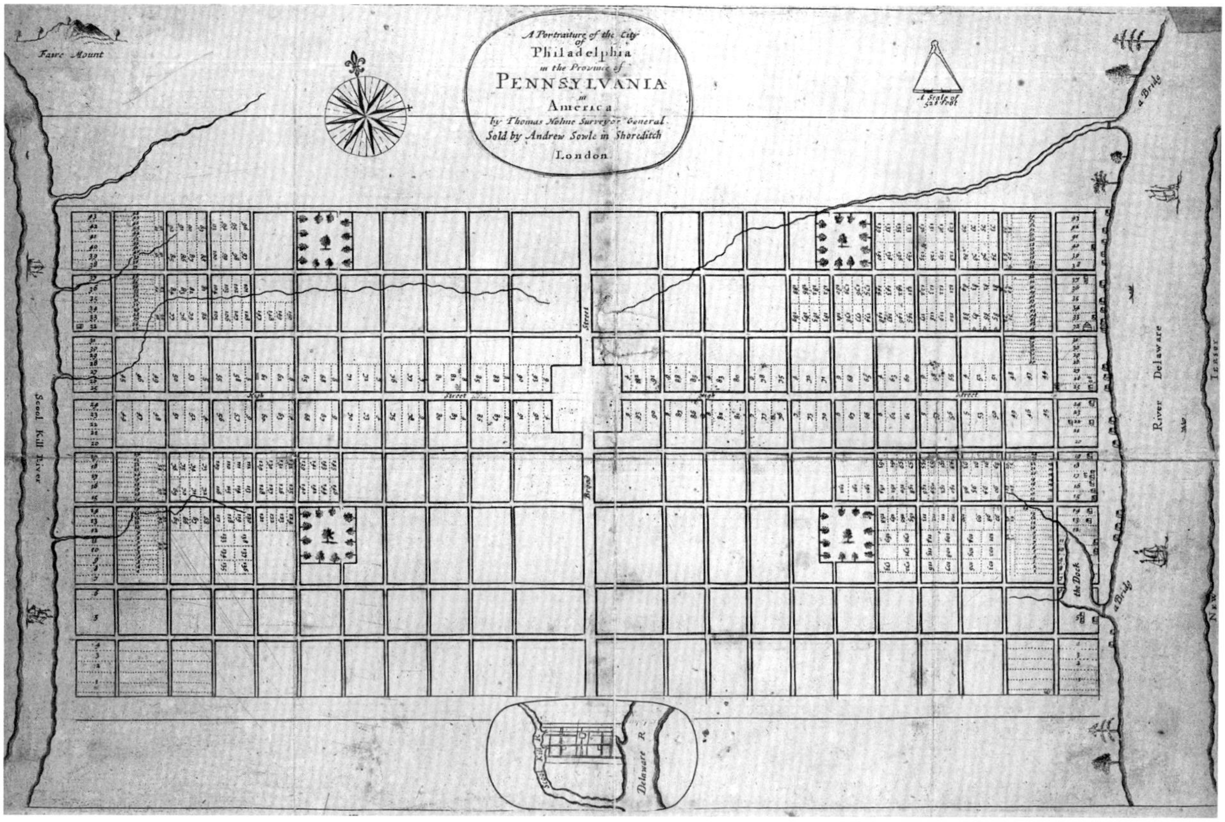

leaders had about the way the City of Zion, and by extension Mormon society, should function, and each in its own way helps us understand the landscape "style" that began to emerge during these formative years in the church's history. As the term is used in this book, style refers broadly to "the way in which something is done, produced, or expressed" and becomes a critical tool for landscape analysis because it sheds light on the thought process that went into the production and use of various spaces. Style is visible in the inherent qualities of an artifact, whether a town plan, a meetinghouse, or a dwelling, and includes such things as size, shape, organization, and decoration, to name a few main characteristics. Historians assume a connection between style and mind: the object we see results from the desires, preferences, and values (both practical and aesthetic) of the maker and user.[24]

Figure 2.7. Neoclassical urban form, plan of Philadelphia, Pennsylvania, 1683. I. N. Phelps Stokes Collection, Miriam and Ira D. Wallach Division of Art, Prints, and Photographs, New York Public Library, Astor, Lenox, and Tilden Foundations.

In practice, style has two principal duties. The first is more common and acts as a "unifying force" in society, denoting a consistency in artifact production that emanates from a shared set of ideas and values. To put it another way, we may say that a common landscape style signals the presence of a common cultural idea—a disposition within a social group toward a way of "doing, producing, expressing things" that most closely satisfies their needs. When we see stylistic similarities in the landscape, we relate them to the structuring power of an underlying set of cultural assumptions. A second function is opposite: style serves to divide one group of objects from another by communicating *difference* or *otherness*. Stylistically dissimilar things signal divisions in the values of the people who make and use them, one group favoring one form and another group a different one. Through such distinctions, a sorting of the material world occurs along the lines of stylistic preference. Again, we can infer that when we find groups of people using different forms, they also hold different values, using objects to both consciously and unconsciously distinguish themselves from others.[25]

Style is a dynamic concept best understood as a kind of *performance* in which people present themselves through their public actions (which include the acquisition and display of possessions) to various audiences to elicit desirable reactions or responses. For example, choosing one city or house style over another is a communicative act that sends a message expressing either a social (race, class, gender) affiliation or cultural (mythic) value. Boundaries are drawn between various constituencies in society, while at the same time reinforcing internal bonds in the old "us" versus "them" equation. In an era when Americans, and this includes the Mormons, were obsessed with the performance of refinement, "all that distinguished [gentility]," Richard Bushman points out, "was the manner of the people and *the style of the objects that surrounded them*."[26]

The style of the City of Zion plan is a relatively easy read. A hint of biblical precedent—it was a city that "lieth four square"—gives way to a more pronounced connection to the gridiron favored in American "genteel" culture, lending the upstart religion an air of legitimacy through its refined pedigree.[27] The other three components, the prescribed low population density, the temple in the center, and the village living structure served to unite the Saints internally, binding them together as a chosen people, while at the same time distinguishing them from the American landscape norm characterized by crowded cities, secular and commercial centers, and individual family farms. Slowly the Mormon symbolic universe was falling into place, and not surprisingly it was one that was different, but not too different, which as we shall see becomes a recurring theme in Mormon landscape history. In striking a new path forward, the Saints did not turn their back on the past, or on the country in which they lived. They kept one foot in the door, so to speak, not just politically but also aesthetically, making Zion at once radical and familiar.[28]

The City of Zion plan developed slowly as a series of iterations, each building on what had come before. The first LDS communities in Kirtland, Ohio, and Independence, Missouri, had been previously platted by others and required no special plan. Following the expulsion from Jackson County, resettlement efforts to the north in Caldwell and Clay Counties initially followed the dispersed American pattern,[29] though attempts were made to establish uniquely Mormon cities at both Far West and Adam-ondi-Ahman by implementing Smith's original "plat." While both of these settlements were quickly abandoned in the face of intense persecution, one feature in both, the reduction of the size of the central ecclesiastical zone (to two blocks at Adam-ondi-Ahman and one at Far West), endured to become standard practice in the future.[30]

The lessons learned from Nauvoo are harder to pinpoint. In laying out this city, Smith chose not to follow the City of Zion plan; rather, the principal streets, Main and Water, met at the river's edge at the Nauvoo House, a church-owned commercial establishment built to provide "comfortable" accommodations for what Smith envisioned would be a plethora of visiting dignitaries. Like Young after him, Smith understood the importance of style, speaking of the house as a "cornerstone of Zion, which shall be polished with the refinement which is after the similitude of a palace."[31] The temple was sited more in the center of town on the hilltop above the river, at some distance from the Nauvoo House. The two buildings, considered by the prophet to be of equal importance, divided the city spatially and this, coupled with the fact that many of the Saints lived on their farms in the surrounding countryside, resulted in a rather sprawling community with two centers, one by the river in the commercial district and the other on the hill around the temple. It is possible to see in this duality a precedent for what was to come in Utah, when the temples were moved out of the town center to adjacent higher ground, though there is no indication in Brigham Young's writings that the Nauvoo experience influenced his subsequent actions to any degree.[32]

If anything, Young took heed of the dangers of a contested city—a power struggle developed at Nauvoo between those on the river and those on the hill—and returned to the older centralized grid to prevent the "scattering" of his flock as they were driven from Illinois. The western exodus that began in 1846, however, presented the Saints with the unlooked-for opportunity to develop and refine their city-building skills. During the migration, in Winter Quarters and numerous trail camps, the order of the grid became a device for holding the emigrants together. It performed the same function in the expanses of the Great Basin. In the valley of the Great Salt Lake, which was uninhabited (Indian homelands were generally farther to the south), the Saints for the first time enjoyed the freedom to build their City of Zion as they wished. Or as Young wished, for in the church hierarchy all power rested with the prophet and president. In spirit, Young adhered to Smith's basic plan in laying out Salt Lake City, but added his own touches, which included a series of public parks along the lines of those found in cities like Philadelphia (Figure 2.8).

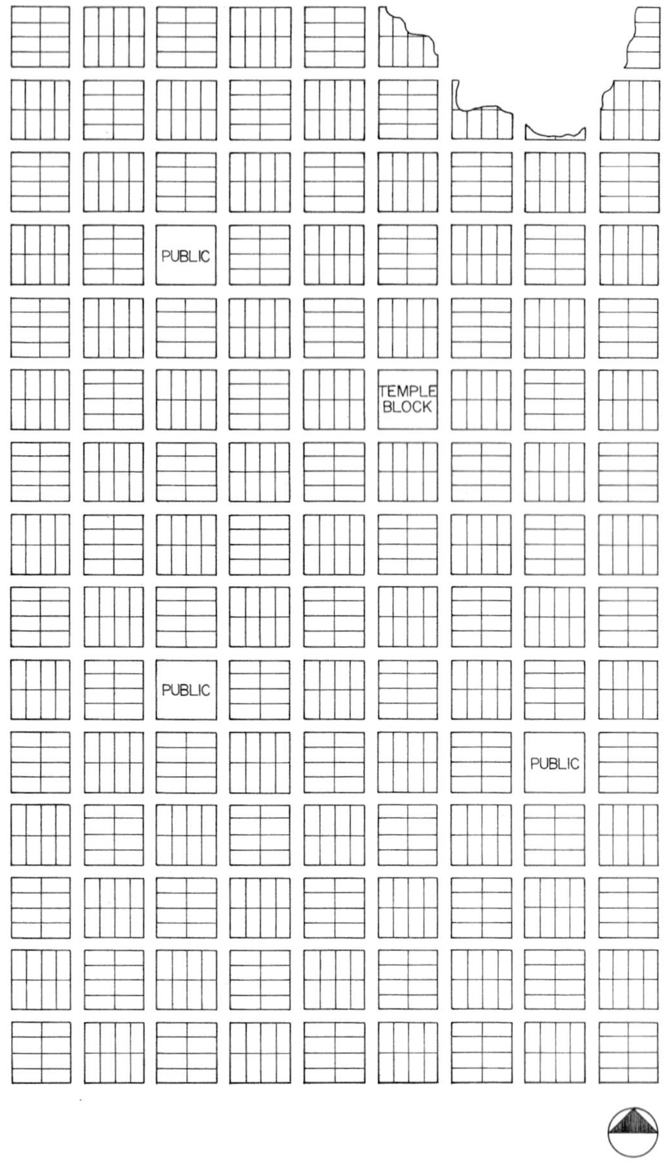

Figure 2.8. The original 1849 plat for Salt Lake City, Utah. Note the individual house lot orientations and the presence of public squares. The plat is asymmetrical because of its arrangement around the sacred temple site and the foothills to the north.

The impact of Penn's plan on Mormon city design seems evident, both in Young's Great Salt Lake City and Smith's earlier City of Zion plat. The most striking similarity between them is their low-density suburban quality, which seems to echo Penn's 1681 pronouncement: "Let every house be placed, if the person pleases in the middle of its plat, as to the breadth way of it, that so there may be ground on each side for gardens or orchards, or fields, that it may be a green country town, which will never be burnt, and always be wholesome."[33] Neither Smith nor Young was so free in revealing his intentions or inspirations, but the cities they envisioned and built for the earth's "latter days" had a "green" feeling, with wide streets, prescribed open spaces, and garden lot housing, all strongly reminiscent of Penn's own idea for Philadelphia.[34]

If considered a nightmare by twenty-first-century city planners bent on increasing density in America's cities, Salt Lake City was well thought of by early visitors, one of whom recalled it as a "large beautiful city, the houses all separate—each with its garden—wide streets, with a pebbly stream running on each side."[35] Another traveler began by admitting that "the general impression given by Salt Lake City is an agreeable one," and after calling attention to the city's ten-acre blocks, wide streets, geometry, streams, tree-lined sidewalks, fruit trees and gardens, concluded, "Altogether, few towns have been so judiciously designed and so perfectly built; few enjoy so great natural advantages, which have been cleverly made the most of. The barren country we passed through would have prepared us to appreciate any place where there might be a spare blade of grass, but Salt Lake City would be considered beautiful anywhere."[36]

Topography and circumstance lay behind some of the inconsistencies found in Salt Lake City's plan. The temple site had been dedicated when the Saints first entered the valley, and it was placed to the north, near the mouth of what came to be called City Creek Canyon. Such a location may have been divinely inspired, but it meant that the temple could not occupy the center of a symmetrical grid, since the nearby foothills precluded much settlement to the north. This resulted in the grid appearing incomplete, with its northern half largely missing. It is true that as later additions were appended they helped fill out the grid to the east, west, and south, thus giving the city more of a finished appearance.[37]

After gaining a foothold in the Great Salt Lake Valley, the Saints pushed out in all directions into the Great Basin, establishing nearly 300 towns by the end of century. In nearly all cases, the far-flung settlements were established under the direction and guidance of the LDS Church's central administration, and particularly President Brigham Young, whose organizational talents earned him the sobriquet, the "Great Colonizer." In terms of a general land policy, clearly the Saints had one: their goal was the orderly occupation of as much of the Great Basin as possible. Equally evident, too, was the fact that Young and other church leaders maintained firm control over its implementation, setting priorities, choosing new town sites, and wielding power sufficient to "call" already settled Saints to found new colonies.[38] At the same time, the system was hardly monolithic. Men and women acting very much on their own and often in their own best economic interests founded many Mormon towns. Such was the case in the Sanpete Valley colony, which started life with a command decision in Salt Lake City, but whose subsequent growth came largely at the hands of enterprising individuals following no specific script. Again, it is hard with these early Mormons to disentangle individual and church interests, since the two were inextricably bound together in the Gospel of Works—the Saints would build the Kingdom by building their personal kingdoms.

Sanpete Towns

Given its location, just off the main north-south settlement corridor, the Mormon colonization of the Sanpete Valley was perhaps inevitable. Yet the specific inspiration for moving settlers into this remote mountain area at such an early date—just two years after the founding of Salt Lake City—came not from church leaders but in response to a request by the local Ute chief Wakara (anglicized to Walker) for the Mormons to come and teach the Indians to build houses and plant crops.[39] Wakara would live to regret the invitation, for the coming of the whites brought nearly two decades of sickness and war to the Utes and ultimately caused their removal to a reservation in the barren northeastern corner of Utah.[40] At first blush, however, the attraction was there, and in the summer of 1849 the chief traveled north to meet with Brigham Young. The LDS president responded favorably and quickly dispatched a delegation under Apostle Parley P. Pratt to visit the Ute encampment. Pratt was impressed with the settlement opportunities afforded by the valley and returned supporting the idea of planting a new colony at a site in the southern end of the valley.[41]

That fall Young chose fifty families under the leadership of patriarch Isaac Morley to colonize the valley. His party made camp at the present site of Manti, although according to one member of the group, Adelia Cox Sidwell, a number of families wanted to travel farther south hoping to find a more suitable location. Morley, however, held fast to his orders, saying, "We behold the stake driven by Parley P. Pratt in his explorations of this valley. This is our God appointed abiding place, and stay I will, though but ten men remain with me."[42] They stayed, but not all were happy. Sidwell later reported that during the first winter "the United Order, every person sharing and faring equally with his neighbor," prevailed, while at the same time complaining that fort building would have been aided by "more unity among the colonists."[43] It was a hard thing, reconciling church duty and self-interest, and it was, as we shall see, a problem that did not disappear. Still, the small band held together and after a winter huddling in wagon boxes, tents, and dugouts—experiencing "all the disadvantages subsequent to new settlements" was how George Peacock put it—the colonists began setting in crops and laying out a city, which they named Manti after a principal city in the Book of Mormon.[44]

During that first summer Brigham Young and one of his counselors,

Heber C. Kimball, visited the nascent colony and filed the following report in the Fourth General Epistle of the Church, issued in September 1850:

> On the last of July Brothers Young and Kimball left home on a visit to Utah and Sanpete [Counties] and returned on the 12th of August, having found a place for a good settlement, located a city at Sanpete [Manti] and noticed several intermediate sites worthy [of] the attention of smaller colonies which we anticipate will be settled this fall, making a pleasant and safe communication from this [Salt Lake City] to our most southern habitation. The Sanpete settlement will also be strengthened and others will spread on the north to and beyond Ogden, so that when the emigration of this season should close there will be a continued line of villages, at short distances, for more than 200 miles in extent.[45]

The letter outlines the church's basic settlement policy: towns were to be placed at regular intervals, usually about five to ten miles, so that horse-powered intercourse between them could be easily and safely maintained, and an unbroken line of communication effected between the peripheral colonies and the core community in Salt Lake City. This objective was met in the Sanpete Valley, though not in the way one might expect. Resistance from the Utes greatly slowed the settlement process, and when expansion did come and a series of new towns were platted, it was not so much the result of a unified plan as the initiative of local families.

Growth in the Sanpete Valley was fueled by a steady influx of new immigrants. After the first official "call" for settlers when Young ordered Morley's group to Manti, the in-migration was largely driven by opportunity; Sanpete was a good destination for new arrivals, and slowly the word spread. In one case Brigham Young himself recommended Sanpete to David Candland, an old acquaintance of his who had arrived in Salt Lake City, saying, "There is splendid land in Sanpete County, take your families there, settle on a farm, and these young sons will some day run it for you, you will do well and good will come of it."[46] More formal advertisements would come later, like this one published in the *Deseret News:* "A few miles north of Manti in Sanpete County the settlers are building a new fort . . . and as it is pleasantly situated and immediately surrounded by good soil and an extensive range, it may be well for those in search of a location to visit the new Ft. Ephraim."[47] Or one sent in from Moroni: "Our recently constructed canal is a success, and will furnish plenty of good water to the settlement, and having accomplished that work they now invite settlers. There is room there for 100 families more. Farming and hay land can be had for the fencing and getting the water to it."[48]

And many Saints responded. The advantages of Sanpete are outlined in an 1853 entry in Danish immigrant Christian Nielson's diary: "It was stated that there was plenty of grass and forest at that country place [Sanpete] and there was a good opportunity for emigrants to get around and have a house erected . . . The best ground around Salt Lake City was already divided out, or bought, and, of course, nearly everyone of ours did not have the dollars to buy with. Our oxen and other animals that belong to us could likely find more grass to eat in San Pete than around Salt Lake City, where grass fields were limited. Further, it took three days to get a load of cut down trees taken from the mountains to Salt Lake City and a small load will cost $6. For the different reasons stated, it was recommended by our church authorities, and accepted by us, to journey down to Sanpete."[49]

Mobility within the Latter-day Saint population was also a factor, with many church members moving from one settlement to another looking for the right fit. Take, for example, Redick Allred, whose diary chronicles his family's wanderings: "[in the spring of 1850] I attempted to get some land 8 miles north of Salt Lake City in Sissons [Sessions] Settlement [present-day Bountiful] but altho there were only six [families] there they said the water was all taken up. . . . Then we went to Big Cotton Wood [at the southeastern end of the Salt Lake Valley] and located near the mouth of the Canyon, where we had plenty of water but little land."[50] Next he went on a church proselytizing mission to Hawaii, then lived for a time in Kaysville, north of Salt Lake City, before moving to Nephi in Juab County during the Utah War of 1858. Then, finally, "in the fall of 1859 I sold out [in Nephi] and moved to Sanpete Valley, where Geo Black and others were relocating the place from whence Uncle James Allred and others were driven by Indians in 1853 [Spring City]. I put up the first or second cabin in the place."[51]

On their 1850 visit, President Young and Apostle Kimball helped lay out the Manti townsite, which closely followed the revised City of Zion plan (Figure 2.9). Under their direction, the land was surveyed into 110 blocks, each 26 rods (416 feet) square and separated by streets uniformly 6 rods (96 feet) wide. It is noteworthy that the temple block at this time was placed in the center of the town, and no parks were penciled in, though city land records show that one was actually established on block 73 in the northwest quadrant. Each block contained eight lots placed at right angles; in practice, however, the lots were distributed in sets of two so that the customary number of lots per block is four, each containing an acre and a half of land.[52]

The Manti Saints built several forts. The first, encompassing a single city block, was completed during the summer of 1852. Too small to offer much protection, this stockade was replaced by a larger fort in 1854 that enclosed nine city blocks in the center of town, including the temple block. The "big fort," as it was aptly called, was a combobulation of various materials and technologies: part of it was rock while other sections, according to one resident, were

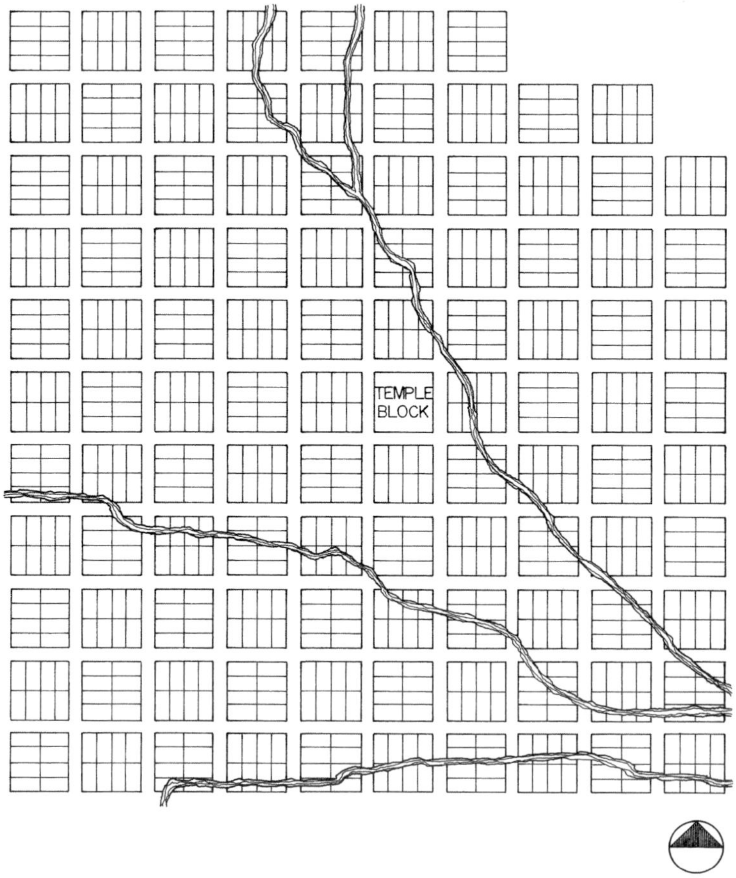

Figure 2.9. Manti City plat, 1852. The original temple block is in the center.

"built in the old Spanish style, by making a frame of wood and filling this with mud, and some of it was built with large adobes."[53] Each family received a city lot, a fort lot, and acreage in the meadow. Narrow east-west-running house lots were laid out on the fort blocks, and land was set aside for farming in the natural meadows located to the west, in the Sanpitch River bottomlands. A common fence enclosed the whole of the meadow, but it was not communally farmed. Rather, narrow strips of unequal size were individually owned and operated (Figure 2.10).[54]

No record survives of how the farmland was actually divided in Manti, but settlers apparently anticipated the practice used several years later in Fort Ephraim, the second town to be established in the valley. In Ephraim, the amount of farmland each family had was determined by how much hay its members could cut in a day. Rural sociologist Lowry Nelson describes the process as follows:

> It was agreed that no one should cut hay in the meadow until after midnight on the evening of July 25. Everyone who wished to cut some hay would naturally desire to get it where it was most accessible and of the best quality. Accordingly

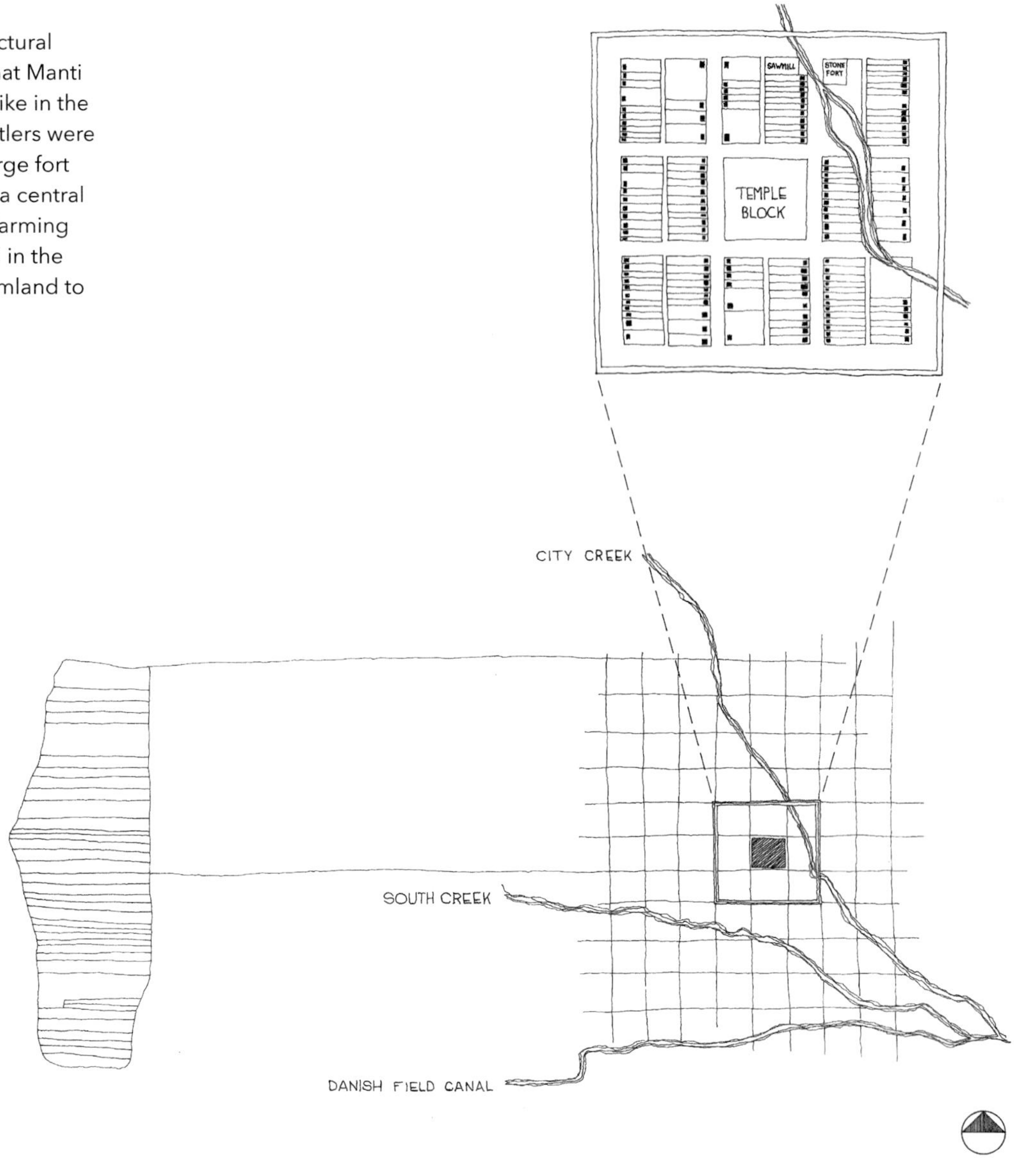

Figure 2.10. A conjectural reconstruction of what Manti would have looked like in the mid-1850s. Most settlers were still living inside a large fort constructed around a central temple square and farming narrow strips of land in the Sanpete River bottomland to the west.

> there was a premium attached to getting on the ground first. A community dance would be held until twelve o'clock when all would yoke up their oxen and make a dash for the hayfield. There was, however, always this provision—each man, without any assistance should cut a swath with the scythe around the hay which he desired. But he must not encircle more than he could cut, single handed, in one day. For if there was any hay left standing at the close of the day, anyone could come in and take it without interference. After the first day there were no restrictions.[55]

Strange as it may seem, the Ephraim model for dividing property exemplifies Mormon practice generally, for it emphasizes an "everyone according to their need" philosophy found in all facets of community life. The Latter-day Saints viewed equality not in the sense of all members having identical shares, but rather, that church members would share according to their needs and presumably their abilities. For example, a large family would "need" more than a small family, an enterprising one more than a lazy one, and so forth. Inherent in such a system were both opportunities for advancement and inequities in distribution. Need, after all, was a relative matter.

Within a few years, the Manti town lands were surveyed and divided into individually owned and operated fields. Because the Sanpete settlement predated the federal land survey, farm lots in the valley do not follow established section lines; instead, they are unequal in size and conform more to the local topography than to any imposed grid overlay (Figure 2.11). Land distribution again seems to have involved both privilege (leading citizens had first option to the best ground) and chance (leftover parcels were dispensed through the drawing of lots). Each family was apportioned acreage according to its needs,

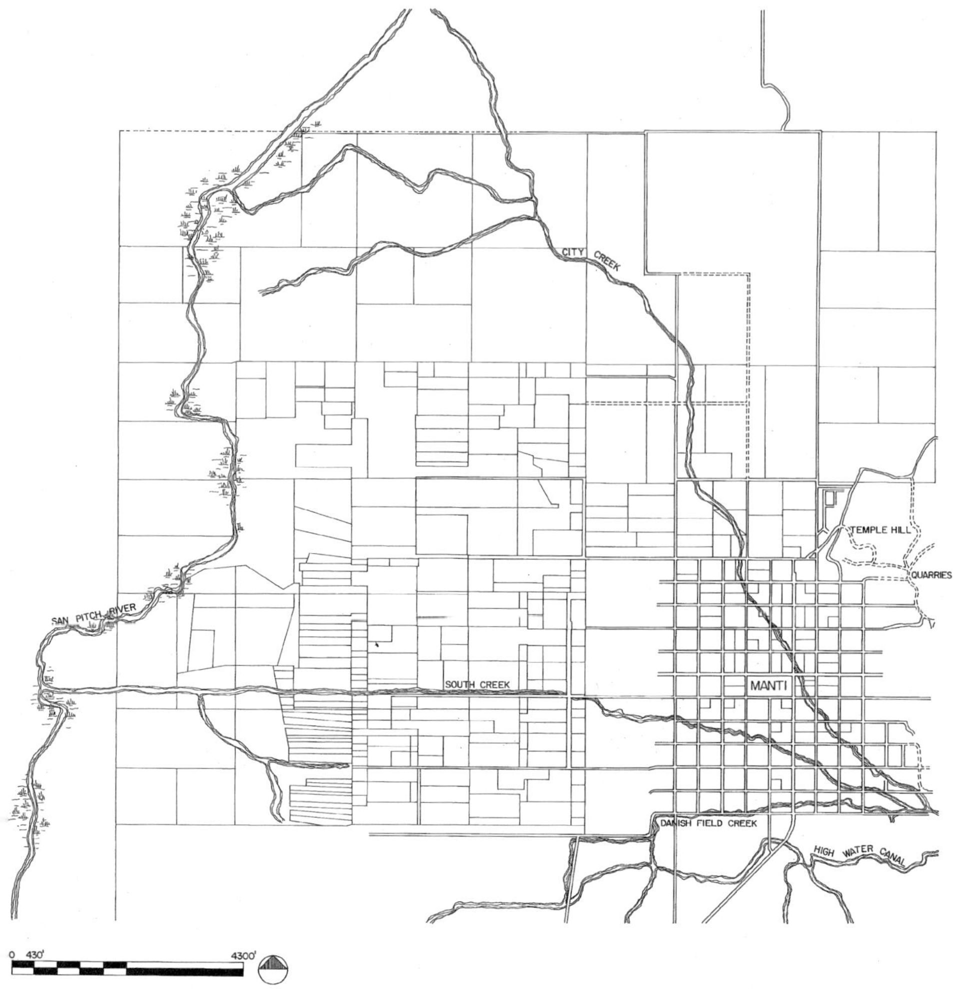

Figure 2.11. Manti City and farmlands, circa 1880. In the late 1850s and early 1860s, the ground to the west and north of the city was divided into separate farms. The plot sizes vary according to topography and size of individual holding. Notice that the original strip farms have endured.

though land records reveal a healthy amount of buying and selling as the settlers attempted to consolidate and improve their holdings. The federal agricultural census for Manti in 1880 lists 137 farms with an average size of 35 acres. The majority of farms, however, were smaller, consisting of 10–15 acres, a figure offset by a number of families falling in the 50- to 70-acre range, with five families possessing more than 100. The census also enumerates the value of each farmer's "land and improvements." Since barns and granaries were constructed in town, improvements on the land would primarily be fencing and irrigation ditches. Clearly some land was better and held a higher value. John Patten's 37 acres were appraised at $2,000 while George Snow's 20 came in at only $200. Similarly, Soren Christopher had 70 acres with a value of $5,000 and Richard Hall's 120 were listed at only $1,000.[56]

Most issues dealing with the running of the towns were left to the city council. Mormon leaders saw the westward migration not as secession from the Union but rather an opportunity for them to create their own (albeit enormous) state within the Union, and thus quickly established American-style civil institutions. Ostensibly church and state functions were separate, each having its own organization. On the ecclesiastical side, the levels of government consisted of the church, the stake, and the ward. The church was governed by the General Authorities, a group that included the chosen president, who was also considered to be a prophet, aided by two counselors and the Quorum of the Twelve Apostles. Next in importance were the stake officials, including a president and his counselors, who presided over the various "stakes" of Zion. The church is divided into stakes (metaphorically anchoring the tent, which was the larger church) that are further subdivided into wards, the congregational building blocks of the religion. A lay official called a bishop administers the ward. Small rural communities are sometimes designated as branches and are led by a branch president. During the early years of settlement, most Sanpete towns consisted of a single ward, although Manti and Ephraim were larger and both were divided into two (north and south) in 1877. Curiously, during the 1850s Manti was considered both a ward and a branch, and had both a bishop and a president. Orson Hyde, a member of the Quorum of the Twelve Apostles, was the de facto ecclesiastical leader of the Sanpete colony until his death in November 1877, shortly after the valley wards were formally organized as the Sanpete Stake of Zion with Canute Peterson of Ephraim appointed stake president.[57]

Whatever pretense there was of church–state separation broke down in practice simply because most if not all civil positions were filled by leading members of the church. The bishop, for instance, often served as the mayor. The Saints, of course, did not view this overlap as a problem. In fact, they expected it. In talking about the prospects of the new town of Mount

Pleasant being incorporated as a city with its own government, Orson Hyde reminded the brethren that "all legitimate power originates in the Church of [Jesus] Christ [of Latter-day Saints] and all political powers must be acknowledged by the church in order to have success," further adding that the people should choose public officials who "are known to be faithful to the [church] leaders of the town."[58]

The Utah Territorial Legislature incorporated Manti as a city in 1851, although a city council with Dan Jones as mayor had been elected by the membership a year earlier.[59] There is some question, however, about who was actually in charge. On the council sat both Isaac Morley, president of the Manti Branch, and Bishop John Lowry. When Jones had to step down after being called on a proselytizing mission for the church, the council moved that Morley nominate a "Person to fill the place," revealing something about his status with the group.[60] Interestingly, Morley chose Jezrell Shomaker, who after being confirmed by the council admitted "it was his main object to carry out the [counsel] of Pr. Brigham Young."[61] When President Morley "said it was the Bishops duty to superintend all public Works,"[62] he was not disputed, for Mayor Jones instructed the council "not [to] disobey any direct [counsel] of Prst Morley."[63]

Acting in the interests of the church, then, the Manti City Council oversaw the affairs of the town. Not surprisingly, the first ordinance it passed outlawed swearing and blasphemy.[64] Then council members turned their attention to such things as building setbacks: "no person shall build their house or houses nearer than twenty feet to the street" (Figure 2.12);[65] beautification: "every holder of lots within the bounds of said City are hereby required to set out in front of their lots such trees for shade as shall in their opinion be the best qualified to adorn and Beautify the City, and to plant said trees not to exceed one rod apart –[except] for gate ways and not to exceed two feet from the line of said lot and lots on a [parallel] line with the side walk";[66] infrastructure: "moved . . . that [a] bridge be built across City Creek on the second street south of the farming land, near Levi W. Hancock's house";[67] business licenses: "any person or persons keeping a tavern, grocery, beer, or liquor shop within the limits of the city shall be required to obtain a license yearly";[68] and public education: "on motion it was carried that the school committee go ahead and build a school house according to their plan as fast as possible."[69]

Another aspect of town life falling under the council's jurisdiction was public health, and this involved regulating waste disposal, both animal and human. Germ theory, the correlation between disease and microorganisms, was in its infancy, but enough of this thinking had filtered into the system to make people aware of the need to protect potable water sources. Thus the council ordained in 1851 that "that no person or persons shall be allowed

Figure 2.12. The standardizing effects of the twenty-five-foot house setback zoning ordinance in Manti (after 1898 Sanborn Fire Insurance maps).

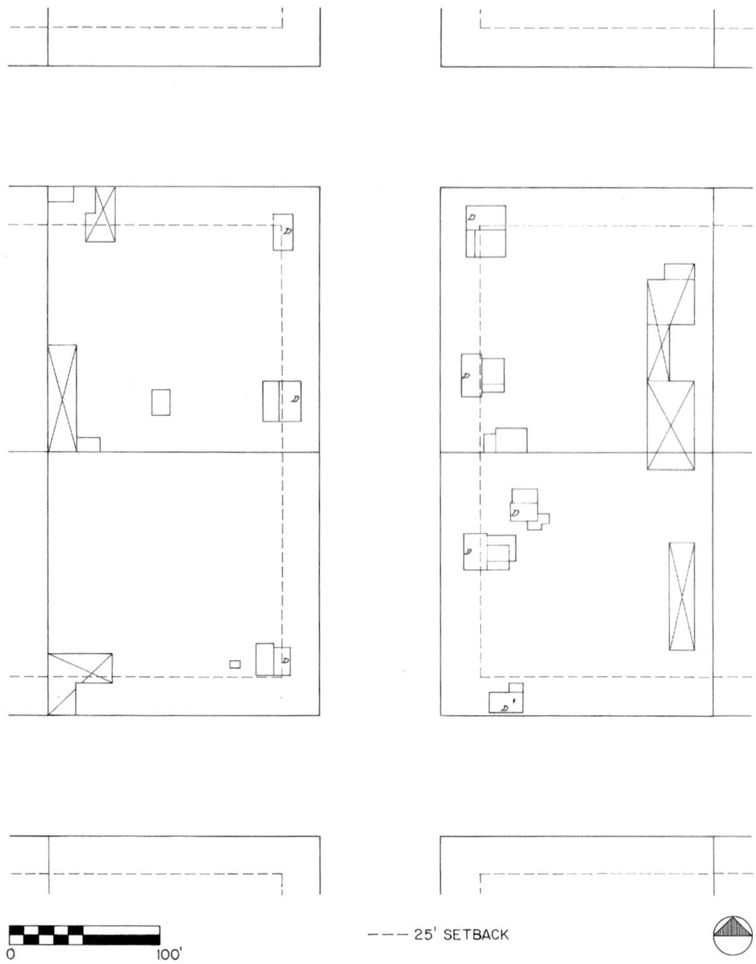

to erect or place cow sheds or yards, stables, privies or to deposit any filthy substance in or so near any of the water course of this City nor in or near the stream which runs through this City so as to affect the Waters thereof."[70] A complaint lodged in Mount Pleasant by the local newspaper editor demonstrated that such actions were necessary: "Look at the washing of dirty filthy clothes in the Water. Look at the water as it comes out of corrals deeply colored for the people below to drink. Is not God merciful that we do not sicken and die. Take your microscope and look at the myriads of live things in clear water. What must there be in the filthy, highly colored liquid called water. Come around our way Mr. Supervisor and see for yourself."[71]

The funds to pay for city programs came through the town councils' ability to levy and collect taxes. The Manti City Council placed a school tax on wheat, "determined at $2 a bushel for in kind payment,"[72] and for general revenue, it agreed to "assess all taxable property within the city limits at its fair cash value."[73] Most taxes were paid in the form of produce or work, as in the case of William Bench and twenty-one other Manti citizens who petitioned the council "for a grant of the privilege to work out their taxes on the erection of a bridge to be situated south east of the city fort outside the same where the City Creek crosses or intersects the road."[74]

How to enforce the various laws and ordinances always posed a problem. Sanpete towns had no real constabularies or jails until the 1860s, and even then they were largely an afterthought.[75] This neglect does not mean there was no conflict or crime. Plenty of both existed, but in most cases they were handled by the church either through the bishop or the bishop's court system, which monitored civil as well as ecclesiastical behavior. One indication of the church's power surfaces in a fencing case that came up repeatedly before the Manti City Council during the 1850s. During the early years of settlement, a single common fence enclosed the individually owned farm lots and hay meadows located outside the town limits. Families were obliged to construct and maintain a portion of fence commensurate with the amount of acreage they owned in the fields. The city council, which set fencing policy for the town lands, had to admonish settlers to comply with the program. In Manti, the situation deteriorated to the point that as a last resort "many of the Council expressed their feeling [of] being in favor of turning it [the fence issue] into the hands of the Bishop and his Council."[76]

Power lay in the pulpit, and church leaders often resorted to the threat of public humiliation as a way of getting the Saints to perform both their civil and their church duties. In one case, James Jones, the bishop of Fairview, rose in church and "stated that many were not living their religion, and wanted the Presidents of Quorums to look after their members and also wanted the Clerk to make out an account of the public work that each man had done, and read it from the stand."[77] Or as a final resort, there was the threat of expulsion. Again Bishop Jones in meeting "spoke of some of the brethren stealing Birch Creek water from Mount Pleasant. They [the perpetrators] would be disfellowshiped for he had counseled them all the time not to take one drop more than what belonged to them, said it was serious matter with him to disfellowship anybody."[78]

It deserves repeating that the Mormon towns were not monolithic in appearance or governance. Subtle differences existed in all the town plans (Figure 2.13), and the leaders in each town responded in different ways to the problems faced in getting their communities up and running. When it came to making decisions, the church-dominated councils appeared as slow in reaching consensus as their Gentile counterparts. Take the case of building the first fort in Manti. After arguing about everything from where it would be located to what it would cost to how to actually build it, the subject was simply dropped, leading one visiting church official to remark, "Truly this is

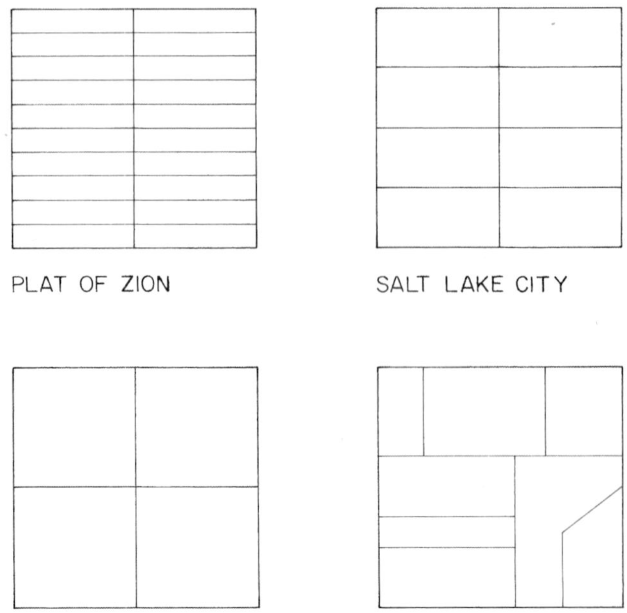

Figure 2.13. Variations in block arrangements: Plat of Zion (twenty lots per block); Salt Lake City (eight lots per block); Manti (the typical Sanpete type with four lots per block); and Ephraim (an exception with from four to twelve lots per block and often with odd and irregular shapes).

a people of great faith; for they rely upon little else for protection. They settle out upon their city lots and farms with all the freedom and apparent sense of security that the people of Illinois and Iowa do upon their prairies."[79] In 1867, at the height of Mormon–Ute hostilities during the Black Hawk War, fort talk resurfaced in the form of building a wall around the whole town. An editorial in the *Manti Herald and Sanpete Advertiser* extolled the virtues of such a project: "We believe it is an accepted fact or idea that Manti is to have a city wall. Now when we say 'City Wall' we mean one of those substantial rock and mortar concerns that will not only enclose but increase the value of property immensely, and through its solidity and workmanship-like finish will stand for ages as a monument of credit and intelligent industry on the part of the builders."[80] The wall was never started.

Expansion

After 1850, expansion in the valley was fueled both by a steady influx of new settlers arriving from the northern colonies and Scandinavia, and a general desire on the part of the Saints to seek out new and more attractive settlement locations. Through the 1850s and 1860s, eight new towns were founded, each with its own story. The drift of settlement was to the north, the result of what seems a constant pressure for new towns. What we see is a hiving off of the Manti population, as Smith had advocated in his original City of Zion plan, but significantly, at least in the Sanpete Valley, this action came with no apparent overcrowding. Rather, families just wanted more or better land, or wanted to live by themselves. Good examples of this kind of opportunism can be seen in the first two settlements established outside Manti; the first came in 1852 and lay seven miles north at Pine Creek, later called Fort Ephraim or simply Ephraim, and the second in 1853 at Canal Creek, about fifteen miles northeast of Manti in a community named Springtown, later Spring City. To repeat, Manti was not overcrowded in 1852. The initial land surveys were still in progress, and President Morley, an old communard, had initiated a policy whereby latecomers would receive land rights similar to those of original colonists. Anthropologist Michael Raber, in what remains one of the best studies of Mormon settlement practices, calls attention to the fact that "the continuing availability of land [in Manti] and the relative remoteness [of both Pine and Canal Creeks] . . . implies that anyone moving there in 1852 had to find [these sites] themselves and do so for reasons other than land shortage."[81]

Motives of those who founded these new towns went unrecorded, but both Raber and Dell Upton, who has also written on Mormon material culture, suggest that habit may have been the culprit. Most American Saints were born and raised in the tradition of independent family farms, and an abiding memory of this kind of living may have driven them to set out on their own to found new and more dispersed communities. The first family to move north to Pine Creek was that of Isaac Behunin, and they hailed from rural New York State. Similarly, the families desiring land along Canal Creek were all Allreds and natives of Tennessee. The actions of both parties reveal a streak of dogged independence among the Sanpete Zionists, and if not for the threat of Ute attack the human landscape of the valley might have evolved quite differently.[82]

Behunin was first. He moved from Manti with his wife and nine children and spent the winter of 1852–53 in a shelter dug into the banks of Pine Creek. In the spring and summer the Behunins farmed about forty acres of land.[83] As the season wore on, a number of other Manti residents ventured north to Pine Creek, including Reuben Allred, who came with fifteen families, "impelled," he said, by the "land and water and delightful situation for a colony."[84] Behunin, however, was hardly welcoming, a decisive sign of his lack of the "Kingdom-building" spirit. As potential new neighbors arrived, he warned them off, saying there was only enough water for one family. This is how one of the newcomers, Augusta Dorius Stevens, put it: "There had already settled on this creek one man and his family by the name of Bahannan who had cultivated some land along the creek and had his cabin [there]. . . . Considerable objection was waged against the settlers by Bahannan as he contended there would not be enough water in the creek for his sheep and to water the small tract of ground he had cultivated."[85] The point was moot, however, because the fledgling settlement had to be abandoned in the fall of 1853 due to Indian hostilities, with the Behunins and their begrudgingly accepted neighbors heading back to Manti.[86]

The Pine Creek settlement was reoccupied in force in 1854, and a small stockade called Fort Ephraim constructed for protection. Good farmland, located north and west of town in the alluvial fan created by the northwesterly flowing creeks, was quickly surveyed "for that purpose."[87] Initially the settlers embraced a communitarian ethic that centered on farming a large "common field" and erecting a fort. One early settler commented that "the cooperative or Typical Teutonic plan was adopted by the original Colonists and one common field, irrigated from the waters of Pine Creek, through union ditches, was occupied."[88] The same cooperative spirit prevailed in the fort, where it was reported: "In building the wall [of the fort] most of the brethren took turns in spending two days of each week working on the wall, while others would work on the canyon road and haul wood and timber. The wall was finished, so far as it ever was, some time during 1855."[89]

Within a short period, however, a more individualistic way of life returned. A town site with individual city lots was surveyed in 1859, originally three-quarters of a mile square, six blocks each way—second west to fourth east, and third north to third south—with a addition of two rows of blocks on the south coming within a few years (Figure 2.14). A history of the city reads:

> Around the outside streets garden lots were located. These varied somewhat in size and the distance they extended into the fields. The greatest number were west of the highway north of town and west of second west where they extended one fourth mile into the fields.
>
> The cultivated fields were divided into five-acre lots except where natural barriers such as creeks, hills or hollows interfered. Eight five-acre lots were to form a block of four acres with a two rod road all around. The main roads were to follow the slope of the land, while the access roads to the five acre plots inaccessible by the main road were to go across the slopes. This pattern is very visible today.
>
> Thus the land was divided into various fields, all with designed ditches for watering, and mostly fenced with large poles from the mountains. In addition there were the meadows to the north and west of these fields. The hay meadow beginning from the Spring City hayfield on the north was divided into eighty-seven strips three rods wide and two miles long east to west, and south of this there were forty-eight shares of the same width but only one mile long east and west. The Ephraim West Meadow had shares five rods wide and a mile long, containing ten acres. . . .

> The plans were that each family was to have a city lot, a garden lot if they so chose, five acres in one of the fields near town and five acres under Pigeon Hollow or Willow creek, a cow share and a hay lot. This would make a total of about twenty-five acres.[90]

Most Ephraimites were eager, once the survey was finished, to "leave the fort and build on their city lots."[91] Land distribution was intended to be fair; according to Amanda B. Cox, "the land was also divided by each family drawing ten or twenty acres according to the size of the family and the quality of the land."[92] Again, according to need.

A similar pattern played out in the settlement of Spring City, which occurred as in Ephraim without any oversight beyond that of the chief instigator, James Allred, who wanted to settle a large area with a few of his own

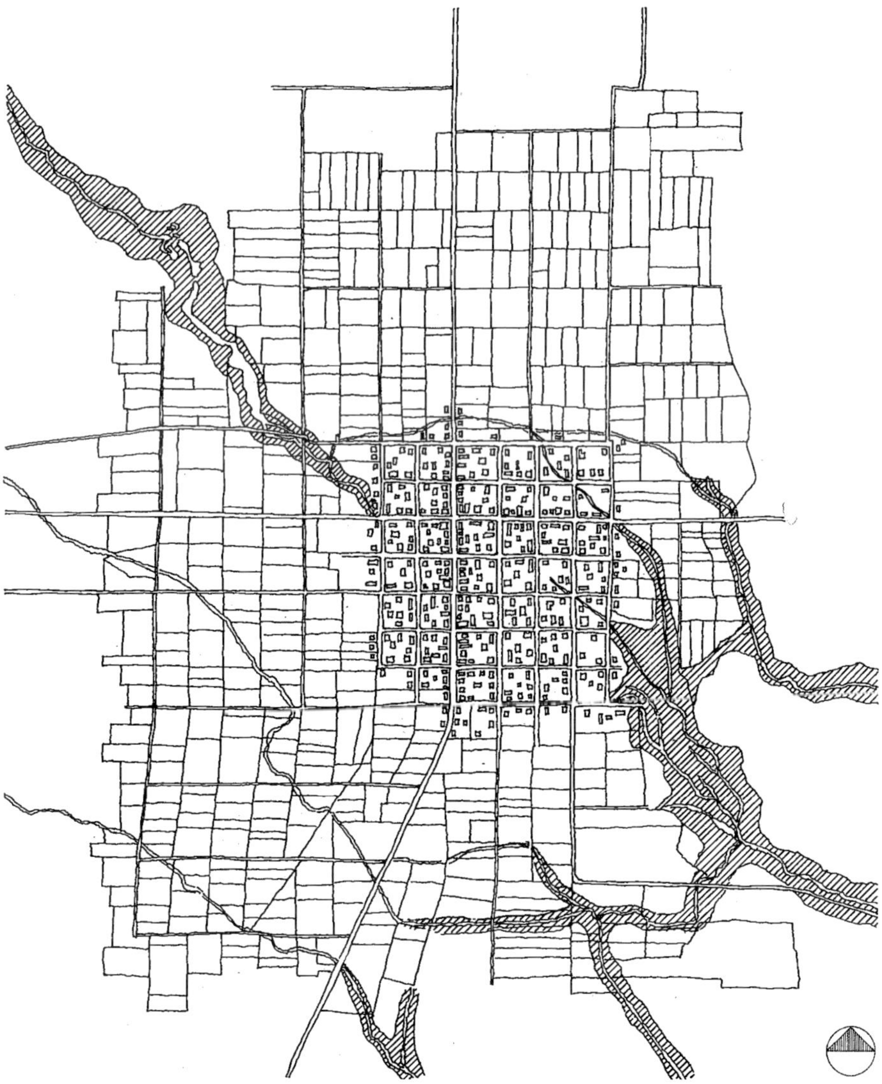

Figure 2.14. Ephraim City and surrounding farmlands, circa 1880.

family members, something he could not do in Manti.[93] A stalwart in the church who had held leadership positions in the East, Allred was a figure of some independence and authority. And certainly he had experience in frontier life. Allred family histories show a people on the move since the late eighteenth century, starting in North Carolina and moving west through northern Georgia and finally into south-central Tennessee. In 1830 several Allreds moved to Missouri, where they joined the Mormon Church in 1832 and, according to Michael Raber's research, "appear to have settled in a pattern of contiguous farms occupied by close relatives." This pattern of familial clustering, Raber argues, was carried over to Utah, where "generations of experience as pioneer farmers," coupled with a tradition of settling "in large groups of kin and affines," shaped their settlement preferences. In short, Raber writes, "being confident in their pattern of living on contiguous farms, they wanted to simply reproduce it in Utah," in direct contradiction of church policies for nucleated settlement.[94]

Spring City began life as Allred's Settlement, and if the family had had their way the name might have stuck. Patriarch James Allred arrived in Salt Lake City in 1851; he was sixty-seven years old and a longtime church member. He knew Isaac Morley from their days together in Illinois. Within a year he moved to Manti, where one of his sons, James T. S., had already located, probably because of the family's relationship with Morley. Before leaving the capital city, tradition has it that Brigham Young advised Allred to "select a place for settlement in the Sanpete Valley where [you can] locate with [your] numerous posterity and kindred and preside over them."[95] Primary documents do not substantiate Young's counsel; however, Allred's actions make it clear that this is exactly what he intended to do, for as soon as he arrived in Manti he petitioned Young for permission to establish an Allred family settlement. This petition probably came early in 1851, for in a sermon later that year Young recalled that Allred "had previously been to me not only to know if they might settle in San Pete, but if they [the Allred family] might separate widely from each other, over a piece of land about two miles square, each having a five acre lot for his garden, near their farms" (Figure 2.15).[96]

Young apparently told Allred, as he would others in the valley, to gather together and build a fort. But Allred, perhaps because of his close friendship with Young and his status as a longtime loyal Latter-day Saint, kept his own counsel and moved to Canal Creek in the early spring of 1852. There he and families members effected an even more scattered type of settlement than originally proposed. Raber's research shows that instead of a central town site, one of the Allred cabins was situated "just north of Canal Creek, another near one of the larger springs in the present townsite, and another for James Allred near Cedar Creek, about a mile north of the others" (Figure

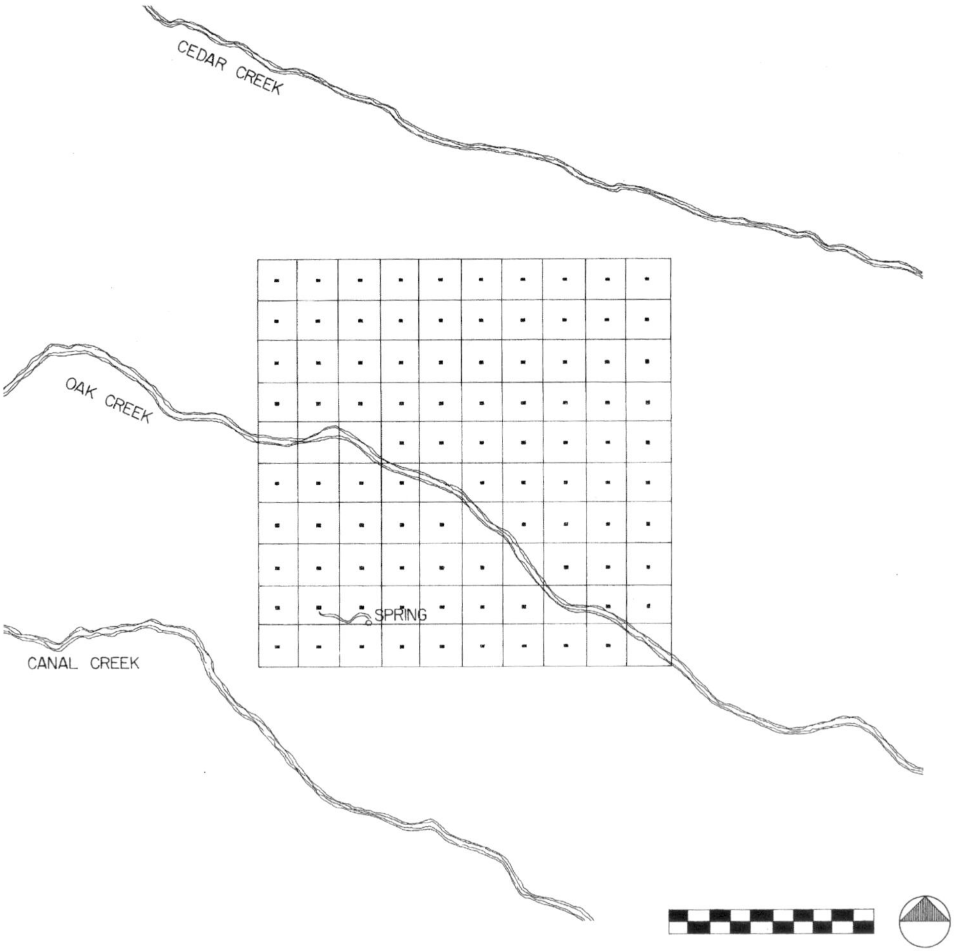

Figure 2.15. Reconstruction of Allred's Settlement, later renamed Spring City, as it was initially proposed in 1851.

2.16).[97] Apostle George A. Smith encountered this arrangement when he visited Sanpete later in the summer, notifying the *Deseret News* that Springtown was settled "by Elder James Allred, with his numerous family and a few relatives, each one building in the vicinity of a spring, in a somewhat scattered condition." Smith "advised [them] to gather together in a fort, upon which they moved some of their cabins closer together."[98] But the family's hopes for a dispersed kind of settlement were not shattered until, like the Behunins in Ephraim, they were forced to regroup in the face of fierce attacks by the Utes during the winter of 1852–53.

The next summer the small Allred family settlement was reinforced by a large contingent of Danish converts—"an influence [having been] put upon them," as one Dane said, to go to Springtown. The fort was enlarged, but by the end of 1853 a general removal occurred as the isolated community proved indefensible when full-blown warfare with the Utes broke out.[99] The town site would not be reoccupied for another six years. In 1859 a chastened

Figure 2.16. Reconstruction of Allred's Settlement as it was originally configured in 1852.

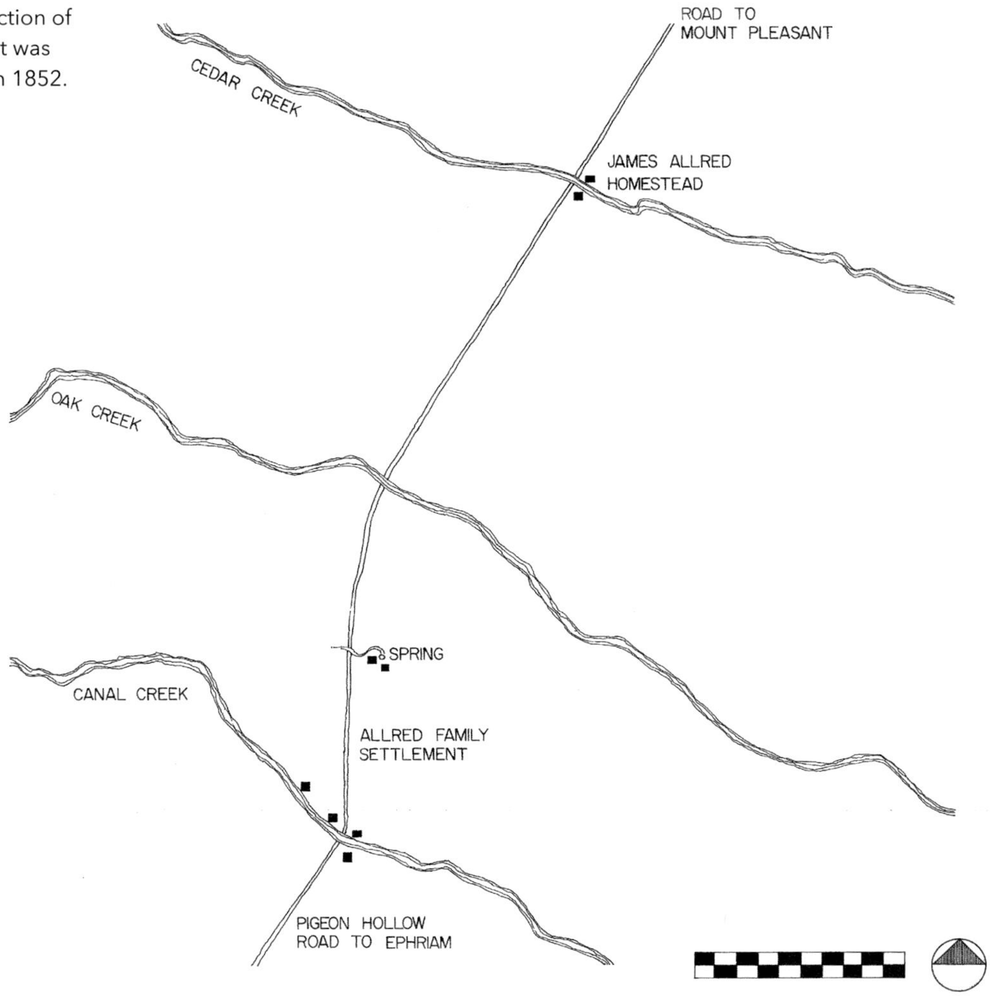

band of Allreds, now under the leadership of George Black and J. T. Ellis, returned, bringing with them Albert Petty, the church surveyor, who laid out a grid type of settlement in Mormon fashion and 640 acres surrounding it for farmland (Figure 2.17). Immediately, the following advertisement for reinforcements appeared in the *Deseret News:* "We have been informed of a new settlement. . . . The facilities for farming are said to be good, surpassed by few, in any, in the Territory, and if peace prevails in these mountains, a thriving village will soon, no doubt, spring into existence there."[100]

The next town settled was Mount Pleasant, located on Pleasant Creek about eight miles north of Spring City. In the winter of 1851–52, "Madison Hambleton and Gardner Potter built a sawmill [at this site] . . . with the object of getting out lumber for the market, the other adjacent canyons presenting such hard conditions of access."[101] The Indian raids of 1853 drove out these enterprising men, but it wasn't long before a number of families

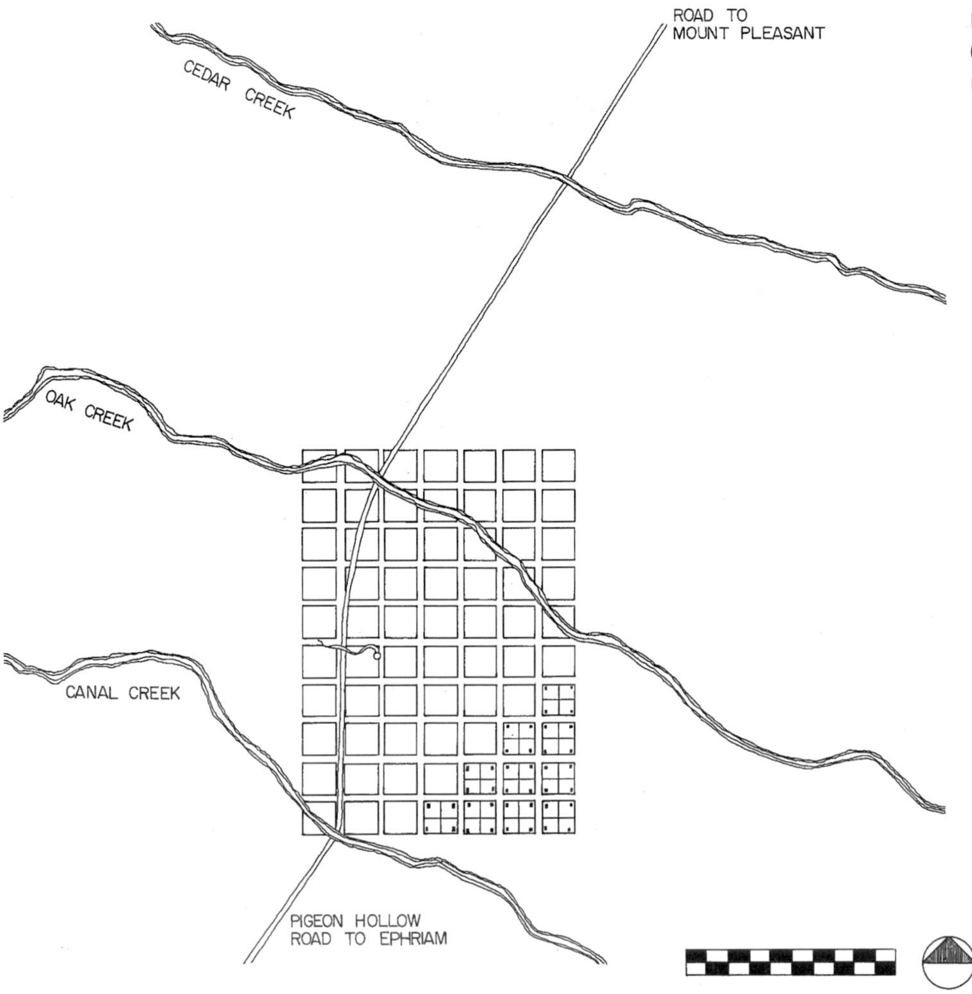

Figure 2.17. Plat of Spring City (Allred's Settlement) after its resettlement in 1859.

from Ephraim expressed a desire to reoccupy the site and start their own town. Again, no evidence exists that Ephraim was overcrowded. In 1858, the would-be settlers chose a committee to "select a location for a new settlement in the north part of the valley." The scouts returned having decided on the Hambleton-Potter mill site on Pleasant Creek. A petition signed by about sixty Ephraim families was entrusted to three men—James Ivie, Joseph Clement, and Isaac Allred—who served as a "deputation to wait upon Pres. Brigham Young, in order to obtain his advice in regard to the founding of the proposed settlement." The emissaries traveled to Salt Lake City and presented the signatures to Young, who after reading the document, said he was "perfectly satisfied that a settlement should be made on Pleasant Creek." The petitioners wanted Young to choose a leader, but "he would not do this, but sent a letter of instructions" for a fort to be built and settlers to gather close together for their protection.[102]

This time the colonists followed Young's instructions. One pioneer recalled that the fort

> inclosed the block later known as the Tithing Yard. 26 rods by 26 rods, enclosing about five and one-half acres of ground. . . . It was made according to instructions and was built of native rock, taken from the surface or dug out of the ground. It was laid with mud mortar. The wall was 12 feet high, four feet wide at the bottom, tapering to about two feet at the top. This wall, in order that the maneuvers of the Indians could be watched from the inside, was built with port holes every 16 feet. About seven feet from the ground. The holes were about two feet wide on the inside, and about four inches on the outside and about 18 inches high. Later the inside of the wall was utilized for one wall in the erection of houses, 16 feet square, with one port hole in the middle of the one wall of each house. There was a flat roofed house in the northwest corner of the fort upon which guards could stand and view the country.[103]

Shortly after, the town site was laid out and the surrounding town lands divided into twenty-acre farming parcels. The settlement thrived, and by 1880 Mount Pleasant had become the largest town in the valley with a population of around 2000.

The year 1859 also saw towns founded at Fairview, Wales, Moroni, and Fountain Green. The impetus for the Fairview settlement followed the pattern in other Sanpete towns, as the thirst for more and better farmland led a number of Mount Pleasant families to move eight miles north and start the town of North Bend, later renamed Fairview. As the settlers gathered in their new location, the newly chosen bishop, James Jones, spoke, saying that he "wished the brethren to be united, and work to build up this place, and make it a beautiful location, worthy of the good wishes of the Servants of God."[104] There may have been some hard feelings on the part of those left behind in Mount Pleasant. In the 1860s the Fairview Ward minutes report that "sum three weeks ago Bishop William Seeley of Mount Pleasant sent a herd of cattle within three miles of our Settlement on land that we had surveyed as we needed more land. Bishop James N. Jones requested him to move them away, which he refused to do, he then sent him a letter with [another] request to move them, but he still refused. Then President [Welcome] Chapman [of Manti] wrote him a letter requesting him to move them away and restore good feelings but still to no purpose."[105] So much for unity of spirit in building the Kingdom of God.

Wales's (Coal Bed) reason for being is traceable to the discovery of coal in a nearby canyon. In 1856, two Welsh converts, John Rees and John Price, were living in Ephraim when they heard from the Indians about the presence of coal in the west mountains. Since they had been coal miners in their homeland, the heavily industrialized Glamorganshire region of southern Wales, they conducted initial investigations. In 1859 Rees returned with fifteen Welsh families to begin mining operations in what became the first coal mine in Utah.[106] Coal from this site, appropriately named Wales, was hauled northward by wagon to Salt Lake City. The coal in the canyons above Wales was never of high quality, however, and the company failed by 1880.[107]

The settlement of Moroni and Fountain Green, in contrast to the other towns, seems to have been more centrally directed. In the winter of 1858–59, Brigham Young asked George W. Bradley of Nephi to settle the Moroni site, which he did with forty families in the summer of 1859. Moroni was supplied with a grid, though to the north of town a series of separate—"scattered" the census taker called them—houses were arranged in a line village pattern (Figure 2.18).[108] In that same year, Young also instructed George Johnson to establish a town at Uinta Springs, a favorite camping spot for families traveling to Manti through Salt Creek Canyon. Johnson's town, now called Fountain Green, was immediately platted in a grid fashion by Albert Petty, the Sanpete County surveyor.[109] Young's reasons for founding these two towns may

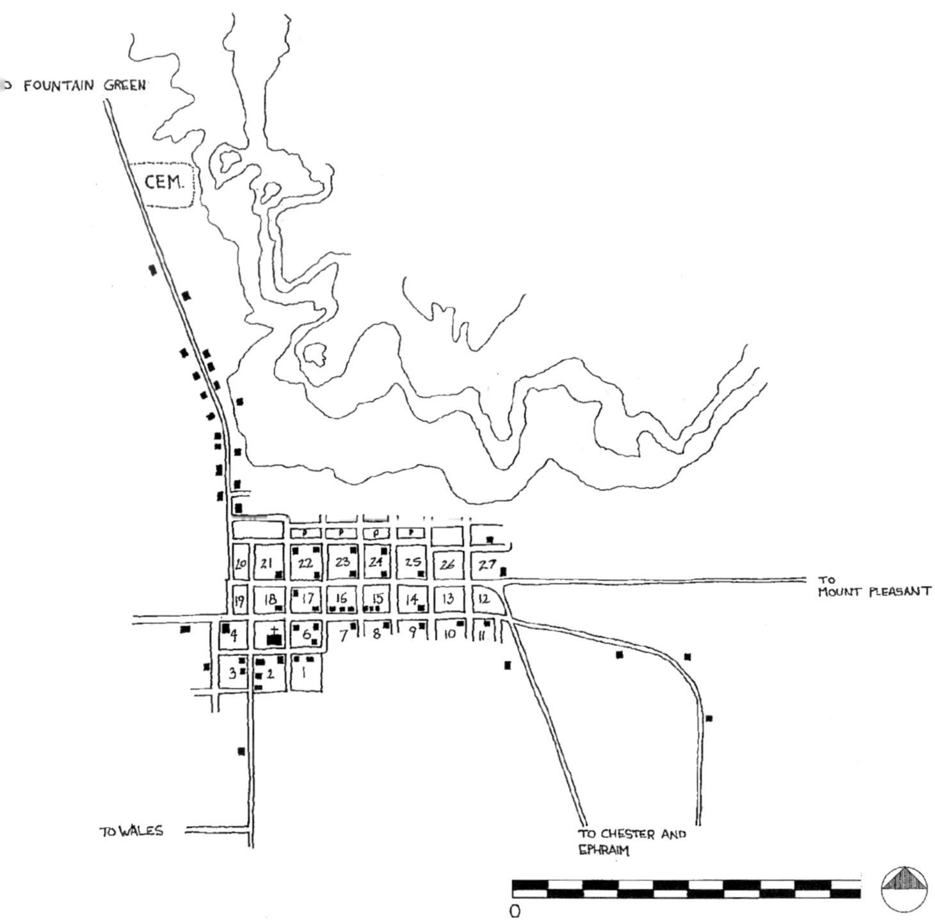

Figure 2.18. Plan showing Moroni's unusual L-shaped layout and linear northern extension composed of individual holdings.

reflect a feeling that his original 1850 plan for a line of connected settlements had gone unrealized and the settlers needed his help in getting things done properly. Neither town had the water resources possessed by communities on the east side of the valley. In Moroni in particular, water was scarce and the settlers had to bring it over from the Sanpitch River in a four-mile-long ditch.[110] Since these were hardly conditions to make unsolicited settlement attractive, Young stepped in.

Each Sanpete town went through similar stages of development: a town was platted, a fort was built, settlers lived in the fort through the 1850s, and finally by the early 1860s the town sites were occupied. Overall, the settlement of the valley transpired as a mixture of church and individual action approximating the general outline of a "communicating network" emanating from Salt Lake City. Opportunity rather than overcrowding or central planning was the overriding impetus for expansion. Later arrivals could take up the leftover land in the established communities, as it was available, or buy from residents at market-driven prices. Demand for personal advantage in both size of farm and quality of land remained the primary factors leading families to strike out on their own to settle new towns. It also put pressure on the village system itself.

Scattered farmsteads, those where families lived outside the city limits on their land, were present in all Sanpete towns, though the number of such outliers was always small. The principal exception was Chester, which from the beginning was a community of dispersed holdings. In 1870, after the lessening of Indian hostilities, Mount Pleasant resident David Candland, a friend of Brigham Young and an irrepressible entrepreneur, decided to expand his personal estate by laying claim to the rich bottomland along the Sanpitch River. According to his biography, "The Territorial legislature had enacted the Homestead Act [1862], whereby settlers could file on large tracts of land, live on it so many years and thus become the owner. Here was the chance. . . . The lands of [Candland's] choice lay ten miles west of Mt. Pleasant, adjacent to a deep rushing stream called 'Canal Creek.'"[111] In 1870 Candland, along with Hans Beck, his Danish business partner, made "the first entry . . . on three quarter sections and Hans Beck followed suit with two. [Beck] was to become David's farmer, built three houses for David and two for himself and moved all the [polygamous] families into them while David furnished farm implements, clothing, shoes and other necessary articles from Salt Lake City."[112] Candland found the Canal Creek District settlement, later called Chesterfield and then shortened to Chester, attractive because it afforded his family "more land and resources."[113]

Chester, organized as an LDS ward in July 1877, was described in 1900 as including the "scattered population residing on both sides of Canal Creek, south of Moroni, and covers farming and meadow lands which formerly were included in the Mount Pleasant and Moroni hay fields. . . . All the people live on their farms, as no townsite has been surveyed as yet" (Figure 2.19).[114] Chester never achieved the status of a real town, instead being something of a "crossroads" type of community with "a [log] meetinghouse, a school house, a store, and a few residences."[115] The attraction for the settlers here was well-watered and incredibly productive soil, with "75 bushels of wheat per acre not uncommon" (compared to the valley average of about forty bushels per acre).[116] Reuben Allred writes about Chester: "B[ishop Frederick] Olsen [of Spring City] . . . sent me to locate a qua[r]ter Section in the farming land in Cannal bottoms with the same promis of reward [basically that the ward would pay him for it for the benefit of the town], but neither was realized, so I proved up on the Land in Chester for myself and moved upon it. After which many others did the same making quite a nice settlement."[117] Allred ended up selling his city lot in Spring City and then moved the "remainder of my family to the new farm. My Bros Isaac and Sidney and my son Redick R. located there [Chester]."[118] Reuben describes the community as it appeared around 1877: "the place grew to quite a prosperous settlement—[people] living on their farms."[119] The rush to claim the open land caused some jealousy on the

Figure 2.19. Chester, circa 1880. This community was established after the initial settlement of the valley. It had a small gridiron plat at its core, but primarily consisted of dispersed homesteads spotted along fertile bottomland between Oak and Canal Creeks.

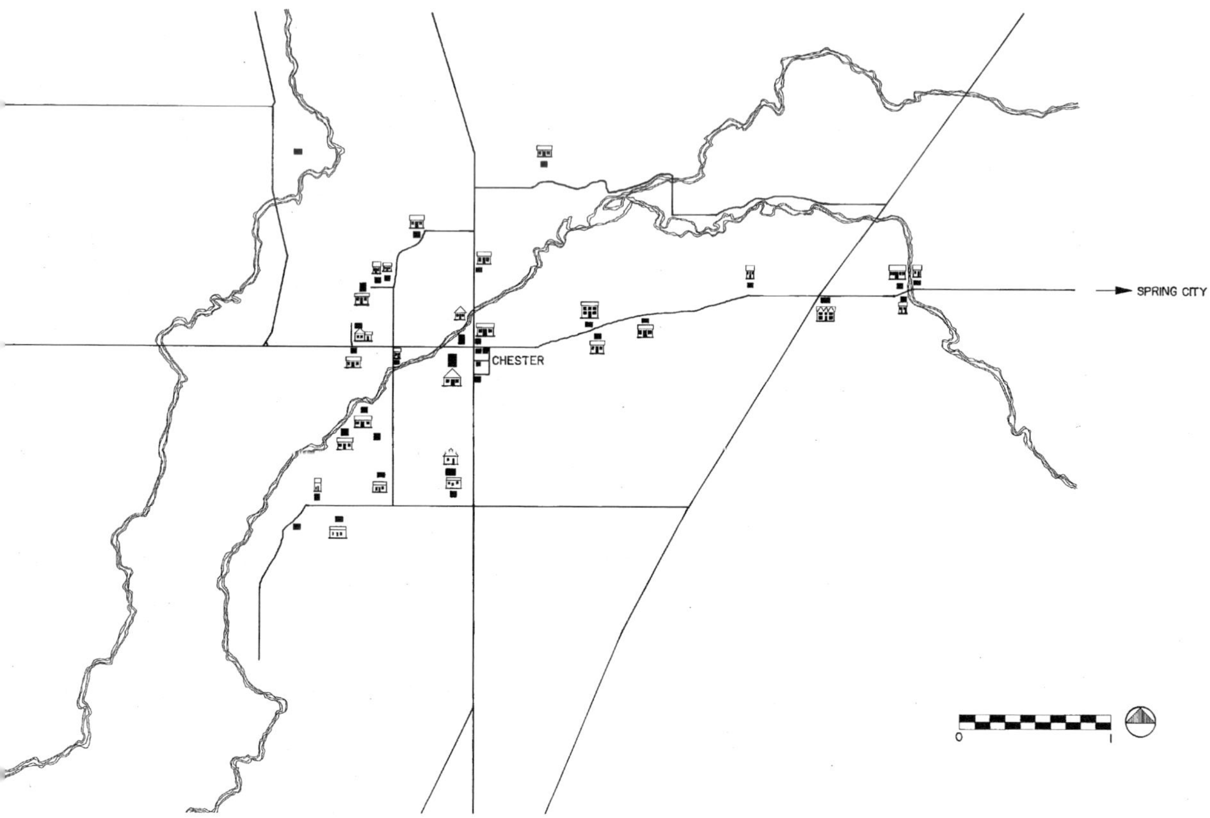

part of the families that stayed in town, making Reuben feel a bit guilty, for later he writes, "I divided up my qua[r]ter section with three poor families keeping only 60 acres for my family to keep down [prejudice] to keep from being called a land jumper."[120]

Would the Chester pattern of dispersed holdings have become the new standard for Mormon western settlement if it had continued through the 1880s and 1890s? It is hard to know. The drive for expansion had pretty well exhausted itself by this time, and besides, the most advantageous locations for farming had been taken up. Using some examples from southern Idaho, where Mormon settlement continued into the early twentieth century, it appears the answer would be yes, since the American style of market towns and individual farms and ranches seems to have been the preferred arrangement. In those areas where villages were established, as in Grouse Creek, along the Utah–Nevada border and in Kelly, Wyoming, outside Jackson, the line village form, with ranches about a half-mile apart, was adopted. In Chesterfield, Idaho, the settlers kept the grid, but stretched it out in a way that only the Spring City Allreds could appreciate, with each block consisting of twenty acres, enough so that you could barely see your neighbors. Times and people change, of course, and by the end of the Kingdom-building period in 1890, the village concept was largely an anachronism.[121]

Another major change in the composition of the Mormon western landscape that occurred late in the Zion-making period was longer lived, and more profound. This involved moving the temple from the center to the outskirts of town, a detached, contemplative site that it has occupied ever since.

Temple on the Hill

During much of Sanpete's early history, local residents referred to the center of Manti as the "public square" or, more commonly, the "Temple Block," since President Young had proclaimed in 1850 that a temple would be built on this site.[122] By the early 1870s, however, things had changed. The talk in the valley now focused on "temple hill" and the great edifice that the Saints would soon erect there. What happened? What caused Young to alter the original town plan and shift the temple from the central block to the top of a nearby hill? The decision was momentous for it required a fundamental restructuring of the Mormon symbolic universe. The strong pull of the sacred center was replaced by a more ambiguous but in the end equally powerful cosmic alignment in which sacred (temple) and profane (town/house) could peacefully coexist. The full implications of the move will be more fully treated in subsequent chapters, but any discussion of early Mormon town planning must confront the simple truth that it transpired. Something happened between around 1870 and about 1875 that made Young change his mind about temples and their place in Zion.

What it was we will never know, for nowhere in his writings or sermons does Young explain his motives. In fact, in speaking of siting temples outside Salt Lake City, he appears incredibly nonchalant, matter-of-factly stating that the temple will be "built here because God ordained it" and leaving it at that. Clearly, however, the millennial world of the early church was ending, and once the decision on temple siting had been made, the change was both swift and complete. After the Salt Lake City temple, sited before the transformation took place, all subsequent nineteenth-century LDS temples were located out of the town center (Figure 2.20).

The first temple built according to the new plan was in St. George, the principal town in southern Utah's "Dixie" region. The decision to build the

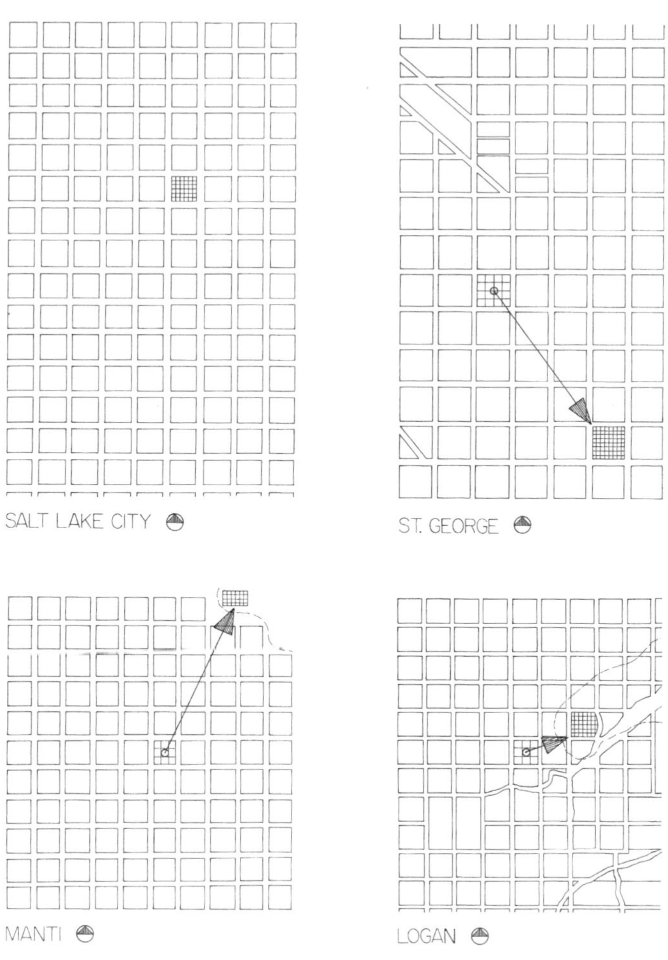

Figure 2.20. Sacred city to sacred point, moving the temple out of the town center: Salt Lake City was laid out around a centrally located temple square (1847), but in St. George (1871), Manti (1875), and Logan (1877), the temples were placed off-center, either out of town as in Manti, or on sites just adjacent to the central block (containing the meetinghouse), as in St. George and Logan.

second Utah temple in the remote town of St. George stemmed from the economic plight of that colony, founded in late December 1861. St. George (named for the Mormon apostle George A. Smith, who headed colonization in southern Utah) figured prominently in Young's plan for the Great Basin Kingdom. It was located in the extreme southwestern part of the territory, on the Arizona border, and conventional thinking claimed the warmer climate would provide the Saints with a location to grow year-around crops, particularly cotton—hence the name Dixie. Transplanted Easterners, English, or Scandinavians all, the Mormon leaders had little inkling of the desert environment whose harshness proved almost insurmountable from the beginning. Extreme aridity, poor soil, the omnipresent desert with its perpendicular (though spectacularly beautiful) red rock landforms, all conspired to defeat the colonists. The summer heat scorched them, and their irrigation systems were destroyed by cloudbursts, infrequent as they were, which released torrential rains that washed away dams and flooded fields. Life for the Dixie-ites was precarious at best. By 1864 their numbers had been cut considerably by sickness, death, and desertion, and Young realized something had to be done: the church would either have to abandon the colony or provide some kind of relief.[123]

Beginning early in 1865, President Young sent flour to St. George to keep the settlers alive and then instituted a "public works" program whereby Dixie Saints would receive payment for their work on a tabernacle, with Young "committing the tithing receipts of all towns in southern Utah to the construction." When it became clear that further stimulus money was needed to sustain the community, a temple was proposed. In the words of one historian, "The St. George temple would . . . be an even larger public project than the tabernacle; this prospect gladdened men like [St. George stalwart] Isaiah Cox, who 'rejoiced great at the news [of plans for the temple], as now I could feed my families.'"[124] Residents thought the temple would be built in the center of town, as was the custom; instead, during an 1871 visit Young, according to the temple's chief mason, Edward L. Parry, chose a site on the southern edge of town "a little elevated above its surroundings." (Figure 2.21)."[125]

As work progressed, the St. George temple builders discovered that the site Young selected was compromised by a "wet and soft" underpinning, and the newly dug foundation trenches quickly filled with alkali water. The church president returned to find some in town favoring a more central location, "building at the head of [Main] street, on another terrace above the city." Young, however, remained adamant, saying that "he had diligently sought of the Lord to know the right location for this Temple, and he was well satisfied that the place at first selected was the right place."[126] Completing it would take some additional engineering, but the building was finished and dedicated in 1877, the year work commenced on two other regional temples, one in the north, in Logan, and the other in Manti.

Both the Logan and the Manti temple followed the pattern established in St. George: they were large public works projects designed to provide economic support to outlying communities, and both were constructed on high ground outside the city. In Logan, the temple was placed on a flat narrow bench to the east of the city center, where the tabernacle stood (Figure 2.22). Young selected the site barely two months before construction began, proclaiming that God had shown it to him in a vision.[127]

The selection of the Manti site appears to have been similarly ordained, though Young remained circumspect about its providential inspiration. On

Figure 2.21. View of St. George from the east, taken circa 1880 by an anonymous photographer. Note the tabernacle slightly to the right, in the center of town, and the temple on the far left, on a slight rise to the south of the city center. Reprinted by permission of Utah State Historical Society; all rights reserved.

Figure 2.22. The temple sits on the hill above Logan in this anonymous photograph from around 1890. The town center is visible on the upper right, clustered around the tower on the city's tabernacle. Reprinted by permission of Utah State Historical Society; all rights reserved.

June 25, 1875, the church president arrived in the Sanpete Valley with an entourage that included a "who's who" of church leaders: Daniel H. Wells, John Taylor, Orson Hyde, Lorenzo Snow, Erastus Snow, F. D. Richards, G. Q. Cannon, Brigham Young Jr., A. M. Musser, J. A. Young, Lorenzo Young, John Van Cott, and "several Bishops." The group pushed south and according to Jens Weibye, one of the best chroniclers of life in Sanpete (who figures prominently in this book), "took a view of Several places in Manti, also of Manti Stone Quarry, and was up on top of it."[128] Weibye described an afternoon meeting in the Ephraim meetinghouse as follows: "Prs B. Young presided. All the Settlements in Sanpete were [re]presented and some from Juab and Sevier Countys, they all want to help build a Temple in Sanpete County, and then they expressed their views where to build it." Most of the leaders listed above called out for the Stone Quarry site at Manti, but "Prs. B. Young did not say where but will [soon] tell us the place."[129] "Soon" was indeed *soon,* for in the Historical Record of the Manti Temple, Weibye reported that "at 4 o'clock the same day [President Young] said the Temple should be built on the Manti Stone Quarry" (Figure 2.23).[130]

Figure 2.23. The Manti Tabernacle was located north of the town center, which stands just out of sight on the right. The Manti Temple is on the left. Photograph by George Edward Anderson, circa 1890. Reprinted by permission of Utah State Historical Society; all rights reserved.

Sacred and Profane

With the temple situated on the hill above Manti, the defining piece in the Sanpete Valley Mormon landscape fell firmly into place. In the end, having one part rather than the whole landscape sacred proved advantageous since it allowed the LDS community to retain its corporate religious identity (closeted in the temple) while at the same time letting its alter ego (the now secular town) develop naturally, unfettered by an all-encompassing and potentially oppressive sacrality. The temple remained the linchpin in the system, but its integrating presence became less explicit, its centrality more symbolic than literal.

The same may be said of the church's role in planning settlements. Because they appear so similar (following the grid-village layout) and strategically placed (at regular intervals down the length of the valley), Sanpete towns give the impression of being part of a vast church-run operation. While the goal, clearly stated in the Fourth General Epistle of the Church (cited earlier in this chapter), may have been to establish a chain of small towns throughout the region that would be linked both to each other (through proximity) and to the capital in Salt Lake City (through their regular spacing), as we look more closely at the way the valley was settled, only three town sites—Manti, Moroni, and Fountain Green—were selected by Young; all the others came into being through the actions of the local Saints. If land was expensive (or unavailable) in one town, the pioneers simply founded another and then went to Brigham Young for approval. That the towns were bunched together (all about eight to ten miles apart) speaks to the unseen power of the church and its mission rather than to direct supervision from Salt Lake City. While looking out for their own interests, the Sanpete Saints kept in mind the larger goal, which was to build up the City of Zion, and it is this formula, of individuals working for the good of the whole, that figures as the central theme in this study. It is even more evident in the way the towns and town lands were divided into home lots and farms, the subject of chapter 3.

3 ACCORDING TO NEED
FAMILY STEWARDSHIPS AND THE DISTRIBUTION OF RESOURCES

> Do all your work well, and it will pay every time, make your fences good and farms and houses, and have everything in its place.
>
> —*Orson Hyde, Fairview, June 19, 1864*

In February 1851, Bishop John Lowry of Manti rose in Sunday meeting and spoke on "the importance of every one looking to himself and setting his own family in order showing the order of God in this principle [and] showing the blessings desired there from by families being set in order."[1] Lowry aimed his words at members of the ward, but historians should listen as well, for his remarks remind us that more than anything it was the family that drove the Zion-making project forward (Figure 3.1). For the Latter-day Saints, God's "order" centered on an individual's faith and works, virtues that had to be cultivated within the membership and then channeled toward a collective end. "I have looked upon the community of the Latter-day Saints in a vision," Brigham Young said, "and beheld them organized as one great family of heaven, each person performing his several duties in his line of industry, working for the good of the whole more than for individual aggrandizement; and in this I have beheld the most beautiful order that the mind of man can contemplate, and the grandest results for the upbuilding of the kingdom of God and the spread of righteousness upon the earth."[2]

As we have seen, except for a brief period at the beginning, when frontier conditions necessitated group action, the Mormon western pioneers seldom acted as a heavenly family and, despite Young's visionary rhetoric, were not particularly communitarian. This word describes a communist or socialist society in which property is collectively owned, labor is organized to pursue common goals, and members of the group share political power equally. None of these applies to Mormonism in the second half of the nineteenth century. Most of the property within Latter-day Saint communities was privately owned; the Saints worked for themselves as well as for the church; and authoritarian church government hardly resembled a political collective.[3] It is true they flirted with communitarianism early in their history. In

Figure 3.1. A Mormon family's stewardship: the William and Ellen Major family house, 527 South 200 West, Spring City. The house was built in 1868 and was considered "a mansion" at the time. Photograph by George Edward Anderson, circa 1884. Reprinted by permission of Utah State Historical Society;

some ways they were obliged to, since purifying the world in anticipation of the Second Coming demanded a program of reform, both spiritual and temporal. In earthly matters, Babylon was synonymous with capitalism, a free-market economic system wherein individuals operate on their own initiative for their own profit. Competition is encouraged, the practice supported by a Darwinian belief in the ultimate triumph of intelligence and industry. The underlying premise—the essential mythology of capitalism—is that if people work hard and invest wisely, they will succeed financially, find happiness, and the whole society will benefit.[4]

Reformers of all eras have pointed out the downside of capitalism: it creates disparities of wealth that are inherently unjust and, for some, even immoral. Self-interest and material accumulation are elevated in importance to the detriment of cooperation and spirituality. The welfare of the community is lost in a frenzy of competition and avarice; mammon becomes the new God. For utopian-minded millenarian movements like Mormonism, the inherent inequities of the capitalist system, coupled with its tendency to alienate people from each other and God, was not the basis on which to build an ideal society. Rejecting Babylon thus meant rejecting capitalism and embracing a communitarian ethic, which Joseph Smith initially did. In the Vision of Enoch, called by anthropologist Steven Olsen the "single most significant revelation to give sanction and definition to [Zion]," the Lord tells the prophet that "[He] called his people Zion, because they were of one heart and one mind, and dwelt in righteousness; and there w[ere] no poor among them."[5] And further, "If ye are not one, ye are not [God's]," Smith declared, adding, "If ye are not equal in earthly things, ye cannot be equal in obtaining heavenly things."[6]

This reformist mind-set produced Smith's "Law of Consecration and Stewardship," also called the "Order of Enoch" or "the United Order." This doctrine, instituted in 1831, stipulated that all converts donate or consecrate their property to the church, which would hold it in collective ownership. The church would then redistribute it in the form of stewardships to individuals according to their "needs and abilities." A degree of free enterprise was retained, since each family was allowed to manage its property as it saw fit, but the program did call for a radical redistribution of wealth: the estates of the richest members would be reduced in size to provide land and resources for the worthy poor. Families, too, were required to consecrate their annual surplus—what they produced in excess of their basic subsistence needs—to the church, which would use it to assist the poor and fund projects such as temple building. Church leaders could also direct some of the surplus toward "stewards who needed funds for improvement and expansion." In short, the church would direct the flow of capital toward purposes it "felt were necessary and desirable."[7]

Attempts were made to implement the Law of Consecration and Stewardship in both Ohio and Missouri, but opposition quickly arose. For one thing there were legal issues: did members forfeit their right to reclaim their consecrated property if they left the church? Second, a disincentive existed for enterprising individuals when they knew that all their increase would revert to church storehouses and coffers, leaving them little for their efforts. And finally there was the question of best use: could the poor, many of the rich Saints asked, be expected to use their newly acquired property as wisely as those who had proved their entrepreneurial abilities?[8] In the end, the social leveling thrust of the stewardship system proved untenable. It was suspended in 1834 and replaced in 1838 by what the Saints considered an "inferior" law that scaled back expected contributions: converts were directed to consecrate only their surplus property when they joined the church and then pay an annual 10 percent tithe on their increase rather than surrender the whole amount. This modification met a similar fate as the original, however, especially since it came amid the turmoil caused by the removal from Missouri and the building of Nauvoo.[9]

After a hiatus of several years, when the lesser law was not enforced, Smith settled on the Law of Tithing, revealed in 1841 and in effect since. With the tithing system, which required members to donate one-tenth of their annual production to the church, Smith abandoned all attempts at economic reform and achieving social equality within the group. From 1841 on, property among the Mormons was privately owned and operated; capitalism had won because the free enterprise tradition ran too deep.[10] Later, lamenting a lack of collective spirit in the membership, Apostle Orson Pratt called attention to the strong current of individualism that ran within the church, saying, "Ever since we entered these valleys [in Utah Territory] every man has been for himself more or less," while admitting that "the inordinate desire for riches is a gentile tradition that we were taught before we came into this church. We brought these feelings into the church; and when we embraced the Gospel we verily thought it was all spiritual and had nothing to do with temporal matters. We came to this valley filled with these notions and traditions."[11]

Old habits die slowly or maybe, in capitalism's case, don't die at all. What seems remarkable about Mormon Zion making, however, is the way such cultural dispositions—in this case those relating to modes of production—were integrated through the Gospel of Works mythology into a cooperative society, though not cooperative in the conventional sense. Cooperation for the Saints did not mean collective ownership of property and profit. This did not work for them; what did work, beginning early in the Utah period, was a system whereby one-tenth of a family's yearly earnings was paid as tithing to the church, which then used it for the mutual benefit of the community as a whole. Church leaders continued to have the prerogative to invest tithing, both cash and in-kind contributions, in public works projects of various kinds, directing the flow of capital toward things that most needed it, especially the construction of temples, meetinghouses, and industrial buildings like mills and factories. Despite its managed nature, Mormonism remained a capitalistic society not only because private property and free enterprise were retained but also because capitalism's core philosophy, the mythic assumption that society benefits when individuals profit, survived intact. Cooperation figured into the equation as the sum of an individual's works and the blessings received for doing those works. As the Saints prospered, the Kingdom would rise.

The fundamental building block in the Mormon economic system remained family stewardship. Stewardships (alternately called "inheritances") came primarily in the form of land: the individual lots the Saints owned in the towns and the surrounding town lands. Town lots contained houses, barns, granaries, orchards, corrals, and gardens—all of a family's "improvements." Out in the town lands lay the farms and pastures. The distribution, size, placement, and organization of the town and farm lots constitute a key set of data in the history of Zion making, for these factors greatly help us understand how the Saints negotiated a productive alliance between private and public interests while maintaining a class-based social organization that was strongly reminiscent of the world they had left behind in the American Babylon.

Land

The integration of capitalism and cooperation within the church tithing system occurred during the early years of western settlement, and it was this "one-tenth" philosophy that built the Sanpete Valley colony. The Sanpete Saints knew the drill. Private property was sacrosanct: in Manti in 1851, ward member John Chase "arose and expressed his mind in regard to some men trampling upon the rights of others such as making roads across others land, picking melons, etc., stating that if he should see any one taking his property willfully he would shoot him or put a ball through them and many other remarks upon Principles for the General Good."[12] Making a profit was a good thing, as Apostle Orson Hyde in 1864 reminded the Fairview Saints: "You have been told about the multitude [of new converts] that are coming from the East and from the West, North, and South and I should not wonder if Flour should be worth thirty dollars a hundred pounds next year. Clear your field of blackseed and do your farming well, manure your land, and plow well, water well, and in seasons, and you will be well paid for your labor."[13] And always pay your tithing: Bishop Jones, speaking in Fairview, said "he wanted the brethren to pay their tithing [since they] cannot be instilled *[sic]* to full fellowship in the Church without it, said he wanted the Teachers to look after the loafers and not allow the idler to eat the bread of the laborer."[14]

The genius of such a program lay in the fact that it put the energy of American individualism to work for the benefit of the church group as a whole. As we have seen, equality in wealth was not a strong Mormon cultural value: Apostle Erastus Snow, visiting Manti in 1858, "referred to equality [and said] this could not exist long in our imperfect state for we were not all economists [and] not all use our talents alike, nor are we [the] same in Character or ability."[15] Hard work, however, was. Dan Jones of Manti said, "it was by merit that every one would attain to the blessings of God that are held out to everyone."[16] Put the two together, add in a belief that wealth was a blessing connected to the grace of God, and you find many Latter-day Saints eagerly working to better their church by first bettering themselves.

Historians of early Mormonism have repeatedly exposed the strong capitalistic strain within LDS culture, but somehow the older story about the communal Zion fighting it out with the American Babylon endures.[17] Landscape historians have done little to further the revisionist cause, remaining in thrall to the grid, which in its uniform division of blocks and lots has routinely served as a symbol of social equality. Mark Leone, an anthropologist who has written about Mormon towns in northern Arizona, makes this point: "There is a nonarbitrary connection between equal-sized pieces of space available to farmers and egalitarianism."[18] One lot, one family, all the same. The trouble with this interpretation, of course, is that land division in Zion was never equal. While the grid offered the potential of equal-size lots, the way they were apportioned and used was based on a "to each according to need and ability" formula. Some families, usually the wealthiest, needed more land, so some Saints ended up with a great deal of property, many very little, and others none at all.[19]

The standard process for allocating town and farm lots was developed in Salt Lake City and then applied to outlying communities like those in Sanpete. The church initially claimed title to the land, though it was not distributed randomly or equitably. A preferential treatment prevailed, for some lots were more attractive and therefore more valuable than others. Those located in the center of town, close to the symbols of power—the temple block and Brigham Young's residence, for instance, in Salt Lake City—were highly coveted. Likewise, city and farm lots along the main waterways were desirable, as were those that generally fell in the fertile alluvial deposit zones formed by the mountain-fed creeks. Access to power, prestige, drinking water, and productive farmland were all considerations in property distributions. In Salt Lake City, an initial distribution to church leaders came soon after the plat was finished in 1847. With the General Authorities receiving first claim, it is not surprisingly that their holdings are found clustered in the downtown area (Figure 3.2). The Thirteenth Ward, lying just east and south of Temple Square, became the city's most prestigious address. Because these families were often polygamous, they received more than one town lot, and a number of them had a great many. It was only after the leadership was accommodated that Apostle Heber C. Kimball, working with surveyor Thomas Bullock, formed a committee to allocate the rest of the city lots.[20]

The same system was used in the Sanpete Valley communities, although in some cases a drawing of lots was held after the leadership was accommodated. In Manti, for example, ward histories talk about using the lottery method for parceling out lots, but the land records reveal a clustering of spiritual and economic elite in a neighborhood just north and west of the temple block, as well as around the temple block generally. Such an arrangement could hardly be coincidental (Figure 3.3). In fact, that part of the city lying north of the temple block also appears to have been the preferred residential district for the most affluent of Manti's citizens (Figure 3.4). The local gentry, if we may use this term, thus dominated the entire northwest quadrant of the town and its outlying town lands, an area that took in the alluvial fan created by the northwest-flowing creeks, making this land the most fertile and therefore most valuable (Figure 3.5). Those who came later, particularly

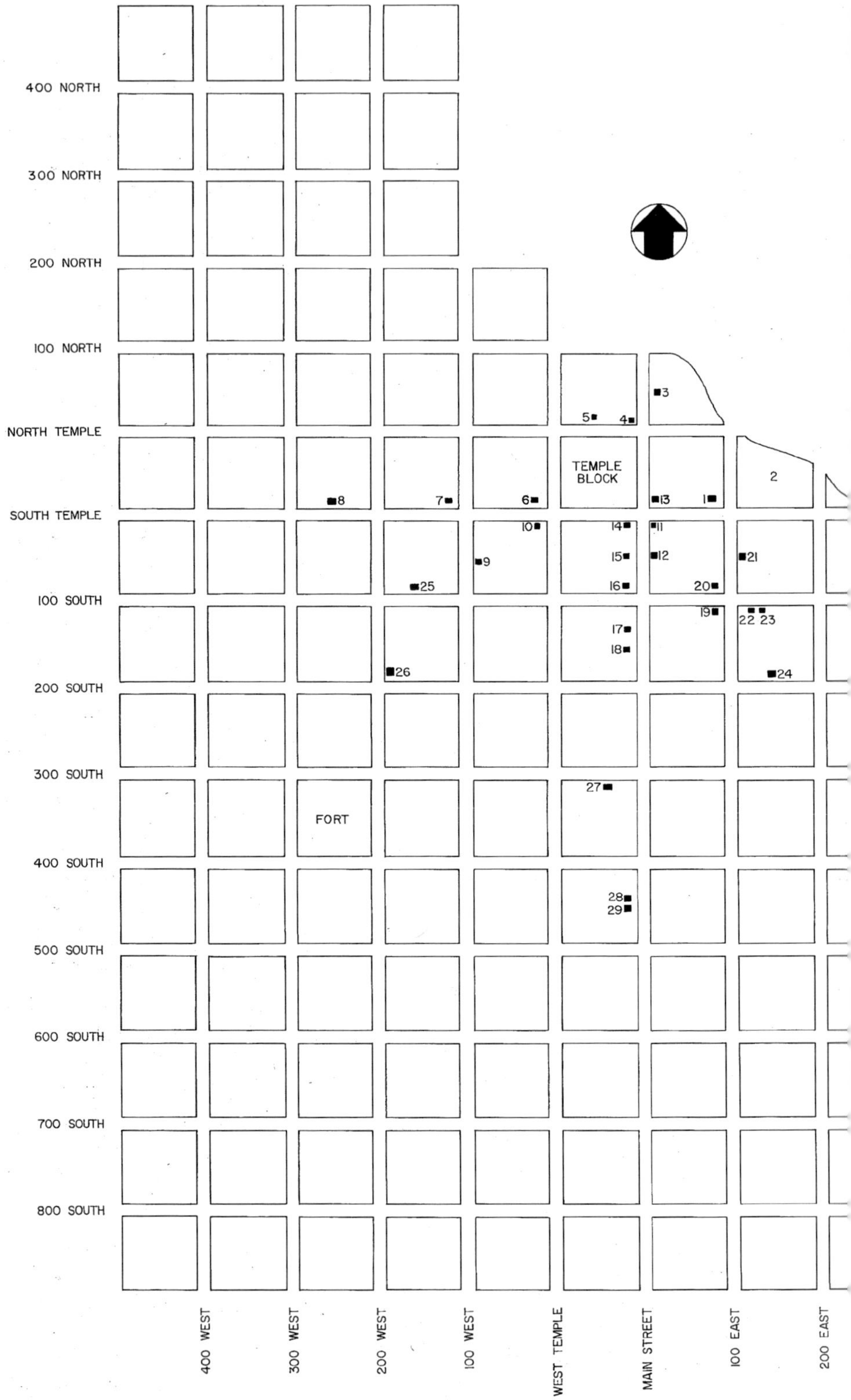

Figure 3.2. Central Salt Lake City, showing the location of homes of prominent men and institutions. 1, Church President Brigham Young's Beehive and Lion houses; 2, President Young's family compound with houses, barns, and school; 3, Apostle Heber C. Kimball's Plantation House and family compound; 4, Apostle Albert Carrington; 5, Apostle Orson Hyde; 6, Apostle George A. Smith; 7, George Q. Cannon, counselor to Brigham Young; 8, William Staines, leading businessman and banker; 9, Apostle John Taylor; 10, Apostle Wilford Woodruff; 11, Apostle E. T. Benson; 12, Presiding Bishop Edward Hunter; 13, Church Tithing Office; 14, original Council House; 15, Livingston-Kinkead store; 16, Kimball-Lawrence store; 17, Daft commercial block; 18, Town Clock store; 19, Seventies Hall of Science (unbuilt); 20, Salt Lake Theater; 21, social hall; 22, city hall; 23, new city hall; 24, Thirteenth Ward Meetinghouse; 25, music hall; 26, federal courthouse; 27, Independence Hall (Gentile church); 28 and 29, Walker Brothers (Gentile merchants).

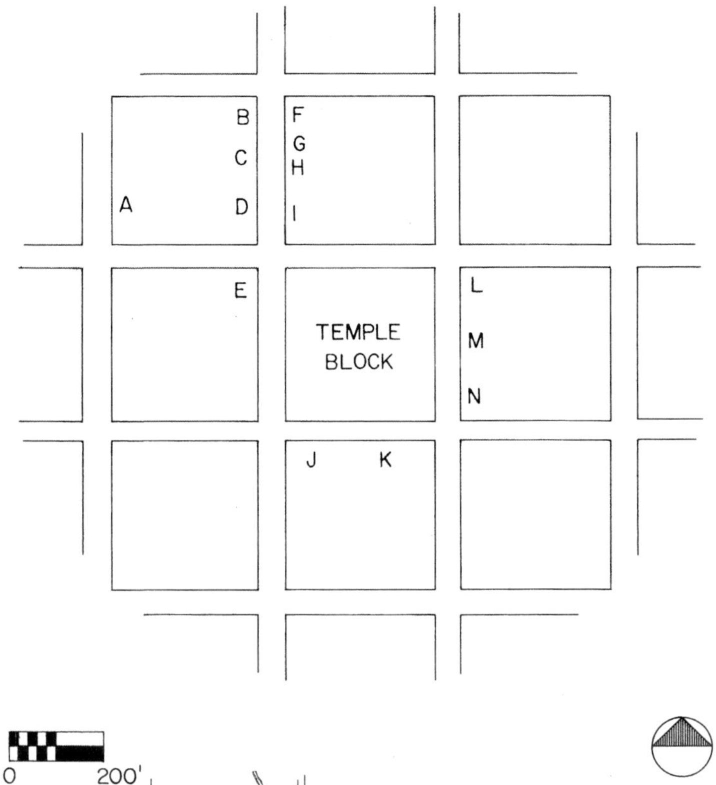

Figure 3.3. Detail of Manti, showing the central location of the houses of the city's leading men. A, Daniel Henrie, farmer and businessman; B, John Lowry Jr., city councilman and county assessor; C, John P. Squires, farmer and businessman; D, Fredrick W. Cox Jr., farmer and son of one of Manti's founders and leading citizens; E, Franklin Spencer, farmer and businessman; F, Fredrick W. Cox Sr., city councilman and wagonmaker; G, Jemima Cox, plural wife of F. W. Cox Sr.; H, Orville Sutherland Cox, city alderman, and later Jezreel Shoemaker, Church High Council; I, Freeborn Demill, Church High Council; J, Isaac Vance, farmer and tanner; K, Elisha Edwards, farmer; L and M, Warren Snow, presiding bishop; and N, Hans Jensen, businessman.

Figure 3.4. Manti in 1880, showing distribution of lots by economic class. The lots shaded with vertical hatching lines were owned by families with a net worth of more than $2,000; those with diagonal hatching were the property of families with a net worth between $500 and $2,000; and lots with no hatching were owned by families with a net worth of less than $500.

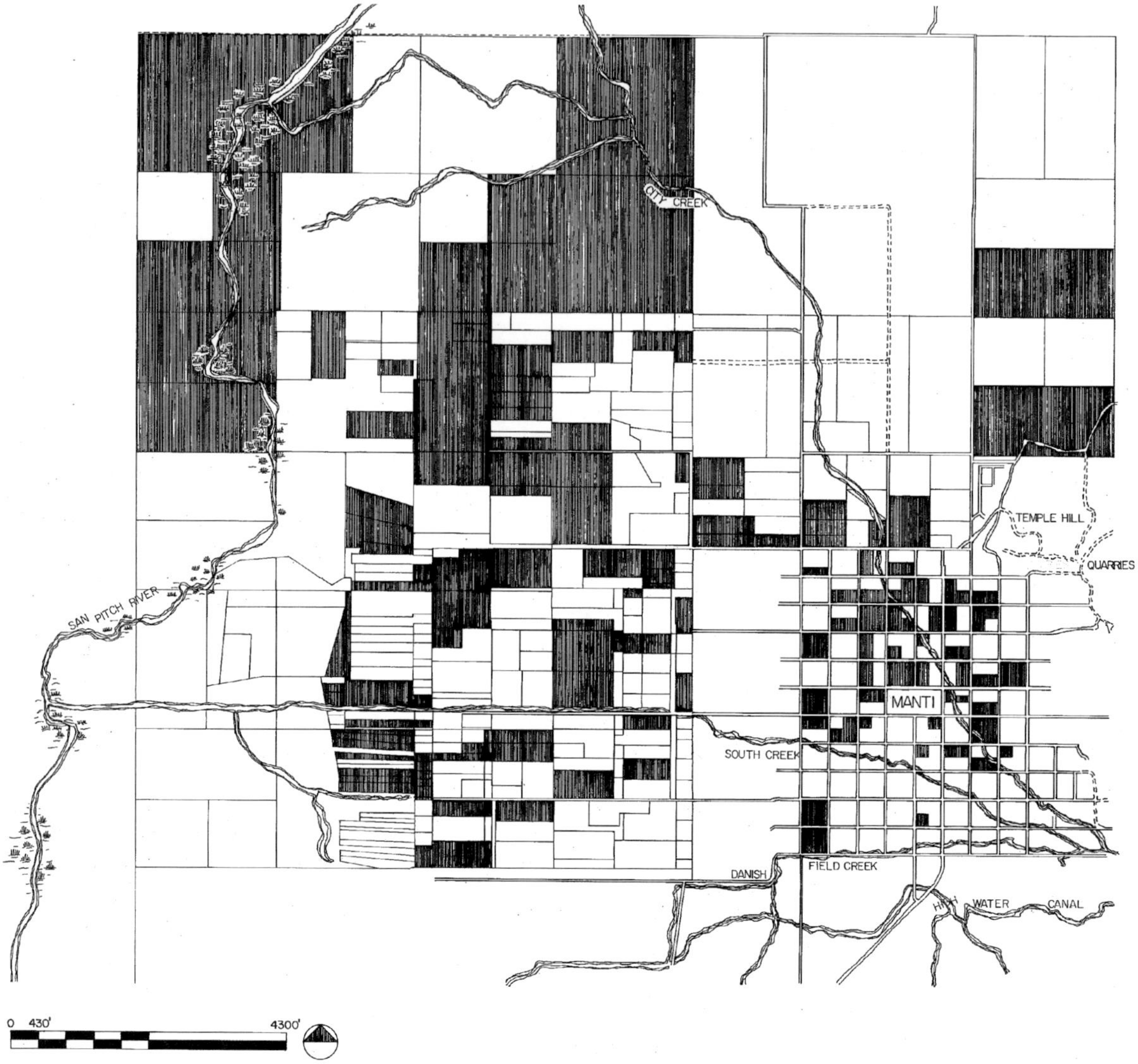

Figure 3.5. Manti city and farm lots showing ownership of the fertile northwest quadrant by the city's elite families. Shaded lots are owned by town residents with an 1880 census evaluation of more than $500.

the Danes and other Scandinavian immigrants, were left to take up unclaimed lots in less desirable districts, buy lots at market rate from previous owners, or start their own towns.[21]

Church leaders generally discouraged land speculation. Lots were basically free: those members who were present at the time the towns were surveyed paid a minimal recording fee for their lots. We also have to remember that Mormons were squatters on the public land until 1869, when the federal survey reached the territory—and the idea that individuals might profit from this windfall was anathema to many. Still, if the land records are a reliable indication, buying and selling town lots and farm acreage became a favorite Mormon pastime. A healthy real estate market existed in all Sanpete County towns from the outset of settlement, for good land was a valuable commodity and much in demand. Men practicing polygamy needed more lots for multiple wives and families, but buying up lots for speculative investment and rental income became common as well.[22]

Church leaders also discouraged speculation because it took land out of circulation in determining community work assessments. An 1867 editorial in the Manti newspaper noted: "It has been suggested that the [fort] wall work be apportioned to each Citizen according to the amount of property he has to enclose. This seems to be the best and fairest way; for it is evident that the more property a man gets enclosed the more he is benefited. It has always been an acknowledged principle of right that 'the strongest horse should have the heaviest load.' Now if the wall is to be built on the above plan, and a man finds that he owns more city lots than he can possibly build wall for, he can sell lots to those without any homestead, and who will be very glad to build wall for them! And thus our city 'farmlots' will find occupants and the city itself (as it should be) become more compact and city-like."[23]

The general mobility of the Mormon population also stimulated land sales during the settlement period. Many Latter-day Saints found themselves on the move, looking to better their circumstances, wanting to be close to friends and relatives, responding to environmental or economic conditions, church callings, conflicts with Indians, or simply from being restless. The transient nature of the society led Apostle Hyde to counsel Sanpeters to stay put and "be contented . . . those that stay where they are and keep improving will always be able to buy out those that are continually on the move."[24]

Land was parceled out in much the same manner in the other towns. In Ephraim, Danish immigrant Anders Thomsen recorded in his diary that he lived in the little fort until 1860, and then "about the time the city was laid out and in casting lots I drew the lot where the old home now stands. There we built a three-room adobe house."[25] In Mount Pleasant, a surveyor came from Manti in 1858, a year before the town was occupied, and laid out a fort and "about 1300 acres of land in 29 acre lots." By mutual agreement, the land was "subsequently divided among the settlers by balloting."[26] A year later, after the town site had been occupied, more land was surveyed and "given to new-comers as they arrived from different settlements."[27] In Spring City, after the 1859 relocation a lottery was held for city lots, and "the farming land, which had been surveyed into ten and five acres lots, was distributed among the settlers and no head of a family was allowed more than fifteen acres."[28]

Despite the lotteries, it should come as no surprise that in all these towns siting favored the local elite. In Ephraim, Stake president Canute Peterson's lot stood across from the tabernacle on Main Street, surrounded by those of other dignitaries. In Mount Pleasant, Bishop and Mayor William S. Seely owned two lots in the center of the city, on the main thoroughfare adjacent to the church block; and over in Spring City, Apostle Orson Hyde's principal house lots were on Main Street directly east of the meetinghouse block, putting him conspicuously in the middle of the action. In the other towns the preferential pattern recurs: the houses of prominent citizens stand close to the center of town while those of lesser means and influence found themselves on the peripheries. One entry in the Spring City Ward minutes reveals the deferential treatment local leaders received: "Motion was made . . . that [Branch] Prest [Frederick] Olsen have a piece of land by the adobie yard containing 10 acres . . . and also his choice of 20 acres more where it would be most convenient for him."[29]

If the ward minutes from Fairview are any indication, the inequities of the land distribution process did not go uncontested. Fairview was surveyed in the fall of 1859 and the initial talk stressed unity: "About twenty of the brethren were present at the surveying of the land, and said they desired all to enjoy equal rights and privileges."[30] Branch president and later bishop James Jones was granted authority to parcel out the land, both city and farm plots, under the general guidelines that farms would be located south of town while the land to the north would be reserved for grazing herds. As Jones proceeded with the distribution, however, the communitarian spirit quickly broke down. One family almost immediately rebelled. While Bishop Jones was absent attending a church conference in Salt Lake City, he left Elijah Jones in charge. The bishop received a letter from Elijah saying that "Lewis [Zebriskie] and William his son came to me and said the 60 acres that the Bishop had given them was not worth farming, there was only 20 acres of it that could be used." Elijah noted that he felt their dissatisfaction came only after they saw better land to the west of the city, by the stone quarry, and so he told them to go ahead and farm the 20 acres, at which point, the elder Zebriskie answered that "he never would stick a Plow in it again, but wanted me to give him 60 acres at the Stone quarry. I told him that I should not give more than 20 acres to any man, and then he wanted 30, which I refused to give."[31]

The Zebriskies were not finished. James Jones returned and after receiving a sustaining vote by the people that they only farm south of town, "William Zebriskie said he would be dam[n]ed if he did not go and stake of[f] some of the land and would hold it by Law and Lewis C. Zebriskie his father followed and they got their homes and went to the land north of the town by the quarry against the will, and the vote of the people when I told him positively to let the land alone."[32] Apparently the reprimand worked, for Lewis later repented, asking in Sunday meeting for "the forgiveness of his brethren." Still, the point is that however the lots were divided, by lottery or by the bishop, dissension surfaced. In Fairview, Bishop Jones was frequently accused of favoritism, though he defended himself in 1864 by saying that "he had tried to give out the land and make men even."[33] To which one member,

Lindsay Brady, responded that the real problem was that the land "should have been given out in five acre lots in the beginning, but it has never been dealt out right and fairly, and he knew it, but did not want to blame any body, as he believed the Bishop have done the best he understood."[34]

A second kind of social sorting occurred around ethnicity, a term used to denote national, racial, or even religious differences in the cultural identities of a country's population. In nineteenth-century Utah, the dominant group was Anglo-American, people who had been born in the United States but were of English descent. Added in were immigrant converts from the British Isles, a number that included members from Wales and Scotland as well as England, and Scandinavia, with Denmark being the largest contributor, although there were also Swedes and Norwegians.

The first settlers in Sanpete were largely drawn from Salt Lake City and reflected the New England–Midwest origins of the early LDS Church membership and bore family names like Cox, Morley, Lowry, Billings, Bradley, and Shomaker. The cultural makeup of the valley was soon to change, for the influx of immigrants, the vast majority of them from the Scandinavian countries, began in 1853, and soon each town had its share of Jensens, Nielsens, Christensens, and Sorensens. Census figures record the change in the population. In 1850, the valley consisted of only American-born settlers. By 1860, the population stood at 3,815, but now only about 60 percent were born in the United States, while the rest listed foreign countries as their place of birth. By 1870, the median year for this study, the pattern of ethnic diversity was firmly established, the census takers reporting 6,174 residents, with 57 percent American-born and 43 percent from foreign countries.

Using the 1870 census figures, the foreign population of 2,896 can be broken down into specific nationalities. By far the greatest number, 1,641 (57 percent), were Danish; the next largest group, 624 (22 percent), were from the British Isles; 476 (16 percent) came from Norway and Sweden; while the remaining number included immigrants from Canada, Germany, France, and Switzerland. Each Sanpete town had its own ethnic makeup. Manti in 1870 had 241 households; of these the largest number, 102 (42 percent), were Scandinavian, 52 (22 percent) were British, and 75 (31 percent) were American, and the remaining 12 (5 percent) were from Canada and Continental Europe. Manti's Scandinavians all hailed from Denmark, and of the 52 British families, 39 were English with the rest divided among Scots, Irish, and Welsh. The 75 American households were broken up into 32 from the Northeast (including New York State), 27 from the midwestern states, 10 from the South, and the remaining 6 from Pennsylvania.

The ethnic topography of Manti resembled that of class. The North Ward was almost exclusively Anglo-American, with families born in the United

States or the British Isles accounting for about 80 percent of the total. On the other hand, the South Ward contained mostly Scandinavians (i.e., Danes), who constituted roughly 75 percent of the population (Figure 3.6). Spatial segregation like this was not unusual for the valley, with immigrants tending to settle near friends and neighbors when possible. Some of Manti's polarization may also be attributed to differing arrival times. When the Scandinavian immigrants started showing up in the mid-1850s, American and British families had taken up most of the best lots lying to the north and west; the newcomers were naturally shunted off to the available lots in the rockier southern part of town. Joseph Hansen, from Copenhagen, came to Manti in 1853 with the first group of Danish immigrants and noted that "the [farm] land lying west of the north half of Manti was assigned to the Scandinavian settlers, the land north of the city having been put to cultivation by those who had previously settled in the colony."[35]

Two decidedly "ethnic" towns did exist. One was Wales, which true to its name was filled with Welsh miners and their families. In 1870, only 16

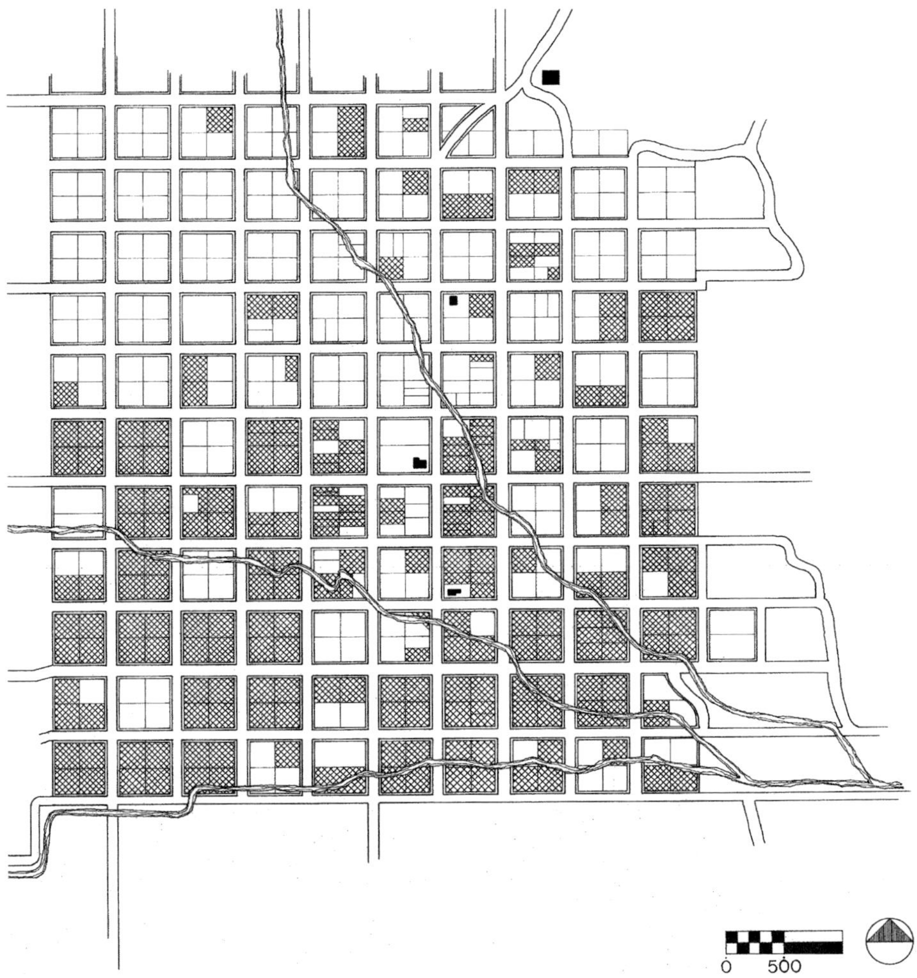

Figure 3.6. Manti city and farm lots showing distribution by ethnicity. Anglo-Americans dominated the northern half of the city (unmarked town lots), while the majority of Scandinavian families lived on the south side (lots with crosshatching).

families resided here, but 10 were from Wales, with another 4 from England. There were only 2 American-born families. The other was Ephraim, known locally as "Little Denmark" because of its sizable Scandinavian population. Of Ephraim's 245 households in 1870, 168 (69 percent) were Danish, 30 (12 percent) Swedish, and 14 (6 percent) Norwegian. There were only 33 non-Scandinavian families, roughly equally divided between British and American Saints.

Despite the mixing of cultures, ethnic conflicts were surprisingly few. Most studies indicate that both the British and Scandinavian Saints melded rather seamlessly into the mix. A *Deseret News* writer had this to say in 1857 about the settlers in Ephraim, "the majority of whom are Danes. . . . The old settlers of Sanpete speak in the highest terms of the industry, energy and perseverance of the Danes and seem to like them well as neighbors."[36] Ethnic tensions were partially allayed by church leaders allowing Scandinavian-language meetings (obviously no such language barrier greeted the British immigrants). There was also a great deal of intermarrying, and even in Spring City, where oral tradition maintains a strict division between the Scandinavians in the north half of town and the Anglos in the south, land ownership patterns reveal a much more diverse and ethnically integrated community (Figure 3.7).

In language and material culture, then, the Scandinavian converts moved slowly but steadily toward acculturation—the adopting of the dominant

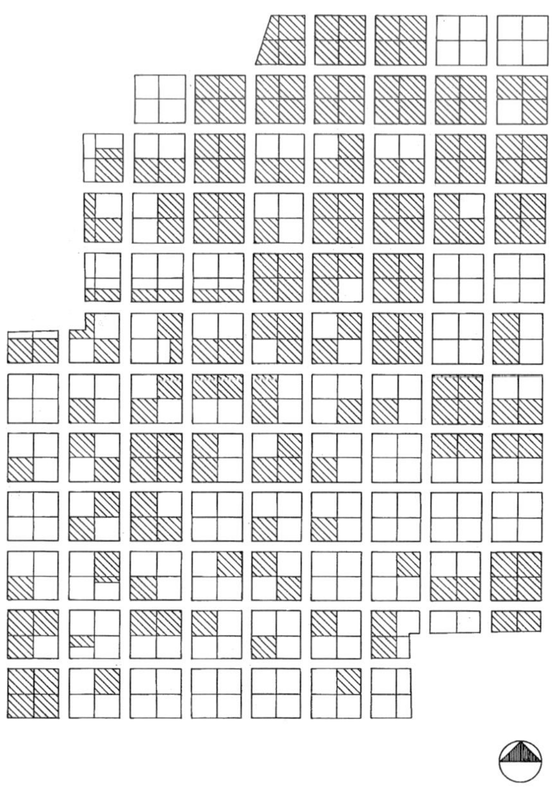

Figure 3.7. Map of Spring City showing 1880 population distribution by ethnicity. Town lots owned by Anglo-American families have no markings, while those belonging to Scandinavians are represented with diagonal lines. A preponderance of Scandinavians lived on the north side, although the mixing of nationalities appears more prevalent than is often thought.

Anglo-American culture. In the immigrant generation, a wide range of responses can be observed, with some families holding rather tenaciously to native tongue and housing forms, others dropping all vestiges of the Old World and assimilating rapidly, and everything in between. As late as 1867, John Hougaard wrote to the *Deseret News* "on behalf of the Danish Saints in Manti to express our gratitude and the obligations felt for your courtesy extend in publishing articles of Danish reading. . . . I read them myself with much interest and feel confident that they will be productive of much good to the Danish people, many of whom can neither speak, read nor understand the English language and imagine themselves too old or for other reasons unable to learn it."[37]

It may be that diversity proved easier for the Saints to accept because, for one thing, all members of the church were relatively recent converts, and even the Americans came from widely disparate parts of the country. The New Englanders, those who joined the church in the 1830s, remained in nominal control, occupying most leadership positions, both civic and religious. But the society itself was an incipient one and a true melting pot of cultures. The reality was that no single group, whether Yankee, British, or Scandinavian, clearly dominated. Rather, church members existed as a multicultural society bound together by a common commitment to the building of the Kingdom of God. One wasn't so much a New Yorker or a Dane as a Mormon.[38]

Water and Work

Figure 3.8. A wooden flume carries water from Canal Creek to the Spring City irrigation ditches in 1979. The flume dates from the early twentieth century.

Rivaling land in importance was water (Figure 3.8). Access to and ownership of water were crucial to the Saints, since whatever land a family had was absolutely worthless without a way to irrigate it during the dry summer months. Historians routinely describe how the Mormon collective approach to water rights differed from the "riparian rights" practices found in other parts of the West (where individuals owned the water adjacent to their property). While water, like land, was claimed by the church rather than by individuals, it is also true that church officials allocated it in much the same way as they did land, which means that it was not distributed evenly despite its corporate ownership. Again, the amount of water a family was awarded, measured in "shares," depended on how much property they owned; quite simply, the more land, the more water shares. Additionally, getting water to the town and farm lots required the building of elaborate networks of canals and ditches (Figure 3.9), and each family was supposed to labor on ditches in a similar way: for every town lot or acre of farmland, a proportional levy was applied for ditch work. Eventually, the church ceded its water rights to water cooperatives, run by vested shareholders.[39]

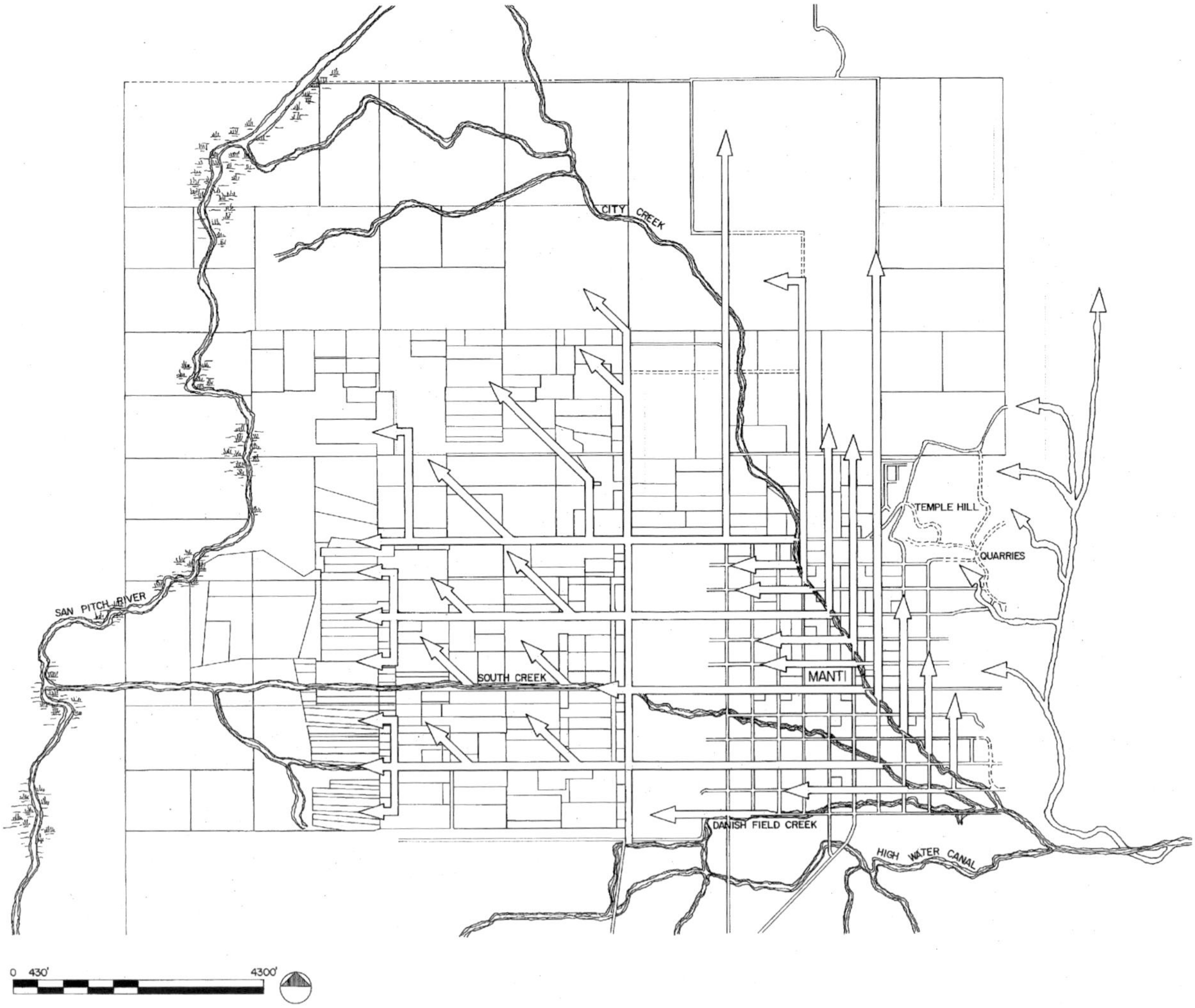

Figure 3.9. Diagram of the gravity-powered irrigation system in Manti. The arrows indicate the directional flow of the city's major watercourses, both natural and human-produced (after Gary Peterson, *Sanpete Scenes*).

Water in Utah was very much a commodity to be bought and sold, along with land, at market prices. The water companies, like the farmers, operated on a for-profit basis. One example is the Manti Hay Land and Forage Company, which constructed a canal, 5 miles long, 6 feet wide and 2½ feet deep, "to intersect Cottonwood and Spring Creeks, and to turn their course at proper seasons from the Manti hay fields into said canal, and thus not only obviate the difficulty attending cutting hay in wet swamps, but extend the area of the meadow lands." The officers and shareholders of the company are commended, in a letter to the *Deseret News,* for the "speedy and energetic manner in which the work has been managed and accomplished, and doubtless the vast advantages that will accrue, will amply repay them for the capital expended."[40]

Disputes concerning water rights could fill a separate book, but suffice it to say they existed and remind us again how central this resource was in the life of the Sanpete Latter-day Saints. Conflicts could arise between towns for the rights to certain watercourses, or between individuals, particularly "among original settlers and those coming in [later]."[41] Things got so bad in Fairview that beleaguered Bishop James Jones in 1860 compared the watermaster's task to the "trials of Job," saying "he feared that some had not been honest and faithfull[;] thought the watermasters had done justice to the brethren, and if we had been True and faithfull we might have had the . . . water out."[42] For newcomers to the valley, Apostle Hyde had this advice in 1878: "With regard to water the old settlers are entitled to the first use of the water as far as it may be necessary. By giving newcomers the right to use surplus water in the early part of the seasons, you beguile them into difficulty from the fact that a continual deviding of water would result in the partial destruction of the crops of all."[43] So much, it seems, for the United Order.

Some ongoing cooperation proved necessary, however, if the settlements were to grow and prosper. Certain projects, usually those that had to do with the personal interests and well-being of individual church members, readily attracted volunteers. Wood was always needed for heating and other purposes, so the Manti ward minutes noted that the "the brethren . . . turned out to open a [road] up City Creek Canyon to obtain timber and poles."[44] Or for infrastructure: when a notice was posted in Manti for road workers, "men volunteered to build bridges."[45] Ditch cleaning, especially to prevent spring flooding, was another area of cooperation; in his daybook entry for February 11, 1876, Jens Weibye noted, "We were a good many of the Manti Brethren out in Public and cleaned the Big Creek trough [of] the City of Manti, and preparing for high water."[46] Self-interest was a powerful motivator, especially when it might affect one's social life: Weibye wrote, "I and family attended a Dance in the Meetinghouse, there was 88 numbers there, but we went not there for the dancing alone, but the Dance was got up for to raise means and give Brother Hans Westenskow a new violin."[47]

Zion making was a complex undertaking—a contract between the leaders and the membership. In Sunday meeting, Spring City Bishop Isaac Behunin reported that he had found a good stand of timber and poles "that would last the people of Springtown for years, and would pay well for making a good road to it, which he thought could be done if every able bodied man would work 5 days each." A good number, seventy-four, volunteered, but to make sure they showed up, Behunin went on to say that "any who has or may give their names to work 5 days and fail to do so shall pay for each day they are delinquent a fair price" and that "any man who does not work on the road, [will] pay for the use of it at a price that the committee may establish per load."[48]

For the most part, the Sanpete Saints performed their community work either to pay off their municipal taxes or to fulfill their tithing obligations by following the 10 percent plan. Bishop Lowry of Manti may have said it best in 1852, when he announced that it was his official policy to get the brethren to "pay their Labor Tithing every tenth day, it being his [Lowry's] policy to forward the public works."[49] Lowry's effort caused the *Deseret News* to report: "Work progressed with rapidity and with that zeal that ever fires the heart of a true Saint of God when he is commanded to strike forth his hand for the rolling forth and upbuilding of the Kingdom of God in this the last dispensation."[50]

Remember too that the line between church and public work was for all intents and purposes nonexistent. In 1861, the bishop of Mount Pleasant asked permission of Brigham Young to use labor tithing to build the "Spanish Fork Canyon Road," today's U.S. Highway 89.[51] In a letter dated July 15, 1861, Young authorized the expenditure, saying, "I take pleasure in informing you that you are at liberty to expend labor tithing (now due) to the amount of $4000, in making a road from Thistle Valley to Springville, and a Bridge across Spanish Fork [river]. I wish you to allot a fair, in your judgment, portion of the road to each Ward, in proportion to its share of the labor tithing due, as shown in your list, and see that each Ward does its portion well, which I presume they will do for it will be to their interest."[52] Even when the work was in their interest slackers could be found. In 1861 Bishop Jones of Fairview said "he wanted a strict and correct record kept of every mans public work, so it can be seen who has build up the place."[53] Also in that city, Apostle Hyde noticed that "among the teams sent to haul rocks for him, was one owned by a certain man and an other man was to pay him for it as he would not go himself. Brethren, the greater weight you carry for brother Hyde the lighter will [be your] own."[54]

So cooperation had its limits, and this seems particularly the case in the area of fencing, which appears to have been the most problematic of community work efforts, judging from the number of calls made in church meetings for the brethren to fulfill their fencing obligations. In fact, enforcement often required draconian measures (or at least the threat of them). In Spring City, J. T. Ellis presented to the ward a "resolution that any one failing to put [up] their fence after a reasonable time being set by the Committee shall forfeit their land, and the committee dispose of the same, to put up the fence."[55] Similarly in Fairview: "Bp Jones spoke upon the condition of our field, and said it have been motioned and seconded that we make it a matter of [church] fellowship, if the brethren do not use their best endeavors to keep their Cattle out of the field south of Town and see that their fence is up forth with."[56]

Family Stewardships

In addition to farmland, an inheritance in Zion normally included a home lot in town. As we have seen, several families had many and others had none (and rented). Still the ideal called for every family to have land sufficient to support itself and, by extension, contribute to the building of Zion. Except in Ephraim, where an irregular division occurred, Sanpete town blocks were quartered into lots of an acre to an acre-and-a-half apiece. Whereas the original plat for the City of Zion called for barns and other farm-related buildings to be located outside town, in the Great Basin all these structures, accompanied by pastures, orchards, and gardens, were moved to the family's home lot. Jens Severine Jensen's lot in Spring City is a good example (Figure 3.10). The house faces west and is surrounded by shade and fruit trees. Directly east is the barn, which had its own small corral to the south. Privy, granary, chicken coop, and summer kitchen were located between the barnyard and the house, while the south half of the lot was left open for pasture and a vegetable garden (which originally stood directly to the south of the house). A small open-sided animal shelter in the pasture completed the ensemble.[57]

Identifying a typical home lot is difficult because they vary so much. Generally speaking, lots break out along class lines, ranging from high to low in amount of acreage and number of buildings. In Spring City, for instance, Apostle Orson Hyde stood at the top of the social scale. Not only did he own eight city lots, but both his original house, built of log, and a later more

Figure 3.10. Jens Severine Jensen's home lot, 276 North 300 East, Spring City, Utah, circa 1870. The round object in this 1993 aerial photograph is a trampoline.

permanent stone one, sat on double lots adjacent to the meetinghouse block. The second lot (Figure 3.11A) contained a two-story stone house, finished in 1875 (see Figure 5.14), a large barn with two side stables, a combination stone granary and root cellar, a small stone building of unknown function (a luxurious privy?), an orchard, and a vegetable garden. The east end of the double lot undoubtedly served as pasture for Hyde's horses and perhaps a few sheep.[58] Also on the upscale side was the home lot of farmer Isaac Behunin, another Main Street resident (Figure 3.11B). Behunin's was but a single lot, yet the noticeably large size of the 1883 stone house, coupled with the double-stable barn standing diagonally to the rear, gave it an impressive appearance. On the lot were the ample gardens and pastures, as well as the original Behunin log cabin, which had been moved off the corner to make way for the new rock house.[59]

More middling are the home lots of the William Osborne (Figure 3.11C) and Marinus Petersen (Figure 3.11D) families. Osborne was from England and Petersen from Denmark, but their lots appear much the same, with the only difference the placement of the barns. For the Osbornes, the barn was placed behind the house on the back of the lot. An open-sided shed, workshop, granary, and privy filled in the space between the house and the barn, with an orchard and gardens to the side. At the Petersens', the substantial log barn was lined up parallel to the side of the house and was of the two-level type favored by Scandinavians. Between the house and barn stood an orchard, and behind the barn was a farmyard containing an adobe granary and open-side stable, sometimes called a loafing shed. Pastures and gardens filled up the remaining space on the lot.[60]

Toward the bottom of the economic ladder are two lots owned by Danes Iver Petersen (Figure 3.11E) and Jacob Nielsen (Figure 3.11F).[61] Neither had a regular barn per se, though the Petersens' livestock were kept in a small open-sided stable to the rear of the small stone house. On the lot, however, were a sizable stone granary and ample space for pasture and garden. The Nielsens were probably lucky they had any land at all, for many in town did not and were forced to rent.[62] Still, the Nielsen lot, which measured out at about a third of an acre, was big enough for a small one-room log house, a log granary, and a corral.

Houses were invariably placed on the corner closest to the street intersections, yielding a crossroads effect (Figure 3.12). Although considered urban spaces, Mormon towns were spread out in a way that resembles a more rural landscape. This was especially true before the lots began to be subdivided and filled in with additional houses during the late nineteenth and early twentieth centuries. In the early days they were characterized by small clusters of houses standing at each intersection separated by large open spaces on the

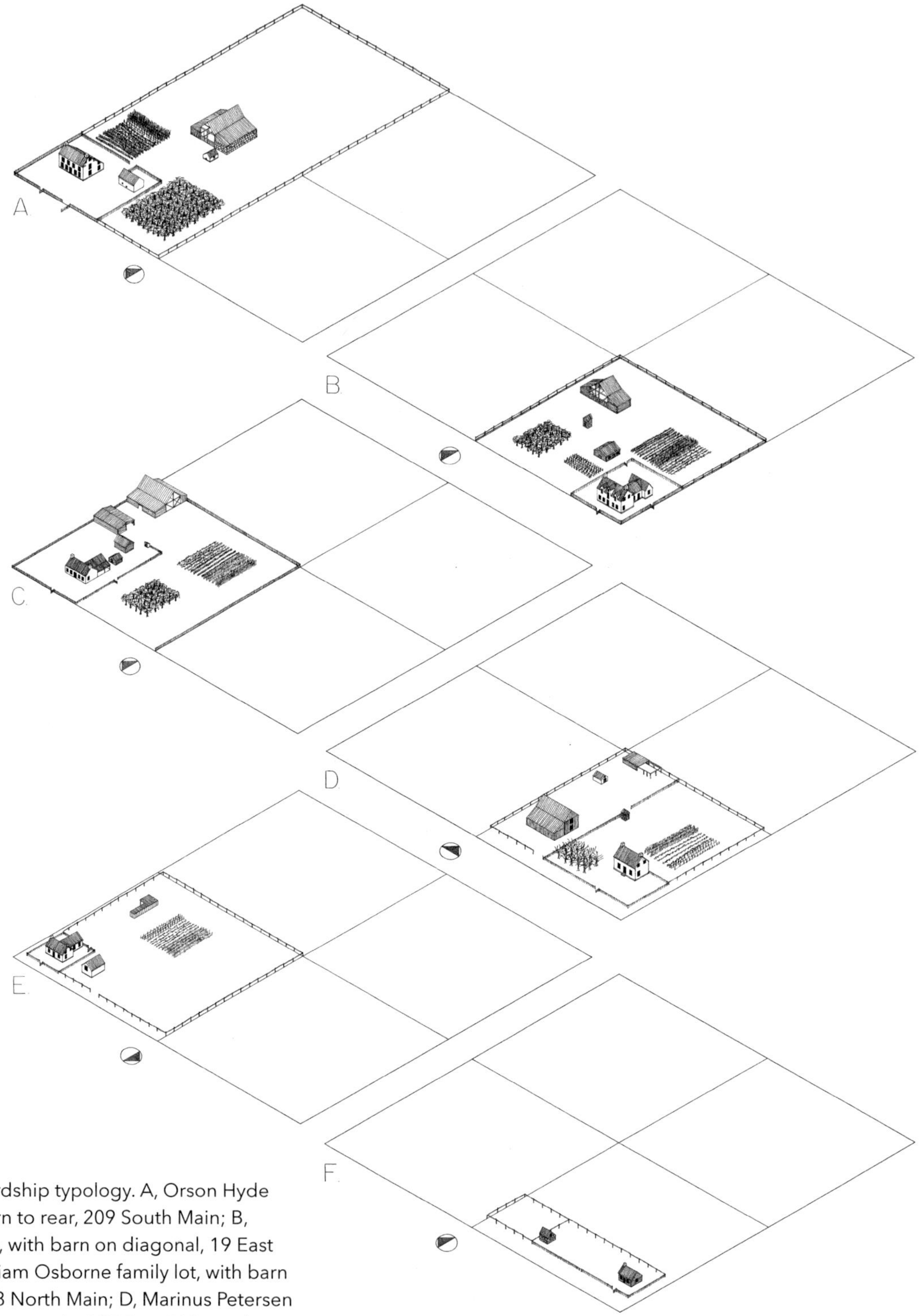

Figure 3.11.
Spring City stewardship typology. A, Orson Hyde family lot, with barn to rear, 209 South Main; B, Behunin family lot, with barn on diagonal, 19 East 100 North; C, William Osborne family lot, with barn behind house, 398 North Main; D, Marinus Petersen family lot, with barn to side, 287 East 500 North; E, Iver Petersen family lot, with rock granary but no barn, 309 North Main; and F, Jacob Nielsen family half-lot, with log granary but no barn, 190 West 300 North (demolished).

block interiors. Such positioning created problems for house builders, however, for the corner placement gave the house two possible fronts. Many Mormon families solved this problem by using house designs that had essentially two principal elevations, one symmetrical and the other off-balance, usually the end of the front-facing wing with a side wing at a right angle. The "houses with two fronts" pattern becomes an idiosyncratic aspect of the Mormon town that often goes unrecognized (Figure 3.13).[63]

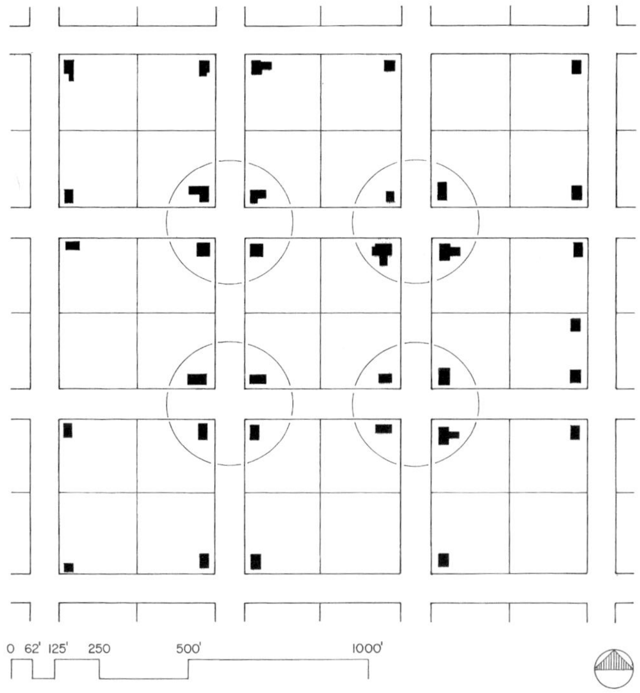

Figure 3.12. Crossroads urban settlement pattern in Manti (taken from 1898 Sanborn Fire Insurance maps).

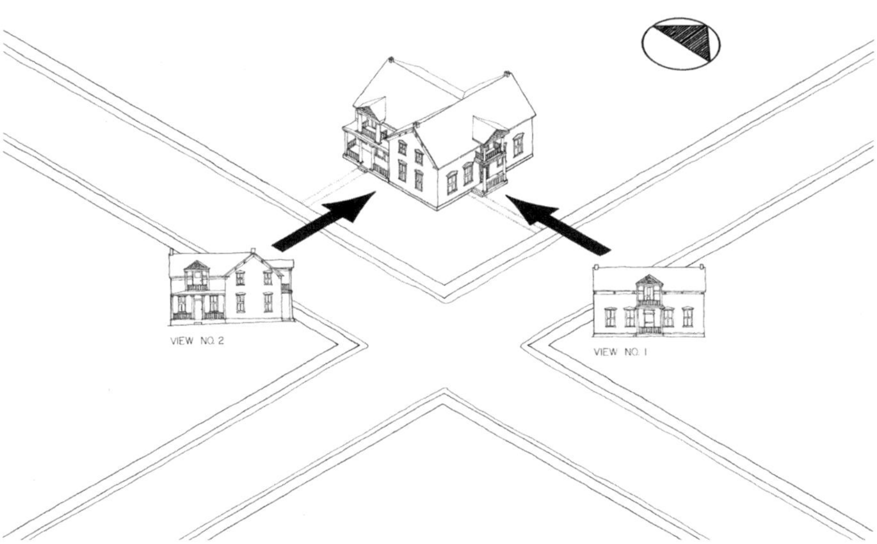

Figure 3.13. By the 1880s, many Mormon families designed their houses to be viewed from two directions. A good example of this corner-lot design is the James Staker family house, 211 North Main, Mount Pleasant, circa 1885. From the east (view 1) it is a symmetrical center-passage house of five bays, while from the south (view 2) it is an asymmetrical cross-wing type of house.

Fences were essential to the home lot and served a number of purposes (Figure 3.14). Most importantly, they created boundaries, or "petitions" as Jens C. A. Weibye called the one he put up between his lot and W. H. Peacock's.[64] They marked property lines and created enclosures, keeping a family's animals (which might include a team of work horses, several saddle and carriage horses, a cow or two, and perhaps some sheep and goats) in and those of others out. Unprotected gardens and orchards were fair game to loose animals that often roamed the streets, and these marauders, allied with deer from the nearby foothills, could devastate a family's much-needed home food production.[65]

Another function was decoration. Picket fences were immensely popular among the settlers, adding a degree of refinement to a family's home lot. When David Candland's shingle and sawmill opened in Mount Pleasant, a contributor in 1868 noted in the *Deseret News* that "lath and picket are to be added, and soon our town will have a decent array of fencing."[66] In addition to keeping people and animals out of the dooryard, fancy picket fences delineated the domestic or civilized portion of the lot. Grass was planted at an early date, a landscape feature that along with the picket fence signaled a special nonfarm use for this space. Whereas the fencing for the farmyard

Figure 3.14. Picket fencing encloses the front and side yards of the S. C. Petersen family house in Ephraim. The photograph shows the house, which probably dates to the mid-1870s, as it looked around 1890. George Edward Anderson Photographs, MSS P-1, L. Tom Perry Special Collections, Brigham Young University.

Figure 3.15. Types of nineteenth-century Sanpete Valley picket fences.

was of the common board variety (rails with broad vertical boards nailed to them), pickets came in a variety of shapes and sizes (Figure 3.15)—the beauty lay in the attention to detail.

Traditional patterns of gender separation were most likely perpetuated on Mormon home lots, with men responsible for the outlying farms and in-town farmyards and women for the dooryards and gardens. One Manti resident recalled, "My mother . . . worked much in the garden. We always had a very good garden, had three different kinds of wild current, also a good patch of serviceberries, also strawberries. Then later my Mother knit socks and paid for quite a number of fruit trees and some shade trees."[67] The male/female distinctions were less than rigid, however, for undoubtedly men, women, and children shared in all duties required to make the farm work as a successful economic enterprise.[68]

Easily the most important building found on a family's home lot after the house was the barn. By the time the Mormons got to Utah, it was customary throughout the United States and much of Northern Europe to integrate a number of farm-oriented functions in a single large building called the barn.[69] During the initial years of western settlement, however, such barns were relatively scarce, since the pioneers directed their attention instead to the immediate tasks associated with establishing towns and constructing houses. Most Mormon farmers and ranchers initially reverted to an older architectural system whereby a set of small outbuildings served in lieu of a single large and expensive barn. Wheat, oats, and corn were stored in granaries; hay was stacked in the open, often with the help of a portable stacker or derrick; farm implements were stored in sheds; and what livestock there was on the home lot (most of the cattle and sheep herds were ranged outside of town) were confined in corrals with perhaps an open-sided and flat-roofed stable placed along side to protect these valuable animals from the elements. These straw-covered and rather primitive stables/barns (Figure 3.16A), sometimes called by farmers "loafing sheds," proved both practical and cheap and were employed throughout the Mormon region as well as the West generally. The simplest of these structures consisted of cedar posts driven into the ground and covered by a flat or extremely shallow-pitched "dirt" roof. Such roofs consisted of log rafters overlaid with a mesh of willows or small branches, which in turn were covered by straw, layered like thatch, and then an additional coating of dirt. Usually the back and perhaps one or both sides were enclosed with stone or sometimes log. More elaborate examples have sections divided into tack rooms and stables.[70]

By the 1860s and 1870s, frontier life in most Sanpete towns gave way to the routines of permanent settlement. Stability brought with it a degree of prosperity that translated into the appearance of real barns, those that reintegrated all farm functions under a single roof. In these buildings, farmers stabled their livestock, mainly horses but also some milk cows and birthing cows; did the milking; stored their equipment and such things as buggies and carriages; and kept feed and hay. These barns were of two kinds, older traditional barns resembling in their form and construction those built in the eastern United States and Europe, and barns of a newer type specifically suited to the Great Basin.[71]

Barn building during this phase was characterized by a variety of types. As we will see in the houses, Mormon pioneer families tended to build in the manner of their homelands. Probably the most common of the larger barns was what is called the *English barn,* a type carried to North America by English colonists and found throughout New England, New York State, and the Upper Midwest. English-type barns are large rectangular buildings consisting of three internal bays (Figure 3.16B). Large double doors front the building and open into the middle or central bay, usually symmetrically composed. This central bay could have a board floor to be used for threshing wheat. One side bay served as a stable for the animals, while the other was a haymow. Some English barns in Sanpete were built of heavy timber frame construction, but a good number were of log, usually found with open central passages. These log variants of the English barn are sometimes called *double-crib barns* (Figure 3.16C).[72]

A second frequently encountered barn in Sanpete is a *bi-level barn* with Northern European antecedents. These barns could be built of adobe, stone, or log, or a combination of materials such as a stone first level and an upper level of logs (Figure 3.16D). The haymow was located above, stabling for saddle and workhorses below on the ground floor.[73]

By the 1880s, after years of frontier expediency and individual experimentation, a degree of consensus emerged in barn building. Gone were the large and expensive eastern and European types of barns, replaced by an ensemble of outbuildings that resembled that of the first settlement years, only with a

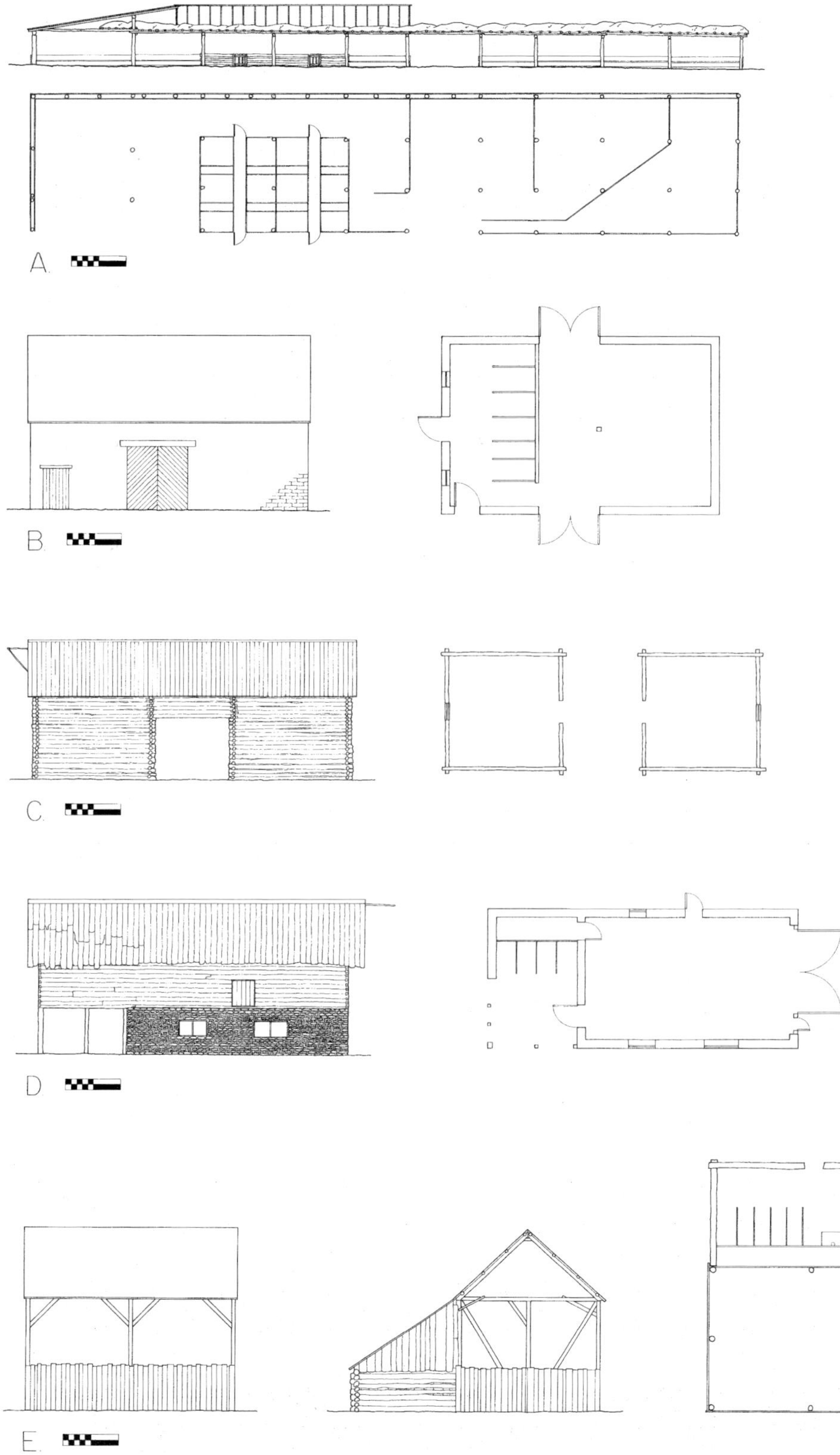

Figure 3.16. Nineteenth-century Mormon barn types. A, open-sided barn with straw-covered roof, between Manti and Ephraim, U.S Highway 89, circa 1890 (demolished); B, Jacob Johnson English barn, 390 South 100 West, Spring City, circa 1875; C, double-crib log barn, West Center Street, Wales, circa 1870 (demolished); D, Neils Peter Ostensen bi-level barn, 300 West 100 North, Fairview, circa 1870 (demolished); and E, William Black, Intermountain barn, 470 South Main, Spring City, circa 1890. Drawings by Collin Tomb and James Gosney.

new type of barn named by geographer Richard Francaviglia the *Intermountain barn* for its common occurrence from northern Arizona to the Canadian border. The Intermountain barn appears to have been a product of the American West, growing naturally from the need of the region's farmers and ranchers for an efficient and locally adapted form of hay storage and animal shelter. The main feature of the barn is the central haymow, which can be enclosed to the eaves with unchinked round logs or loose-fitted vertical or horizontal planking, or simply left open above the ground level (Figure 3.16E). The roof is carried on a light box frame of dimensional lumber. The entrance stands on the narrow gable end. Hay is loaded with a Jackson fork that runs along the ridgeline on an iron track. To one or both sides is added a stable, insulated against the winter cold and summer heat with walls of adobe, stone, log, or brick-filled balloon framing. These barns were cheap and easy to construct and provided a minimum of cover for both hay and livestock.[74]

Accompanying the new barns was an array of outbuildings that included privies, chicken coops, hog pens, icehouses, workshops, summer kitchens, and smokehouses (Figure 3.17). The most plentiful of these were granaries, which were used to store wheat and oats, fundamental fixtures in the family's diet. Granary design reflected both use and national origins. Most adhered to a standard plan: the door, placed centrally either on the long side or the gable end, opened into a passage with storage bins arranged to both sides. Farmers initially had to shovel grain into the bins, but later conveyor systems were developed that made the loading process easier. Most early granaries

Figure 3.17. A photograph from 1993 of a multipurpose work building on the Peter Molter family lot, 300 East and 200 North, Spring City, circa 1870. The design for the projecting gable roof probably came from Molter's homeland in Schleswig-Holstein, which was part of Denmark until 1864.

were constructed of log, often with Scandinavian notching, like the Swedish double notch found on the Poulson family granary in Ephraim (Figure 3.18). Some granaries had a refined quality that belied their utilitarian role, as in the case of one commonly built in Wales of a light timber frame and sheathed with clapboards; the Gothic-inspired finials give the small building an added flare (Figure 3.19).[75]

Figure 3.18. Lars Poulson granary, 100 West and 100 South, Ephraim, circa 1865 (photograph from 1978). Poulson emigrated from Sweden and built this granary in the style of that country, using a double-notch form of corner timbering and fitting the logs closely together with long horizontal grooves.

Figure 3.19. Frame granary on the Thomas Davis family lot, 100 North Main Street, Wales, circa 1870 (photograph from 1978). The Davises were from Wales.

Collective Individualism

In describing the American character, historian Michael Kammen uses the term "collective individualists," and it is tempting to borrow it here for our Mormon Zion makers.[76] The trouble is that the Latter-day Saints turned Kammen's paradox around: where he finds individualism enabled by a collective spirit (a degree of personal freedom is sacrificed in the name of social order), in Mormon communities it was the opposite; the collective spirit was facilitated by individualism (the social order was strengthened by the participation of church members acting on their own). We shall see more of how this equation worked in the next chapter on house forms, but the essentially meritocratic nature of the City of Zion, a place where resources were unevenly distributed on a best-use basis and community well-being factored out as the sum of its individual parts, stands as a hallmark of early Mormon culture. To paraphrase a line from the writer Gertrude Stein (quoted by Kammen), the Saints acted as if they "went all together one by one."[77]

4 FRONTIER FASHION

DOMESTIC ARCHITECTURE AND INDIVIDUAL DISPLAY

> [President Young] counciled the brethren to build good houses and make good fences around our gardens.
>
> —*Manti Ward Minutes, April 28, 1853*

SOMETIMES THE BEST WAY to make a point is simply to repeat it so often that it finally sinks in. This certainly seems the case when it comes to Mormon housing, for church leaders spoke a great deal about domestic architecture and the message was always the same: "If you wish to build a house," Brigham Young told the faithful in Salt Lake City, "build as good a one as you can imagine."[1] Similarly, Apostle Heber Kimball preached: "Build good houses and adorn them."[2] Local Sanpete leaders followed along: one of Manti bishop John Lowry's main duties, he explained, lay in "stimulating the brethren to build Good Houses,"[3] and in Manti meetings, President Welcome Chapman often made remarks "encouraging the people to Build good houses."[4]

Given the number of times the "build good houses" line surfaces in the Sanpete documents (and those of the church as a whole), even now it is hard not to get the point, but at least two questions do remain: Why the preoccupation with good houses? And what in fact did nineteenth-century Mormons think a good house was? Such questions figure prominently in Mormon landscape history, for a house was the single most important thing a person or family owned (or rented). Like Americans generally, the Utah Latter-day Saints paid great attention to how their houses looked. In return, the buildings served them well as both shelter and sign, protecting them from the elements while at the same time advertising social standing and cultural identity.

The domestic architecture found in the Sanpete Valley is typical of Mormon western communities during the settlement period: masonry construction, adobe and stone initially, and later brick, predominated over wood; the neoclassical aesthetic emphasizing rectilinear massing and symmetrical composition was universally accepted (though not always fully realized); and fashionable effect was achieved by applying trim packages of Federal, Greek, and later Gothic and Italianate decorative elements. Houses came in a variety of sizes, from big to small depending on the finances and tastes of the family that built them, or better, had them built, since the Sanpete Saints, like their counterparts in other Mormon communities, relied heavily on a set of professional builders and carpenters for their architectural needs. This approach to residential architecture was established early in the church's history and reflects a concern for worldly appearances consistent with the American populace generally. The pious Saints were not above putting on airs when it came to house style and fashion.[5]

The Genteel Tradition

Mormon leaders never precisely explained their idea of a good house. There were short rants against log construction (Figure 4.1), like this by Brigham Young in Salt Lake City: "I marvel to see you contented to live as you do. I have passed much of my life in a log-house, but do I like bed-bugs and darkness? No. I love light. Were I obliged to live in a log-house, I would have it plastered and whitewashed that it might be neat and pleasant."[6] Or Apostle Orson Hyde conveying the same message to a Sanpete congregation: "Some men never get any thing better than a log cabin and it [is] full of buggs."[7] But for the most part platitudes sufficed for the simple reason that everyone, leaders and followers alike, was on the same page: a good house was one in fashionable neoclassical style, which at its most basic was a rectangular masonry building with a door in the middle and symmetrically placed windows (Figure 4.2).

Mormons early on gained a reputation for asceticism, a rejection of worldly affectations.[8] This characterization now seems rather misguided. They did embrace communalism during the Ohio and Missouri years, and throughout

Figure 4.1. Fountain Green log house belonging to the John Green family. Anonymous photograph, circa 1860. Reprinted by permission of Utah State Historical Society; all rights reserved.

Figure 4.2. The new house the Green family built in Fountain Green around 1870. John was a teamster, and he and his wife Elizabeth had six children. Anonymous photograph, circa 1880. Reprinted by permission of Utah State Historical Society; all rights reserved.

the Utah settlement period Brigham Young preached self-sufficiency and abstinence,[9] yet there is little indication that the Latter-day Saints were anything but good American consumers. A consumer is, of course, someone who buys things. As it is used here, however, the term applies more broadly to someone who makes purchases with the implicit assumption that a direct and readily discernible connection exists between such possessions and a person's, a family's, or even a community's identity.[10] This materialistic ideology resides at the heart of the capitalist enterprise and informs to a great extent the obsession Mormon leaders had with good houses. If, that is, the Latter-day Saints hoped to gain legitimacy as a mainstream American religion, then they had to prove themselves worthy. One easy way of demonstrating worthiness was by living respectable lives in refined houses. We saw this mind-set in town planning, where the orderly style of cities became part of a church-wide performance of community gentility. The style of houses was equally symbolic, with the symmetrical house becoming an explicit sign of cultural refinement, the three-dimensional equivalent of the gridiron city plan.[11]

No matter where they came from, whether New York or Tennessee, Birmingham, England, or Aarhus, Denmark, Mormon converts arrived in Utah conversant with both symmetry and neoclassicism. As a design concept, symmetry (dividing an object down the middle to yield two equal halves) is firmly embedded in the Western folk aesthetic, the product of an abiding human need for order. As late as the nineteenth century on the American frontier, people viewed the world in its natural state as irregular, chaotic, and dangerous. By drawing nature through the filter of human-imposed symmetry, a degree of control was achieved that was both literal (the world is made regular) and symbolic (humans have the ability to control nature) that provides both pleasure (beauty in a balanced design) and psychic safety (nature transformed into culture). In traditional application, a semblance of symmetry was all that was required, just enough balance to give people the illusion of being in charge. The arrival of neoclassicism as an Anglo-American cultural style in the eighteenth century, however, had a profound impact on the design process, particularly when it came to architecture. In the hands of the neoclassicists, a symmetrical world became rigidly symmetrical.[12]

As the name implies, neoclassicism resulted from the revival and reapplication of ancient classical designs. At its most literal, this meant copying the outward trappings of Greek and Roman prototypes, a practice that yielded a plethora of little Parthenons and Pantheons complete with monumental temple fronts, porticos, columns, orders, and cornice entablatures. Such replications mostly surfaced as public and religious buildings. In domestic architecture, the neoclassical aesthetic combined with already entrenched appreciation for symmetry to produce a new house form consisting of a horizontal block with a low-pitched roof, a centrally placed front door or projecting pedimented pavilion, classical trim along the eaves and around the doorway, and a balanced and proportional arrangement of openings and decorative elements. In Italy, this type of house is associated with the sixteenth-century architect Andrea Palladio; in England and its colonial peripheries, the name it gets is "Georgian," after the reigning kings of the time (Figure 4.3).[13]

The neoclassical movement started in Italy during the Renaissance and slowly spread northward, first to Northern Europe, then the British Isles, later Scandinavia, and finally to North America, where it dominated the scene in domestic architecture from the 1750s until the outbreak of the Civil War.

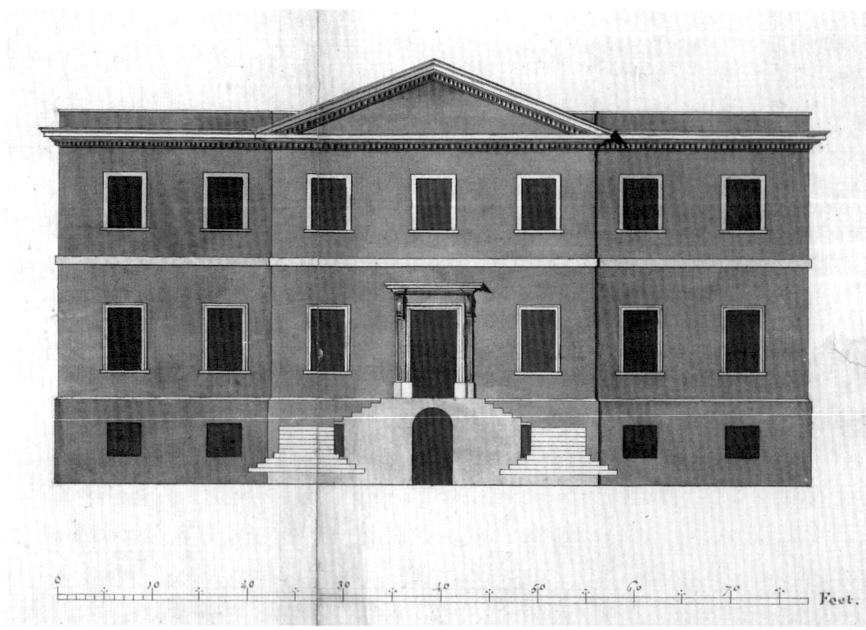

Figure 4.3. English Palladianism. Unexecuted design for alterations to Butleigh Court, Butleigh, Somerset, William Paty, 1758. Reprinted by permission of RIBA Library Collection of Drawings.

One noteworthy contribution neoclassicism made to Anglo-American architecture came in the form of the Georgian house, a block-like residential type that was two stories high, two rooms wide, two rooms deep, had a central stair passage and usually a rear service wing, and could come with any number of decorative trim packages. The Tillinghast house in Providence, Rhode Island, built in the 1760s, is a typical Georgian house (Figure 4.4). Style is expressed principally through form: the symmetrical rectangle is the defining feature, while classically derived decorative features are confined to the eaves, windows, and front door. Here the eaves are plain, but the window heads are graced with a projecting cornice and over the front door is found a dentiled pediment carried by attached classical pilasters.[14]

So popular was this house type with America's landed and mercantile gentry that it remained a staple of upper-class life through later phases of neoclassicism, even when Federal and Greek decorative elements supplanted Georgian details. In this way, for nearly a century the form served as the perfect architectural expression of wealth, power, and refinement. The Francis Hitchings family house in Upstate New York (where Mormonism originated), dating to the 1830s, shows the enduring nature of the Georgian type: here the basic shape and plan of the house are preserved while specifically Georgian decorative elements are dropped, replaced with the heavy entablature, gable-end cornice returns, and front entrance Doric columns of the Greek Revival. In the vernacular design tradition, decorative fashions change while the house form stays the same (Figures 4.5 and 4.6).[15]

It should come as no surprise that wealthy Mormons embraced the Georgian house. Many were built in Nauvoo, including the one constructed in 1843 for Apostle Wilford Woodruff (Figures 4.7 and 4.8). Woodruff's house consists of a classic Georgian plan set inside an austere outer shell characteristic of the Federal brand of neoclassicism. From 1800 until well into the 1840s in the western part of the country, a severely plain architecture was in vogue, where the house block was stripped of ornament, suggesting a bourgeois rejection of Georgian-era aristocratic fussiness. In the Federal mode, embellishment was confined to a transom (often elliptical) and side lights on the front door. On Woodruff's house, small semicircular windows are added in the gable ends that have parapet roofs. Parapet-style end walls, rising above the roof, were useful in preventing the spread of fire in urban areas, though in the loose suburban landscape of Nauvoo it was largely a nod to fashion. Parapet roofs are one of the defining features of Federal neoclassicism and are found through the eastern and midwestern United States in the early years of the nineteenth century.[16]

The crown jewel of Mormon neoclassicism is church president Brigham Young's principal Salt Lake City residence (Figure 4.9). Named the Beehive

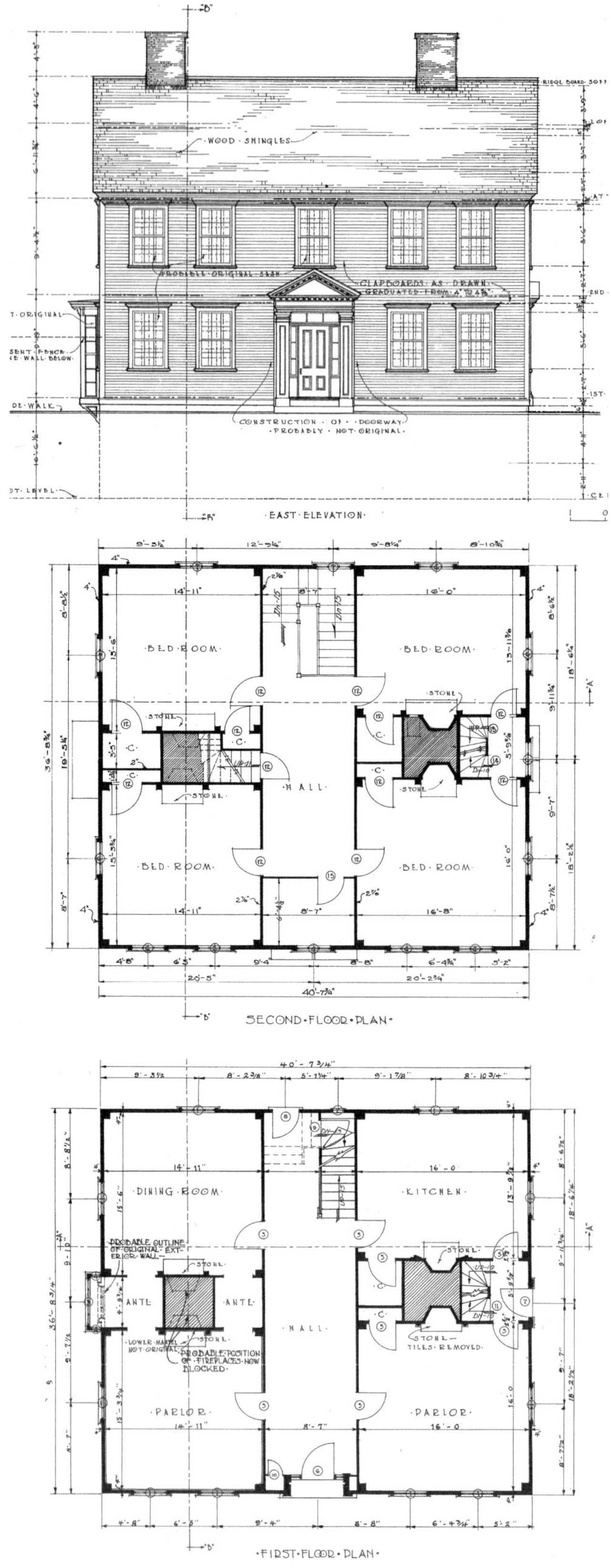

Figure 4.4. The Georgian house. Elevation and floor plans of the Captain Joseph Tillinghast family house, 403 South Main, Providence, Rhode Island, circa 1760. Historic American Buildings Survey, National Park Service, HABS RI, 4-Prov.

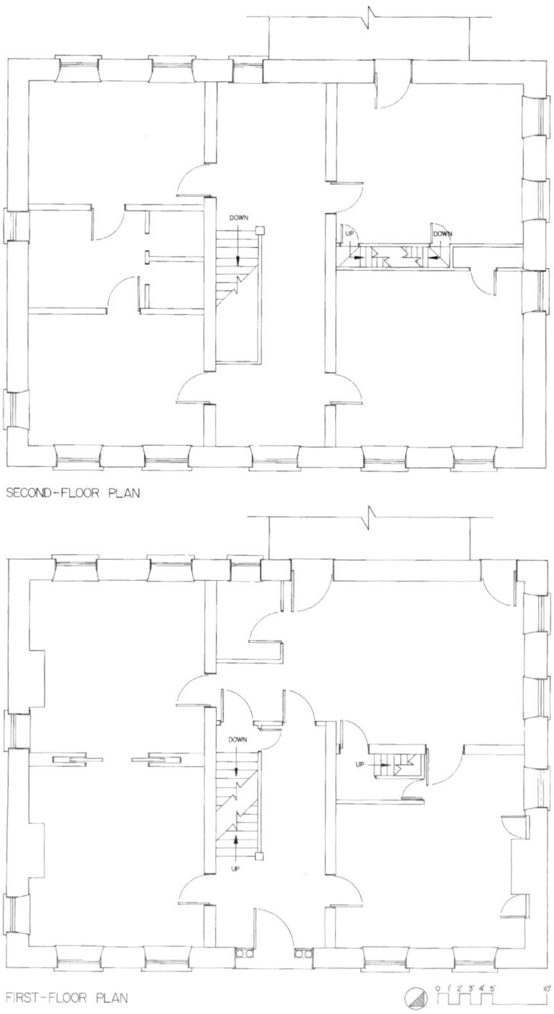

Figure 4.5. Francis Hitchings family house, Summit Street, Lockport, Niagara County, New York, 1834. Historic American Buildings Survey, National Park Service, HABS NY, 32-Lock, 1983.

Figure 4.6. First- and second-floor plans of the Hitchings house. Fieldwork by Virginia Barrett Price; final ink drawing by James Gosney.

House (the beehive symbolizing Mormon cooperation, obedience, and industry) and completed in 1854, the house was designed by LDS Church architect Truman Angell. It has a basic Georgian plan and a rather eccentric decorative scheme consisting of a broad wraparound porch, a Greek cornice with returns on the gables, and a pedimented panel inset midway up the front roof. There is an elaborate balustrade on the ridge and a square observatory topped with the distinctive beehive sculpture. More will be said of Young's living arrangements—he was a polygamist of great renown—but the Beehive House functioned as both residence and statehouse; on the first floor were Young's personal bedroom, bathroom, and parlor, while upstairs were additional bedrooms and another parlor known as the "long hall," which was used for entertaining family and official visitors.[17]

Very few rank-and-file Mormons, of course, could afford such grand accommodations. The vast majority lived in smaller, more modest dwellings like the one built by Isaac and Ellen Vance in the 1860s in Fairview (Figure

Figure 4.7. Neoclassicism at Nauvoo, the Wilford Woodruff family house, Tenth and Hotchkiss Streets, 1843 (photograph from 1977).

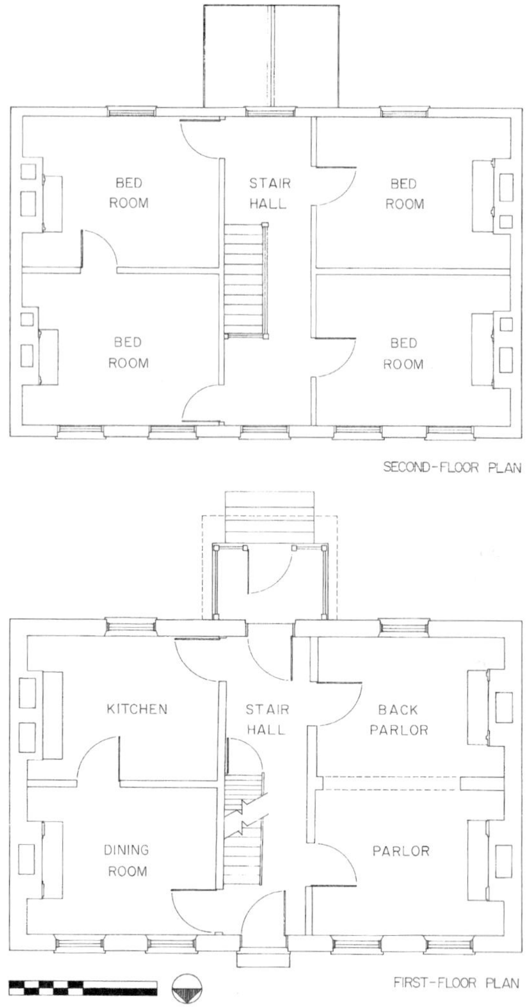

Figure 4.8. First- and second-floor plans of the Wilford Woodruff family house (after HABS ILL, 34-Nau).

Figure 4.9. Neoclassicism in Salt Lake City. Brigham Young's Beehive House, South Temple Street, 1853–55. Courtesy of the Church History Library.

4.10). The house is an example of what scholars have named the I-house.[18] I-houses are downsized Georgian houses, being one room deep, two stories high, and with or without a central stair passage. Customarily too, they have a rear kitchen wing, either included in the original design or added soon after. The Vance house has neither a rear kitchen nor passage, and contains only two rooms per floor, for a total of four. Most Latter-day Saints' houses were even smaller, having a single story and two or three rooms. It should be evident, however, that no matter the size of the house, the umbrella aesthetic of symmetry, reinforced by a transcendent neoclassical styling, dominated Mormon domestic architectural design to the extent that a degree of stylistic unity exists across both geographical boundaries and class lines.

Big or small, city or country, the great majority of Mormon houses from the Zion-making period will have a symmetrical (or nearly symmetrical) facade with a door *(d)* in the middle and one or two windows *(w)* to either side in a *wdw* or *wwdww* pattern, or less commonly *wddw*. The ubiquity of the symmetrical house may be one reason both contemporary and later observers have seen a uniformity in Mormon domestic architecture.[19] A "good house" for Mormons was a fashionable one, and during the settlement period this meant a house that possessed geometry, harmony, and proportion, with their implicit connotations of rationality, balance, and order. It did not matter whether they were large or small, only that they were stylistically right, thereby connecting the architecture to the culture of gentility.

Building materials had similar meanings. In decisions regarding materials, the underlying supposition was simple: the more processed it was, the farther it was removed from its natural state, the better, since processing, like symmetrical composition, demonstrated the capacity of people to master their

Figure 4.10. Neoclassicism in the Sanpete Valley. The Isaac Vance family house, 300 South 400 East, Fairview, circa 1865 (photograph from 1978). Vance was from Ohio and came to Utah in 1849, living first in Manti.

environment. Who could like a log house? It was made of timbers that still resembled trees, suitable perhaps for a first house or for backwoods hillbillies, but anathema to all who valued refined taste and cultured living. For these people, clapboards—trees run through a water- or steam-powered sawmill and cut into smooth rectilinear boards—were the thing; and when painted white to stand out from the natural world, such exterior wall surfaces became the perfect expression of human power and refinement.[20]

In the semiarid Sanpete Valley, as in the Great Basin as a whole, timber was in short supply, and what there was grew in the higher elevations of the Sanpitch Mountains and along the Wasatch Plateau. Every mountain canyon was dotted with sawmills, but the wood coming from them was needed mainly for fuel or to supply the planing and shingle mills that served the local building industry. Masonry houses were therefore the default option, and here too a hierarchy of value surfaced that was linked to the "aesthetic of artificiality."[21]

Kiln-fired brick was naturally at the top, since it required the most processing: clay had to be located, excavated, and transported, then mixed, placed into molds, and finally fired. In the Sanpete Valley two varieties of fired brick occur. One is red because of its high iron content, while the other, with lime, turns out a burnt-yellow color. Both are pleasing to the eye and seem to have enjoyed equal status. Common bond coursing in a five or six stretcher-to-single header row scheme is standard (Figure 4.11A), although some church and business leaders used the more prestigious Flemish bond, which alternates courses of stretchers and headers. Flemish bond brickwork is a subtle but universally recognized affectation whose meaningfulness comes from its pleasing decorative pattern and its conspicuous consumption of expensive bricks (Figure 4.11B).[22]

Next to brick in the hierarchy was stone, and the smoother and more evenly coursed, the more highly it rated. Unlike brick, whose identity as clay is utterly extinguished through processing, stone cannot be entirely divorced from its earthy origins. Still, if worked correctly, it can achieve the balanced regularity so highly sought in building materials. Rubble walling, where the stones are left in their natural state and piled unevenly, ranked at the bottom of the scale, probably roughly equal to log. Square-cut and evenly coursed ashlar walls, however, were much esteemed (Figure 4.11C), especially in the Sanpete Valley, known for its excellent and readily available limestone. The more regular the stone wall was, of course, the more it cost, an equation known to everyone and another example of conspicuous consumption in valley housing. To save money but still get the desired effect, many home builders found it easier to lay up roughly coursed stone that was then given a geometric overlay of raised or scored mortar joints, a technique that lent a degree of refined regularity to an otherwise rough wall (Figure 4.11D).[23]

Finally there was adobe. During the Zion-making period, adobe, the name for unfired or air-dried brick, was the cheapest and most readily available building material in the Sanpete Valley as well as throughout the entire Great Basin. Early on, church leaders touted it as an ideal solution for people building in a desert climate with limited timber resources (either for building or as fuel for firing brick kilns). Adobe became something of a last resort, however, and though it was common it was still never embraced with great enthusiasm. The use of adobe by Mormons may have come, according to many historians, from an exposure to it in the nearby southwest territories and California, where it was ubiquitous.[24] This could be true, though Mormon adobes are smaller than Pueblo or Hispanic ones, and furthermore, adobe making is not all that different from fired brick—just leaving off the final firing stage—making a case for an independent invention. It should be noted too that unfired bricks are not unknown in the East,[25] and are a building staple in Denmark, where they are called *ler tegel* and used mainly as infill "nogging" on timber-framed buildings.[26]

Whatever its origins, adobe with its dull brown color never fit in with the aesthetic of artificiality (Figure 4.11E). At its best it remained the color of dirt, and if not protected from the weather, it quickly flaked, crumbled, and returned to its natural state. One indication of the low esteem in which adobe was held is that if at all possible it was quickly covered with layers of smooth plaster, both to protect it from the elements and to make it more socially presentable. Such plaster veneers were often painted to resemble fired brick and stone as a way of upgrading what was a building material of necessity, not choice (Figure 4.11F).[27]

The emphasis on refinement visible in the houses is also evident in what was being said regularly in Sunday meetings. (NB: The Mormon code word for refinement was "improvement.") Bishop George Bradley of Moroni observed, for example, that "the people [in Moroni] are generally blessed with health, and . . . are energetically striving to make their homes the abodes of all that is elevating and refining in the correct scale of progressive improvement, socially, morally, and religiously."[28] Or read what George Peacock, one of the leading citizens of Manti, wrote in the *Deseret News:* "A vast amount of plowing and sawing are being done in this county, also building houses, improving roads, bridges, etc., and penetrating the [canyons] for timber, poles and wood. While all these are going on, the people are not forgetting the formation of societies for education and advancement, to meet the present as well as future necessities, sustaining their friends, building up homes and making it desirable."[29]

Did the Mormons suffer from an inferiority complex? Certainly. They had to prove both to God and the world at large that they were respectable

Figure 4.11. Beyond necessity: the art of masonry in Sanpete Valley architecture. A, common bond brick, 100 South 400 West, Manti, circa 1870; B, Flemish bond brick, Llewellyn family house, 265 West 200 North, Fountain Green, after 1876; C, ashlar stonework, Petersen family house, 287 East 500 North, Spring City, circa 1870; D, ribbon joint masonry construction, 100 West 200 North, Manti, circa 1870; E, common bond adobe, Garlic family house, 300 South 100 East, Fairview, circa 1865; and F, adobe covered with bricking veneer, Clawson family house, 184 East 200 South, Spring City, circa 1880. Photographs from 1978–79.

A B C D E F

Americans. In some ways, their whole existence was viewed as something of a test, as Bishop Jones of Fairview reminded them: "The Lord," he said, "has given us the worst part of the Earth to see how we will manage it, and if we will prove our selves worthy of any better."[30] But there was another audience too, and this was the American population, who generally viewed this new religion and its acceptance of modern revelation with suspicion, skepticism, and outright scorn. How were LDS Church leaders to convince the religious establishment that their new church was legitimate? For much of the nineteenth century Mormons resided outside mainstream society, and more often than not were portrayed in the popular press as uneducated ne'er-do-wells, drawn from the impoverished soil of New England and Upstate New York, the slums of Liverpool, Birmingham, and other British industrial cities, and the hardscrabble farms of Denmark, southern Sweden, and frigid Norway. Add polygamy to the mix, with its undertones of promiscuity, and a tough press was inevitable. The need to display refinement—improvement—in the built environment was one way to counter this impression and demonstrate the divine nature of the religion.

Frontier living compounded the image problem. In Ohio and Missouri, then considered the West, the persecuted Saints never had the opportunity to prove themselves; they were pushed out before they had a chance to build their communities. In Utah, they got a reprieve, being out of reach for a time at least. And here, behind the sheltering bulwark of the Rocky Mountains, Zion would be built as a sign to God of the church's temporal worthiness, but also to send a signal back east to the United States, of civility and taste, the contemporary marks of respectability. David Candland, writing to the *Deseret News* from the nascent town of Mount Pleasant, noted: "The progressive is a feature of this new-fleged city in the agricultural, mechanical and spiritual . . . bonafide homes are better than the miner's camp."[31] Families had to sacrifice, but refinement was worth the effort. Philip Hurst of Fairview wrote a letter to his mother, saying, "[My house] has took so much time and means that it will cramp me for a while but if I can get it done it will be some satisfaction to have a house that we can enjoy ourselves in."[32]

Live within your means but still aspire to refinement and respectability was the mantra. Unnecessary extravagance was not countenanced (though church leaders often failed this test). Sanpete Stake president Canute Peterson, talking to a church conference in Mount Pleasant, "showed the folly of buying so much merchandise and manufacturing noting [he] had mad[e a] calculation that there was not grain enough raised in the Stake to pay for all the merchandise that had been imported and sold in the Stake during the past year."[33] Overextending was problematic, but hoarding and deferring were also to be avoided. Apostle Orson Hyde addressed the Saints in Fairview in

November 1862 and said, "We should make our selves comfortable houses, and many other coviniencess for our own comfort and happiness, and we should enjoy them and not cut our days short by starving our selves of the Things that God so abundantly has blessed us with, as the future may not be ours."[34]

There is a strain of LDS rhetoric calling for abstention and avoiding the "ways of the world." Such antimaterialism, however, was largely just talk. If we look at the things they built and bought, from the leadership down to the lowliest farm laborer, Mormons certainly were aware of style and how it worked. They may have to make their own clothes and furniture, but these items would still be as refined as was humanly possible. A recent book calls the Mormons a "people of paradox," since they preached spirituality and abstention but practiced worldliness and accumulation. It could be argued that such capitalistic behavior was quite natural, even expected, especially given the emphasis placed within the society on the Gospel of Works and the blessings received from doing good works.

It was one thing to talk about gentility, of course, but such a lifestyle had to be paid for, and during the years of Kingdom building the Sanpete economy was robust enough to sustain an appropriate level of consumption. Save for the first years of subsistence, the local economy was market driven with profits and increases going into tithing but also possessions of all kinds. Carl Dorius of Ephraim mentioned in April 1871 that there was news of rich silver and gold discoveries in Pioche, Nevada, and exclaimed, "There will be a market for our produce."[35] Christian Larsen described the entrepreneurial spirit found in his family: "Grandfather was an ambitious man and had keen vision and confidence in the potential wealth and growth of the West. He started a freighting business, buying produce such as eggs, butter, and cheese and hauled it by horse and wagon to Salt Lake City, many miles away. With the money the produce brought, he purchased dry goods and other hard to get items which he freighted back to a little store which he had started in his home. Grandmother and her daughters sold these articles. He did a modest business and helped others to get a start in business. During an early period he freighted produce as far as Pioche, Nevada."[36] Emma Jane, wife of George Tucker, wrote in 1872: "[George] has gone to Pioch[e] with a load of barley, expects to be gone almost a month. A great deal of grain has been freighted out of there."[37]

A Mormon Housing Style

Temporary living conditions characterized the valley during the initial settlement period. Even into the 1860s Sanpete families preferred the protection of a fort to the exposure they felt out on their town lots, which, despite the compactness of the village, were still widely separated on five-acre blocks. A report out of Ephraim in 1860 declared, “No elegant mansions were constructed but the houses were built of logs and adobes or stone as each family could afford.”[38] After 1867, however, as the threat of Ute raids diminished, house construction increased. The transition from fort to town living was rapid in each of the communities, for few found the cramped conditions within the fort walls attractive. Joseph Hansen, a Danish immigrant, spoke for many when he told his diary that “to people throughout their lives that had had good, comfortable homes with plenty of the necessities of life this condition must have been very hard to bear.”[39]

Most of the pioneer-era houses in the Sanpete Valley date from 1865–1885, a twenty-year period characterized by intense building activity of all kinds. The houses constructed during this time convey important clues about the City of Zion and the kind of place the Saints wanted it to be. Again, no pressure came from church leaders to build this or that type of house. They only called for good houses, and everyone knew what they meant. In the end, the buildings themselves are the best evidence for understanding the Mormon style of housing. For our purposes, three general patterns stand out. First is variety. Within the prescriptive framework of neoclassicism, great latitude existed as to what individual families could do with their houses, and they took this to heart, creating a remarkable multiplicity of designs. Second is what scholars call an “open plan” approach to housing, with direct entry to the family’s living space from the outside. The final pattern is evident in a differentiated housing landscape in which ethnic and class distinctions were obvious and accepted. If doubts persist about the Latter-day Saints’ love affair with capitalism and consumer culture, then it is only necessary to look at their houses.

Diversity of Design

Students of Mormon housing have customarily approached the design topic from a perspective of cultural convergence. The incoming convert population, consisting of Saints from all over the eastern United States, the British Isles, and Scandinavia, quickly forged a unified cultural identity around their shared commitment to the Zion-making project.[40] One sign of this convergence is housing, where a multiformity of immigrant housing possibilities was reduced into a single unified architecture, with the Yankee style of the core converts, those from New England and Upstate New York, providing the model. In what to date is still the most comprehensive survey of early Mormon housing, geographer Leon Pitman tested the convergence hypothesis and concluded that "elements of house form or shape became similar throughout the [Mormon] culture region, indicating that an assimilation process occurred in folk housing concepts and that a common material folk trait complex emerged."[41] Further, Pitman attributed this uniformity to a "willingness and ability on the part of the Mormons to assimilate into an accepted mold, regardless of their diverse cultural origins."[42]

The trouble with Pitman's study is that, like others, he mistook the repetitiveness he rightly saw in the housing as something peculiar to Mormonism, a product of their collectivist leanings. It was not. If Mormons might be known for their obedience to the church, unity of spirit, and zeal for Kingdom building, they were not drones—little worker bees in Zion's Beehive. In their everyday actions, they were remarkably, even stubbornly, individualistic, holding on to their old identities as Southerners, Danes, capitalists, shopkeepers, or whatever, while at the same time gradually embracing their new Mormonness. The pervasiveness in western folk tradition of the symmetrical house and the global popularity of neoclassicism, with neat sets of proportions and geometries, made it extremely likely that the Saints would build similar-looking houses no matter where they originated, since the architectures of their homelands were that close in appearance. Still, there are subtle differences of great import. Within the basic formula, individual Mormon families enjoyed broad freedom in designing and buildings houses of their own choosing, and this they did to great effect.

It is customary, scholars of these subjects tell us, for immigrants to build in the manner they were accustomed to in their home countries. Depending on the diversity of the incoming population, there is the possibility of great variation in immigrant building practices, especially in the first generation, which knows little else.[43] Given the diverse nature of the Mormon convert population, both native and immigrant, we should therefore expect to see a wide range of housing types and construction methods in Mormon settlements like those in the Sanpete Valley. And we do. In fact, variety is one of the chief characteristics of Mormon housing everywhere. To repeat: Mormon converts came from all parts of the United States, the British Isles, and Northern Europe, where neoclassicism was firmly established at the time of immigration, so a certain sameness was inevitable. There are nevertheless significant differences in the houses.

Take, for example, the James A. Allred house in Spring City (Figures 4.12 and 4.13). It dates from around 1875 and appears to be a fairly standard central passage I-house. Yet noteworthy is its wood construction. As indicated earlier, timber in the valley was relatively scarce and required a great effort to procure from the nearby canyons. Thus wooden buildings are rare here even after the railroad's arrival in the late 1880s and 1890s made lumber more

Figure 4.12. An I-house built in the southern style by James A. Allred, 297 South 100 West, Spring City, circa 1870 (photograph from 1979).

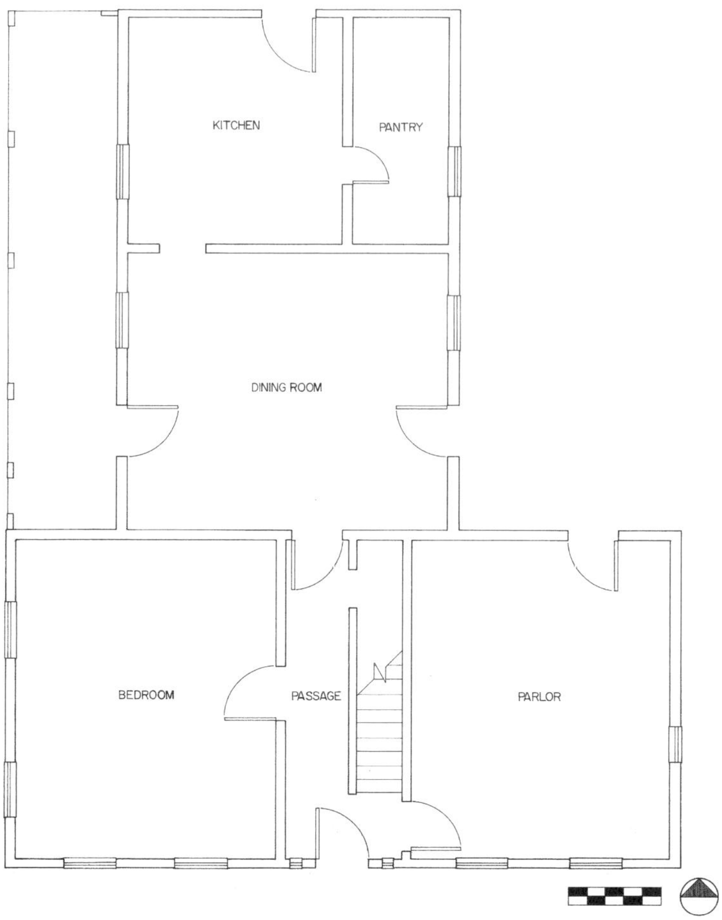

Figure 4.13. Ground-floor plan of the Allred family house.

readily available. The Allred house, however, is completely wooden. It has a light box timber frame that is covered with imported redwood clapboards. The exterior is classically Federal, with relatively little decoration save for the transom above and sidelights around the front door. So why use wood when it was more expensive and harder to get? The answer is simple: the Allred house is not just an I-house; it is a *southern* I house.

James A. Allred was born in Bedford County, Tennessee, in 1819. His family joined the Mormon Church in the 1830s and removed to Missouri, where they homesteaded a 600-acre tract of land. Driven back to Illinois, the Allreds lived in Pike County, south of Nauvoo. Here in 1844 James married Elizabeth "Betsy" Parks, a Missouri native. The couple moved west to Salt Lake City in 1861 and then to Spring City in 1865. Successful in both farming and the livestock industry, Allred became president of the Spring City Cooperative Store and for many years was the town's bishop. He married two other wives: Mary Ann Pollard in 1866 and Elizabeth Brough in 1878. In the 1870 census, James, Elizabeth, and Mary Ann are living together, probably in an adobe house he owned just east of Main Street. Shortly thereafter, James contracted for a substantial house to be built for first wife, Betsy, like the ones the couple had known back home in Tennessee and southern Missouri. This meant it would be an I-house, since this was the house of choice throughout the Upland South, and it had to be built of wood. James had the money and spared little expense on the house, even having redwood siding imported from California. In 1880, he and Betsy lived here, while Mary Ann and Elizabeth had their own separate houses in town.[44]

If the Allreds could have a house that reminded them of Missouri and the South, then Alma and Elizabeth Staker could have a northern one (Figures 4.14 and 4.15). Actually, the Stakers were Canadian, from Cataquera, Ontario. Alma's father, Nathan, converted to Mormonism in the early 1830s and joined the Gathering first in Kirtland and later in Jackson County, where Alma was born in 1837. When things became dangerous, the Stakers retreated back to Illinois, where they also lived in Pike County. By 1853 they were in Utah, where Alma, now of age, struck out on his own, settling in Mount Pleasant and marrying Elizabeth Young (no relation to Brigham) in 1856. Alma worked as a sawyer and carpenter, and in the 1860s built a large adobe house that closely resembled those he had known in the East.[45]

The design the Stakers chose is what historians call a temple-form house. The type gets its name from its temple-like appearance: the gable roof points forward and the low-pitched roof and cornice returns intimate the kind of full-blown pediment found on classical temples. Such houses were popular during the Greek Revival phase of neoclassicism and were particularly numerous in the northern Midwest, from Ohio's Western Reserve (which included

Figure 4.14. The temple-form house type was popular in New England and the northern Midwest during the second quarter of the nineteenth century. They are rare in Utah, probably because they were fading from fashion about the time the Mormons moved west. A good example of the house type is the Alma Staker family house, 81 East 300 South, Mount Pleasant, circa 1865 (photograph from 1978).

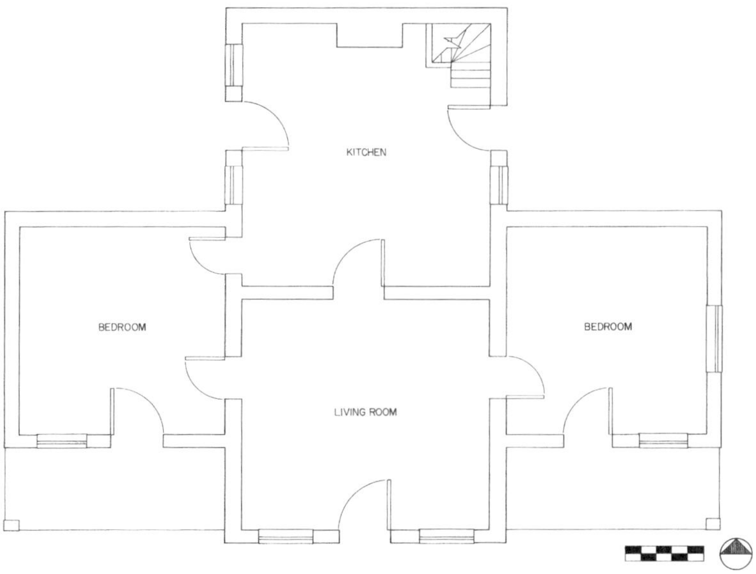

Figure 4.15. Ground-floor plan of the Staker family house.

Kirtland) into the upper parts of Indiana and Illinois as well as all of Wisconsin and Michigan. Temple-form houses were built in Nauvoo (Brigham Young chose this plan albeit with a Federal rather than Greek exterior) but were going out of vogue by the time the Saints reached Utah. The one the Stakers built in Mount Pleasant is unique, a testimony to the variety of domestic architecture found in the valley and state as a whole.[46]

English and Welsh converts also contributed to this housing hodgepodge, though their buildings are often hard to identify. Common throughout the British Isles is the hall-parlor house, composed of two main floor rooms, the larger being the hall or combination living room and kitchen; and a smaller side parlor or chamber that was a "best" room or parents' bedroom—in Utah it was invariably the latter. If there was an upstairs, it contained extra bedrooms or possibly a workroom for spinning and weaving. Hall-parlor houses date to the late medieval period and were exported to the North American colonies early in the seventeenth century, where they became a fixture in the Anglo-dominated landscape.[47]

In the British Isles, hall-parlor houses predate the coming of neoclassicism, and while they often approximate bilateral symmetry, rarely are all their doors and windows exactly in line, as is the case with the house John and Sarah Oldham built in Mount Pleasant in the mid-1860s (Figures 4.16 and 4.17). The Oldhams were English converts and their house harks back to English tradition, being slightly off-balance, the door in the larger of the two rooms and the openings grouped around it in a way that leaves a gap between them and the corners. John farmed, and together he and Sarah raised seven children in this adobe house, which incidentally was never plastered.[48]

Of all the Zionists, Scandinavians seem the most foreign, coming as they do from outside the Anglo-American cultural zone. Consequently, their houses have received the most scrutiny as a kind of litmus test for conformity. The essential question has been, did the Danes (the largest of the Scandinavian immigrant groups) build Danish-style houses in Utah? The answer is yes, but it requires some qualification. Scandinavians—Danes, Swedes, and Norwegians—did build Old World houses in the Mormon West. However, the designs they chose were not those we might expect. Most converts came from the lower rungs of Scandinavian society—it was the poorer sort who emigrated—and had lived in small peasant-type houses either of log or timber

Figure 4.16. A typical hall-parlor house built by Englishman John Oldham around 1865 (photograph from 1978). The house has been demolished, but once stood at 400 East 200 South in Mount Pleasant.

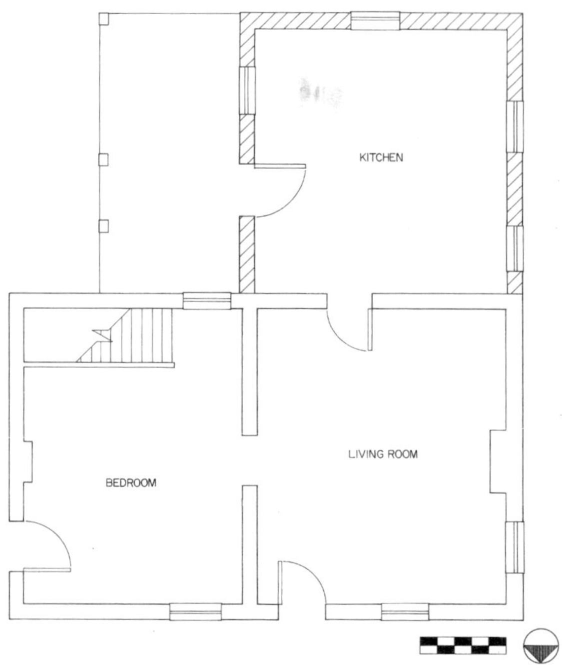

Figure 4.17. First-floor plan of the Oldham family house.

frame and thatched roofs. Once in Zion, however, many of them fooled everyone by building not traditional houses but rather newer ones favored by the Scandinavian bourgeois class, both rural and urban. Such houses they might had seen but could never have afforded in their former lives. When they became farmers in places like the Sanpete Valley, they quite naturally built houses suitable to their new social status. Some imitated their American neighbors, but many chose a three-part villa design that had become popular in the Nordic countries as neoclassicism spread among the newly affluent classes in the first part of the nineteenth century.[49]

The Hans Otterson house in Manti, built in the 1860s, is a one-and-a-half-story example of the Scandinavian three-part house (Figures 4.18 and Fig. 4.19). The name comes from its tripartite plan—three rooms arranged axially under a gable roof—and in many cases (though not Otterson's) a tripartite principal elevation as well. This last was achieved by setting off the central room in some way or another. It could be a cross-gable, a porch, or even just the way the openings were arranged, a *w/d/w* cluster in the middle, with a gap (indicating the location of the internal walls), and then the outside windows. The center room is most often, as in the Otterson house, the kitchen or combination kitchen and living room. One side room serves as the best room or parlor and the other as a bedroom. Upstairs rooms again function as bedrooms or workrooms. In the Otterson house they were unfinished. Hans was born in Aalborg, Denmark, in 1834, joined the LDS Church and immigrated to Utah in the mid-1850s, and lived in Manti as early as 1860. Here he farmed and worked as a stonemason. Hans never married and probably built this house sometime in the mid-1860s, doing the stonework

Figure 4.18. This three-part Scandinavian house belonged to Hans Otterson. It was constructed about 1860 and is located at 202 South 200 West, Manti. Photograph from1978.

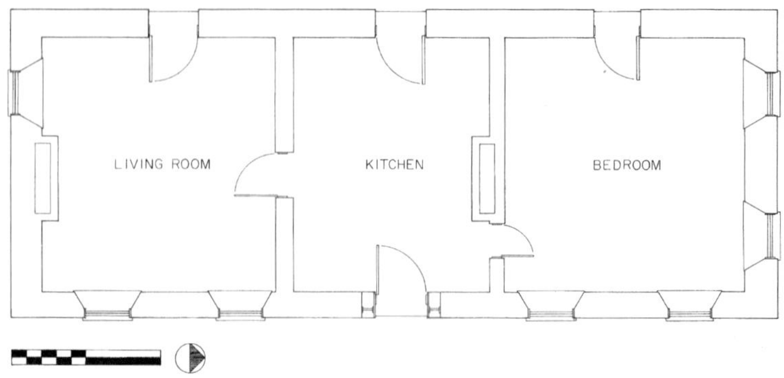

Figure 4.19. Three-part floor plan of the Otterson house.

himself. It is nicely coursed limestone, and an early photo indicates that the front was originally plastered, while the other three walls were left stone. Sadly, Hans was brutally murdered by two men during a robbery attempt on the house in 1884.[50]

The housing landscape of the Sanpete Valley City of Zion is, then, remarkably varied. At the same time, a degree of visual consistency remains evident due to the general acceptance among the settlers of both traditional (western folk) and popular (neoclassical) design principles. Within this overarching structure, however, latitude existed within which individuals could work and express themselves. An example of this openness is a set of one-story, two-room houses found in the valley (Figure 4.20). All were built between 1860 and 1870, and all have the basic two-room plan. In such houses, putting the door in the center to achieve symmetry is impossible because of the internal wall.[51] Each builder thus had to solve the problem of balancing the facade in his own way. The designer of the David Allred family house (Figure 4.20A), located in Spring City, decided to go with a single offset door and ignore symmetry; for Eric Sandstrom's house (Figure 4.20B), also in Spring City, the builder went with an unbalanced four-bay facade, the presence of the door weighting the design to the left; in a small house in Manti (Figure 4.20C), bilateral symmetry was achieved by giving the house two doors (one of which was never used); Jens Severine Jensen of Spring City arrived at another variation (Figure 4.20D), including two doors but not bothering to center them in the two rooms. Finally, there is the James Clawson family house (Figure 4.20E), built in two stages in Spring City; each side got equal treatment with a door centered between two windows. This kind of variation within the tradition is common and characterizes vernacular design in the valley during the Zion making years.[52]

The design tolerance in the valley was extremely high and carries over to the decorative process as well. If one word could describe the way Sanpete owners and builders approached embellishment, it would be "eclectic," since the usual pattern was to mix and match fashion elements from many different

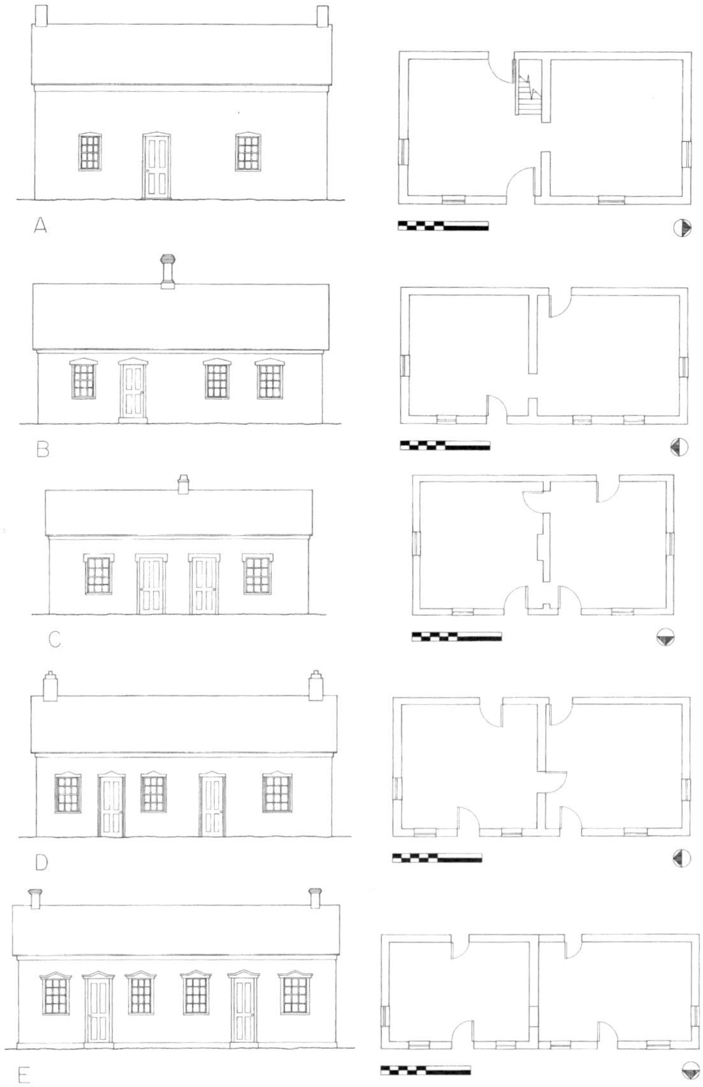

Figure 4.20. The diversity of design options for two-room houses in the Sanpete Valley. A, David Allred family house (window-door-window), 490 South 200 East, Spring City, circa 1865; B, Eric Sandstrom family house (window-door-window-window), 400 East 400 North, Spring City, circa 1865; C, house (window-door-door-window), 350 East 400 South, Manti, circa 1865; D, Jens Severine Jensen family house (window-door-window-door-window), 276 North 300 East, Spring City, 1870; E, James Clawson family house (window-door-window-window-door-window), 184 East 200 South, Spring City, circa 1870–80. Drawings by Collin Tomb, Cory Jensen, and James Gosney.

sources: Georgian plans, Greek cornice returns, Gothic Revival cross-gables and dormers, Italian brackets, and so forth. Such a combobulation of features is evident on the I-house Hans Peter Olsen built in Fountain Green (Figure 4.21). Olsen hailed from the Jutland area of Denmark, converted to Mormonism, and immigrated to Utah in 1858. He first lived in Moroni and then in 1867 moved up the road to Fountain Green. He occupied leadership positions in the local ward, prospered as a farmer, and built this impressive house in 1877. Olsen's eclectic detailing includes Greek pedimented window and door heads on the ground floor, Roman arched openings over the upstairs door and windows, an elaborate, almost Federal-inspired front door transom and sidelights, a molded cyma-curved brick cornice, and Greek cornice returns on the low-pitched dormers. We should not judge such excesses harshly; in all, the Olsen house is a bold statement of the local design aesthetic, reflecting

Figure 4.21. Eclecticism in Sanpete Valley house decoration: the Hans Peter Olsen family house, 215 South State Street, Fountain Green, 1877. Photograph from 1978.

not so much naïveté as it does the freedom the Saints felt in creating beautiful houses for the Kingdom.[53]

In thinking about Mormon artifacts of all kinds, the tendency has been to assume "order produces order"; an orderly society, that is, will naturally produce an orderly material culture. It is good to remember, however, that order can also allow disorder. People comfortable with themselves and their world can often accept diversity in ways those living under more socially turbulent conditions cannot. Disorder to an extent demands order, for when it spells danger then it is quickly quashed. When nonthreatening, as in a state where people feel safe and their collective house appears in order, then nonconformity in individual behavior can be more easily indulged. Ironically, odd-looking houses in this way may be indicative of a healthy society.[54]

Open Plans

In their book *Everyday Architecture in the Mid-Atlantic,* Gabrielle Lanier and Bernard Herman divide housing into two kinds, those with *open* and those with *closed* plans. According to these authors, open plans are "those that provide access from the outside directly into a heated living space." Closed plans are "characterized by access into the living areas of the house through an unheated stair passage or entry."[55] This delineation is crucial for understanding Sanpete Valley and Mormon housing, for the opposition denotes something more than simple convenience. House form, as we have seen, is tied to culture. The way houses are constructed and arranged facilitates certain actions that reflect particular social structures that are in turn validated by cultural mores. What this means is that open-plan houses are typically found in communities where privacy, the ability to physically shut oneself off from family members and neighbors, is neither a high priority nor something that enhances one's social position. Conversely, in those communities where closed plans predominate, privacy and social segregation are valued and the architecture advances this ideology. In houses the difference between an open and a closed plan is often nothing more than a stair hall or passage, but it is a significant difference nonetheless because of the larger cultural implications.[56]

The Sanpete Valley is an open-plan landscape. This aspect of the Mormon housing style is best understood from the vantage point of what architectural historian Dell Upton calls a "social molecule": the rooms a society feels adequate to most fully satisfy its everyday needs.[57] Mormon house design and use during the years covered by this study were based on what may be thought of as a basic three-room social molecule that included the old hall—also called variously the "sitting room," "front room," or more commonly the "living room (LR),"[58] a bedroom for the parents (BR), and a kitchen (K) (Figure 4.22). Other rooms could be added as the need arose. The most common of these extra rooms were the circulation/stair passage (PS), a true best room or parlor (PA), a dining room (DR), and a pantry (P). Additional bedrooms and workrooms were often found on an upper story, when there was one. In the basic house, children were tucked away in the living room or kitchen for the night.[59]

These spatial conventions coalesced in the years before 1890 in the hall-parlor house, a house of English origin and American omnipresence in which the living room and parents' bedroom were placed in the front section and the kitchen, as a service area, was contained in a rear ell. The hall-parlor form could be expanded to accommodate additional rooms. Many families, like that of William and Ellen Major in Spring City, settled for the basic

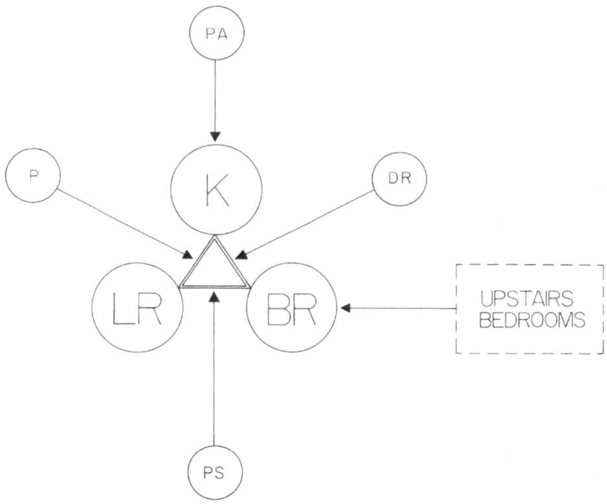

Figure 4.22. The Sanpete Valley basic three-room "social molecule" for house design. The main rooms are living room (LR), bedroom (BR), and kitchen (K); the ancillary rooms are passage (PS), parlor (PA), dining room (DR), and pantry (P).

three-room plan but supplemented it with an upper half-story that was used for extra bedrooms (Figure 4.23; see also Figure 3.1). William was born in England and came to Spring City when it was resettled in 1859. He was a farm laborer who became a farmer and had this small stone house built in the early 1860s. The living room fireplace has a tasteful Greek mantle, while the appearance of the closet-type staircase is enriched with beaded paneling.[60]

The vast majority of Sanpete Valley houses were of the hall-parlor type.[61] As we saw with the Oldhams, such houses were no strangers to immigrants from the British Isles, since they were part of the housing stock found there

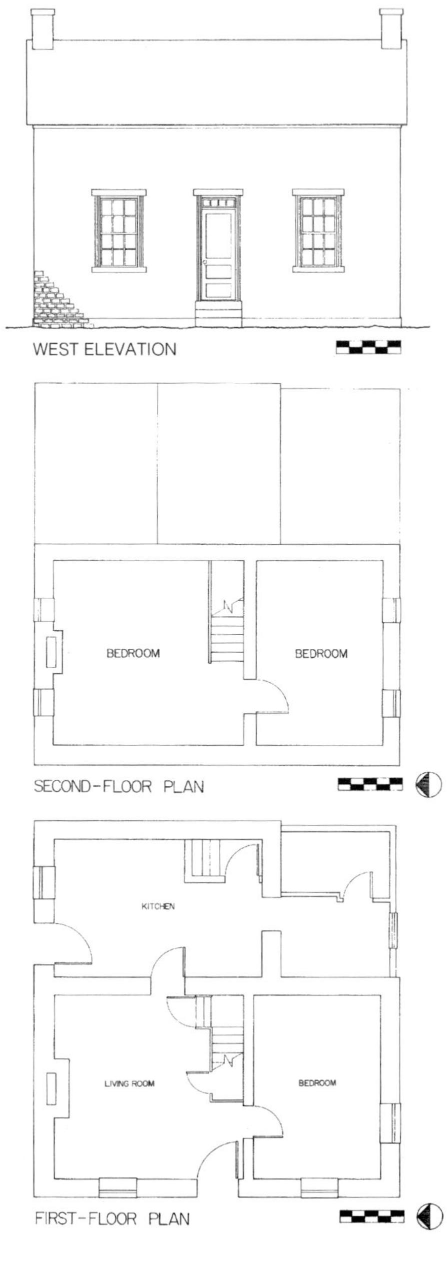

Figure 4.23. Principal elevation and floor plans of the William and Ellen Major family house, 527 South 200 West, Spring City, 1868.

since the late Middle Ages. For Danes, Swedes, and Norwegians, however, it was a new house form and undoubtedly required some getting used to before it felt right. In the Scandinavian countries small peasant cottages and workers' houses were common, but they lacked a rear kitchen wing and often were broken up into a number of small rooms, including an entrance lobby.[62] The jump to the two rooms with rear kitchen, open-plan hall-parlor form (and three-room social molecule) is one area where acculturation occurred, with many Scandinavians, such as Soren Jensen, a Dane living in Spring City, finding the new house (Figure 4.24) not merely an inexpensive solution to their housing needs but also a convenient sign of their new Mormon identity. Jensen did not give up his Danishness completely, however, for the rear kitchen/service shed is built in the Danish half-timber manner with vertical studs (placed directly into the ground) mortised to a plate and infilled with adobe bricks (Figure 4.25). And remember, too, just down the street were a number of three-part Scandinavian houses, so assimilation became an individual decision.[63]

Adding a circulation space to a house was something families of modest means could not usually afford: a passage or stair hall took up valuable room that in a small house could best be used for living and sleeping. Indeed, in many one-and-a-half-story hall-parlor houses the upper floor was reached via an exterior staircase, thus avoiding the need to sacrifice square footage in the main ground floor rooms. One of the most interesting things about

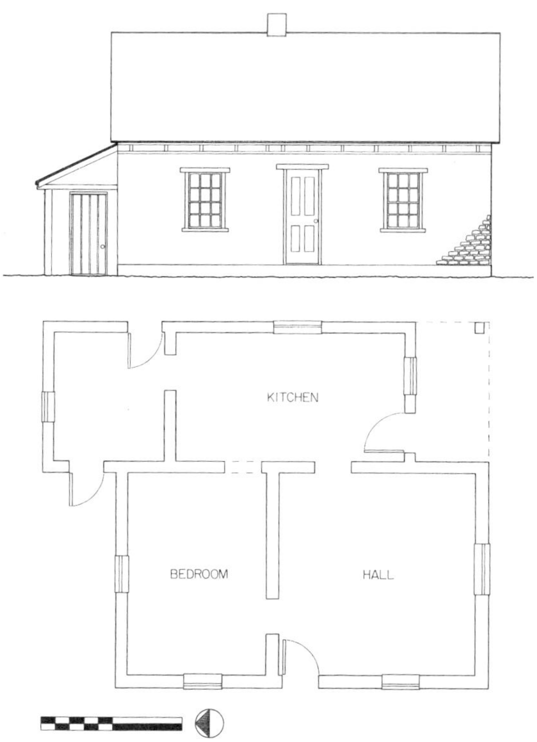

Figure 4.24. Principal elevation and floor plan of the Soren Jensen family house, 488 North 100 East, Spring City, circa 1865 (demolished).

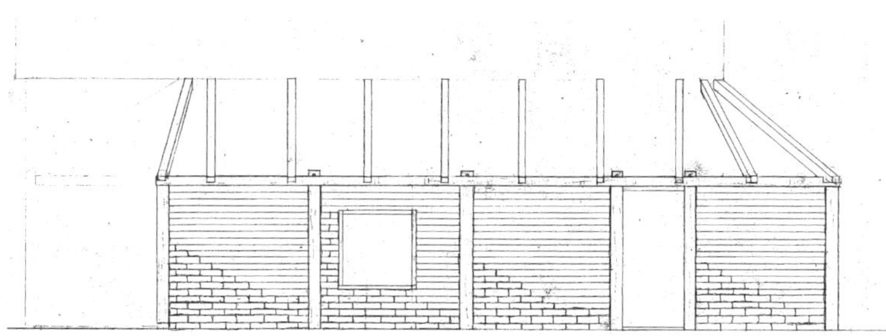

Figure 4.25. East rear elevation of the Soren Jensen house, showing its earthfast studs and half-timber construction.

early Sanpete housing is that many of the larger houses (of all types) have open plans, indicating that some of those who could afford the luxury of a circulation passage often refrained. A closed plan was something people had to feel was important, and this does not appear to have been the case. Historians have long assumed that Mormon I-houses contain central passages, since this is usual in other parts of the country.[64] Curiously, however, many of these large two-story houses in the Mormon region, like the one Jabez Faux built in Moroni in 1867–68 (Figures 4.26 and 4.27), have open plans, being simply larger variants of the hall-parlor type. Faux was from Yorkshire, England. His house is constructed of fired brick rather than the more common adobe, and it sports a bit of Italianate flare in its use of paired brackets along the eaves (the porch is a late nineteenth-century addition), but conceptually it conforms to the basic housing style of the community.[65]

There are, of course, exceptions. In the more urban and cosmopolitan setting of Salt Lake City, closed-plan houses appear to have been more prevalent, and in rural colonies like the Sanpete Valley, a small elite composed of the wealthiest families lived in houses that had entrance halls or passages. The Luther and Lola Tuttle family house in Manti exemplifies this closed-plan segment of the architectural landscape (Figures 4.28 and 4.29). Tuttle, a native of New York State, was Manti's leading merchant and businessman. He was a banker, a livestock dealer, two-term mayor, and a member of the Church High Council. He had this stone I-house built in the mid-1860s. The plastered exterior is original. In 1870 Luther was living here with his wife, Lola, seven children, and a domestic servant. The central passage originally opened into a lean-to shed that extended out from the south side of the kitchen wing.[66]

Why was the open-plan so popular in the City of Zion? Economy played a role, but seemingly not an overriding one. We can also rule out climate, since

Figure 4.26. Jabez Faux family house, Highway 132, Moroni, 1867–68. Photograph from 1978.

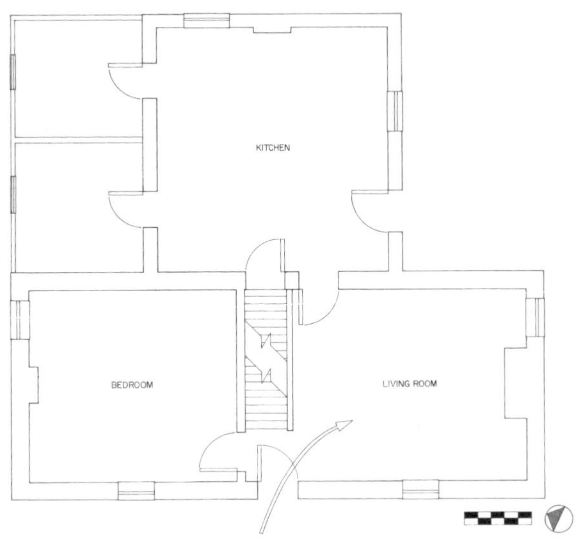

Figure 4.27. Ground-floor plan of the Faux house with arrow indicating direct entry into the open hall-parlor plan.

Figure 4.28. Luther Tuttle family house, 300 North 100 West, Manti, circa 1865 (demolished). Photograph from 1978.

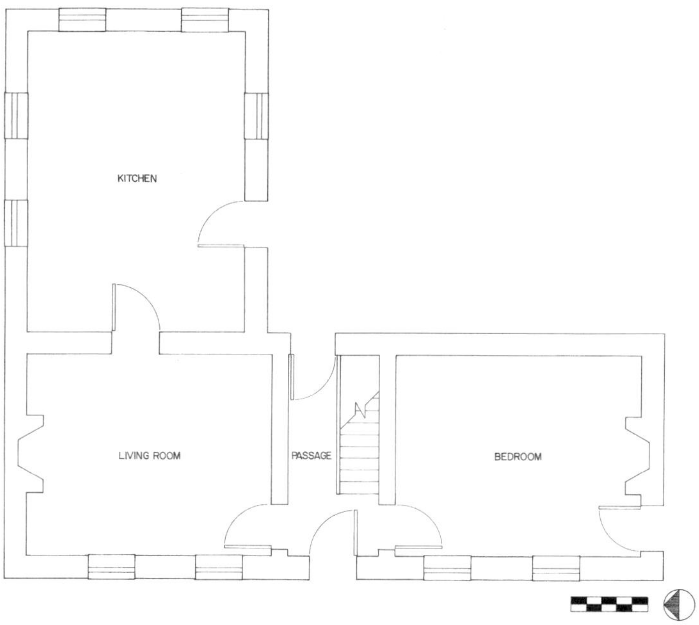

Figure 4.29. Ground-floor plan of the Tuttle house.

the cold winter temperatures and heavy snows characteristic of the Sanpete Valley, if anything, would have favored having house interiors closed off from the weather. The choice of the open plan in Mormon communities most likely results from a cultural disposition toward community engagement, an attitude fostered by the close-knit social fabric of village life. With the Saints living close together, and sharing the deep bond of religious belief, a degree of social integration was achieved that rendered buffering devices like hallways and passages superfluous. Most houses were fronted by picket fences, barriers through which visitors had to penetrate, but once inside the gate the going was easier. Remember, too, that during the settlement years, the years of the Experiential Zion, a kind of psychic cohesion permeated Mormon group consciousness. Cultural boundaries, the conceptual lines separating insiders and outsiders, were drawn at the community's edge and not around individual households; thus there was even less need for internal barriers.

This proclivity for open plans spills over into the newer Victorian-style houses being built in the late 1870s and 1880s. One thing about Mormon architecture: it may have been a bit *retardaire,* lagging behind the times in terms of fashion, but this was not because the Saints were opposed to worldly display. They simply lived too far away to stay abreast of current trends. In Salt Lake City, the gap between East and West was not so great, especially after the railroad was finished. Church leaders in particular rather quickly adopted, in the name of taste and refinement, the newest designs. And what was new was the *picturesque* style, an approach to architecture diametrically opposed to the neoclassical, with its obsession over symmetry and artificial order. In its stead came an architectural aesthetic based on the revival of even older premodern principles, those of the Middle Ages, and especially the Gothic. The name for it was the picturesque, because it was intended to evoke a "picture" of the world in its natural state. Asymmetry, irregularity, and the organic qualities of nature now came into vogue, bringing with them a range of new houses and decorative schemes associated with the Victorian period of architecture in the late nineteenth century.[67]

A few picturesque-style houses appeared in Salt Lake City during the 1850s. It may be an extension of the belief in continuing revelation mentioned earlier, but it does seem that the Saints were never keen on holding unnecessarily to the past. Apostle John Taylor said it best when he told the Saints: "The subject of architecture should receive attention from you; and your children should be encouraged to improve in the building of houses, and not be satisfied to merely copy after what their fathers did in the days of their poverty."[68] Or perhaps he really meant the "days of the neoclassical." One of the first examples of the new "Gothic" fashion was LDS Church architect Truman O. Angell's 1851 design for the first Salt Lake City Tabernacle (see Figure 7.2), which resurfaced several years later in Brigham Young's 1854 Lion House (see Figure 5.2), designed by another Mormon architect, William W. Ward. Numerous Gothic cottages were built in the capital for the city's leading citizens, including those with the cross-wing shape and plan, an asymmetrical house composed of two wings set at right angles.[69] Another picturesque fashion popular in the Mormon capital was the Second Empire, an exotic French import (see Figure 8.23) characterized by its curvilinear mansard roof. These Utah French houses date from the early 1870s, an indication that the Mormons rather closely followed fashion trends in the East.[70]

In rural Zion, isolation prevented the early acceptance of the new architecture. Picturesque designs, however, made their entrance, however timidly, in the 1870s and 1880s, most often with the open-plan interior arrangement. A good example is the large two-and-a-half-story Gothic house Peter Greaves built for his family in Ephraim (Figures 4.30 and 4.31). Jens Christian Breinholt, a stone and brick mason, mentions in his journal building a "large rock house for Peter Greaves" in 1875.[71] The house has the basic cross-wing plan. In the front-facing wing were the parlor and a bedroom, and to the side was a dining room/living room. A kitchen extension stood off the rear. Again, curious by its absence is a passage, which normally would have been included in the design. In the Greaves house, as was the custom in Mormon communities outside Salt Lake City, the door opens directly into the family's personal space. Other than that, all the essential elements of the new Gothic-type house are evident: the steep-pitched roof and wall dormers, the finials on the dormers and gable end, the scroll-cut gingerbread along the raking eaves, and the front bay window. Greaves was born in New Jersey in 1837. His family moved west into Ohio where they heard the Mormon gospel and were baptized into the faith in the 1840s. Young Peter struck out on his own in 1852, landing in Ephraim four years later. He was a carpenter by trade but quickly established himself as a "buyer and shipper of wools, hides, and grain."[72]

Figure 4.30. Peter Greaves family house, 118 South Main, Ephraim, circa 1875–80. This was one of the first houses in the valley designed in the new Gothic Revival mode.

Figure 4.31. Ground-floor cross-wing plan of the Greaves House.

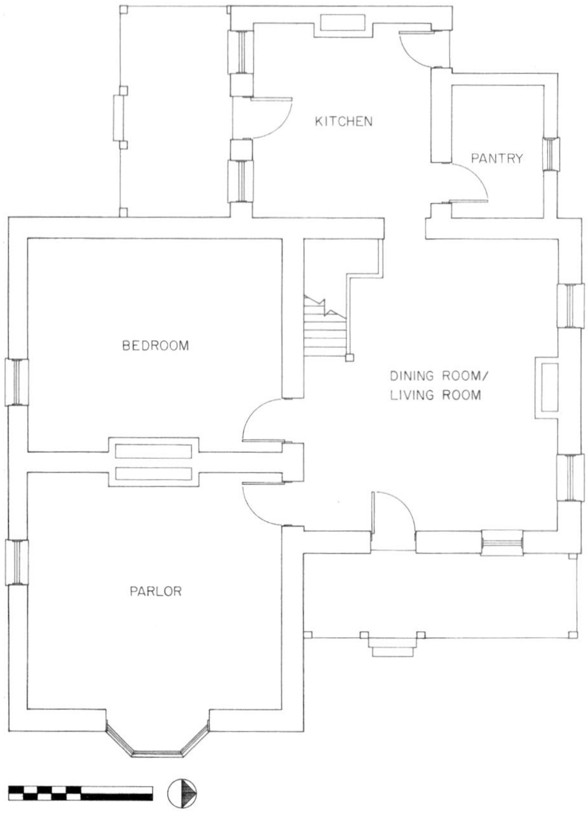

Differentiation by Design

Style, as indicated earlier in this chapter, can unify or divide. On one level, the general acceptance of the neoclassical style created a bond between people of all backgrounds, abilities, and classes. Within the symmetrical tradition, however, distinctions could be made that created distinctions within the society. We have seen some of these already, particularly in the area of ethnicity (the Scandinavian three-part house) and house plans (the choice of closed plans by the affluent). Probably the most obvious distinctions in the City of Zion landscape were those established along class lines. The closed plan belongs in this category, though it is relatively innocuous, or at least not so aggressively apparent as house size, which was the principal vehicle for calling oneself out. All Mormon houses shared the same design aesthetic, but some were big, others small, and most fit somewhere in between.

Inequality in housing (and life) was a fact of life in the Sanpete Valley, as it was throughout the Mormon Great Basin empire. It is important to note that no attempt was made to explain or apologize for disparities in wealth that the houses reveal; it was simply part of the story. Two houses illustrate this point nicely, one built for Sanpete Stake president Canute Peterson and his family in Ephraim and the other for the Paul Kofford family in Spring City. These two houses represent the highs and lows of housing in the valley.

At the very top of the social scale stood Canute Peterson and the house he had built in Ephraim (Figure 4.32).[73] Peterson was one of the first Scandinavians to join the LDS Church. He was born in 1824 in Eids Fjord, Hardanger, Norway. His parents immigrated to America in 1837, bringing Canute with them to LaSalle County, Illinois. After leaving home, he converted to the Mormon Church and as a missionary helped spread the gospel throughout the Upper Midwest, and particularly in those areas with large percentages of Scandinavian immigrants. After Nauvoo was abandoned, Peterson set out for Utah. En route he married his first wife, Sara Ann Nelson.

When the couple reached Salt Lake City, they found the good land taken, so they moved south to Lehi in Utah County. Canute contracted for a log cabin to be built and moved in with Sara and the couple's two-year-old son. Almost immediately Peterson was called away, this time to serve a four-year proselytizing mission to Scandinavia. He was a skilled orator and a champion missionary, bringing nearly five hundred converts from Denmark, Sweden, and Norway back with him, including Gertrude Maria Rolfson, a native of Christiana, Norway, whom he took in 1857 as his second wife. The Lehi log house was enlarged and the two wives lived there together with their shared husband quite amicably. Yet another mission called Canute away, again to Scandinavia, and once more he married one of his converts, this time twenty-two-year-old Charlotte Amelia Extram, a Swede.

In 1867 Peterson was summoned by Brigham Young to move south and serve the Sanpete Valley as stake (regional) president. Canute immediately purchased a home site on Ephraim's main street, across from the meetinghouse, and started planning a new house. His wives remained in Lehi until the house was completed, probably in 1869. In terms of its design, the Peterson house is easily recognizable as a Georgian-type house, similar to Brigham Young's Beehive House and others built by LDS church leaders in the West. It has a five bay façade with a boxed cornice and returns on the gable ends. The soffit features paired brackets, dentils, and a decorative frieze. Inside, the woodwork was faux-painted to resemble marble and oak, and there was an elegant curved staircase leading to the second floor.[74]

The census enumerator in 1870 found the whole family reunited in the Ephraim house: Sara and her five children; Gertrude and her five; Charlotte with one; and a boarder, John Thompson, for a total of sixteen counting Canute. It is unclear how the house was divided up. Most likely each wife had one of the three large upstairs rooms for sleeping, with the two smaller ones used for overflow, work, and children (an unfinished attic may have been for

Figure 4.32. West elevation and first- and second-floor plans of the Canute Peterson family house, 10 North Main, Ephraim, circa 1868–70.

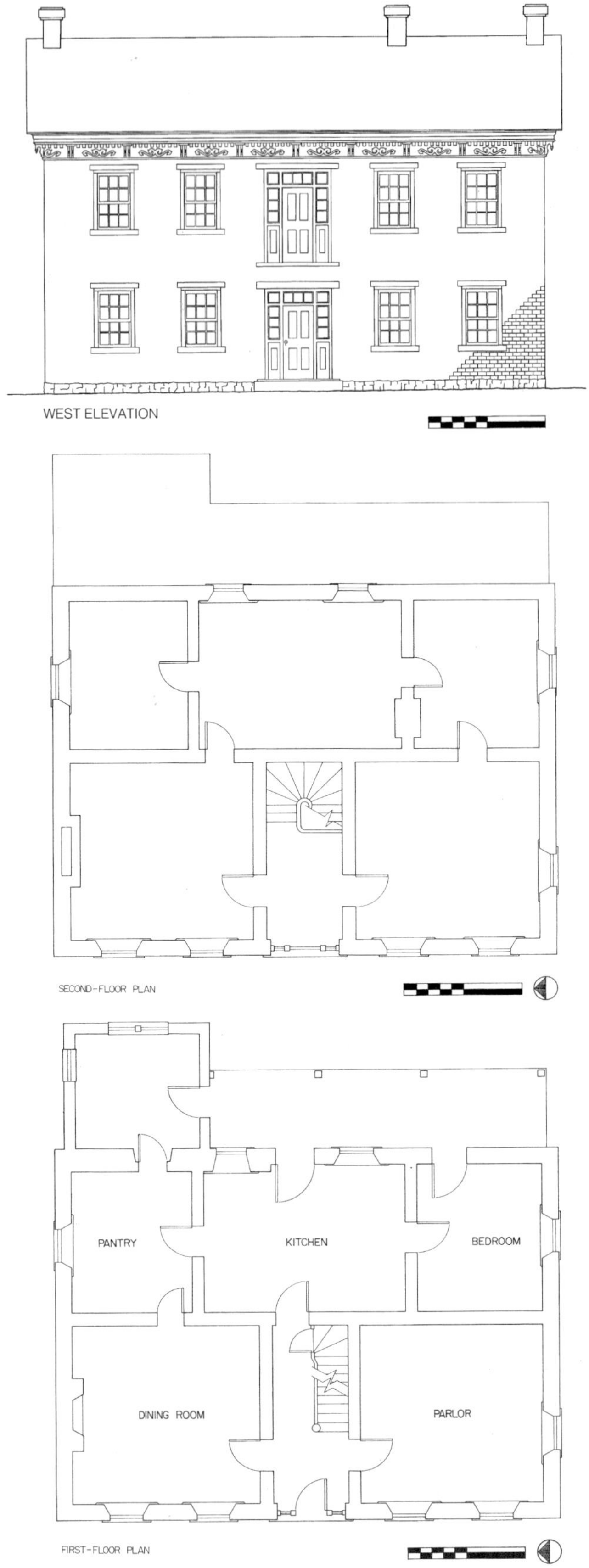

the children as well). Thompson, the boarder, could have slept in the room off the kitchen. The front rooms included a parlor and a dining room.[75]

At the bottom of the three-room housing group is the Paul Kofford family house in Spring City (Figure 4.33).[76] Kofford was Danish and came to Utah in 1853, settling first in Manti and then moving to Ephraim, where he served as ward bishop from 1856 to 1859. The Koffords joined the resettlement of Spring City in 1860 and shortly thereafter contracted to have Christian Nielson Olsen build them a stone house. Olsen's journal records the event: "I have agreed to do the masonry on [Kofford's] house for a steer not quite 2 year old."[77] The bill seems about right. It is a very small house, even with the requisite three-room minimum. The front room was an all-purpose room, used for cooking, eating, and sleeping. One of the rear bedrooms may have been reserved for Paul and his wife, Anna, who was also Danish. The other could

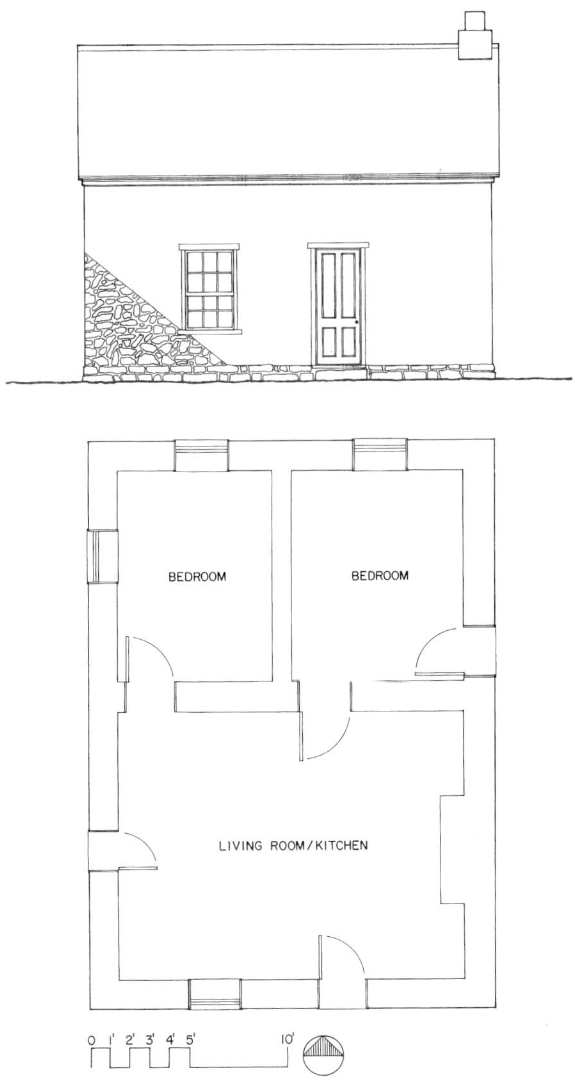

Figure 4.33. South elevation and ground-floor plan of the Paul Kofford family house, 11 East 100 South, Spring City, circa 1860.

have been a bunkroom for the children, which by 1880 numbered seven. In such cramped quarters, one thing is certain: the Koffords knew each other very well.

We should not lose sight of the fact that for a man like Canute Peterson, the building process was relatively easy, or at least it came more easily than did spelling in his adopted language, as this letter about the Ephraim house to his wives in Lehi attests: "Tuesday I was up to the sawmill to get som sawing don, I got some of the Door fraims and some of the Window fraimes don. It takes a great deal of lomber to Do that only 21 winders and 15 doors, and Lintels over them all and then think of all the joce [joists] and then all the reast. . . . The brick is Small but good. I think it will take about 20,000. . . . I have 12,000 adobies Made, and I will need about 10 or 11,000 mor. . . . The foundation is nerley don. You know how hard it is to git so Much or miney materiels to gider. Lime to lie the Bricks in. Sand has to be huld about 5 mills over a bad road. I have begun as it ware Withy my Eyes Clost and I do the same to Day, about Bilding this Big Hous but I do not lik to take my Family from a good home, and put you in a hummel [hovel]."[78]

All Peterson had to do was place an order for what he needed and then go pick it up (or have it picked up). The process was not so easy for those without a surfeit of money. Danish convert Peter Madsen of Ephraim noted: "Now in the year 1860 I began to build a house on the city lot. I had to labor much and hard for to get a place to live in, I had to go to the mountains and cut the trees down and haul them to the Sawmill for to get time [?] and lumber, and I had to haul all the rocks and I was the mason also to lay the rocks in the wall, nails was 40 cents lb and windows lights 8x10 was 40 cents each, I did not get the roof on the first year, and I had to build some kind of hous for our domestic animals also, and I had to attend to the farm business also."[79] Madsen's account leaves one tired from just reading it, but this kind of effort is echoed in diaries throughout the valley. Getting a roof over one's head came at great expense, either in money or labor.

As a peripheral colony, the Sanpete Valley saw a smaller gap between rich and poor than did Salt Lake City. But it was present and clearly not considered a divisive issue. No complaints about disparities in wealth surface in the written documents, and certainly no hesitancy to flaunt it existed in the houses. The Saints were all together but unequal, some contributing more to the Zion-making process than others, particularly in the area of refinement. If the admonition was to "build as good a [house] as you can imagine," then that is what people did. And they worked hard at it, driven forward by an ethic of consumption that is rather surprising. These are not plain buildings in any way, and sometimes the degree of ostentation is surprising. Certainly this is the case with the house built in Fountain Green for Bishop Rees R. Llewellyn and his family.

Llewellyn was born in 1828 in Aderdale, a town in the heavily industrialized area of Glamorganshire in southern Wales.[80] Rees went into the coal mines as a small boy and remained there until emigrating to Utah as a Mormon convert in 1856. His wife, Ann, who accompanied him, had also worked in the mines. The couple arrived in Salt Lake City in the fall of 1857, destitute, and after a long winter there they headed south, first to Utah Valley, where they lived for four years in Santaquin, and then on to Fountain Green, which was being settled. Rees became the town's first postmaster, built a one-room log cabin, which he soon enlarged for his growing family. By the mid-1860s, the Llewellyns had accumulated enough capital to build a two-story brick house, the first one in Fountain Green, which served both as a post office and a boarding house. Rees eventually became one of the town's leading citizens, serving in the church leadership, as president of the town council, and even as a member of the state legislature. Around 1876, after he returned from a mission to Wales, the Llewellyns moved into their newly built two-story brick house (Figures 4.34 and 4.35); they had come a long way from their previous lives working in the mines.

The Llewellyn family house is a classic brick I-house with a rear kitchen ell. One of the downstairs front rooms was a master bedroom, while the other, the one to the north, served as a parlor. Upstairs were more bedrooms. Not a great deal has been said here about house interiors (due to space limitations),

Figure 4.34. East elevation of the Rees R. Llewellyn family house, 256 West 200 North, Fountain Green, circa 1876. Photograph from 1977.

Figure 4.35. First- and second-floor plans of the Llewellyn house.

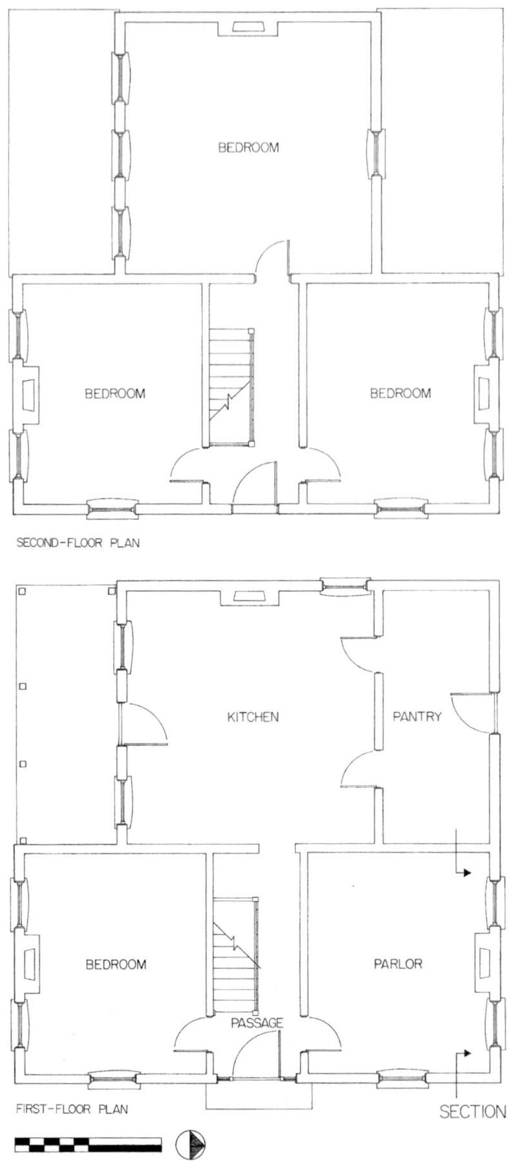

but to understand the significance of the Llewellyn house we have to pay attention to finishes, particularly that found in the parlor, which is covered with decorative painting (Figure 4.36).

Such extravagance is actually not that uncommon in the Sanpete Valley, or in other parts of the Mormon West. LDS families were keen, if they could afford it, to add fancy painted finishes to their home interiors. These could be simple stencilings, which seem to have been preferred by many Scandinavians (Figure 4.37), though simulated architectural details were more widespread. Such things as wooden or plaster paneling, wainscoting, and crown molding were prohibitively expensive, so people hired painters to artfully approximate

Figure 4.36. Decorative painting on the north parlor wall of the Llewellyn house.

them in oil. Faux painting, graining, and marbleizing have a long pedigree in Western tradition, beginning with the Renaissance. They enjoyed a revival during the neoclassical period and were practiced extensively throughout the United States during the nineteenth century, as well as the British Isles and Scandinavia.[81]

Mormons painted just about everything in the house. Pine (actually Douglas fir) was the available wood, and it had a wide grain and a surfeit of knots. To dignify it, in keeping with both the culture of refinement and the aesthetic of artificiality, it had to look like some fancier and more costly material, such as mahogany, oak, or walnut, or, even better, marble. Sanpete Valley cabinetmakers met most local needs for furniture and were particularly adept at faux graining.[82] House painters too were in demand and were quite accomplished in their work. Pine doors were transformed into oak, maple, or walnut doors. Pine mantles were disguised as marble (Figure 4.38). Parlors like those in the Llewellyn and Hans Peter Olsen houses got fancy paneled wainscoting that is hard to distinguish from the real wooden kind (Fig. 4.39). All in the name of gentility.

Figure 4.37. Wall stenciling, Andrew Olsen family house, 269 East 300 North, Spring City, circa 1860–65. Photograph from 1977.

Figure 4.38. Faux marble painting on the rear parlor mantle at the Greaves house, Ephraim.

Figure 4.39. Faux-grained wainscoting in the parlor of the Hans Peter Olsen family house, Fountain Green.

Good Houses

Housing is an important barometer of cultural process. It is a simple thing: when attitudes and values change within a society, house style will likely change too. Form follows desired function. In the case of Mormon housing, we might therefore expect something dramatic to have happened around 1870 as the church's isolation breaks down, cultural boundaries shift, and the temple/town dichotomy takes hold. This does not happen, however. Some superficial changes occur a few years later; by around 1890 picturesque/Victorian designs replace neoclassical ones, but the defining features of the Mormon housing style, design tolerance, open plans, and hierarchy, remain largely intact. We might say that the secondary characteristics changed, while primary principles endured.[83]

The main point to draw from the houses is that from the outset they display an unmistakable worldliness. There is nothing plain or reticent in their design. Salt Lake City led the way, of course, with newer eastern fashions in operation well before the railroad made its appearance. The colonies followed. *Good houses* were desirable signs of both individual and group merit and it is important to recognize that neoclassicism was favored, not as a symbol of Mormon order or orthodoxy, but because it represented the refined taste of its time. When trends changed, the Saints went along, replacing their older symmetrical houses with new irregular ones. As good consumers, the Mormons knew full well the importance objects had in establishing both cultural legitimacy (demonstrating refined taste to the outside world) and class distinctions (sorting the population along economic lines). The style of the houses makes this point rather nicely.

Although living on the frontier and only tangentially connected to the cultural core, the Latter-day Saints replicated as well as they could the housing of their previous homelands and made good houses a prominent feature in the City of Zion landscape. Better, cheaper transportation after 1870 certainly meant more goods, a wider range of choices, and news of the latest fashions, but the underlying idea that objects (their appearance, size, and location) determined a family's place in society was a fact of life in LDS western communities. The railroad might have made them better consumers, but they already knew the value of shopping.[84]

5 POLYGAMY AND PATRIARCHY

WOMEN IN THE LANDSCAPE

> I will here state that since my first trial in receiving the principle of celestial marriage I have never doubted its being the work of God and know that it is the most "glorious dispensation of the fullness of times" destined to usher in the millennium, when peace shall reign on the earth.
>
> —*Mary Ann Price Hyde, 1880*

CONSUMPTION FOR MANY SANPETE MEN meant owning a fine house, but during the Zion-making years they could also have satisfied the drive for accumulation by having more than one wife (Figure 5.1). Data from the 1870 census indicates that almost a third (30 percent) of all Sanpete households were polygamous, and if we add to this number their monogamous relatives and friends, the number of people directly and indirectly involved in the institution rises dramatically. In much the same way as the South before the Civil War was a "slave society," even though only a small percentage of Southerners actually owned slaves, Utah and the larger Mormon-settled area of the West must be considered a "polygamous society" in the second half of the nineteenth century, since living in Zion during this period required many to participate in the practice and the community to accept it.[1]

In Nauvoo, many Latter-day Saints greeted news of Joseph Smith's 1843 revelation introducing the principle of celestial marriage with outrage and revulsion. A schism opened that cost Smith his life and nearly brought down his church. Yet less than a decade later, when in 1852 Brigham Young openly proclaimed polygamy a pillar of LDS Church doctrine, no such outcry occurred. The dissenters had left (many eventually gravitated toward the Reorganized Church of Jesus Christ of Latter Day Saints, which was established in 1860 and opposed polygamy), and the "Brigham" Saints (those who went west), whether they joined in or not, nevertheless acquiesced and went along with the "principle," as it was known. By the time of Young's announcement, plural marriage had been absorbed into the routines of Mormon life. One consequence of this acceptance was the need to invent architecture for it, for no precedent existed for housing multiple-wife families.[2] The choices made figure significantly in the social topography of the Mormon Zion, though rarely have historians fully appreciated the subtle genius behind this distinctive vernacular building tradition.

Figure 5.1. Fairview polygamist Aaron Hardy with two of his four wives, Emma and Amy, circa 1880. Hardy clerked in the cooperative store and taught school. He was from Manchester, England. Author's collection.

Unorthodox Orthodoxy

Ask almost anyone in Utah today about polygamous housing and they will quickly point to Brigham Young's Lion house, a large dormitory-like residence that stands next to the Beehive House in downtown Salt Lake City. And they would not be wrong (Figure 5.2). Built between 1854 and 1856, the Lion House (Young was known among the Saints as the "Lion of the Lord") served as home to many of the president's wives: the main-floor apartments were reserved for wives with children, the upper-floor rooms (behind the dormers) for the childless wives, and the basement level contained the kitchen, dining hall, pantries, and servants' quarters. In all, at the peak of its existence as a multifamily dwelling, the Lion House housed a fraction of Young's fifty-six wives; the rest lived elsewhere in the city in separate houses or in other towns like Provo and St. George.[3]

Figure 5.2. Lion House, South Temple Street, Salt Lake City, 1854–55. Courtesy of the Church History Library.

The trouble with singling out the Lion House as a model of polygamous architecture is that doing so promotes an older "plural marriage was the exception not the rule" approach to the history of Mormonism's "peculiar institution." Thinking of polygamous architecture in terms of a few exceptional houses supports the idea that only a few of the most prominent church leaders participated. If we accept the society as a polygamous one, and we should, then dwellings like the Lion House, for all their prurient charm, are historically deceptive. Even the most cursory survey of Mormon housing practices shows that the vast majority of plural families opted for the exact opposite, choosing instead inconspicuous, normative houses and then adapting them to multifamily needs.[4]

The Andrew Petersen house in Manti is a typical example (Figure 5.3). From the outside it is impossible to tell the house is a polygamous dwelling since it looks very much like all the others in town (and in the valley and the state for that matter). Yet once a visitor is inside, he or she sees that the plan betrays its true identity (Figure 5.4). Nicknamed "Holy Ander" because of his pious ways, Andrew took two wives, Anna and Petrea, and lived with them in this rather plain adobe house during the 1860s and 1870s. In designing their house, the Petersens opted for a central passage, but placed two staircases in the space where normally there would have been but one. In this way, each wife got her own separate apartment consisting of a downstairs parlor and an upstairs bedroom. The long shed placed at the rear apparently acted as a common kitchen. Presumably, as was the custom, Holy Ander moved between the two spaces as circumstances and inclinations allowed.[5]

Why such an orthodox architecture for a clearly unorthodox (and at the time extremely sensational) practice? A number of factors may account for this. For one, there was, as pointed out earlier, the issue of polygamy's prevalence. With so many families involved, one hardly needed to highlight it in the landscape with a distinctive house design. In Manti, for instance, with almost a third of the families during the 1870s living in plurality and their residences and properties scattered throughout the town (Figure 5.5), no matter where residents went they would have been exposed to and aware of the new state of matrimonial affairs.[6] Another reason relates to polygamy's relatively short fifty-year lifespan: insufficient time elapsed for the Saints to develop a consistent answer to the question of how to house multiple wives and their families. Experimentation was the rule, with everyone trying something different according to individual needs, which were many and remarkably varied. Some families got along and lived together, others bickered and lived apart, some did both, and as we shall see in the case of Jens Weibye, sometimes the situation changed almost daily. Given such a moving target, it is hard to imagine anyone coming up with a consistent approach in architecture.[7]

On a deeper level, one wonders whether the Saints unconsciously chose a nonconfrontational architecture as a way of hiding their martial nonconformity. Traditional house forms would serve as "masks of orthodoxy" so to speak, thereby downplaying polygamy's impact on the society and giving less ammunition to Gentile critics who decried it as immoral and oppressive to women. Certainly it would be tempting to throw up a disguise, making the practice invisible except to insiders who would know who the polygamists in their town were and where they lived. The Lion House and a few other large polygamous compounds seem to discredit this explanation, since they

Figure 5.3. Andrew Petersen family house, 300 South 400 East, Manti, circa 1870. Photograph from 1978.

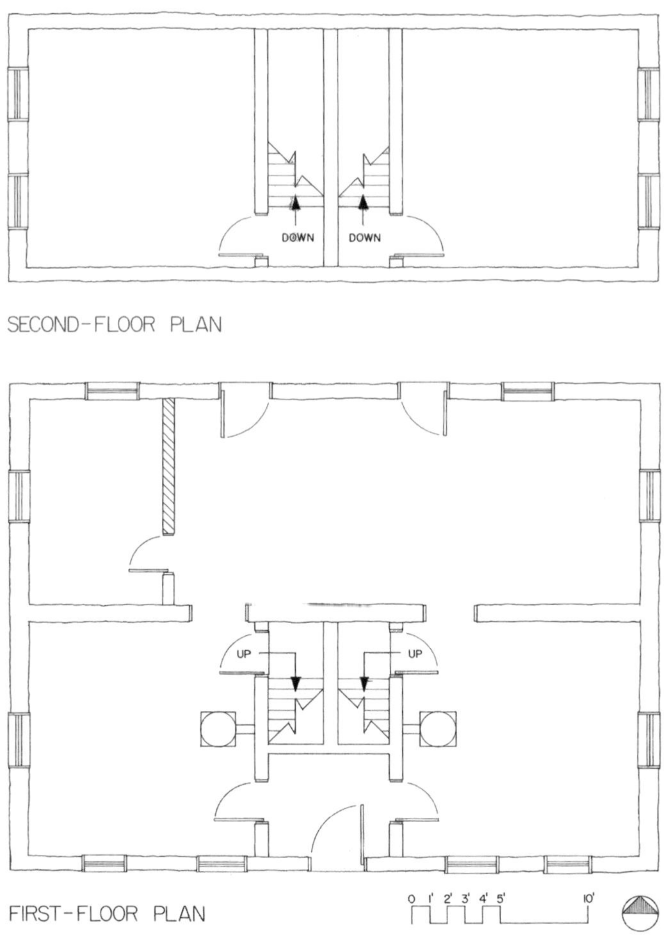

Figure 5.4. First- and second-floor plans of the Petersen house in Manti. Note the two staircases and partitioned second-floor bedrooms.

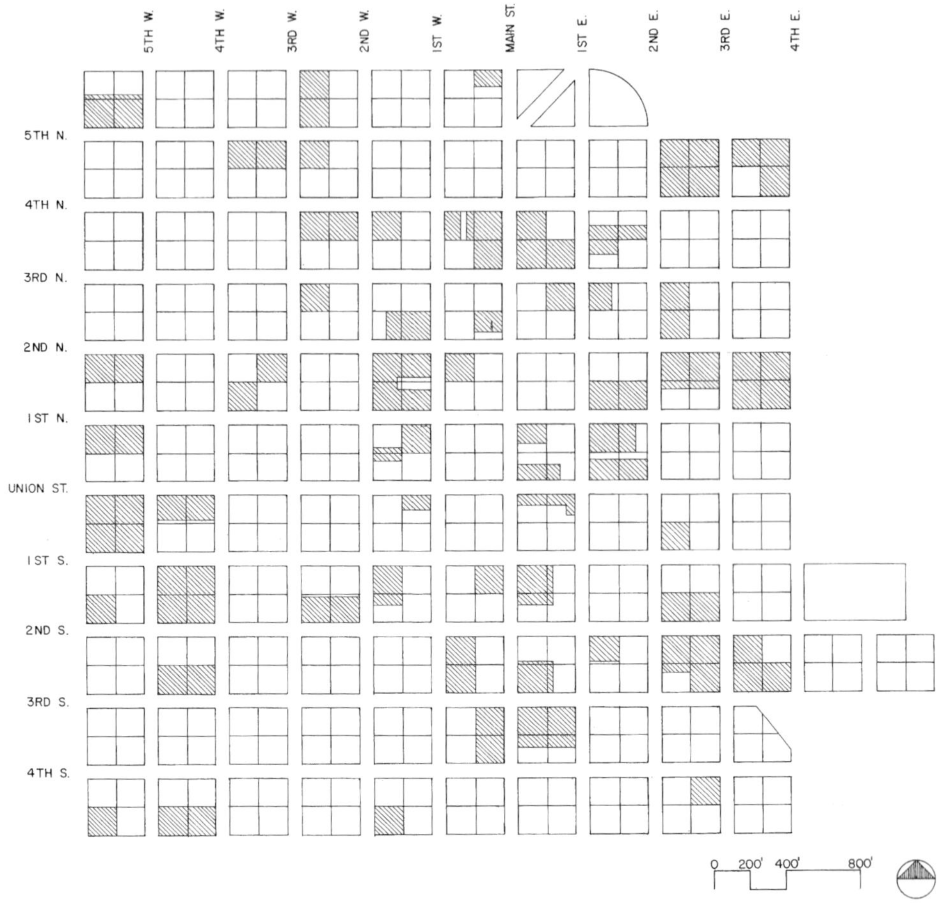

Figure 5.5. Lots owned by polygamist families in Manti, circa 1880 (with diagonal hatching). Not all the lots contained a house, but the physical presence of the practice was nonetheless considerable.

aggressively asserted polygamy's presence in the landscape—and they were noticed and commented upon by many visitors to the Mormon capital.[8] Perhaps in the end it was simply the degree of normality that the Saints attached to polygamy that determined how the houses were built. Generally speaking, church leaders defended plural marriage from two positions. First, it was a righteous institution sanctioned by God, and second, it was carried out in accordance with both civil and ecclesiastical law. The charge of immorality was absurd, the argument went, because polygamy was nothing more than American-style marriage carried forth as usual but with more wives for each husband. Adultery and sexual dalliance were illegal, and the rituals of courtship and marriage were strictly observed. Given this rather nonchalant business-as-usual attitude, it is no wonder that the architecture of polygamy would follow suit, with the Saints on the whole adopting traditional housing solutions for what they perceived (and presented) as a logical extension of normative (and biblically sanctioned) practice.[9]

Certainly this was the case in the Sanpete Valley, where given the limited range of options within the traditional housing repertoire, two general patterns emerged. On one hand, husband and wives could live together in a single house, a solution Mormons and Gentiles alike named "cohabitation," or simply "cohab" for short. On the other, each wife could have her own house, thus preserving the basic one-on-one housing arrangement found in monogamous marriages. It was not an either/or proposition, of course, and most polygamous families tried one or the other or both at different times depending on the circumstances. The architecture invented for polygamy in the Sanpete Valley resembles that found in other parts of the western Zion and illustrates the rather ingenious nuances of what can only be read as a peculiar chapter in American housing history.[10]

Cohabitation

In the Sanpete Valley no houses on the scale of the Lion House were constructed. No single man accumulated such a large number of wives. Nor were any dwellings conspicuously polygamous. The two largest cohab houses were those belonging to Canute Peterson of Ephraim (see Figure 4.32), who married three times, and Frederick W. Cox of Manti, who had five wives (Figure 5.6). Both men employed the Georgian house form, though Cox's shows best the degree to which a traditional plan could be modified for multifamily use.

Frederick Walter Cox Sr. was born in 1812 in Plymouth, Oswego County, New York, in the heartland of the Burned Over District. He converted to Mormonism in 1834 and a year later married Emeline Whiting, the daughter of a fellow Latter-day Saint. The couple made their way to Far West, Missouri, where the church was gathering, but soon were "driven from there" and forced back to the Nauvoo vicinity, where they made their home "in the [Isaac] Morley Settlement near Lima, Illinois."[11] Here in 1846 Frederick Walter took two more wives, Cordelia Morley (daughter of Isaac) and Jemima Losee. In entering polygamy it was later said of Cox, "No man could have

Figure 5.6. West and north elevations of the Frederick Walter Cox Sr. family house, 94 North 100 West, Manti, 1854–61.

tried more than he to live up to the high standard of men it takes to live up to that kind of life."[12]

In 1852, the Coxes followed the Saints who had earlier been expelled from Nauvoo west to Utah. After a short stay in Salt Lake City, they landed in Manti where they were reunited with members of their extended Illinois family who had migrated as a group to Salt Lake City and then on to Sanpete Valley in 1849. Cox noted that they were welcomed to town by "Granpa Morley, Uncle Edwin Whiting [his first wife's father], Uncle Joseph Allen, Uncle Orville [S.] Cox, and Sylvester Hewlett in whose house we lived the rest of the winter."[13] After renting Hewlett's house for a year, Cox built a small rock house in the southwest corner of Manti's Little Stone Fort consisting of two sixteen-foot rooms. Here the family, now counting four wives—Lydia Losee (sister of Jemima) was added as wife number four in 1855—and nineteen children lived for nine years.[14] A Cox family history offers a description of the fort house:

> Aunt Emeline's room was [lighted] by one small window, one door, and an open fireplace, and had room for two beds with the foot boards coming close together. There was scarcely room for her family to gather around the fire opposite the beds. The next room being the corner one had a door facing the east; a window faced the north. The partition walls were straight west from the door and south from the window. Aunt Jemima had two beds in here and Aunt Lydia one. They had no fireplace but used a step-stove for cooking and heating. Aunt Jemima had a family but Aunt Lydia had not been married long. They did all their work, lived, and ate in this one room. Mama [Cordelia] had [her own] small bedroom a little more than half way up the side of the fort. In it there was space enough for one bed and a small one on the floor. There was a corner fireplace with room for mother's "half" chair where she sat to knit and we gathered around her and the fire."[15]

By the mid-1850s Frederick Walter's family (which now included his oldest son and his wife) totaled twenty-five and there was clearly need for a bigger and more permanent house. Work started on the "big house," as it was called, in early 1854, with family members cutting and hauling rock from the stone quarry and carrying timber from mountain canyons. Cox hired a team of local masons and carpenters, and the house took seven years to complete. The house was planned with twelve rooms (Figures 5.7 and 5.8) on three floors (including the large basement) plus an open garret in the attic for a children's dormitory. The west rooms on the second floor were left open, becoming a long room for school, religious services, and dancing. The minutes of the Manti Ward mention "a private Social Picnic Party was held in the F. W. Cox House Ball Room; Saturday PM 19th [of January 1861]. Most of [the] Church Authorities here being pres[ent]."[16]

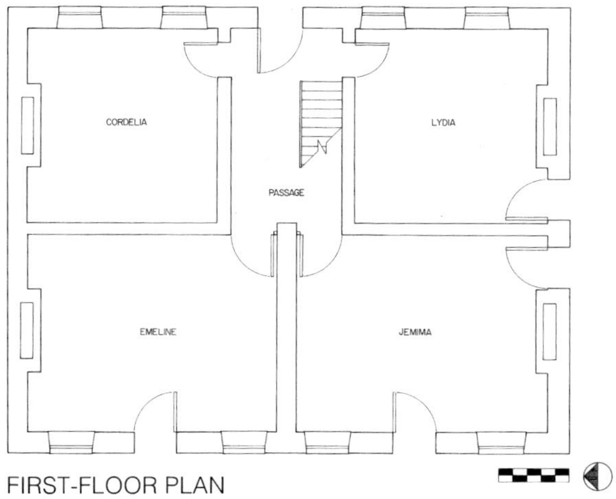

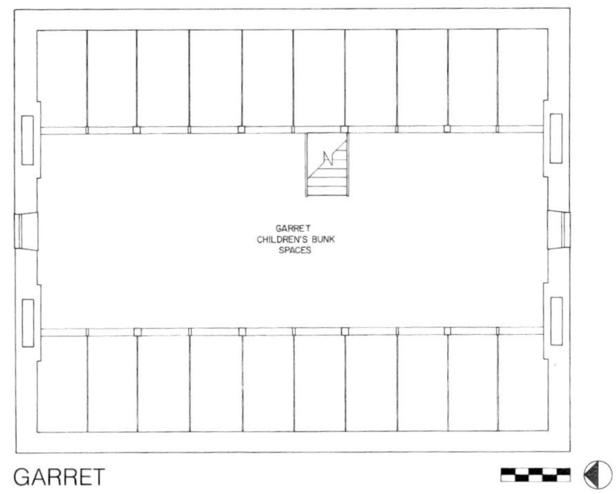

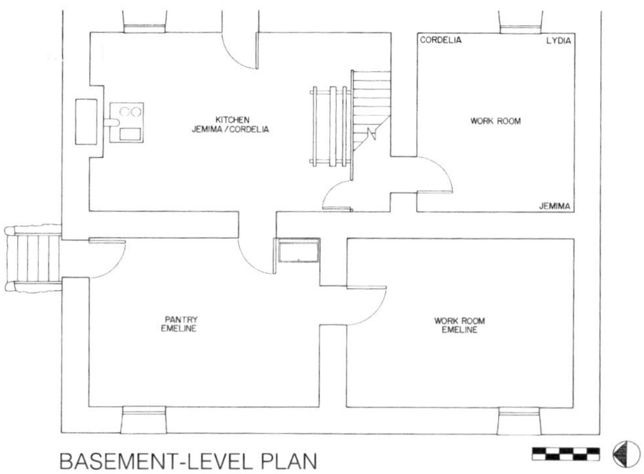

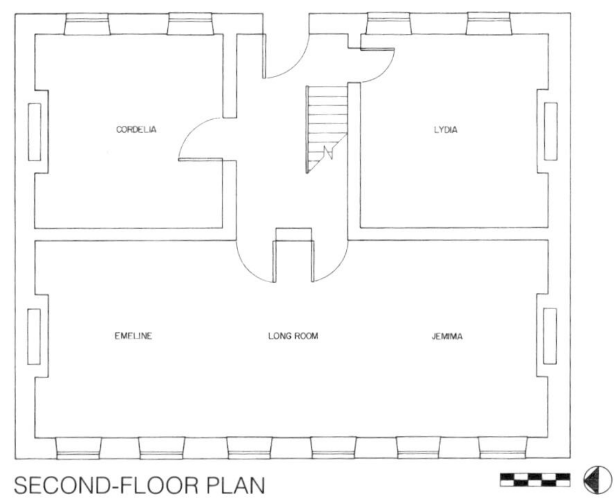

Census records indicate that all four Cox wives lived together in the Big House, which according to Cordelia's daughter Theressa was "quartered like a pie and each of the four wives received a section."[17] In all probability, the house was constructed to face east toward the interior of the fort since that is the orientation of its formal center-passage entrance. Each of the four ground-level apartments was accessible from the passage, providing an equality of access that polygamous wives seem to have desired—a door of one's own to the outside was a fundamental right.[18] Two more outside doors are found on the west main-floor rooms; this elevation became the front of the house after the fort was demolished and the regular city plat reinstated.[19]

When Cox took young Emma Petersen for a fifth wife in 1869 (she was eighteen and he fifty-seven), he had a separate house built for her next door (Figure 5.9). Justifications for the new house run from overcrowding in the old one to jealousy toward the young newcomer on the part of the older wives. Whatever the case, Emma's house is quite curious (Figure 5.10). It originally had a two-room chambered hall plan (one room above the other) and a fireplace on the front west wall, with the chimney disguised by inclusion in a

Figure 5.7. F. W. Cox Sr. house, basement and first-floor plans. Cooking and dining took place in the basement, with work and storage spaces divided among four wives, who each had an apartment on the first floor.

Figure 5.8. F. W. Cox Sr. house, garret-level and second-floor plans. The second-floor arrangement is more ambiguous. Spaces were allotted for the four wives, but Emeline and Jemima shared the "Long Room," which was often used for dining, entertaining, and dancing. Children were relegated to cubicles in the unfinished garret.

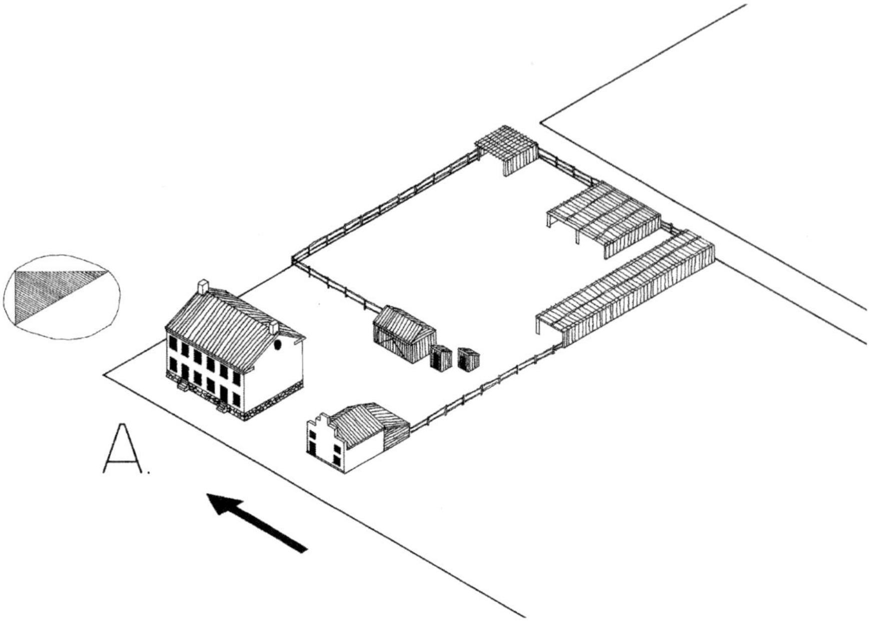

Figure 5.9. View of the F. W. Cox Sr. family compound, showing the Big House to the north of a small one constructed for fifth wife, Emma Petersen Cox.

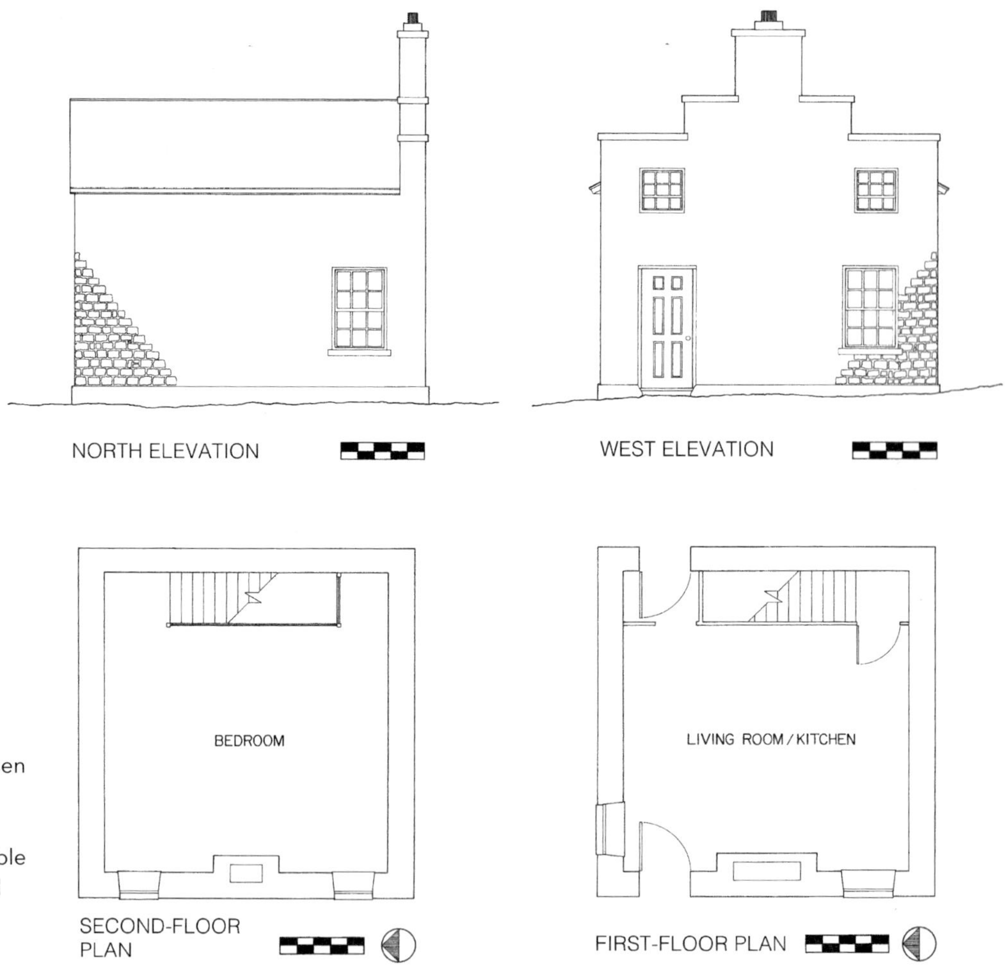

Figure 5.10. Elevations and floor plans for Emma Petersen Cox House, 90 North 100 West, Manti, 1869. The stepped parapet on the gable adds a dash of architectural fashion to this small stone house.

parapet wall similar to those found in Nauvoo. To my knowledge, this is the only stepped-gable Federal house standing in the Mormon region, though at one time they were undoubtedly more numerous.[20]

Another example of the design complexities faced when attempting to accommodate multiple wives is found in the houses that Orson Hyde built in Spring City. Born in Oxford, New Haven County, Connecticut, in 1805, Hyde embraced the Mormon faith in 1831, after his foster family had moved to Kirtland, Ohio. Part of the original core group of LDS converts, Orson was a gifted speaker and intensely spiritual. He served proselytizing missions on the East Coast and in England, visited Zion's Camp in Missouri as an emissary of Joseph Smith, and even made a pilgrimage to Jerusalem. In 1835 he was chosen, along with his friend Brigham Young, to serve on the newly formed Quorum of the Twelve Apostles, making him one of the highest-ranking members in the church hierarchy.[21]

Orson had married Marinda Johnson in 1834. She continued to live in Kirtland while he was off on missions and other church-related journeys. Shortly after his return they moved to Missouri in 1838, just before the persecutions and subsequent removal of the Saints to Nauvoo. Here in 1843 Orson married twice more: first Martha Browett and then Mary Ann Price. Both women hailed from England and lived discreetly as servants in the Hyde house, since polygamy at the time was still a clandestine activity. After Smith's martyrdom and the exodus of the main body of the church, Hyde helped direct the westward migration from Kanesville (later Council Bluffs), Iowa, where he and Martha divorced in 1850. Orson, with Marinda and Mary Ann, departed for Salt Lake City two years later. In tow was a servant and divorcée, Charlotte Quindlin, whom Hyde married in 1852 after arriving in Salt Lake. A year later the entire family was living in a fine new house that stood just north of Temple Square.[22]

Throughout the 1850s Apostle Hyde kept busy setting up and administering Mormon colonies first in Wyoming and then in California, though he still had time to court and wed Ann Eliza Vickers in 1857. Ann Eliza's addition was countered by the subtraction of Charlotte, who in 1859 asked for and received a divorce. Then Young placed Hyde in charge of the Sanpete Valley colony, and in the spring of 1860 the indefatigable Apostle moved south, choosing Spring City as his new hometown. Mary Ann Price Hyde later reminisced: "In 1850 we moved to Salt Lake City where he [Hyde] made a comfortable home, but was soon after called on a mission. On his return he took another wife [Ann Eliza], and was appointed to preside in Sanpete Co. This was a new country and sparsely settled and Mrs. Hyde [Marinda] preferred remaining in the City with her children. So it was agreed upon that I should go to Sanpete."[23]

Marinda stayed in Salt Lake City along with Ann Vickers, who recently

Figure 5.11. The south elevation of Apostle Orson Hyde's first house in Spring City. It stood on the corner of 100 West and 200 South and consisted of a two-story log front section and a one-story rear kitchen wing built of stone. The large adobe house in the rear of the photograph is unidentified. Photograph courtesy of Myrtle Hyde.

had given birth to her first child. Mary Ann later wrote that "my husband took three young wives after settling in Sanpete Co. and for several years we lived together until the offspring became so numerous we were compelled to have separate homes."[24] The three young wives were Julia Reinert (age twenty-one), married in 1863; Elizabeth Gallier (twenty-four), 1864; and Sophia Lyon (eighteen), 1865. Hyde contracted to have a large house built several blocks west of Main Street (Figure 5.11). The house was standing by April 1863, when it was described by a member of President Young's traveling entourage: we "halted before the residence of Elder Orson Hyde, who, with his usual blandness of manner and a countenance which betokened a good heart, received his distinguished guests and welcomed them to the hospitality of his home. His house is of hewn logs, one and a half stories, with a stone kitchen."[25]

The Hyde house slowly filled up. At first there were only Mary Ann and Orson. Then, by 1862, Ann Eliza had arrived with her infant child, and in 1863 Julia came. In 1864 Elizabeth and her family arrived, then Sophia in 1865. By 1868, five wives and eleven children were crammed into the house's five rooms, and it was probably at this juncture that Julia decided to have a house of her own. The 1870 census shows her living away from the main family with her two children, probably renting a small two-room adobe house located on the east side of town (Figures 5.12 and 5.13).[26] The house was certainly modest, but then Hyde never was a wealthy man and depended heavily for his livelihood on donations from the Sanpete brethren. In 1876, for instance, when Hyde was seventy-two years old and "43 years in the Church," Jens Weibye of Manti visited Spring City and noted that Hyde "has 25 persons in his family, his hired help cost him $350 a year, $100 a year for Shoes to his family, and $100 Schoole Bill. [He] told us what he want[ed] and need[ed] for his family."[27]

Figure 5.12. Local tradition ties Julia Hyde to this small adobe house on the southeast side of Spring City. She probably rented it in the late 1860s and early 1870s. The photograph was taken in 1978, shortly before the house was knocked down.

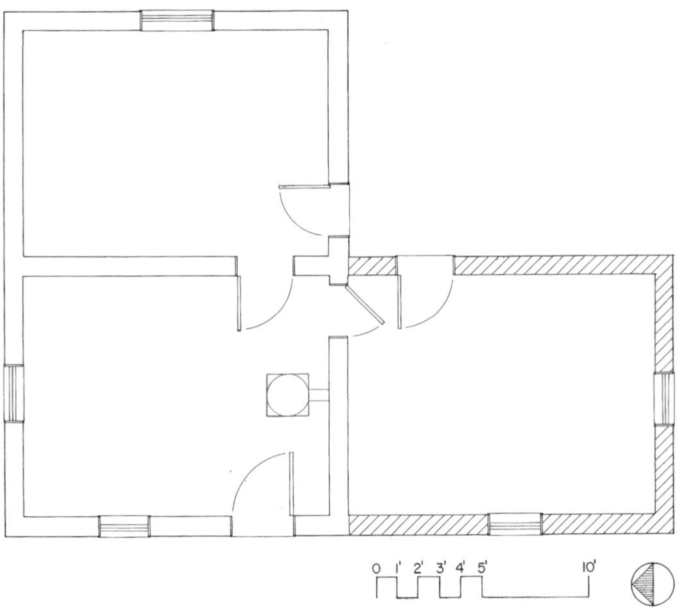

Figure 5.13. Ground-floor plan of Julia Hyde house. The original house consisted of the north room (the one to the left in the drawing), which probably dated to the early 1860s. It had a large fireplace on the north wall that was turned into a window when the south room was added, perhaps when Julia was living here with her two children.

In 1870 Marinda left the family, receiving a divorce that year.[78] Shortly after this Orson finally began construction on a house commensurate with his standing in the Sanpete community. Built in the years between about 1872 and 1876, it stood prominently on the town's main thoroughfare across from the meetinghouse. Its I-house profile added to its stature, as did its finely pointed rock walls and dignified Greek trim (Figure 5.14). The open plan is consistent with valley practice, though still surprising since a house of this size, built for the valley's leading citizen, might be expected to have a central stair passage. The Hydes, however, chose the open hall-parlor arrangement on the first floor, whereas on the second they reconsidered, adding a

Figure 5.14. The Orson Hyde family house, 209 South Main, Spring City, 1872–76 (photograph 2005). A long one-story kitchen and service shed extends along the back of this two-story stone I-house.

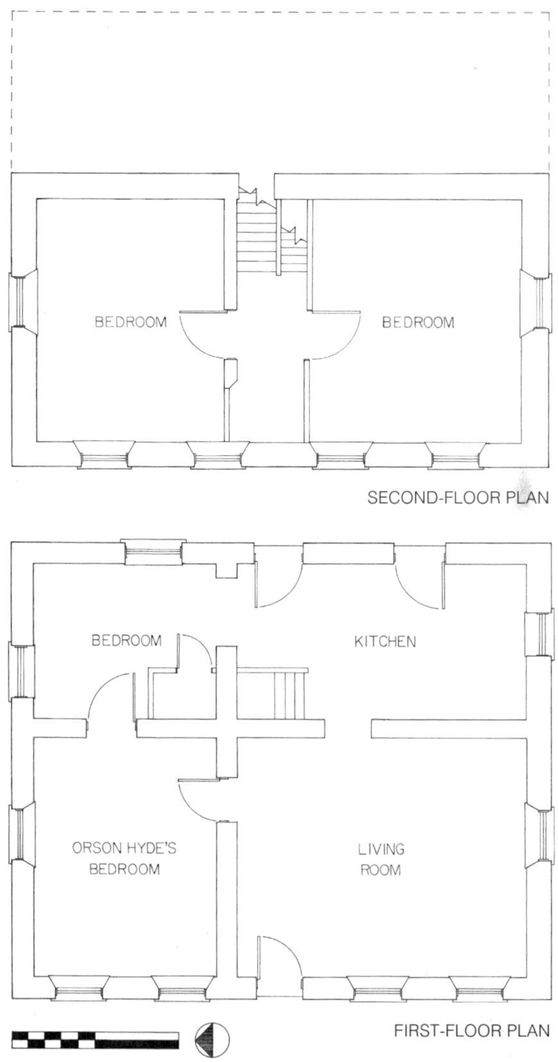

Figure 5.15. First- and second-floor plan of the Hyde family house. The open plan on the ground level is unusual for a family of the Hydes' stature. A passage was awkwardly inserted into the upper floor, with a wall bisecting one of the front windows.

hallway to separate the two upstairs bedrooms and provide their occupants more privacy. An unfinished basement and attic gave the family added storage space, and a rear shed-roof extension provided an extra bedroom as well as a kitchen. It is unclear where everyone slept, though records do indicate that Mary Ann, Ann Eliza, Elizabeth, and Sophia all lived in the house after its completion in 1876, and before Orson died in 1877 (Figure 5.15).[29]

Another common Sanpete Valley house enlisted for polygamous purposes was the three-part type favored by Scandinavian immigrants (Figures 5.16 and 5.17). The house's tripartite plan was ideally suited to a family of two wives: each wife and her family would have a side room and then presumably share the middle room for cooking and eating. Norwegian polygamist Jens Jensen figured this out when he was faced with providing spaces for his two wives, Katrina Sophia Sorensen and Anna Maria Nielsen, both also from Norway. The Jensens lived in Spring City, where plat records show the family living together in this one-story adobe house. The house is quite early for Spring City, probably dating to the early 1860s. It is unusual with so few windows, perhaps as a precaution against marauding Utes. In 1880, after Jens's death in 1877, Katrina and Anna Marie are shown living here with their eight children.[30]

Figure 5.16. The three-part Scandinavian type house of the Jens Jensen family, 200 South 200 South, Spring City, circa 1860. Census records indicate that Jensen lived here with his two wives, Katrina and Anna Marie. Photograph from 1978.

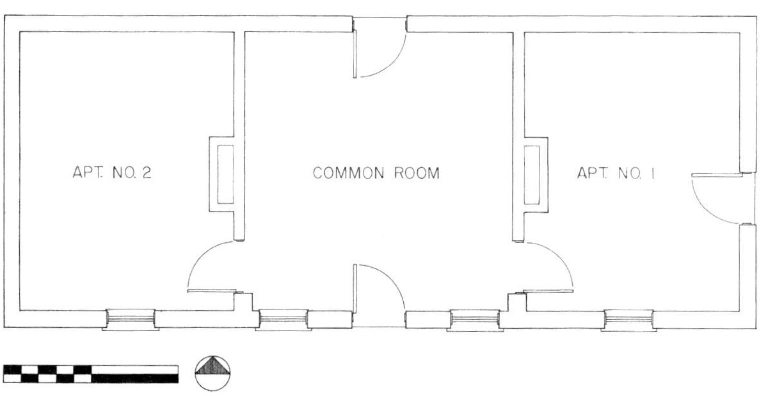

Figure 5.17. Ground plan of the Jensen family house. Presumably each of Jensen's two wives had one of the outer rooms for her own, while the middle one was shared.

Separate Houses

Building houses for each wife was another alternative for polygamous families and one perhaps requiring a less dramatic change in behavior, preserving as it did a semblance of single-family routine. The decision for more houses often was, as in the case of both the Coxes and the Hydes, the result of outgrowing the original cohab space. Reuben Allred, for example, arrived in Spring City with two wives, Lucy and Jane, and later wrote, "We lived as one family for many years—until our children multiplied to such numbers that we separated for convenience."[31] Separate houses also proved more convenient after the federal "raids" against cohab polygamists began in the 1880s. Allred recalled in 1889 that "as soon as it was convenient I prepared a home for my first wife in Spring City to make a show of keeping the law, my second wife and family [remaining] in Chester on the farm."[32]

Much depended on a family's wealth. John Crawford of Manti was one husband who could afford two houses. He was a successful farmer and rancher who also owned an interest in both a sawmill and a limekiln. Born in Wickston, Scotland, in 1829, Crawford joined the Mormon Church at the age of fourteen and immigrated to Utah in 1849. After living for a while in Salt Lake Valley, he moved to Centerville, north of the capital, and then in 1853 Brigham Young called him to Manti to help strengthen that vulnerable settlement. It was a turbulent time, what with an Indian war and all sorts of fort building going on, but John still managed to court and wed twice, first to Cecelia Sharp in 1853 and then Elizabeth Snow in 1856.[33]

Crawford owned two lots in block 87 of the Manti City survey (Figure 5.18). A large stone house was built on the east lot, where John lived with Cecelia (household 107 in the 1860 census) and four children. Elizabeth and her two children lived on the west lot (household 108). The size of the east house proclaimed it the family's headquarters, and this is undoubtedly where John lived most of the time. In architectural style too it was noteworthy, being a two-story I-house with a hall-parlor plan and a fashionable Gothic Revival cross-gable on the front (Figures 5.19 and 5.20). An unusual feature of the house is the large chimneystack that sits at the back of the two-story front section, serving both the front living room and the rear kitchen. Most chimneys are found along the ridgelines, either at the ends or middle. The chimney's location here follows an older British tradition and may reveal something of John's Scottish heritage. Elizabeth's house is less imposing: it is a one-story hall-parlor plan dwelling with a five-bay facade and constructed of uncoursed rock. It does have elegant pedimented window heads, but the obvious disparities between the two houses may or may not have caused problems between the wives (Figures 5.21 and 5.22).

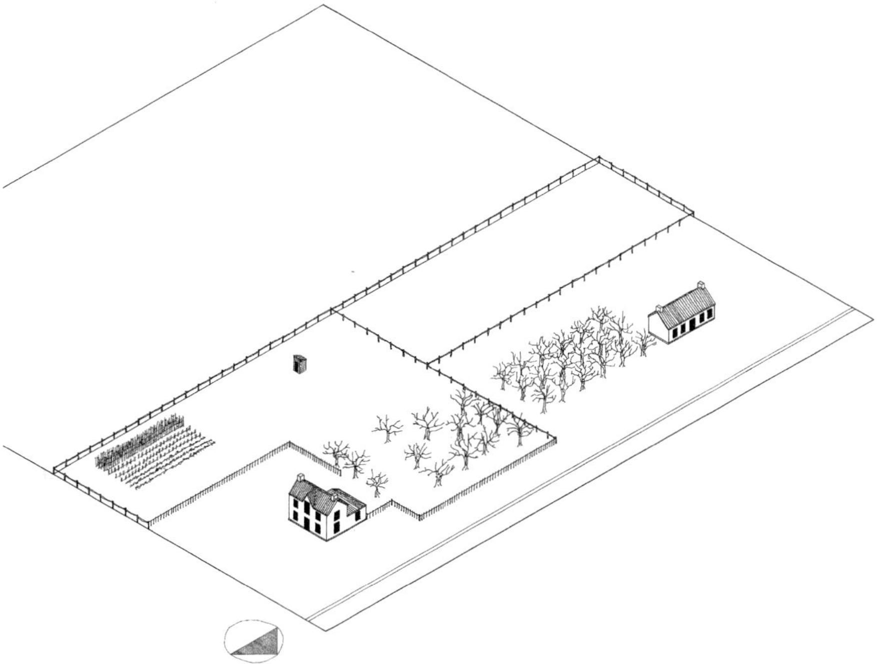

Figure 5.18. John Crawford owned two city lots on the north side of Manti and built separate houses there for his two wives, Cecelia and Elizabeth. He lived most of the time with Cecelia in the larger two-story I-house (to the left in the drawing).

As a rule, when wives had separate houses, they were spread out through town—the husband apparently not being able to buy adjacent lots as he added more wives and families. Arrangements were more often than not ad hoc affairs, with houses located here and there throughout the town and territory. The families of James Guymon are indicative of this pattern. Guymon was born in 1816 in Jackson County, Tennessee. At an early age his family moved to Illinois, where James's mother and father joined the Mormon Church in 1835. James soon followed suit. After his first wife, Sarah Davis, died in childbirth in 1838, he married Mary Ann Couch and after the expulsion moved west,

Figure 5.19. John and Cecelia Crawford family house, 203 West 300 North, Manti, circa 1865–70.

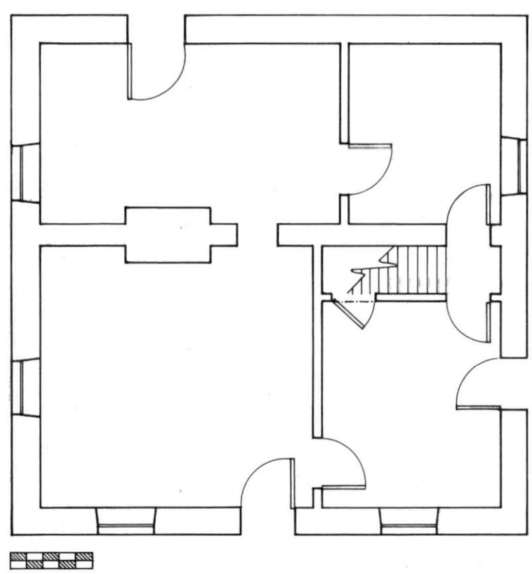

Figure 5.20. Ground plan of the first John and Cecelia Crawford family house

Figure 5.21. John and Elizabeth Crawford family house, 295 West 300 North, Manti, 1865–70.

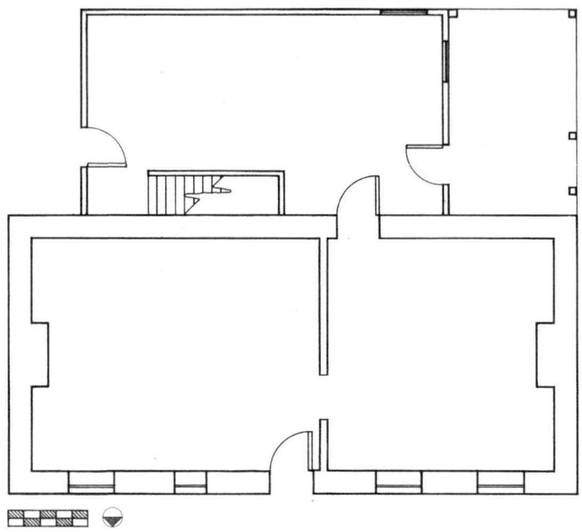

Figure 5.22. Ground plan of the John and Elizabeth Crawford family house.

first settling in Kanesville (Council Bluffs), Iowa, where in 1847 he married a second wife, Rhoda Leach. The whole family—James, Mary Ann, Rhoda, and all their children—moved on to Utah, settling in Salt Lake Valley before picking up and moving to Springville, in Utah County. In 1857 James was called to work in the Iron Mission being established in Parowan, in (appropriately enough) Iron County.

In Parowan, James married again, going this time for young Mary Boden (she was eighteen years his junior). For the next seven years, until 1864, the Guymons lived together in Parowan. When his mission was completed, James decided to move to Fountain Green in the Sanpete Valley. Mary Ann remained behind in Parowan and died there in 1868. James, now with two wives, Mary and Rhoda, bought several available lots in Fountain Green (Figure 5.23). One was on Main Street, while the other was to the west on 100 North Street. James lived in this latter house with Mary and third wife (fifth overall) Martha, whom he married in 1866. In 1870, Mary had five children and Martha had none. We do not know how they divided the space, but the house has two front-facing wings and presumably each wife had her own wing. For a time, James ran a small store in the house as well. Rhoda's house, over on Main Street, probably started as a one-room log house. The Guymons were not rich, and when they added to the house, probably in the late 1860s, a single-story brick hall-type house was all they could afford. Here Rhoda lived with her nine children.[34]

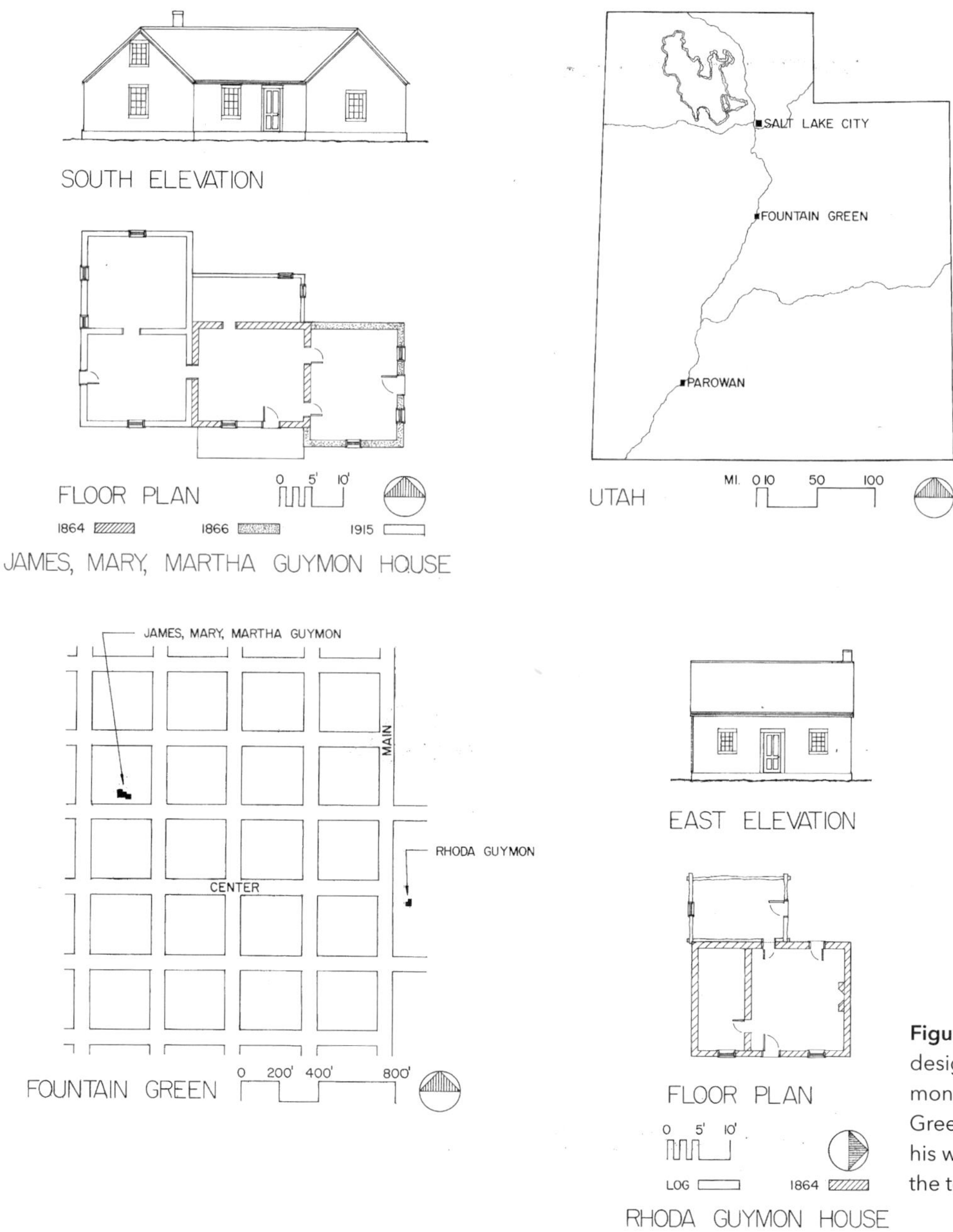

Figure 5.23. The location and design of the James Guymon family houses in Fountain Green, circa 1875. Another of his wives lived to the south, in the town of Parowan, Utah.

Fluidity

The variety of individual solutions is remarkable in these house histories. How much money the family had and what the relationship was between husband and wives and between the wives at any given time determined what kind of housing they had. This is one of the reasons writing about the architecture is so difficult—one day one arrangement and the next day something completely different. To get a sense of how complicated and fluid the housing situation could be, it is useful to look at one Manti family that left behind a rather full account of its trials and travails in plurality. We have met Danish immigrant Jens Christian Andersen Weibye before: no history of the Sanpete Valley could possibly be written without consulting the voluminous daybooks he kept throughout his life. His comments regarding the dynamics of multifamily living are both poignant and enlightening. Preserving the original spelling makes them all the more engaging (remember that Weibye's first language was Danish).

Born in Hjørring Amt (County), in the vicinity of Aalborg, Denmark, in 1824, Jen Christian Andersen Weibye converted to the LDS Church in 1854, though he remained in his native land for almost a decade before heeding the call and gathering to Zion. He continued working as a tailor, preached the gospel, and courted Sisilie Marie Pedersen of Hjørring, whom he married in 1860. Two years later, the couple made the journey to Utah, arriving in Salt Lake City, where they lived in the "8th Ward's campground" for a year. The next December he and Sisilie moved to Sanpete, where in early 1864 he bought an "adobie house with two rooms in, and a city lot of Harrison Perry Fugate in Manti for 35 bushels of Wheat (wheat $2.00 a bushel) and our three year old heifer, reconed to 15 bushel of wheat . . . that is the same as $100.00 in all." He also traded "the family's tent, worth $50, for 10 acres of land in the midle field of Hans Ottesen," while admitting that the house he bought from Fugate was "in a rather poor condition (only two pane of glass)."[35]

Looking to better their lot, the Weibyes sold the Manti house in 1865 and moved to Richfield, a newly opened town about sixty miles south and west of Manti. Here Jens contracted for a small adobe house to be built, though the investment would be in vain. Brigham Young ordered the Richfield settlement to "break up" on account of the Indian troubles there. Weibye dutifully moved his family back to Manti in April 1867, where he now had to rent his old house, with payment in wheat futures—what he hoped to raise the coming year. Ever optimistic, he wrote, "We moved our things, and feel now at home in our old place."[36]

Well, maybe not completely at home. While visiting friends in the town of Mount Pleasant on June 7 (he was there because it had "frosted" in Manti and he could not work), Jens impulsively bought a city lot on the south side of town and started building a house. He spent the first days of June in Mount Pleasant, "breaking" up a load of rocks, and "commenced to lay foundation to my new house here in town," which was finished by June 18. On June 21 he returned to Manti and declared that he was "glad to see [his family] all well."[37] The month of July was spent back in Manti, fixing up the house there: "I put some mud on our house, and a board on the bottom of the roof [presumably to hold the dirt in place]."[38] Then it was back to Mount Pleasant, where now he started to make adobes. It seems that in one day of continuous hard work he could make eight hundred! The next day he took time out to write "a letter to my wife" but still "mad 354 adobies," which was his daily average for the month. Through the late summer he worked as a laborer harvesting crops and only returned to Manti at the end of September, where Bishop Andrew Moffit asked him to be tithing clerk in that city.[39]

Moffit's offer proved a turning point in Weibye's life. In November 1867 he notes that "Bishop Moffit bought Sister Lewises House of Isaac Vorhees to me for 150 Bu[shels] of wheat, he [Vorhees] is to have 50 bushels of wheat down, and 100 bu after harvest 1868," and "I moved with my family to Blok No. 77 lot 7 and 8 in a Stonehouse where there is a Cellar also."[40] Through the year he continued to farm and work at the Manti Tithing Office and make preparations for constructing a new house. This meant that he had to "break down" the extant house during early October 1868, perhaps because it was poorly built or otherwise ill suited to their needs. First he took down the south room of the two-room house and used the rocks for what was the cellar of the new house, measuring "6½ feet high, 9 feet long, 7½ feet broad inside. The wall is 1¾ to 2 feet thick."[41] He and Sisilie went to a dance in the council house, then he worked covering the cellar with "floor beams," which "takes about five days." The couple lived in the north room, which he upgraded by buying a used door to cover the fireplace so that he could heat it with a stove rented from Brother Jens Christensen "for $1 a month."[42]

In January 1869 he mentions in his daybook that he had brought the woman who would be his second wife home to meet Sisilie. He mentions nothing of Sisilie's reaction to Maren Kirstine Gregersen, but she must have acquiesced because Jens and Maren did marry and he then began the process of housing his new wife. Apparently he planned to settle each woman in her own house: "I helped [Maren] to move into Albert Smith's north room where I am to pay two dollars a month in rent and is to have it a few months til I get [a house] build for her."[43] Then the three—Jens, Sisilie, and Maren—traveled to Salt Lake City, where Maren was sealed to him in the Endowment House as his "second wife."[44]

What happened next is unclear. The old stone house he had bought from

Isaac Vorhees was still partly dismantled, but he wrote on May 7, 1869, "to day my second wife Maren Kirstine moved from Albert Smiths and home to me, because I have room for her now. I did not have any room for her before."[45] This entry is a month before he began work on a completely new house, mention of which first appeared only on June 9: "Peter Larsen commenced to day to build my [new] house with Rocks, it is to be 26½ feet long and 24 feet wide (broad). I tended him, and my first wife [Sisilie], she tended the Tithing Office."[46] Presumably, some refurbishing of the old house had taken place, to make it possible for Maren to move in, though he never stated what it was. Perhaps they were simply all wedged into the north room, warmed by Brother Christensen's stove.

Through the summer, Larsen and Weibye continued to make progress on the new house, while Jens tended the garden, worked in the tithing office, and watered his wheat. In an entry from late June, Weibye was irked by the behavior of Larsen, who disappeared for "11 dais," an absence that caused delays.[47] On July 4, Jens attended the town's Independence Day celebration that concluded with a dance in the council house—he didn't say if he took one wife or both. The masonry work on the house was reported finished on July 30. Larsen charged him "$140 dollars in U.S. Currency, and $114.95 pay on his Emigration [debt]."[48]

Weibye positioned the new house on the west part of the lot. It adhered to the standard one-story hall-parlor plan but had a rear shed extension as well as a small, unfinished attic and a cellar, both reached by stairs in the rear section. What is interesting about the design, which Weibye sketched out in his daybook (Figure 5.24),[49] is the way he modified the conventional hall-parlor plan to accommodate his two wives. Bedroom number one lay in its right place to the side of the living room, though it was reduced in size considerably by sharing the space with a closet and the staircases (one leading up and the other down). In the rear shed, in addition to the kitchen, a small bedroom was tucked into the north end. In this way, the Weibyes expanded the social module for their plural needs: Jen and his first wife, Sisilie, occupied the front bedroom while Maren was relegated to the rear room beside the kitchen.

During August, Jens worked harvesting his wheat, digging potatoes, and helping the carpenter Mads Madsen put the rafters and shingles on the house. Jacob Christensen made the window sash, with thirty-six panes, and at this time they "layed the loft [ceiling] in [Sisilie] Maries Bedroom."[50] Ole Munster was another man Weibye hired to do "carpentering," as well as Christen [Berntsen], who laid up the chimney and did other finishing masonry work. Weibye shingled the house himself and also noted that he whitewashed "our two new bed room," and plastered our "clothing room [closet that opens

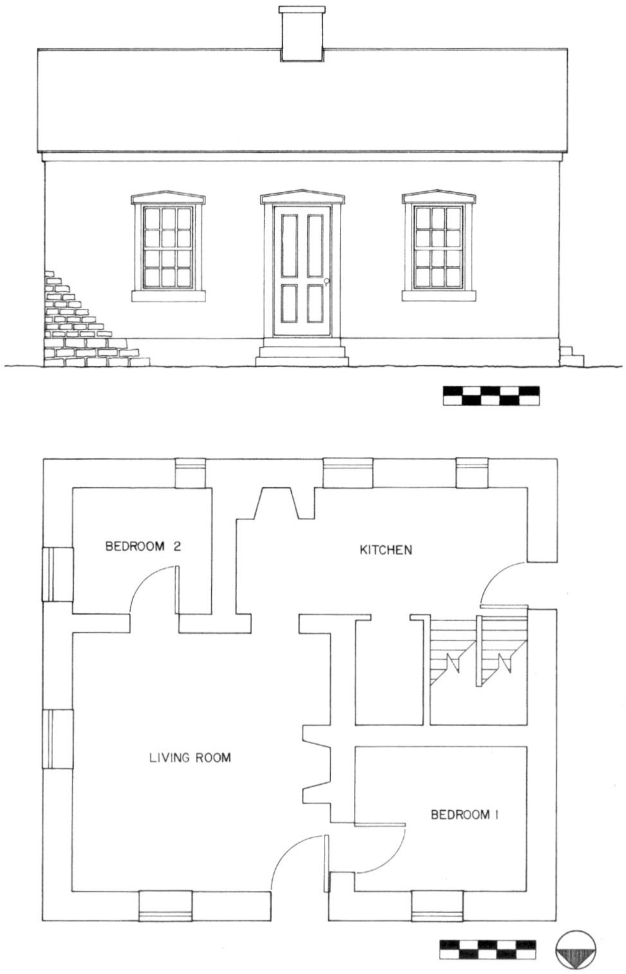

Figure 5.24. Principal elevation and plan of Jens Weibye's new house, 90 East 200 North, Manti, 1869–70.

into the kitchen]." On September 26 the work was done to the point that "my two wifes moved their beds in to our new bedrooms in our new house, and fixed them up nice."[51] All seemed to be well: on October 30 Jens stated that "last night I and wifes was to the Officeers danse in the Council house here in Manti."[52]

The house was livable but still not completely finished. In April 1870 Weibye's journal contained this entry: "we cleane and whitewashed ur old house, and moved some into our new house. [Sisilie] Marie moved our bed into our bedroom No. 1."[53] Then on April 25, "Jacob Christensen layed some loft for us over our seeting-rooms [living room] in the new house."[54] From June 28 through June 30, he had the floor laid in his new house: first carpenters Jacob Christensen and Peter Lund "plain" the lumber, and then they laid the floor, first in the main house and then the "kitchen," assisted by Weibye.[55] Finally, on August 5, Christensen came back to complete the finish work in the "seatingroom," and Weibye put down "78 brick for a hart [hearth] in our kitchen."[56] He also made a "cobert [cupboard] to stand in our Kitchen." It was not enough apparently to placate Maren Kirstine, who at the end of the month moves "her bed into the old house."[57]

Undeterred, Weibye continued to record work on the house: he had Ole Monster make a "kitchen table and sink in our kitchen and I helped him, he made a Cloth box for [Sisilie] Maries bedroom," which cost about "8 bushels for furniture work."[58] Plastering on the house interior continued through October, and on October 21 "my wife [Sisilie] Marie layed down carpet in her bed room for the first time; and today she layed down carpet in the southeast room for [her daughters] Else and Magrethe."[59] This was Maren's old bedroom (2). November the construction was finally over: A. Wilson "points" the stonework, and they purchased a "Parlor Stove (price $17.65)." Weibye then left on a two-year proselytizing mission to Denmark, leaving his wives to fend for themselves for two years and twelve "dais."[60]

On his return, Sisilie Marie came to meet him in Salt Lake City. They arrived back in Manti on October 11, 1873. On December 4, he and Sisilie Marie walked over to the council house to hear Brigham Young speak, but it is curious that through this whole period he never mentioned Maren. She remained in the picture, however. Early in 1874, Jens hired Christian Kjar and P. P. Dyreng to tear down the "old house,"[61] the one where Maren was living. And then among his expenses for 1875 he listed an "Adobie House with Rock Cellar under, Cellar 9½ by 12 feet; house 13½ by 25½ feet, price about 190.00."[62] This long rectangular house was located in the south part of town. More information about it and its occupant is found in the daybook entry for June 28, 1875, where Jens said that he went to the "south house in the evening to stay with second wife Stine [Maren Kristine]." During the night he came down with the stomach flu and was hauled back to the new house so that he could be "home with my wife Marie."[63]

Throughout 1875 the dual household arrangement persisted. Weibye continued working on the new house, digging "a new root cellar of rocks, behind the house, 12 x 10½ feet, six foot high ceilings, also a new granary which also included a washroom." And then he "got a Little nice stove for our Bedroom (price 7.25, Stovepipe and elbo 90 ct, freight 35 cts. Total $8.50).[64] He also spoke of putting carpet down and installing the new stove in Marie's bedroom, which he (significantly, since it indicates where he was sleeping) calls "our Bedroom."[65] Maren was apparently still annoyed with the arrangement and living in the south house. On the whole, the year ended on a down note: "Some body broke 4 window lights on the east end of my House, the reason I do not know, but some men or boy must be made angry at me for some thing."[66]

The next year proved eventful. Things started out routinely enough: Jens built a "correll" on Maren's south lot, and added more improvements to the north one, including "a new Chicken House, a Pig-pen, and moved my correll from the north side of my City lot and south on the southwest Quarter of my lot."[67] Then on October 3 the daybook entry announced that "I moved my 2nd wife Maren Kirstine to my House, where my first wife Marie she lives, it is with united feelings that we ar going to live in One house now as we was before I went on Mission in 1871."[68] Matrimonial bliss returned to the Weibye household! Maren's south house was then rented—"Bro Rasmus Henningsen with family moved into my south house, and is to pay 2.00 per month in Rent for the winter months"[69]—and then sold in late March 1877 to Henry Wintch, who bought it for $275, to be paid as follows: in 1877, 120 Perch Rocks, $80.00; 3,000 feet lumber, $75.00; Cash, $25.00; Wheat, $25.00; and Labor, $5.00; and in 1878, Cash, $25.00; Wheat, $25.00.[70]

With his cohab life working, Weibye contemplated a newer, larger house to match his growing family. This new house would also be constructed of stone and would sit east of the existing house, on the northeast corner of the lot. Mathias Christian Andreasen Hansen and George Braithwaite were hired as masons; work commenced on July 23, 1877.[71] By November the "wall plates" were set and the masons finished with their portion of the project; "there Is 278 perch [of stone] in it, it is 40½ feet long 21½ feet wide and 16¾ feet from the foundation to the roof."[72] And, not to spare any details, Weibye further noted that there were "13,000 shingles—45 days labor to put the roof on." A "Skougaard from Ephraim" was hired to do the roofing.[73]

When completed, the Jens C. A. Weibye house was one of the finest houses in Manti (Figure 5.25). It is yet another I-house, this time graced with elaborate details in the Gothic Revival fashion. The upstairs wall dormers have steeply pitched roofs, finials, and scroll-cut bargeboards. The center one is larger and contains a door leading to a two-story porch with a fancy lattice-like balustrade. On this central dormer, which is larger than the side window dormers (emphasizing the symmetry of the composition), there is woodwork simulating a fancy scissor truss with pronounced finial. Other features include pedimented window heads on the downstairs openings and a white picket fence.

On the inside, the plan predictably follows the one-room-deep arrangement found on local I-houses, but the house does have a central passage (Figure 5.26). In the naming and function of the rooms, it is best to rely on Weibye's own description of the house: "[We] put up upstairs petition [partition] in the south end of the house [part of the central passage is the south room divided into two], got Loft [ceiling] layed, and mantelpiece in the lower Bedrum, and got that bedroom and a little room west of it Plasteredt, got loft laed over the Hall [passage] and after over the Parlor [main living room]."[74] To set this bedroom off as special, Weibye had "wall-paper [placed] in our New House bedroom."[75] One indication that he named the passage the "hall" is

Figure 5.25. This photograph from the late 1880s shows the principal east elevation of Jens Weibye's "newer" house, 190 North 100 East, Manti, 1877–79. George Edward Anderson Photographs, MSS P-1, L. Tom Perry Special Collections, Brigham Young University. Anderson labeled his glass plate negatives on the back; note the reversed writing at the bottom of the image.

found in an entry that describes finishing the "up Stair-railing in my Hall, in my new House."[76]

If there was any question about a consumer mentality prevailing among the Saints, it is dispelled by men like Weibye, who, when they could, went all out to provide material comforts for their family. For example, he wrote about hanging paintings and other pictures in "our Bedroom [the downstairs one which he shared with Sisilie Marie], and the "Room is now considered ready, with Carpet, Curtains, and Pictures, as well as a Grate; the first room finished in our new house."[77] Then in November, "Wm Luke jun whitewashed my dining-room [in the rear wing], and Charles Tennant got ready with plastering my Kitchen and Cellar."[78] In his daybook Jens also talked about having the stair built up to the North [first floor] Porch.

The work went on and on. In July 1879, Jens, along with Brother Peter R. Petersen, "tuck the Roof of my old House and the following days he continued to tear it down the most of it, I am going to rebuild it, and raise it higher."[79] Jens started the rebuilding project at the end of August, with M. Axelsen "doing mason work for me, on my little Rock house."[80] The idea was to get more room on the second floor, so the two put "joices" in over the sitting room and kitchen,"[81] and then Morton Axelsen put "up the last Rocks in the West end of my little Rock house [which] is now rebuilt."[82] The house was now a full twenty-four feet wide and twenty-five feet long. And finally, in October, the workers finished "with the carpenterwork in my [big house] Dining-room and got the Cellar-Stairs made by Hans Jac. Hansen. Jens Carlsen done the Carpenterwork in my Dining-room."[83] It seems that

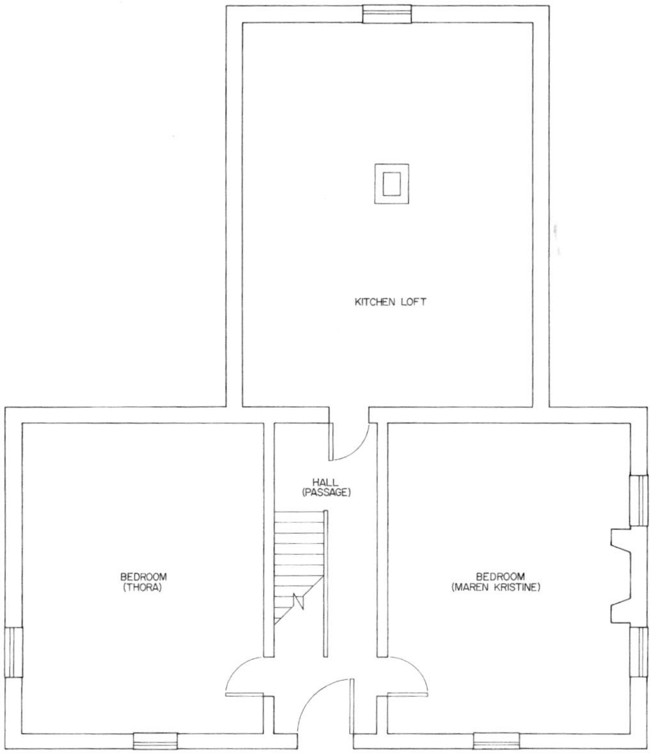

SECOND-FLOOR PLAN

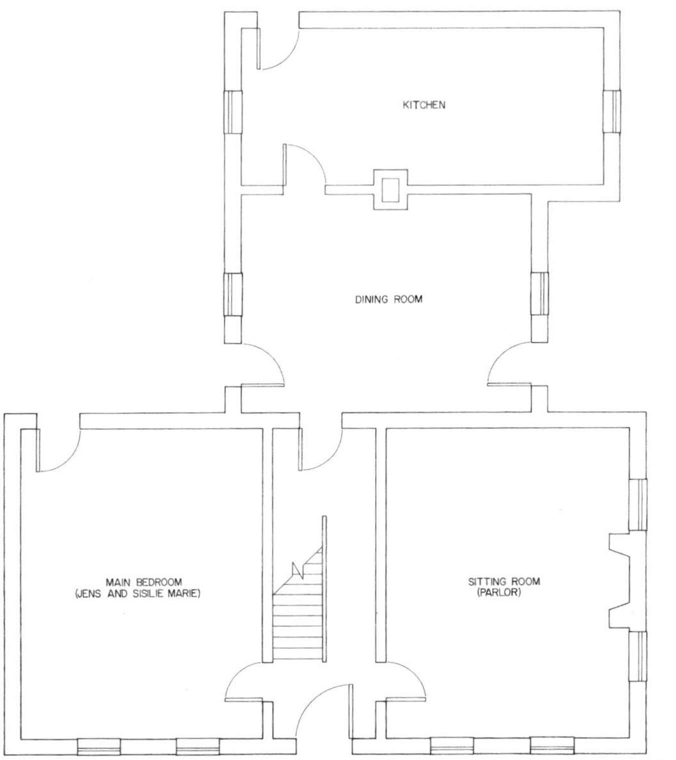

FIRST-FLOOR PLAN

Figure 5.26. First- and second-floor plans of Weibye's 1877–79 house.

domestic tranquillity prevailed, for that month "I and my two wifes attended Bro N. L. Christensen Birth Day Dance in Ephraim house where the Temple Laborers live a good many of them one Block from the Manti Temple."[84]

By November 22, 1879, a Saturday, Weibye wrote that the big house was ready for occupancy, saying, "We moved from our adobie house and up in our New [one], and in our Rebuilt House, and have it very comfortable now, more then we used too have it at anytime."[85] Things were so good that apparently Jens decided it was time to marry again, taking a third wife, Thora Hennriete Twede, who was sealed to him in the Salt Lake Endowment House on April 9, 1880.[86] Even this late, the Weibyes are still purchasing locally produced furniture. In May, one entry reads: "We got a new bedstead made by Christopher Crame Painted by Lewes Hansen, and a Spring Matress . . . the mattress was 8.00, bedstead 15.00, painting 3.00, for a total of 26.00."[87] And the big house was filling up: on August 11, 1880, Jens wrote, "My wife Thora moved in to her room in the South of my New Large House upstairs."[88] At this time, too, Thora took a job "clerking in Manti Relief Society co-op Store, for $3.00 pr. Week."[89] The 1880 Census lists Weibye in the big house, along with Maria *[sic]*, Stine, and Thora. No mention is made of anyone living in the rebuilt house next door.[90]

The Weibyes' peaceful existence did not last long. By the end of January 1881, the household imploded. Jens wrote: "My wife [Sisilie] Marie told me that she would go down to our Daughter Magrethe Kjar['s], and stay there, because she would not live in my family any long[er] when my wife Maren Kirstine is in my House; I then made preparation to move my wife Stine over into Ole Monsters little Rock House." Perhaps anticipating trouble, Jens had purchased the Munsters' house the previous year. Now it was ready, and the day after Sisilie Marie's declaration, he "moved Stine over in Ole Monsters little Rock House. She has now been in my House with me and my first wife Marie since October 3rd 1876. 4 years 3 months 26 days."[91] For some reason, Stine found the Munster house unsuitable, and on February 9, "Bro J. Chr Kjar and Chr Skougaard helped me to move my wife Maren Kirstine from Ole Monsters house to Ane Christopffersens House, which I have rentet for some months at 4.00 per Month to be paid in Tithing, she has been in Ole Monsters House in 11 nights and days. We could not agree with Ole Monster, so I moved my wife, and will Deed his House and lot over to him again which I did."[92] Finally, writing in May 1881, Jens said that he "moved my wife Maren Kirstine into Peter Poulsens House that I have bought for $260.00."[93] In February 1882, Maren Kirstine died at age fifty-four. The family was never reunited.[94]

Some minor details remained unfinished on the big house. In early 1882 it got "carpet and window curtains in the parlor,"[95] and Jens hung pictures in "our parlor and North Room upstairs and changed some in our Bedroom and dining room."[96] Two years later, however, in the fall of 1884, he wrote that the carpenters were still working on the "cornish." Seven years of construction and he admitted the house has "6 windows there is not cased."[97] Everything on the house itself was done by October 1885 and in August that year the final touch, the picket fence, was added. Jens Weibye, a model of frontier refinement and gentility, found the strength to also complete his marrying, taking Isabella Walker as his fourth wife (third living) at the end of the summer.[98]

By this time, the U.S. government began cracking down on polygamous families, and particularly those in cohab situations. Probably this pressure prompted Weibye to commence yet one more building project, a house for Thora. In March 1887 he wrote: "I marked the Size of the House that I am going to [build] for my wife Thora, it will be 15 feet wide and 24 feet long," and was to "be built on that City Lot that I bought of Jens Petersen January 4th 1887 for $100.00."[99] And then, he said, "I moved my wife Thoras Furnite etc. into that new House that I have built for her; the Lot has cost me $100.00 and the House about $325.00. I have borrowed some means to build the House."[100] There was no indication that Isabella ever lived in the big house, and a map Jens drew in June 1887 had the three wives living in separate dwellings. Though he did not say, Isabella likely lived in the small house Jens had purchased in 1881 for Maren (Figure 5.27). But whatever the living pattern,

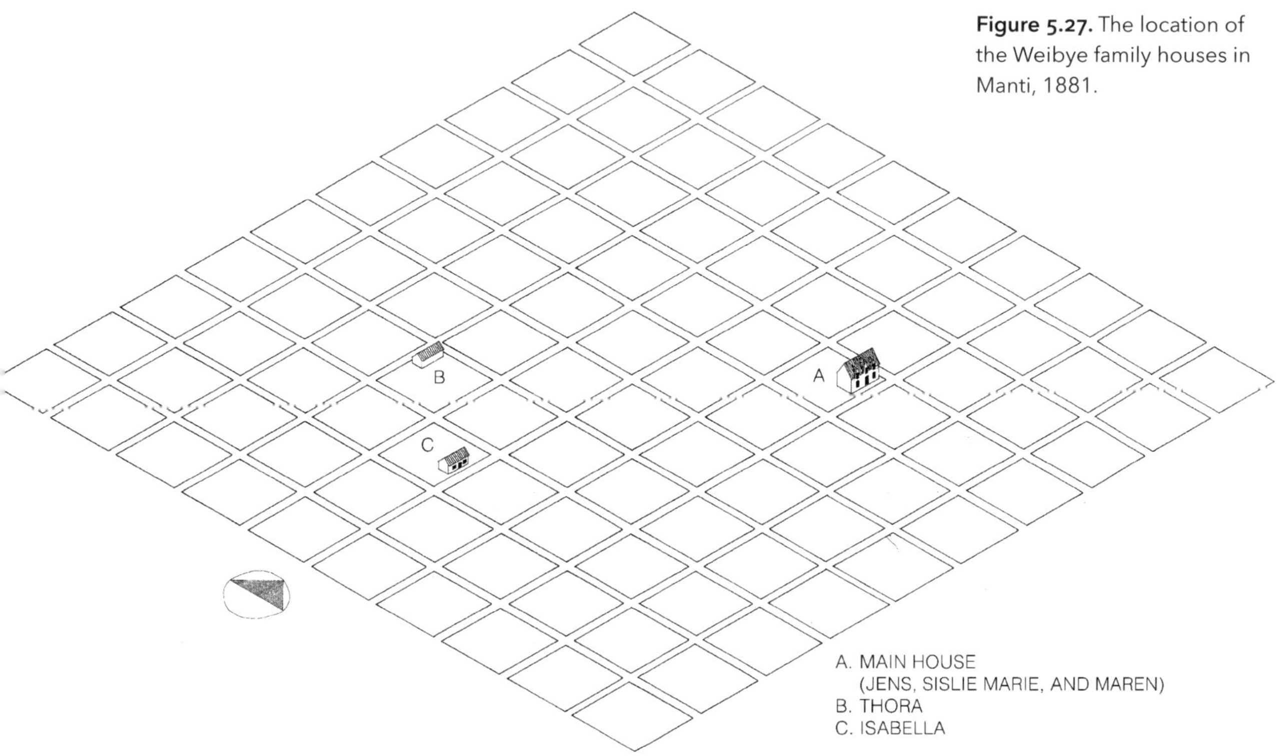

Figure 5.27. The location of the Weibye family houses in Manti, 1881.

and however fluid the housing arrangements were, it is clear that the Weibyes were still a family, at least in the "plural" sense of the word. On June 8 Jens confided that "to night I had my 3 wifes Marie, Thora and Isabella in my House, and we had Supper together that was a joy for me; we are all well."[101] At last.

A Building of Their Own

The lesson of the houses is that polygamy was a tricky business, and it kept the men and women who entered it on their toes, responding to both the vagaries of life and the fickleness of love. The houses also offer some insight into gender relations in the City of Zion that otherwise might go unnoticed. Questions concerning the impact polygamy had on women and their standing in Mormon society go hand in hand with any discussion of the built environment, since the production of the material and social worlds is so closely intertwined. Many have wondered whether this new approach to marriage altered traditional gender roles in any way, perhaps even giving LDS women a stronger voice in the community. Or were the women reduced under patriarchal authority to a state of servitude akin to the concubines of old? Answering such questions lies beyond the scope of this study, but the landscape does offer food for thought, even if not a full-course meal.[102]

How far did polygamy go in changing existing gender practices? Some historians have argued, correctly it seems, that plural marriage did promote increased social awareness and action among LDS women as they sought to defend the institution and themselves from attacks by antipolygamy Gentiles. Suffrage was another area where it made a difference; the Mormons needed all the votes they could get to maintain political control of the Utah Territory and thereby preserve polygamy, a situation that led to women in Utah receiving the vote in 1870 (in state and local elections).[103] And it is possible, other historians say, that plural wives, because they often lived alone while their husband was with his other wives or on a church proselytizing mission, enjoyed a degree of freedom and autonomy unknown to their monogamous sisters.[104]

The landscape offers a rather different (and less positive) assessment. In terms of women and everyday existence, life in the principle seems to have been radical in name only. The way plural marriage worked was much like the housing that sheltered it—older established traditions were tweaked and preserved rather than upended and discarded. Nineteenth-century American society was patriarchal: men ruled both the nation and the family. It was the same with Mormons. The introduction of polygamy did little to change the fundamentally unequal relationship between the sexes. Men could have more wives, but it did not work the other way around. Men owned most of the property, maintaining their time-honored position as spiritual and legal heads of the household (if anything, plurality even enhanced this arrangement since husbands could potentially head many households rather than just one). And finally, polygamy gave the male ego a biblical boost by establishing a direct lineage between the patriarchs of old, such Old Testament figures as Abraham, Isaac, and Jacob, and those of the new City of Zion dispensation.[105]

This does not mean that Mormon society was any more oppressive or chauvinistic than the United States in general, but it was not less so either. It is important to point out, as the Weibye example shows, that wives were not excluded from the conversation. They were perfectly capable of demanding their own living spaces, of helping to design their own houses, and if need be, simply locking the door to keep out an unwanted husband. But at the same time, the spaces they inhabited were not theirs per se, and they were legally obliged to share them when and if the husband arrived.

Another thing to remember about polygamy is that generalization is dangerous. This appears especially so in housing, where it is difficult even to pin down occupancy patterns (which varied so greatly through time). And as soon as we say that some polygamous families tried "equal comforts," with each wife receiving identical space, then we encounter just as many or more displays of favoritism, with one wife receiving a better house or more attention. No, the best history of polygamous architecture would be one that treated every family individually, and this kind of effort will take time. Data need to be collected on plural families, their houses must be identified and documented, and then living patterns described—where the wives lived, for how long, how often the husband visited, and so forth—before venturing further. How would we, for instance, ever know whether women in polygamous households had more or less autonomy than their monogamous sisters? The answer most likely will be that some did, some did not. Not much of a response, but it is the best we can do at present.[106]

The topic nevertheless remains beguiling. For some wives, like Augusta Dorius Stevens of Ephraim, plurality meant living the good life. In the 1850s, at age sixteen, she had married Henry Stevens, a much older man. She wrote: "I thought the principle to be right and became his second wife. . . . There was little, if any, courtship in my marriage." But Henry "was a good man to me and his first wife also and she proved to a good, kind mother to me and my children also that came later." Augusta reported that Stevens's first wife was a "remarkable and good woman and I loved her dearly. She treated my children as if they were her own. In our lonely cabin dug out of the side of a hill where we were each provided with our room we had lived in love and unity."[107]

Counter this experience with that of (a nameless) Mrs. Peter Madsen of Ephraim. Her husband's journal from 1857 noted: "We [the brethren] had lots of preaching and [counsel]. . . . Some of this was about plural marriage, I was obedient but not wise, I married a girl, but she did it more of fright than of love, for that reason it could not last long only about 9 months then she was divorced."[108] And there was hardship, even in the best of circumstances. Manti polygamist Redick Allred was called away on a mission in 1852, just three years after the town's founding. Everyone was still living in the fort and life was precarious at best. After his call, Allred wrote: "I began to make preparation for my journey and to situate my Family as comfortable as possible; but being a man of small capital, I could not provide the many necessaries, which nature required to sustain a family in the absence of a husband and father."[109]

How did the wives feel about being left alone? We do not know, since they rarely talked about such things. Rare, in fact, are expressions of emotion, although they do surface on occasion. One particularly poignant journal entry comes from Emma Jane Tucker of Manti. Emma had but a single husband, but she may have spoken for many of her sister wives, both monogamous and polygamous, when she wrote her family just before Christmas in 1872. In the letter she acknowledged that her husband George was "poor" and worked hard to stay afloat financially. A long-distance hauler freighter, George was often gone, which prompted her to say, "George has gone to Pioch[e, Nevada] with a load of barley, expeces to be gone almost a month. . . . It is so lonesome here without any of you. I'd like to be there for some plum pudding and all the good things to eat." And again, in a letter dating from March 1875: "I'm looking for George to come from the city, but I'm always looking for him so that is no news."[110]

Zion was a man's world. In reading over fifty years of ward minutes for each town in the valley, I encountered no female voice. They were there, but in public at least, perfectly silent. We can hear their voices in journals and diaries, but mostly they speak of their daily routines. Again drawing on Augusta Dorius Stevens, we hear the words of a polygamous wife describing her life: "Milking cows, making butter and cheese, spinning and weaving to make cloth for the clothing of the whole family became a part of my duties besides my general house work. I did a great deal of sewing and prepared the cloth and made the clothing for the men as well as for the children and myself. . . . I used to cook our meals over the fire in the fire place and we thought we made some good substantial meals too." When her husband was disabled by asthma, she supported him through sewing and weaving in her home, and other kinds of work, including midwifery, bringing more than "twelve hundred babies into the world in my practice of obstetrics."[111]

Except in extreme cases, running a polygamous home (or homes) was much the same as doing it with a single wife—it required constant negotiation between the sexes to work out problems, needs, and desires. It was just life but with the added complications of more wives. And if women were not in full control of their domestic spaces, they could nevertheless find points within the landscape in which to gather, to keep up with the latest news, solicit information and advice, and offer congratulations and condolences. Scholars call this kind of intercourse "networking," and it is a fundamental human activity, common to men and women alike. For Sanpete men, it may have occurred while they were walking to the fields, or at the feed store, ward meetinghouse, social hall (or the saloon, for there was a least one bar in every town but Chester). For women, networking happened over back fences, at the streams doing laundry, at the market, in sewing circles, or in Manti at least, at the council house, which had a large fireplace in its south end (Figure 5.28). On cold days, one resident recalled that women and young girls would find chairs or benches and "in short time there would be a circle of mothers and women, some little distance back [from the fire]."[112] Sitting, and talking.

Mormon women also had a specific building of their own, the Relief Society Hall (Figure 5.29).[113] The Relief Society was an LDS female service organization dedicated to helping the poor. At the time of its inauguration in 1842 at Nauvoo, it was typical of women's service groups around the country.[114] After the move west, however, it lay largely dormant until revived in 1868 by

Figure 5.28. "Women at Rag Carpet Bee," Mount Pleasant, late 1880s. George Edward Anderson Photographs, MSS P-1, L. Tom Perry Special Collections, Brigham Young University.

Figure 5.29. Manti South Ward Relief Society Hall, Main Street between 200 and 300 South (west side), after 1892. The anonymous photograph probably dates to the early years of the twentieth century. Courtesy of the Church History Library.

President Brigham Young, part of his effort to shore up Mormon resolve and promote economic self-sufficiency in anticipation of the completion of the Transcontinental Railroad in 1869. Young worried that ready access to cheap Gentile goods would destroy Zion's economy and bring down the Kingdom—one of the first "buy local" movements.[115]

The Manti Ward history provides some background on the Relief Society in the Sanpete Valley: the "relief society [had been] organized in Manti in February 1856 . . . and remained "active through 1861," but "soon after this the society was broken up through lack of patronage and other reasons and Manti had no Relief Society after that until May 11, 1868, when a new organization was effected."[116] At that time the ever vigilant (and seemingly omnipresent) Jens Weibye noted that he and "Brother Hans Jensen" attended a meeting of "13 sisters here in Manti for the porpose to Reorganice the Relief Society again." Rebecca Wareham was elected president.[117] This date marked the rebirth of the Relief Society. The best documentation of Relief Society activities exists for the one in Spring City, where Apostle Orson Hyde's first wife, Mary Ann, served as president.

At one of the first Spring City meetings, Mary Ann Hyde laid out to the gathered sisters the purpose of their calling: "The object of the Relief Societies were to assist the poor, to instruct in every good principle, and to do good at all times."[118] At first the sisters gleaned donations from the community and then parceled them out to the needy. They were, however, admonished not to overdo it. Speaking in 1870, President Hyde urged the women "to go on and do the Best they can [in raising contributions]," but at the same time warned them "she did not wish them to give when they could not afford as this is a relief society and not meant to distress people."[119]

In addition to donations, the Relief Society sisters' income mostly came from selling home-manufactured goods. In Ephraim, receipt records from March 1869 to December 1881 reveal that the Sisters produced "70 quilts valued from $3 to $9 each," six hundred yards of homemade cloth, jeans, and "lindsey," "many yards" of carpet, 6,691 pounds of cheese, and 9,100 dozen "and 10" eggs," which, coupled with "monthly donations have realized $13,220.73."[120] There was also a special attempt at silk production, which required growing mulberry trees for the silkworms. The Manti Relief Society in 1878 listed in its receivables "1 City lot for to plant Mulberry Trees on." The donor of the lot was (who else but) Jens Weibye, his gift valued at seventy-five dollars.[121] In Ephraim, the sisters' property in 1881 included a "hall, 7 acre silk farm, machinery, Co-op shares, sheep, wheat, etc."[122]

Some of the relief societies invested in local businesses, in sheep and cattle, in the cooperative stores, and even availed themselves of usury, lending wheat by the bushel for a return of a "bushel and a peck."[123] The mainstay of their operation, however, continued to be donations. Eggs and wheat were particularly valuable. But they would turn down nothing, as an 1871 account book for the Manti Relief Society testifies: donations that year included a "dress, peticot, boots, shirt, quilt, dress, socks, night cap, calico quilt, many quilts, 31 yard carpet, salt, flour, sugar, beans, butter, soap, coffee, apples, soap."[124]

Disbursements were directed toward the "Sick and Poor," but also to such projects as, in Manti, the meetinghouse and tabernacle funds. Laborers could trade, for instance, their work for credit at the cooperative, but they could also collect their in-kind wages from the Relief Society, as an entry from the society's minutes lists: "Christian [Berntsen] got 3 quilts (valued at $17), Rasmus Petersen 3 quilts (on $15), Christian Halvorsen 1 quilt ($5), labor of Christian Nielsen and Carl [Berntsen] ($5 each); George Braitwaite bot $3.42 worth of cheese for his labor, and Richard Hall '6 yard heans [jeans],'" valued at $6.[125] After 1877, the greatest number of products went toward temple construction, gained mostly in the form of in-kind payment to workers. For example, in 1879, the Ephraim Relief Society donated to the Manti Temple "Quilts ($38.45); Socks ($6.50); Gloves ($6.00); Cheese ($19.68); Cash ($13.00); Labor ($10.00). Total $93.63."[126] One 1881 donation worth mentioning also came from Ephraim: "Before the wards were divided there was given to the [Ephraim] Tabernacle by the Relief Society one silver sacramental service—value $114.00" and also "windo-glass for the building," at the price of $70.06.[127]

The first meetings of the Manti Relief Society were held in the council house (see Figure 7.8). On March 10, 1869, the *Deseret News* reported that "almost every sister in this place [Manti] belongs to the Female Relief Society, and the institution is doing much good. Its members clothe and feed the poor and hungry, visit the sick, and mind their own business generally. I've heard some people say that 'women can't assemble together without gossiping and meddling with everybody's business,' but that's not so. I have visited one of their meetings about two weeks ago, they were all busy. Some were cutting and tearing rags for carpets, and some were making pantaloons; others again were cutting out blocks or squares for quilts and coverlids, and sewing and quilting, and all for the poor, of whom, thank the Lord, there are but very few in this place."[128]

By the end of the 1870s the Manti sisters commenced building a hall of their own, combining it with a store in the manner of the Fifteenth Ward Relief Society building in Salt Lake City, which had a first-floor store and a second-story meeting hall. The Manti building (Figure 5.30) was finished in 1882—a reference to it in Jens Weibye's daybook says he attended their meeting "in their New Hall."[129] Its dual purpose was indicated by the fact that Weibye also wrote: "The Manti Female Store commenced; Alvira Cox and Maria Larsen Clerks, Capital Stock Vallue $200."[130] The Manti hall/store was unusual in that it didn't follow a standard hall plan, with its narrow end facing the street. Rather it was what amounted to a central-passage I-house adapted to new needs. The store was found on the first floor. Instead of ample storefront windows it had two bays projecting onto the sidewalk for displaying merchandise.

It is possible to get an idea of what the interior of the Manti hall may have looked like through the following description of the building's costs: the September 1, 1880, record of disbursements for the Ladies Hall includes "19½ yards linsey ($11.70) for carpenter John Wilson, $7.90 cash for stonemason Thomas Hoggan," and then lists "C. Cramer made Benches ($2.40); lumber for Benches and posts ($30.00); nails and screws ($6.09); 22 Benches made ($26.00); making a Stand ($4.00); 2 benches made ($3.20); planing Lumber ($8.25); lumber of F. W. Cox ($6.00)." At the end of the year, more disbursements were made to the "Ladies Hall," including "1 stove ($11.50); stove piping ($2.10); Freight of Stove ($.85)"; as well as "Painting and Soap [?] ($1.00); 19½ Yard Carpet ($11.70)."[131]

So what went on in the Relief Society halls? We know they sold merchandise, held meetings, made plans for soliciting donations and supporting those in need, both individual Saints and building projects. But what did the women talk about, given the opportunity to be alone, without (for the most part) any brethren standing around? Fortunately, we have the minutes of the Spring

Figure 5.30. Manti Female Relief Society Store (and Hall), Main Street between Union and 100 North (west side), 1882. The ladies' store is sixth from the left, an I-house made into a store with bay windows for displaying merchandise. Reprinted by permission of Utah State Historical Society; all rights reserved.

City meetings, and these documents reveal a range of topics that should not be of any great surprise, given the nature of the halls as networking spaces. One issue that came up was gender equity, getting equal pay for equal work. "Sister Hyde said that she wanted to hear the Sisters speak their feelings . . . as she had . . . understood that some of the Sisters felt bad that there was such a low estimate placed up-on our labor."[132] It seems they were donating time at the cooperative store and received a lower wage equivalent than did the men. Times don't change that much perhaps.

They also talked about fashion, or the avoidance of it. Mary Ann Hyde toed the church line by saying she "was pleased to know that in the [capital] City [of Salt Lake] they [the sisters] were adopting resolutions to discard the fashions of the Gentile world."[133] A speech by Sister Robinson, however, was closer to the mark in terms of what the shopper-friendly Saints wanted; Robinson rose and reported on a trip to Salt Lake City, saying that she "felt well," and "had visited the sisters [in the city] and found all doing well she had visited the commission store in the city and saw a great many beautiful articles there. She wished to do right she saw her one failing [vanity] more than anyone else does."[134]

And then there was polygamy. Where could a sister go to vent about her husband bringing home a new young wife? At an August 1, 1870, meeting, something of an open forum on plural marriage took place. After introducing the subject of polygamy, Mary Ann Hyde asked the sisters to "express themselves" on "the principle." The minutes report that "Sis Mary Olsen said if anyone had been tried in Polygamy she had; but she was glad to say that she now felt better and felt to Sustain her husband in every thing pertaining thereunto."[135] Sister Elizabeth (Betsy) Allred said that "she was glad she had the privledge of obeying the gospel and was glad of her experience in plurality. Not that it was always sunshine all the time, but the knowledge she obtained, and it was a commandment from God and it was her desire to serve [H]im."[136] Hyde herself had thoughts on the subject, and spoke of the "trials which we had to pass through[;] she had been thirty years in plurality and she had her trials in that as well as other things and she had found it well to try to have a bouyent heart."[137]

On a more mundane, practical level, there was home economy. What better place to learn a few tricks to try around the house? At a November 1870 meeting, "Sister Brough gave in her report as to the condition of the Ward and thought it would conduce greatly to the health and comfort of the people if the Sisters would keep their houses clean."[138] In Ephraim in 1869 the talk focused on disease and "advising ventilation in our houses plenty of fresh air, and cleanliness, as the sure groundwork of health."[139] And, in the same year, also in Ephraim, "Sister Ellen Madsen gave some good instruction in regard to making the littl we have to eat look as pretty and neat upon the Table as possible."[140]

Women were also the protectors of community morals, and Mary Ann Hyde referred to the "comencement of the [saloon] and she was sorry that there was any one so low as to establish a whiskey shop on the hay bottoms to sell liqure to our boys while they were at work," and that "some old men would patronize them who did sell liqure."[141] And of course there was faith. Sister Hyde in 1874 said to the sisters: "We ought to be thankful for the many and mercifull blessings the almighty poured out upon us. She urged the sisters to be up and alive in their dutys nd to do all they could for the Society and the upbuilding of the Kingdom of God."[142]

In addition to halls and stores, the sisters also built granaries to house their in-kind donations such as wheat before it was distributed to the poor. The Relief Society granary in Ephraim, dating to the early 1870s, is a good example (Figure 5.31). Shortly after the Ephraim Relief Society was organized, the sisters purchased seven acres of land and planted mulberry trees, one thousand of them in all, to launch the silk industry in that city. The climate, however, thwarted their efforts—it was too cold for the worms. The land was traded for property on Main Street, on the lot to the south of the newly finished cooperative store that stood just to the north (see Figure 6.20). The Ephraim Relief Society granary contained a number of large grain bins. The minutes explain how the system worked: "The wheat stored was changed by selling it when prices were high and using the money to replace the wheat when prices were low, thus changing the old for fresh new and adding a few

Figure 5.31. Ephraim Female Relief Society granary, 90 North Main, circa 1870–75. Photograph from 1978.

more bushels."[143] The Ephraim sisters also purchased the upper floor of the cooperative for use as their meeting hall.[144]

The buildings the Female Relief Societies constructed in the Sanpete Valley and throughout the Mormon region gave women a symbolic presence in the community that was undeniable. These were women's spaces. Unlike their houses, the halls and granaries were public places that the sisters actually owned and over which they had control. There is every indication, too, that whenever possible male assistance in getting them constructed was kept at a minimum in order for the sisters to maintain as much autonomy as possible—they did not want to put themselves in debt to the brethren, nor be patronized in any way. Property ownership and buildings were male worlds, however, which meant the sisters had to venture into unfamiliar spheres. Building lots had to be acquired, builders hired, and work supervised, tasks that necessitated dealing with men on their terms. There was a limit to female power, however, and it probably lay somewhere near the ward bishop's front door, as this remark by President Mary Ann Hyde of Spring City reveals: Hyde said that "she wished the consent and blessings of the bishop on every thing she done in connection with the Society."[145]

In the Sanpete towns, the work on Relief Society buildings appears to have gone quite smoothly. Halls and granaries went up around the valley, the poor were fed, money for the temple was raised, and the networking went on. The best description of the building process is again found in the minutes from Spring City that center on a small stone hall the sisters there built in the 1870s (Figure 5.32). The building was sometimes called a granary, but its plan seems to contradict this tradition. On the first floor was an open meeting and

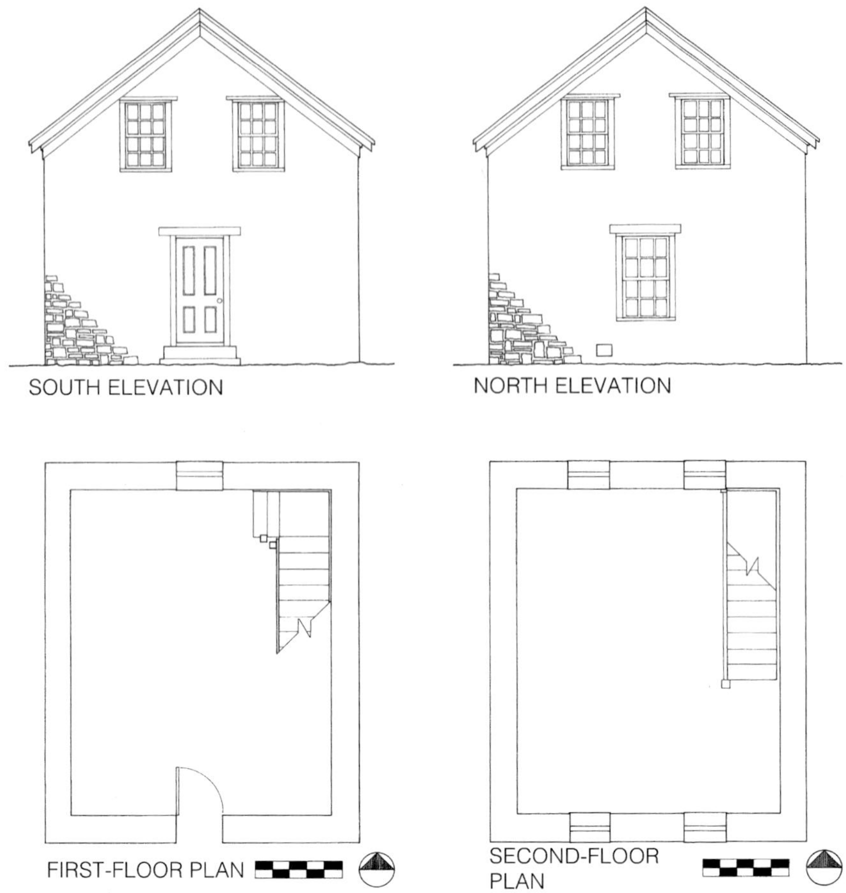

Figure 5.32. Spring City Female Relief Society Hall, 69 West 300 South, circa 1870.

work room, while the upstairs possibly served as additional meeting space or as an office. The stonework suggests two construction phases, a relatively rough one taking the walls up to the first-story level, and then a more ably executed second phase for the upper attic room. An interesting feature is the location of the front door in the rear rather than the front, but otherwise, it is a fairly standard example of the hall-type building in the valley.[146]

After their official organization in 1868, the Spring City sisters met regularly in the sisters' houses (one was the William and Ellen Major house discussed in chapter 3), but the goal from the beginning was to build a hall—to have their own space. A lot just east of the church tithing yard was purchased, probably in late 1868 or early 1869 (the year the first federal land survey began). From the tenor of the discussions it is possible to sense the urgency the women felt about the project. In the summer of 1870, Sister Hyde said, "She would like to have the poor looked after, She did not wish to have the object of the Society to be so far forgot as to neglect the poor, she wished the Sisters to contribute. . . . She felt the Sisters were improving in union but they felt need of a House of their own to meet in."[147] Another Relief Society member,

Nancy Acord, "enquired what the Sisters were willing to do toward getting lime to build the house. She had heard there was some lime to sell at the Coal Bed [Wales] and wished to get some as quick as possible."[148]

On November 10, 1870, "Mary Ann Hyde accompanied by her husband [Apostle Orson Hyde] and assisted by Mrs. Annie Larsen laid the corner stone of the F[emale] R[elief] Society Hall."[149] The women also bought "rock for foundation stone [$50]" and contracted for labor "due on House [$200]."[150] Perhaps in an effort to raise money for the building, the east half of the lot was sold to the local school trustees for a rock school (see Figure 6.17).[151] The work proceeded but in fits and starts. August 31, 1871: Hyde "urged the sisters to use all their influence in forward the erection of the house it would be a great benefit."[152] July 14, 1872: "There had been some mistake about the lumber the Society had got [for] their house but those that had used it seemed willing to make it good."[153] July 21, 1874: President Hyde "asked the sisters their opi[ni]on in regard to the house, the Bishop [Frederick Olsen] had preposed to build the house and have the lower part for a public school room. She wished the sisters to be free and speak their minds on the subject."[154] They apparently did and declined. Sisterly pride? Perhaps. But there were misgivings, too, when they realized that they would, in the words of Elizabeth Brough, have to "put off building the house for awhile as we did not have means enough and could not get the required assistence."[155]

Bishop Olsen soon offered another partnership, now saying the hall could be part of a library, to which Sister Ann Larsen quipped, "It was a very good idea to get a library but she thought we needed a house first to read in."[156] The bishop was persistent, visiting a Relief Society meeting in January 1876 at which he "encouraged the Sisters in ther progress he intended to help them to build their house as soon as he got through with the present public business he had to tend to."[157] In the end, the building was finished. It was combined with neither school nor library, and what help the sisters received from the bishop and other men in the community the minutes never say, but persistence bordering on stubbornness was a necessary evil if the society was to have a house of its own.

Oddly Familiar

How did the institution of plural marriage affect women's status within LDS society? The verdict is still out, but looking at the buildings, which is all that we can do here, the phrase that comes to mind is "oddly familiar." What we see is a landscape of difference (there are all these polygamous houses) with decidedly normative qualities (the houses and meeting halls look the same as most American houses and meeting halls). Thus, while recognizing that the fluidity of polygamous relationships makes it hard to generalize, it is also hard not to, given the unmistakable conservatism of the practice. Presented with the possibilities of change, the Mormons chose not to, or at least, not very much. Houses or halls, they fit rather easily into a landscape that was becoming increasingly familiar, however odd.

6 BUSINESS AS USUAL
THE AMERICANIZATION OF THE MORMON MAIN STREET

> Whatever may be said of this Church by the outside world[,] one thing they can not deny [is] that this people have prospered temporally.
>
> —*John Taylor, Ephraim, November 31, 1881*

A NEWSPAPER DESCRIPTION of Fairview from 1900 reported that the town "contains four general stores, one furniture store, one harness shop, two hotels, one butcher shop, and a planning mill *[sic]*, half a dozen steam sawmills, good public schools and a great number of comfortable homes."[1] Sounds like a nice town. Busy, prosperous, on its way up. The fact, however, that Fairview had a substantial Mormon meetinghouse receives no mention. An oversight? Perhaps, but it also might not have been considered that important. As we have seen, Mormon towns were becoming increasingly secular as the century progressed. That churches helped define Mormon communities is undeniable, but they were not overtly sacred, a designation reserved for temples, and thus lacked a galvanizing presence. Almost by default Main Street became the de facto center of town, both literally and figuratively. Here were located all kinds of businesses, public buildings, and the houses of leading citizens, as well as meetinghouses and other church-related structures. This chapter looks at the architecture found along Sanpete Valley main streets as yet another sign of the changing face of Zion during the later part of the nineteenth century.

Useful in this effort is an appreciation of two kinds of spatial orders, the axial and the nonaxial.[2] An axial landscape is constructed around a visible focal point (terminated axis) that organizes various disparate elements into a single coherent system. The most common axial landscape is one in which the line of sight is directed toward an end point marked by the most important building in the community. In a religious society, the centerpiece would likely be a church (Figure 6.1A), whose preeminent position proclaims the spiritual identity of the community while at the same time establishing a hierarchy of architectural value—the church and then everything else. In this way, an axial landscape creates readily apparent distinctions between the highly valued (sacred) and less valued (profane) spaces around which people order their daily experience.

By contrast, a nonaxial (open axis) landscape lacks both a focal point and the systemic order that goes with it. Here the line of sight is open; the eye travels unimpeded to the horizon (and beyond), and no building is called out for special recognition (Figure 6.1B). In this kind of environment, space is more homogeneous because all parts have roughly equal value—architectural hierarchy is traded for architectural equity. Nonaxial landscapes are generally secular, since religious buildings receive no special treatment. Churches compete with stores, mills, city halls, and houses for attention, with citizens

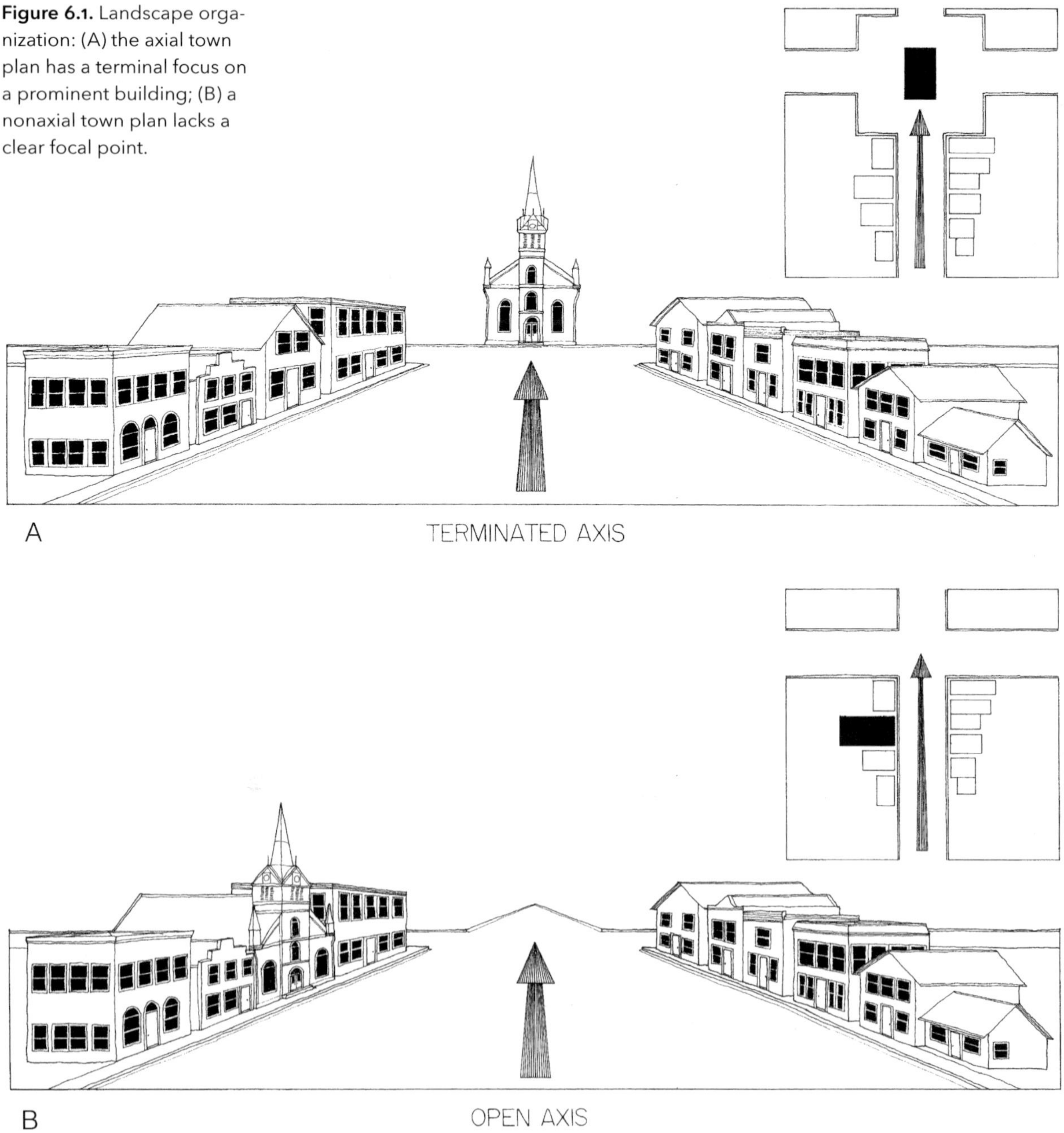

Figure 6.1. Landscape organization: (A) the axial town plan has a terminal focus on a prominent building; (B) a nonaxial town plan lacks a clear focal point.

negotiating their way through the mix with a less clearly orchestrated sense of priorities.

Given its religious nature, it is curious that the Mormon town has a nonaxial structure. Neither Joseph Smith nor Brigham Young planned or executed an axial city, although the temple (on the temple square) or the meetinghouse (on the meetinghouse block) provided excellent termini. Instead, all blocks were treated the same, at least visually, and no attempt was made to draw attention toward a sacred center. For most Mormons in the Zion-making years, the sacred points in the landscape lay out of reach, either back in Jackson County or in the temple towns of Salt Lake City, St. George, Logan, and Manti, existing more as a feeling than a physical reality. And even if a town had a temple, it would not have been situated conspicuously at the head of the main street. They were certainly visible (Figure 6.2), but nevertheless stood slightly askew, leaving the landscape without a clearly defined focus.[3]

What order there was came from several sources. First there was the grid and its ability to organize space, both physically and mentally, by providing a recognizable framework of street names and house numbers. In Mormon towns, streets line up at right angles beginning with a central block (initially the temple or meetinghouse block), and all numbering begins there, as in Salt Lake City, with South, East, North, and West Temple Streets. Counting off in each direction, there are 100 East, 200 East, 100 West, 200 West, 100

Figure 6.2. This photograph from the late 1880s reveals the Manti Temple's off-center placement in the landscape. George Edward Anderson Photographs, MSS P-1, L. Tom Perry Special Collections, Brigham Young University.

North, 200 North, 100 South and 200 South Streets, and so forth, so that the street addresses act as homing beacons, establishing fixed points of reference within the structure of the town grid. In this way, when you are in a Utah town, you always know where you are in relation to the town center, which in turn then makes a larger connection to other town centers and finally the center of Zion in Salt Lake City.[4]

A second organizing device may be seen in the way the towns were sorted geographically by function. In Salt Lake City, for example, a sizable religious zone formed in the blocks around Temple Square (Figure 6.3). Here resided not only the temple (yet to be built but still a factor) and church buildings, such as the Council House and the Tithing Office, but also the houses of church leaders and other prominent individuals who desired to live near the spiritual center of the city. A commercial/retail zone consisting of stores and businesses formed along the north–south Main Street (originally named East Temple Street), and off to each side were found public buildings like the City Hall, Social Hall, and Salt Lake Theater (all to the east on what would become State Street), as well as the County Courthouse (on 200 West). And finally, a small non-Mormon or Gentile neighborhood dangled at the southern end of the Main Street spine. Here were a cluster of retail establishments, a nondenominational Independence Hall for political meetings and Sunday worship, and later the houses of leading Gentile families.[5]

Smaller towns like those in the Sanpete Valley followed suit (Figure 6.4). In Manti, the central block was at Main and Center Streets; Ephraim, Main and Union; Spring City, Main and Center. More important were functional zones. In Manti, to the north lay the public area with its requisite set of civic buildings, but the central commercial zone, which spanned several blocks, was less defined; stores here shared space with the tithing yard and meetinghouse. To the south stood a Gentile church, an unwanted intrusion perhaps but part of the Main Street mix. In Ephraim the pattern was reversed. Religious buildings were placed to the north, next came a string of commercial establishments, and finally the civic zone. Mount Pleasant had perhaps the most distinctive downtown district. Rather than running north to south, like those in other Sanpete towns, Mount Pleasant's main street ran east to west. On the east it bumped into the county road (renamed here State Street), forming a T-shaped pattern where stores, hotels, city offices, and the non-Mormon "Liberal Hall" (purchased by the Presbyterians in 1868) lay on Main Street, while along State Street, at the symbolic head of the commercial district, stood the city's main religious buildings—the tithing office, the meetinghouse, and the social hall.

The full effect of the nonaxial town plan is evident in a reconstructed bird's-eye view of Manti's main street, as it appeared around 1880 (Figure 6.5).

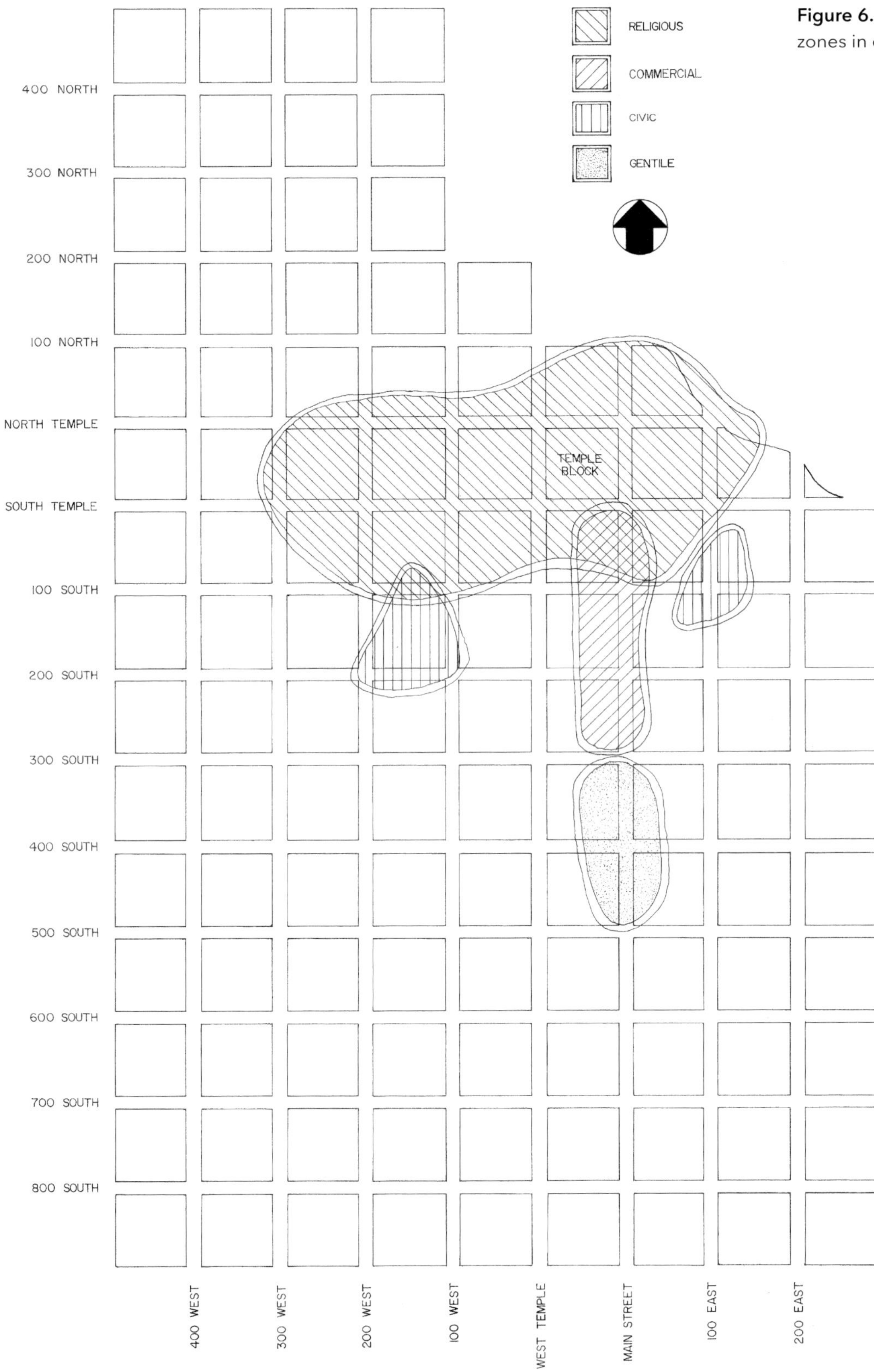

Figure 6.3. Principal activity zones in early Salt Lake City.

Figure 6.4. Activity zones in Manti, Ephraim, and Mount Pleasant.

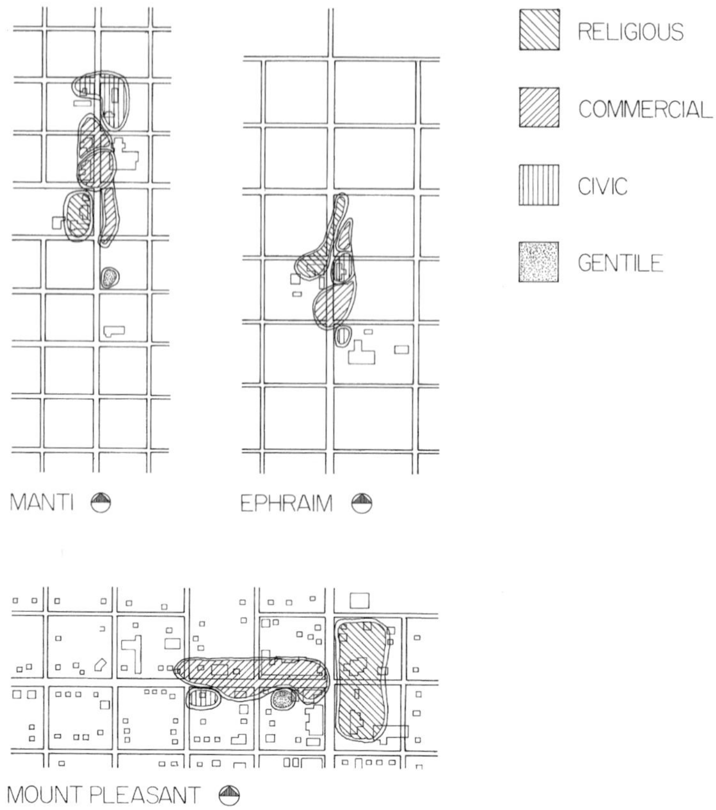

Most noticeable is the lack of an axially defined spatial hierarchy. No building stands out, or at least, the street plan does not direct attention to any one of them in particular. Beginning at bottom right (south) is the steepled Presbyterian church, with its adjacent parish house. The rest of the block consists of houses built during the first years of settlement. Moving on, one then sees on the right (the east side of the street) more houses but also several stores and a hotel. Across the street (on the west side) are the town's main religious buildings: the meetinghouse/tabernacle (still under construction) and the older Council House. In the next block, commercial buildings dominate, though the tithing yard is found here as well. Finally on the north end come the city hall, the county courthouse, and the North Ward School. All in all, the linear configuration is surprisingly similar to a typical American main street—diverse interests are represented, some religious, some not, the whole being a collection of seemingly random parts.

For a brief period in the 1860s, a certain unanimity in nonresidential architecture appeared along the Sanpete main streets that had the potential, if it had lasted, to give the central district a particular Mormon style. Figure 6.6 shows the three phases of LDS main street architecture and helps us to understand the ideological struggles going on within the church. From first

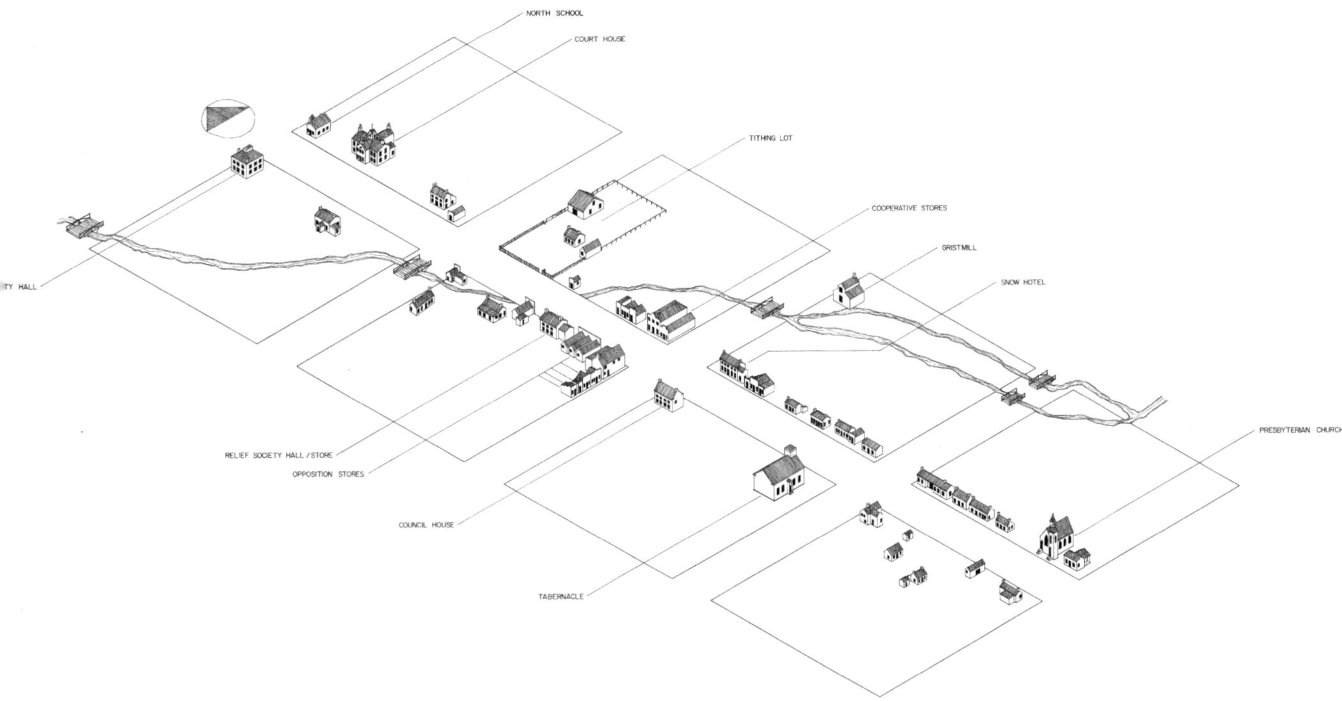

Figure 6.5. This bird's-eye view of Manti reconstructs what the city would have looked like in the 1880s.

settlement in 1849 through the 1850s (top row), we see diversity in building types appearing downtown. This lack of design consistency was undoubtedly due to a combination of impermanence (things were just getting started) and ignorance (the City of Zion, as we have seen, had no blueprint, so no one really knew what was expected). Granted, options were few: the basic compositional unit in architectural design, the rectangle, could be placed either broadside to the street (side gable), so that its front door opened on the long side, or it could have its ridgeline facing the street, with the front door on the narrow end (front gable). During the first impermanent (or experimental) phase of main street architecture, either one could be used for any kind of building, and the link between architectural form and building function (design reveals use) was nonexistent: warehouses looked like houses, houses looked like churches, and churches looked like stores.

From the late 1850s into the 1870s (Figure 6.6, middle row), conditions stabilized and a new architectural protocol surfaced where buildings were sorted generally into two classes: residential and nonresidential. Put simply, houses had side gables, and all other buildings, no matter their function, had front gables. As with houses, designs for public, commercial, and religious buildings could vary considerably as long as they adhered to the front-gable orientation, which for want of a better name can simply be called a *hall.* Halls had rectangular plans of one or two rooms, a front-facing gable roof (which could have a stepped parapet), and any number of facade treatments, though symmetry still figured as the basic ordering principle. There was nothing particularly unique about the hall. It was known all over pre–Civil War America, usually

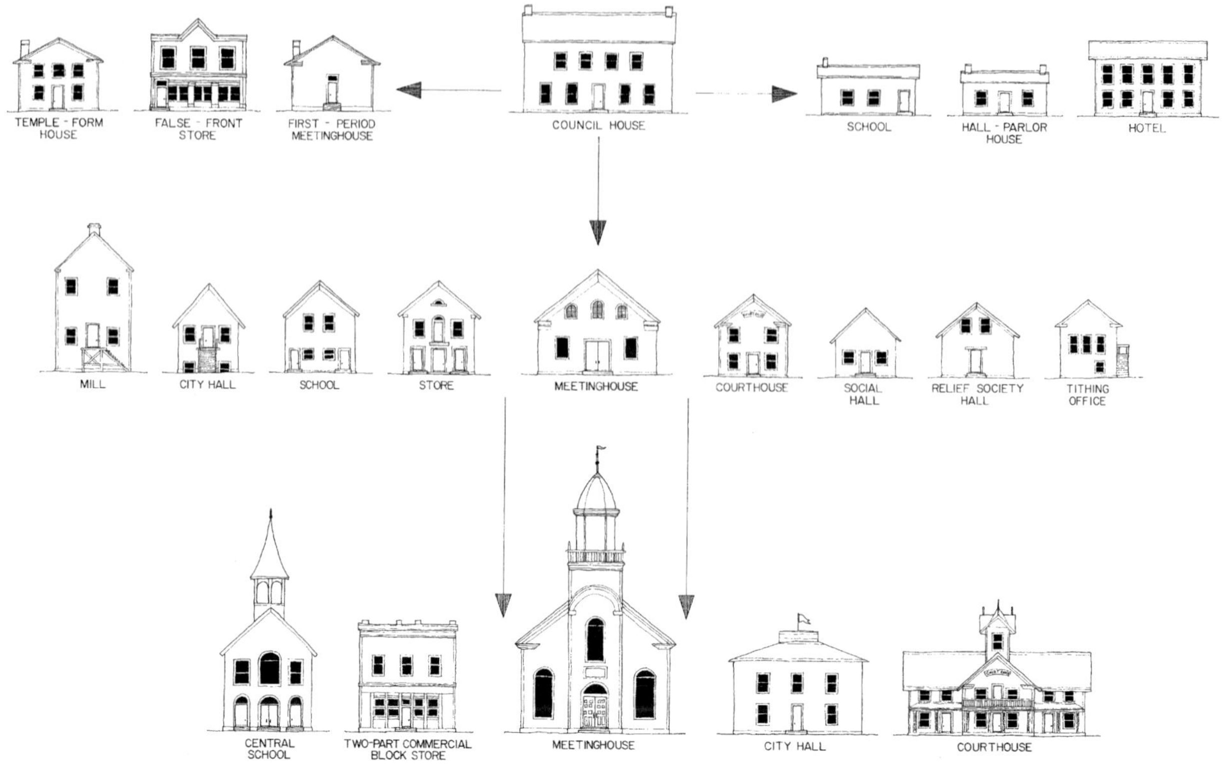

Figure 6.6. The structure of architectural change in Sanpete Valley towns during the second half of the nineteenth century. Top row, 1849–60: function unrelated to building type; middle row, 1860–70: functions unified in a single-hall-type building; bottom row, 1870–90: specific functions advertised by building typology.

performing a nonresidential function. Still, its ubiquity on Mormon main streets during the late 1850s and throughout the 1860s cannot be ignored, for it united a number of disparate activities, from religious to industrial.

The final phase of main street architecture began about 1870 and in various guises has lasted to the present (Figure 6.6, bottom row). During this time, the Saints rejected uniformity in favor of a more conventional design approach in which form and function were adjoined. In place of the all-purpose hall, that is, a new set of designs flourished whose use was clearly identifiable by their architectural typology. Schools came with bell towers, stores became block-like affairs with square fronts, meetinghouses went back to being steepled churches, city halls got truncated hipped roofs, and the courthouse was recognized by its monumental size. What this shift meant was that the downtown went from an *undifferentiated* to a *differentiated* style in nonresidential architecture, a change of major consequence.

A guiding argument in this book is that 1870 figures as a watershed year in LDS architectural and cultural history. It was at this juncture that millennial idealism gave way to pragmatic permanence. The date is not hard and fast, of course. Different communities experienced these changes at different times, usually coming later as the distance away from the cultural core in Salt Lake City increased. In chapter 1, I identified four phases of Zion: the theoretical (1830–41), the experimental (1841–47), the experiential (1847–70), and the enduring (1870–90). The period of architectural uniformity on main street coincides with the third or "experiential" phase, while the move toward differentiation marks the fourth, or "enduring," phase. With the Saints isolated in the West and the Gentile threat minimal, clear "us versus them" boundaries existed that made all within Zion sacred. Hence, little need arose to distinguish between civic or religious or even commercial buildings—all were part of the same Zion-making experience. A corporate mentality prevailed that had its architectural equivalent in the homogeneous appearance of main street.

By the early 1870s, the apocalyptic zeal of the experiential Zion had diminished. There are a number of causes for this change. The one most often mentioned is the end of Latter-day Saint isolation brought about by the completion in 1869 of the Transcontinental Railroad. With Gentiles knocking at the door, the thinking is that the Mormons abandoned their Zion-making schemes and reverted to their former ways, remaking Zion into America. This is true to some extent, but again, it is also too simple, too tidy, especially when we consider the slow cultural drift that characterized the City of Zion throughout its history. A combination of factors is more likely, not the least of which is the transition from a world "coming into being" to a "world in place," the replacing of rapture with routine. Such a transformation was not immediate, of course, and took place gradually through the late 1860s and 1870s, but it was obvious nonetheless. As the corporate community dissolved and a new emphasis on the individual arose, the landscape was rebuilt in a way that helped people understand the new social order. Before, when all activities contributed similarly to the Zion-making project, the ubiquitous hall was enough, a sign of this shared commitment. Afterward, with the millennium deferred, the hall was not sufficient, since the sacred whole was now broken into disparate parts, each with its own identity.

The first step in this spatial reconfiguration, as noted earlier, required moving the temple out of town, thereby creating discrete sacred (temple) and secular (town) spheres. Once this happened, the boundaries of Zion were moved from outside the group to outside the individual church member. Increasingly, Mormonness (and salvation) became a personal rather than a group responsibility. It was no longer who you were but how you behaved that mattered—a harbinger of the Word of Wisdom culture that would soon come. As the sacred canopy lifted, Main Street emerged in its new secular identity, assuming a familiar role as the activity center of town. And since the nonaxial plan inherently undermined hierarchy of any kind—no building stood above any other—a multiplicity of interests consistent with a secular community arose. Homogeneity gave way to differentiation, the old architectural labels resurfaced, and churches became the buildings with steeples.

Buildings on Main Street

Sanpete Valley towns all had main streets, though they went by various names. These streets became active town centers where people gathered, conducted business, shopped, went to the theater, and worshipped. Such activities increasingly took place in spaces designed for a specific use, an evolution away from the older all-purpose hall that signaled an important shift in the psychic structure of valley life. The following section surveys the various building types found along Sanpete main streets within the context of this change.

Tithing Yard/Office

Latter-day Saints were required to tithe 10 percent of their production to the church, and during the nineteenth century tithing took the form mostly of "in kind" contributions, including such things as grain, livestock, and labor. The variety of tithed goods is illustrated by this list of "receivables" taken in by the Manti Tithing Office during 1867 (Table 6.1). One hundred and fifty-one families contributed.

Collecting tithing was always problematic, for tithe paying among the Saints was hardly universal, as an 1871 telegram from Brigham Young to Manti tithing clerk Jens Weibye attests. In it Young asked Weibye to "furnish . . . as near as possible the proportional number of people who pay tithing in your respective ward, and also estimate as nearly as possible the amount of Stock and grain paid in proportional to the amount raised in your ward, if you will make a close examination of this matter you will be astonished, I presume

Table 6.1

Butter, Eggs, Cheese, Chickens	$325.26
Wool	$169.09
Hay	$231.60
Oats	$695.82
Stock, Sheep	$384.92
Pork	$120.20
Labor, Wood	$1,171.97
Potatoes	$570.44
Wheat	$1,781.64
Barley	$1.50
Cash	$60.50
Fruit	$5.28
Merchandice	$31.14
Total	$5,554.86

Source: Weibye, Day Book 2, March 7, 1868.

you will find that not one tenth of that which is due the tithing has been paid and probably not over one third of the people who pay tithing at all."[6] Weibye did not record his response, but comparing his numbers from 1867 (151 households paying tithing) to the number of households enumerated three years later in the 1870 census (243 households in Manti), the compliance rate stands at 62 percent. Young might have been pleased (if not surprised) by the strong showing.[7]

When it did come, in-kind tithing was stored in church-owned barns, granaries, and corrals until it was reallocated toward specific projects, often as we have seen, in the form of wages. These structures were confined to a space in town called a tithing yard, which also contained offices for the bishop and the tithing clerk. Tithing yards in the Sanpete Valley were again patterned after the one in Salt Lake City, which stood at the head of Main Street and encompassed two city lots.[8] They ranged in size from the smallest, occupying but a single lot like the one in Spring City, to a lot-and-a-half as in Manti, or two lots as was the case in Mount Pleasant, where the tithing yard stood north of the intersection of State and Main Streets (Figure 6.7). The Mount Pleasant Tithing Yard nicely illustrates the open, nonaxial nature of the LDS town plan. Like the meetinghouse block to the south, it remained tucked away out of the normal line of sight and thus commanded little overt attention.

Figure 6.7. The organization of Mount Pleasant's religious zone is shown in this bird's-eye view reconstruction of the city around 1890. On the right is the church block, which contains both meetinghouse and social hall. On the upper left is the tithing yard, with an office, barns, and corrals. On the northeast corner of Main and State Streets stands the city's ZCMI (co-op) store, which dates to the 1880s.

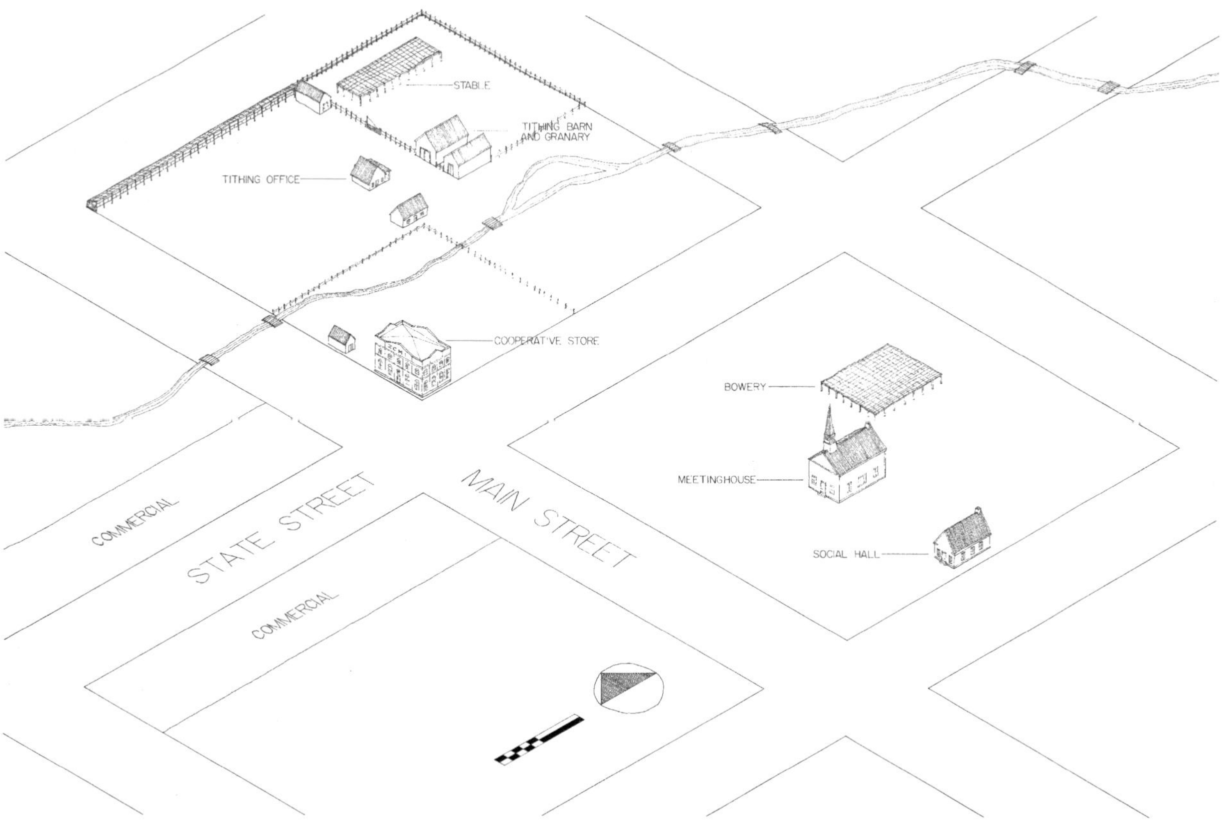

Settlement period tithing offices in the Sanpete Valley were invariably stone or adobe halls with a ground-floor office (or offices) over a partially subterranean root cellar. The one built in Moroni in 1875 is typical in both its bi-level form and its Greek countenance (Figure 6.8). Cornice returns accent the proportional balance of the temple-like east front elevation, a visual effect enhanced by the use of heavy pedimented window heads. On the south the ground sloped away sufficiently to allow access to the basement. Another opening, either a window or possibly a loading chute, is visible on the bottom right of Figure 6.8. The principal door lay to the north, where the main floor was nearly level with the ground.[9]

The Manti Tithing Office is another good example of the type (Figure 6.9). It was constructed of stone and again was originally a single-story temple-front hall with full cellar. This building dates to the 1860s but got a significant remodeling in the summer of 1875.[10] Tithing clerk Jens Weibye recorded the event: on September 30 the brethren "commenced to rebuild [the] Manti Tithing Office, some of it was teared down, and now it is made 1½ Story high; October 29th they got done with the wall and ready for the roof." In November, he continued, "We got the Roof on the Manti Tithing Office and the Chimney, it is the onlyest one of that kind in Manti. I[t] took over 800 brick, they are [also] now reparing our old Meetinghouse outside, and inside."[11] Renovation work took about four months; by January 25, 1876,

Figure 6.8. East elevation of the Moroni Tithing Office, circa 1870–75. Photograph from 1978.

Figure 6.9. Anonymous photograph showing the Manti Tithing Office as it looked shortly after its remodeling in 1875. The original one-story section was completed in the 1860s. Photo courtesy of the Patten House Museum, Manti Daughters of the Utah Pioneers, with special assistance from Clara Beus and Shannon Miller.

Weibye moved his tithing account books into his new office, also saying "to night we had the first meeting [of the United Order co-op] in the North Room in the new Tithing Office."[12]

After remodeling, the building appears to have had four rooms, two down and two up, one to each side of the large central chimney (with a basement cellar). Weibye's journal reveals some of its use: "When Bro Henry Roberts came to his drawer in the Telegraf Office here in the Tithing Office he discovered that his Money drawer was bursted open in the night, and about $4.50 in Cash and about 50 cents in Stamps was tacken but nothering else we are missing, we think they have come in through the west window in Prst [Bishop] J. B. Maiben's Office."[13] Evidence from the crime scene then suggests the telegraph/post office and bishop's office occupied the ground floor, while Weibye's tithing operation was upstairs.

Despite the rebuilding in Manti, tithing office design escaped the more dramatic changes evidenced in most nonresidential architecture after 1870. This may be because no prototype existed for such buildings. Tithing offices were unique to Mormons and to the Mormon West (none were constructed in Nauvoo), making it impossible to fall back on a more familiar typology. When a change did come, it was not until 1908, when the church stopped taking in-kind contributions. At this time, a new type of tithing office was introduced. It followed a standardized plan issued by the church building department in Salt Lake City. Given the late date, these new offices were Victorian in design, built of brick, and had a distinctive hipped roof residential appearance.[14]

Baptismal Buildings

Not until the completion of the temple in 1888 was there a formal baptismal font in the valley. Until that time, baptisms were conducted primarily in the open in creeks or other waterways. In several cases, however, small baptismal houses were constructed. One such building (Figure 6.10) is illustrated in Jens Weibye's journal from 1875. Here he notes, "A house was built about one mile from Manti [over] the Warm Spring for to have a dressing room when they are baptizing, and also for a bade-[bath]house; about 60 days Labor besides teamwork and Materials was spent on this house. Bp. J. B Maiben, W. S Snow and Hans Jensen were the directors for its building."[15] It was dedicated on November 28.

The historical records of Spring City reveal another baptismal building. Ward Minutes for 1888 describe the erection of a baptismal house and font just west of the main spring (near the center of town on Main Street). The building was to be sixteen by sixteen feet square, eight feet high, with "rustic" [drop or novelty] siding and a shingle roof.[16] Several years later the board of directors of the Spring City Ecclesiastical Ward met in the "bishop's office"

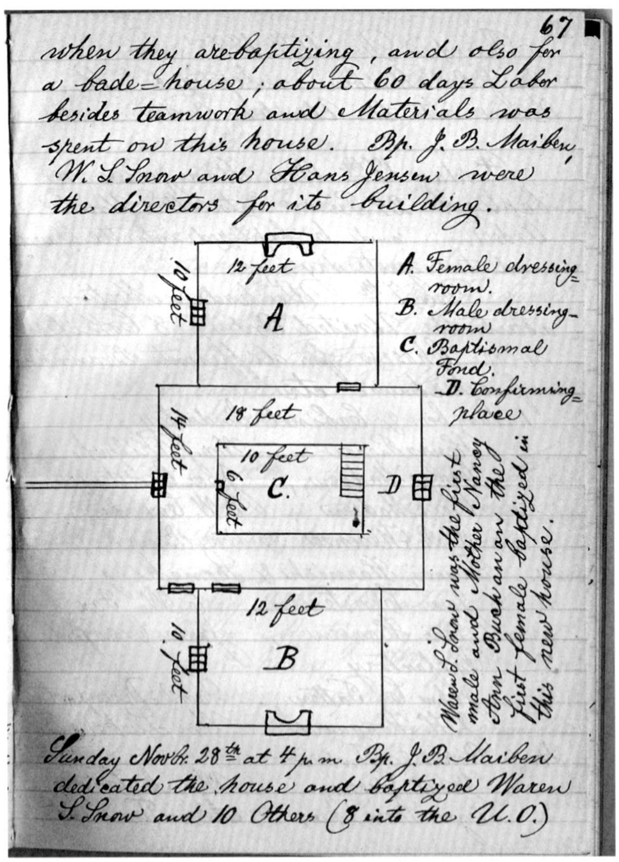
67

when they are baptizing, and also for a bade-house; about 60 days Labor besides teamwork and Materials was spent on this house. Bp. J. B. Maiben, W. S. Snow and Hans Jensen were the directors for its building.

Sunday Novbr. 28th at 4 p.m. Bp. J. B. Maiben dedicated the house and baptized Waren S. Snow and 10 Others (8 into the U.O.)

Figure 6.10. A page from Jens Weibye's journal with a sketch of the Manti Baptismal House, 1875. Courtesy of the Church History Library.

and received a report of labor expenditures that indicated "the Brethren had shown willingness in turning out [to] do the work and also in donating lumber, shingles, logs, pickets, etc. to its accomplicment and that we now had a good and comfortable place in which to attend to the Ordinance of Baptism that is a credit to the Ward."[17]

Churches

Main street was also home to churches. In addition to LDS meetinghouses, which are covered in chapter 7, most towns had a building or two of other denominations, particularly Methodists and Presbyterians, who carried out missionary activity throughout the state but were particularly active in the Sanpete Valley. Feeling that Mormons were good people with bad ideas, officials of these older established religions stressed education as a conversion tactic: once properly educated, the reasoning went, Latter-day Saints would naturally see the error in their ways and abandon their upstart faith. When they did so, the Gentiles would be there to welcome them back.[18]

A number of non-Mormon houses of worship were built in the Sanpete Valley before 1890.The congregations were small but determined. Methodists chose Ephraim and Spring City, where towered Gothic Revival churches were completed in 1885 and 1889, respectively.[19] The Presbyterians struck first in Mount Pleasant and then moved south to Ephraim and Manti. In Mount Pleasant, the Reverend Duncan McMillan united with a group of apostate Scandinavians who had in 1875 constructed a Liberal hall (the name referring to the non-Mormon political party in the territory). McMillian found these disaffected Mormons receptive to his preaching, and soon he purchased the hall, which already had a steeple, and turned it into the Presbyterian church. About the same time, McMillan also was conducting services in nearby Ephraim, where a branch was organized and a "neat stone church" erected in 1880.[20]

McMillan's message likewise appealed to apostate Mormons in Manti. He organized a congregation there in April 1878 with, according to Jens Weibye's calculations, "2 Presbyterians and about 10 Apostate Mormons, there [that] was cut off from the Church in 1877 and 1878. . . . The Apostate Mormons are all Scandinavians."[21] Work began on the new church in 1880, and Weibye places its completion date as November 13, 1881, saying that "it was the first Sectarian Church here in Manti, Mr. W. G. Martin is the preacher, but there is only a few Members not over 10."[22]

Despite their small numbers, Manti's Presbyterians got a fine new church (Figure 6.11). It was conspicuously located at the south end of Main Street and designed in the fashionable Gothic Revival manner by Peter van Houghton, an architect from Salt Lake City. The picturesque Gothic aesthetic is visible in such features as the steeply pitched gable roof, the asymmetrical corner tower, pointed-arched windows and window tracery, and the scroll-sawn bargeboards along the raking eaves, complete with pointed finial at the ridge. The most distinguished feature of the church is the tripartite belfry, which begins with a sloping, truncated hip roof, then moves to the closed belfry and its rounded-arched windows with pointed Gothic tracery, and finally a flared pyramidal tower roof with pointed apex. At the time of its completion, it was one of the finest pieces of architecture in the valley, a fact probably not lost on the dominant Mormon population.

Figure 6.11. Presbyterian church, 185 South Main, Manti, 1880–81. Photograph from 1979.

Social Halls

Given the Mormon preoccupation with refinement, it is not surprising that they carved out space in the landscape for the arts, and particularly music and drama. In Salt Lake City, a social hall was erected in 1853 for lectures, theatrical performances, and dances. It was a typical Greek building—a large rendition of the simple hall form. When a theatre was completed a decade later, in 1862, however, it heralded the coming of the new approach to public architecture, being easily recognized as an entertainment palace. Monumental in size, it was easily the finest building in the territory, complete with two full-height Doric columns on the entrance, a pronounced Greek cornice, and triglyhs along the frieze. The theater anticipated by nearly a decade the move toward self-referential buildings that would become standard practice among the Saints by the 1870s.[23]

In the Sanpete Valley, a building specifically reserved for entertainment and edification was a luxury few towns could afford. This does not mean, however, that the arts were neglected, just that buildings had to serve more than one purpose. In Manti, for instance, the Council House performed a variety of services, including a place for Sunday worship, city council meetings, theatrical performances, lectures, and dances.

Similar mixed-use buildings existed in all Sanpete towns. One of the earliest was constructed in Mount Pleasant, as this ward history account attests: "At a Bishop's council meeting held at Mt. Pleasant June 20, 1862, it was unanimously resolved to build a public building at Mt. Pleasant to be called the Social Hall by selling shares at $20 each. This building, which was also used, primarily, as a meeting house, was built the following fall and dedicated Dec. 7, 1862."[24] It was adobe, measuring thirty by forty-five feet, and stood on the south side of church block (Figure 6.12). After its completion, the town hired a new orchestra consisting of two violins, a clarinet, a cornet, and a bass fiddle. Dances were regularly held with quadrilles and squares particularly favored, although the size of the hall limited the fun to thirty-two couples at one time. No beer was allowed inside, however. The price for admission to a dance or play was a bushel of wheat to pay the orchestra, the actors, and for general maintenance. A design flaw gave the building no side or back doors, so if the house filled up early and the central aisle was blocked, the cast often had to climb through a back window. No mention is made of what happened during a fire drill. The bishop and his family, as well as his counselors and their families, received free tickets. On off days, the hall was used as a council chamber, school, and meetinghouse.[25]

Rees R. Lewellyn of Fountain Green informed the *Deseret News* in December 1869 that "a spacious Social Hall is about to [be] erected in this place, by

Figure 6.12. The principal west elevation and plan of the social hall, Mount Pleasant, 1862.

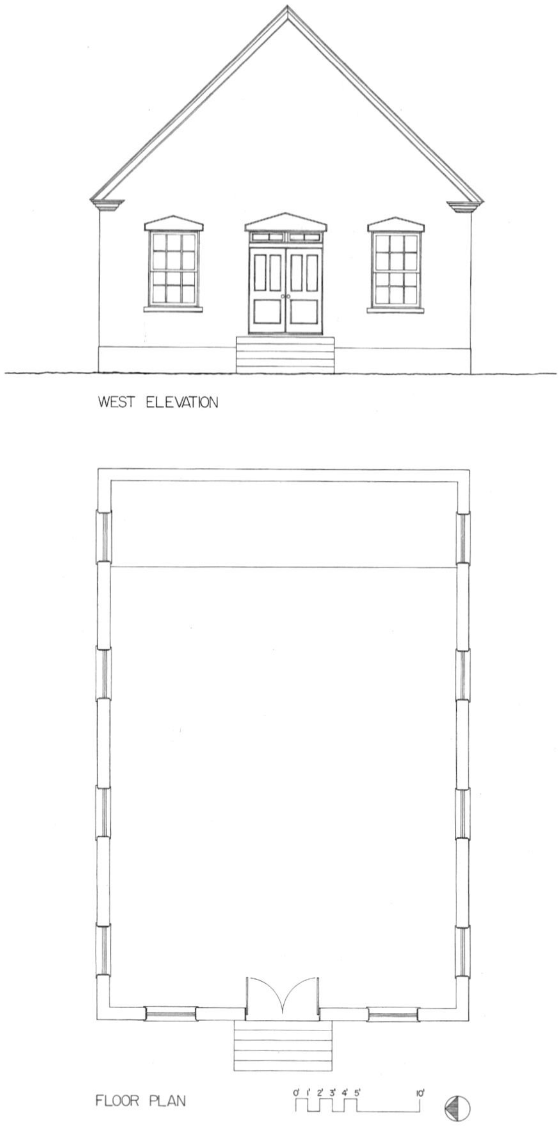

subscription, from ten to one hundred dollars each."[26] Nearby Moroni had its own dramatic association as early as 1865, with comedies like *Charles the Second* and the *Widow's Victim* among the local favorites,[27] although it did not have its own building until 1891, when a fine stone and brick "opera" house was constructed (thirty-five by eighty-five feet in dimension with a seating capacity of one thousand). Until that time, the group used the old log (1862) and then adobe (measuring forty by seventy-five feet and finished in 1870) meetinghouses for its performances.[28] In Ephraim, the straw-covered bowery "held the first musicals for any large gatherings," although the large room on the upper level of the Cooperative store was the favorite venue for lectures, plays, recitals, and dances, as well as meetings of the Female Relief Society after its completion in 1872."[29] The meetinghouse in Spring City accommodated artistic and social gatherings until a large "amusement hall" was erected in 1870 just east of Main Street.[30]

County Courthouse

As a political entity, Sanpete County was organized within Utah Territory in 1852 and George Peacock appointed probate judge. These events are recorded in Peacock's journal: "Commenced my official duties of County Judge in the spring of 1853."[31] At first, Peacock noted, the courtroom and his office were located in the "West room of my house."[32] An official courthouse was constructed in Manti in 1864 and then significantly remodeled, beginning in October 1873, when Judge Peacock mentioned that while "in [Great Salt Lake] City," he "purchased material for the County building."[33] A report published that year in the *Deseret News* confirmed those materials to have been for a remodeling project and not for a new building. In the newspaper article, Abner Lowery of Moroni described a visit to Manti, saying that "the addition of two wings and [an] extension to the Sanpete Courthouse is progressing, the walls of the south wing b[eing] up."[34]

Two years later, on January 3, 1875, Judge Peacock wrote in his journal: "The new Court House was dedicated. I offered the Dedicatory Prayer. 300 persons assembled in the hall of the Court House."[35] A little over a week later he added that on January 11 and 12, "Court [was] in Session. The selectmen were much pleased with the new court house and its furnishing and surprised at the low price it had cost the county. They had estimated the cost at 12,000 dollars, the clerk read the estimate at 5,000 dollars."[36] Jens Weibye's daybook corroborates Peacock's account, writing in January 1875 that there was a "big meeting in the County-hall," which is "now finished."[37]

A photograph of the finished courthouse shows a large neoclassical-style building consisting of a two-story gable-front central block flanked by two-story wings to either side (Figure 6.13).[38] Judging from the preceding commentary, the following building sequence is likely. During the initial phase of construction, the courthouse was a large version of the standard hall building type. Its gable faced forward in temple-form fashion, the classical Greek reference supported by a low-pitched roof and pediment-like cornice returns. The 1873–75 remodeling transformed the simple hall-type building into a rather monumental (for the time and place) public edifice, complete with two-story flanking wings. The elaborate Victorian cupola and two-story front porch were apparently added later, in the 1880s or early 1890s.[39]

Figure 6.13. Sanpete County Court House, 180 North Main Street, Manti, as it appeared around 1900. The hall-type center section was constructed first, in the mid-1860s, and the side wings were added between 1873 and 1875. Reprinted by permission of Utah State Historical Society; all rights reserved.

City Halls

Mormon towns had civil as well as ecclesiastical governments. During the settlement years, city councils often met in whatever space was available. Sometimes this meant convening in a councilman's home, though more commonly gatherings were held in meetinghouses or social halls. Again, the Council House in Manti is a good example of such versatile buildings. Yet when city halls did get built, they followed the design sequence outlined for Main Street building types; the earlier ones, like the Ephraim City Hall (Figure 6.14), were standard hall-type buildings, and those coming later, as was the case in Manti (Figure 6.15), adopted a more clearly defined institutional identity.

In Ephraim, talk of constructing a municipal building began shortly after the city's incorporation in 1868, though the plan was not carried out until 1873.[40] When completed, the Ephraim City Hall was a hall-type stone building with the typical front-facing gable, a boxed soffit, and built-up moldings on the cornice and frieze (without the Greek returns). The principal decorative elements were the headers over the heavy cased windows and door. These were scroll-bracketed pediments with architrave molding. The hall had two floors. On the upper level was the council chamber while below, in the partially below-grade basement, was a "lockup" or jail.[41]

Only a few years later, when the citizens of Manti got around to considering a city building, thinking on the subject was changing dramatically. For one thing, city services were growing more complex, so space for offices as well as meetings was needed. There was also the issue of prestige; Manti was emerging as the principal city in the valley (a position hotly contested by both Ephraim and Mount Pleasant), and city leaders undoubtedly wanted

Figure 6.14 *(left)*. Ephraim City Hall, 38 East Center Street, 1873. Photograph from 1979.

Figure 6.15 *(above)*. Manti City Hall, 191 North Main Street, 1873–82. Stucco over cut oolite limestone. Photograph from 1978.

a building commensurate with such lofty aspirations. And finally, albeit on a more subtle cultural level, it was simply time for a city hall to look like a city hall.

In nineteenth-century America, a popular building type for public activities (principally courthouses and city halls) was a square-shaped structure with hipped roof and central passage plan. It competed with the temple-form type throughout the antebellum period, but Mormons adopted it rather wholeheartedly in the West. Its first use was in Salt Lake City, for the quasi-public Council House (1849–50). More notable were the second City Hall (1864–66), which replaced a gabled hall dating to the 1850s, and the County Courthouse (1855–65). The box-like design was used in Box Elder, Summit, and Washington Counties, among others, and was chosen for Manti's new city hall.[42]

Constructed over a nine-year period (1873–83), Manti City Hall is a fine example of this approach to public architecture. Minutes from a council meeting on July 15, 1873, read: "Motioned and carried that the work on the City Hall be resumed and that A. W. Bessey, A.C. Van Buren, and W. Luke act as a committee to examine the grounds and get up a draft [design] for the house with power to call upon such assistance as said committee may deem necessary." Apparently there was no great hurry. Twenty proposals came in—each containing plans for the building as well as costs for materials, tools, and labor—but a contract was not awarded until March 1875. The job was awarded to A. E. Merriam, a carpenter-builder from Manti, who may have missed a few deadlines, given the late date for its completion.[43]

The building had style, however. As mentioned earlier, it deviated from the older hall design, basically being a large double-pile Georgian house adapted to public use. The ground floor contains four roughly equal-size rooms separated by a central passageway containing the staircase. Upstairs were meeting and courtroom spaces. Merriam's design was typical of the type, though graced by subtle Italian details such as a low-pitched truncated hipped hoof, decorative cornice bracketing, and smoothly plastered limestone walls. Its textured stucco with quoins at the corners is late, probably dating to the 1940s.[44]

Schools

During the settlement years, school-building responsibilities in the Sanpete Valley, as in other parts of the Mormon Kingdom, were left to local LDS officials, who responded by overseeing extensive, if always inadequately funded, building programs. Most work was accomplished either by means of subscriptions (paid by individual families) or a general "school tax" (equitably distributed but not easily collected).[45] In Manti, the city council in November 1851 voted to provide public support for school buildings and teachers' salaries from a "general assessment"; but "each [pupil] attending school should furnish an equal amount of wood for the heating of the school room."[46] Whether the council was acting in a civil or an ecclesiastical capacity is unknown (and irrelevant since the two were one and the same), but by all accounts local officials did make a conscientious effort to meet the spatial needs of a growing school-age population. When schools were built, they followed the general pattern of architectural change found in nonresidential buildings.

Ephraim offers a good example. In 1859 the city's single ward was divided into four teaching districts, and four small rock schools were completed, three in 1863 and the fourth in 1864.[47] These were one-room affairs (Figure 6.16) with a decidedly house-like appearance that remained in service until retired in the late 1870s upon the completion of two new school buildings, one for the South Ward and one for the North, plus the requisitioning of the Quinn/Greaves store and dance hall on Main Street, which was remodeled (complete with bell tower) to become the Central School (see Figure 6.21). Not until 1908 was a consolidated school, one that included both grade and high school classes, finished.[48]

A similar sequence occurred in Mount Pleasant, where in 1863 one log and three adobe schoolhouses had been constructed for the town's scholars. A little over a decade later, however, a large hall-type schoolhouse was finished, as reported in the *Deseret News* on February 1, 1876: "Our new school house was finished last week. It is the best schoolhouse in the county. It is 50 by 28 in

Figure 6.16. "Students and Teacher, Miss Armstrong in front of Stone School," date unknown. This small school was constructed in Ephraim between 1863 and 1864 and used until the late 1870s. George Edward Anderson Photographs, MSS P-1, L. Tom Perry Special Collections, Brigham Young University.

the clear, with about 14 feet ceiling, eight large windows, three on each side, two in the end. It fronts State Street, has a large double door in the front end [gable-front], and a single door in the rear. The ventilation is good. It is finished with three large and elegant blackboards, two good stoves and about eighty-two seats, accommodating one hundred and sixty pupils."[49] In 1896, a large brick central school was built a block north on the old tithing yard lot.

The late nineteenth-century shift in civic building design is evident in two schools, one in Spring City and the other in Manti, that are closely related in age but telling in their differences. The Spring City building, often called the John Frank Allred School (after an early teacher), was constructed in 1876 and remains one of the finest examples of the hall-type form in the valley (Figure 6.17).[50] Its classic styling, testimony to the enduring popularity of Greek fashion among Sanpete residents, consists of the tripartite symmetry, low-pitched roof, and pronounced cornice returns typical of the genre, as is the small pedimented date stone in the gable.

Several years earlier, two schools were built in Manti. John Hougaard, in an April 1874 letter to the *Deseret News,* explained: "Since the circumstances of the people have improved, their interest in the proper training and education of their children has correspondingly increased. . . . We have here in Manti two very good, well arranged and well furnished school houses, one of which was commenced a year ago this Spring and finished last fall, so that school was kept in it all last winter."[51] Both schools (renamed the North and

South Ward Schools after the town was divided into two wards in 1877) were originally Greek front-gable halls, greatly resembling the Allred School. However, in the late 1870s, probably about the time that the courthouse was remodeled, the North Ward School was also reworked, with a clipped gable and bell-tower cupola added (Figure 6.18), both signs of the new interest in differentiated building types. Proving yet another exception to the rule, the South Ward School was curiously left untouched, perhaps because it was located a block west of Main Street.[52]

Figure 6.17. John Frank Allred School, 63 West 300 South, Spring City, 1876. Photograph from 1978.

Figure 6.18. North Ward School, 190 North Main Street, Manti, 1874. The bell tower is a later addition, probably from the late 1870s or early 1880s. Reprinted by permission of Utah State Historical Society; all rights reserved.

Commercial Buildings

As repeatedly stressed, within Mormon society a strong work ethic centered on individual effort prevailed. Bishop Jezrell Shomaker, speaking in Manti during a time of shortages, "said some had complained that he was not liberal with his wheat in this trying time; said he did not intended to see any starve but wished to see those that had fooled their wheat away suffer a little."[53] Mean-spirited? Perhaps, but it seems likely that most of the Saints would have agreed with him, or with James Wareham of Manti, who quipped in Sunday meeting, "Complainers were the idlers."[54]

During the first years of settlement, people were virtually forced to live the United Order, but afterward, when the local economies started to grow, "the practice of sharing was discontinued and [settlers] had to work for themselves."[55] Individually owned and operated businesses and shops sprang up in the downtown districts of each town, entrepreneurs eager to profit by meeting consumer demand, which was considerable. Advertisements in the *Manti Herald and Sanpete Advertiser* attest to the competitive atmosphere. Here are two from the same firm, the Manti Branch of the Eagle Emporium (which was owned by William Jennings from Salt Lake City): "The above Establishment is still in flourishing condition, offering a variety of good and cheap goods for convenient pay. Come On! Come on! Forward! With your butter, oats, eggs, and bacon. Cash not refused."[56] And this one: "Citizens of Manti. You would do well to look in and patronize—Jennings Branch Store, Manti. A few young cows taken in exchange for goods."[57] Anything to make a sale.

Various kinds of businesses lined up along valley main streets. Most sold general merchandise, carrying everything from canned goods to cloth. Specialty shops included those of furniture makers, stone carvers, tinkers, tailors, barbers, lawyers, and doctors. The south side of Block 28 in Mount Pleasant's downtown district (Figure 6.19) included the following in 1880: beginning at the far left, a house belonging to Magnus Petersen, soon sold to Hans Nielsen; then the post office, purchased in 1873 by Niels Nielsen and August Wall, who tore it down and built the two-story brick Sanpete County Co-op, or Swedish Store (Gentile Store); next was P. M. Jensen's saloon, Henry Beck's harness shop, and after several vacant lots, a general merchandise store, probably built around 1875 by Joseph Hutchings and William Liter; then came Warren Child's saloon, dating to around 1878; another saloon, owned by Andrew Oman (sometimes spelled Omenn); a small boardinghouse, a sample room, a sleeping room, and then, on the right end, Andrew Oman's two-story hotel.[58]

The presence of saloons may come as a surprise, given the pious nature of the Sanpete communities. Most Utah towns had them, however; during the nineteenth century alcohol consumption was frowned on but not forbidden.

Figure 6.19. A reconstructed view of a typical Sanpete Valley urban streetscape from the 1860s and early 1870s; the north side of Mount Pleasant's Main Street between 100 and 200 West (lying along the southern edge of Block 28) is shown here.

Moses Thatcher, a church apostle visiting from Logan, spoke at the Stake Conference in Manti in 1883: "When I was here last night and listened to the singing I turned around [and] saw a sign 'Liquors for sale.' I then saw the temple on the hill and I wondered if it could be a saint who stood behind the bar."[59] In Sanpete the presence of so many Scandinavians may have increased the local rate of beer consumption. Thatcher himself was not particularly amused and spoke to the contradictions in both signs and culture: "When we started Co-operation [in Logan] we put up the sign 'Holiness to the Lord' over the door"; "I asked President Young how we could reconcile with our profession [of faith] and then deal in liquor [apparently they sold liquor in the Logan co-op] he answered 'any one who will lift the whiskey cup to the lips of his brethren and continue shall be damned.' It was the last time we sold whiskey in our store."[60] Another forty years would pass, however, before LDS leaders formally adopted the "abstinence only" policy called the "Word of Wisdom."[61]

The cooperative store Thatcher referred to was tied to a distinctive church economic program initiated in the late 1860s and intended to stem the tide of Gentile intrusion into Zion. As the Transcontinental Railroad drew near (it was completed in 1869), LDS officials sought ways to counter what they perceived would be an increased non-Mormon presence in the Kingdom, once transportation became both quicker and easier. They particularly worried about the church's financial resources being siphoned off by Gentiles merchants, and to meet this threat they inaugurated a retail mercantile system designed to keep Mormon money in Mormon hands. It was an old idea; Bishop Warren Snow of Manti as early as 1857 "told [the] brethren to take care of their grain; and that any one in the future who sold it to the Gentiles should be cut off [from] the Church."[62] But by the late 1860s, it had acquired stronger emphasis. Jens Weibye, in a daybook entry for 1868, mentioned attending "two meetings [where] John Van Cott [president of the Quorum of the Seventies] preached to us not to deal with the Jews or Gentiles but trad[e] with our own Mormon Brethren."[63]

Such apprehension led Brigham Young to create the Zion's Co-operative Mercantile Institution, or ZCMI, which established a parent store in Salt Lake City; ZCMI would bring consumer goods into the territory and then sell them to the Saints through a network of sanctioned local outlets, thereby keeping Mormon capital "in-house." The key word in the ZCMI business model was cooperative, meaning an enterprise owned and operated by its users (in this case the Saints). It also denotes a system in which church members would work together to reduce their reliance on the outside world by increasing their self-sufficiency and patronizing stores that carried goods imported by LDS merchants. Make your own or buy local was the idea.[64]

To understand the Mormon brand of cooperation, two things are important. First, the stores were never actually built or owned by the LDS Church. Rather, construction was financed out of each company's existing capital, capital raised by selling shares in the business to local investors. The cooperatives became, in effect, church-endorsed joint-stock ventures, returning a dividend to the shareholders on the basis of their investments. Second, shares in the ZCMI stores were never equitably distributed. People could buy into the cooperatives according to their interest and financial capabilities, and they received dividends on a commensurate basis. In short, some members owned a great deal of stock and others little or none. Not surprisingly, leading businessmen were often the principal stockholders and also sat on the board of directors. In Manti, Weibye listed the officers of the co-op in 1870 as follows: "Bishop A. J. Moffit, President; F. W. Cox, Sen[ior], Vise President; Bord of Directors, Luther Tuttle, Wm F. Maylett, Wm Andersen, Hans Jensen 1st, James Crawford (newly elected), E. W. Fox, Secretary; Wm T. Reid, Treasurer."[65] The names represent a "Who's Who" of Manti's ecclesiastical and business elite. Somewhat apologetically, Bishop W. T. Reid of Manti's North Ward would state at the Stake Conference in 1880, "This principle [of cooperation] should be carried out on a basis of equity and truth. It is not designed for the benefit of a class but for the benefit of all."[66]

Moroni was the first Sanpete Valley town to have a ZCMI store. In 1868 one resident commented that since merchandise sold at an "extortionate" rate, the Saints there concluded to open "a little store and run it on the cooperative principle."[67] Not everyone participated, but several of the town's entrepreneurs, including George Jackson, Jens Nielson, Charles Longston, Lars Larson, and Robert Mallinson, "commenced their business by subscribing

$20 each and sending a team to Salt Lake City after one load of merchandise. This was sold the first day after getting it home with 50 per cent profit, which was very cheap compared with prices previously paid for the same line of goods. Immediately afterwards two more loads of merchandise were sent for and in a short time a flourishing business was established which in 1900 was the leading merchantile house in Moroni."[68]

One incentive for the Saints to support the co-ops, as they were called, involved paying dividends to consumers as well as stockholders. In Spring City it was reported in the *Deseret News* that the co-op paid a split dividend: "An admirable principle has been adopted by the people of Spring City in conducting the co-operative store of that place. The wise policy of sharing the dividends with the consumers, or patrons of the store, has been carried out for some time, and with admirable effect. The buyer has a pass book in which the clerk inserts the amount of each purchase. At the end of each half year, stock is taken, and when the amount of the dividend is known, it is divided by two, one half going to the shareholders and the other to the purchasers. This system appears to greatly benefit the people and is an inducement for all to do their purchasing at the store."[69]

Other towns fared equally well. The ward history of Fairview states: "In 1869 a co-operative store was commenced . . . with a capital stock of $300. The first goods were sold May 10, 1869 in a rented room. This small business gradually grew until it did a great amount of business, thus in 1893 it had a capital stock of $8000, and had a trade amounting to about $40,000 per annum, doing business in a substantial two story rock building. Up to 1893 the institution never paid less than 20% dividend per annum and occasionally as high as 60%."[70]

The co-op store in Ephraim was organized in 1869, and construction on a new building commenced in late 1870. By November 18, 1872, the traveling agent for the *Deseret News* reported that the people of Ephraim are "at work on their new co-operative store, a large, fine building, two stories high. The upper room will be used for a hall for recreation. The building is 65 feet long by 35 feet wide, of white rock, the front smooth dressed. It will be up to the square in about two weeks" (Figure 6.20).[71] By the end of the year the same reporter could write that "a new rock building commenced the year before was finished in Ephraim for the use of the co-operative store [ground floor] and a Relief Society hall [upstairs]."[72] The Ephraim co-op was a large hall-type structure, distinguished by a bracketed cornice, cornice returns, hooded window heads, and a large semicircular blind arch containing a painting of a beehive with the words "Holiness to the Lord," a slogan that signified membership in the ZCMI family of stores.[73]

The official church line on cooperation was voiced by Stake president

Figure 6.20. ZCMI store, 96 North Main, Ephraim, 1871–72. The Female Relief Society used the upper level as a meeting hall. The building has since been restored to its original appearance. Photograph from 1978.

Canute Peterson, who addressed a meeting of the Ephraim priesthood in 1877, saying "he wanted the brethren to sustain the Co Op Stores and avoid the opposition stores."[74] In a similar vein, Apostle Wilford Woodruff, speaking in Manti in 1878, said, "Co Operative Institutions should not fail in the midst of Saints, nor should the Saints build up opposition in their midst."[75] Those whom Peterson and Woodruff labeled in "opposition" were either outsiders (non-Mormons) or LDS businessmen who operated independently of the ZCMI procurement and distribution system (presumably buying from outsiders). In the Sanpete Valley, apart from Mount Pleasant, where a number of apostate merchants set up shops, nearly all opposition came from within LDS ranks, the spirit of free enterprise seemingly irrepressible. Certainly a good many Saints actively endorsed and patronized the ZCMI outlets. At the same time, many did not, preferring to go after their own profits or the best prices, even if doing so meant joining the opposition.

Local church officials made attempts at enforcement, mostly to drive opposition stores out of business (since it appears that they could not force people into boycotting them). One such case in Ephraim involved Christian A. Larsen, who ran a small store in his house, taking produce to Salt Lake City and then bringing back dry goods to sell to his Sanpete Valley neighbors. His daughter recalled later, with a degree of bitterness, "His business activity did not, of course, go unnoticed and it was felt by certain factions that he was doing business in opposition to the co-op store . . . and being a man who was unafraid in the expression of his convictions, no doubt aggravated those who opposed him. He was excommunicated from his Church, to which he had given a full measure of devotion."[76]

Mostly a "live and let live" attitude prevailed, with the cooperative/opposition store split increasing competition and driving down prices. Such nonchalance is visible in the case of a large "four room rock structure" built in 1875 in Ephraim, just across the street from the tabernacle. Its owner was George Quinn, who, although a member of the church, openly announced his intention to compete with the newly completed co-op. His building certainly looked the part, being about the same size and style as the church-sponsored store. Of particular interest were the large round-arch windows on the streetside facade, rivaling in fashion any similar building in the valley (Figure 6.21). Land records indicate that Quinn owned his store for a number of years before selling out to another prominent church member, Peter Greaves, in 1883 for $2,200 (an immense sum at the time). In 1889 Greaves transferred title to the local branch of the LDS Church, which turned the building into its Central School, adding a bell tower to advertise its new pedagogical identity.[77]

A similar situation arose in Manti. By the 1870s, Main Street was divided into two factions. On the east (Figure 6.23) stood the cooperative stores. The first one, a one-story gable-front building with a stepped parapet, was built in 1868–69. Manti resident James Brown, writing in 1868 in the *Deseret News,* observed that "Messrs. [Luther] Tuttle and [Edward] Fox, of this town, have commenced to erect a store on the first block northeast of the Council House, and by the start they have made I should judge it will be a nice building when completed."[78] Another investor in the co-op, county probate judge

Figure 6.21. George Quinn's store, 187 South Main Street, between 100 and 200 South (east side), Ephraim, circa 1870–75. When the store was turned into a school around 1890, a bell tower was added. Later the building was used as a city hall. George Edward Anderson took this photograph in the 1880s and called it "Ephraim Utah Block Parade." Courtesy of the Church History Library.

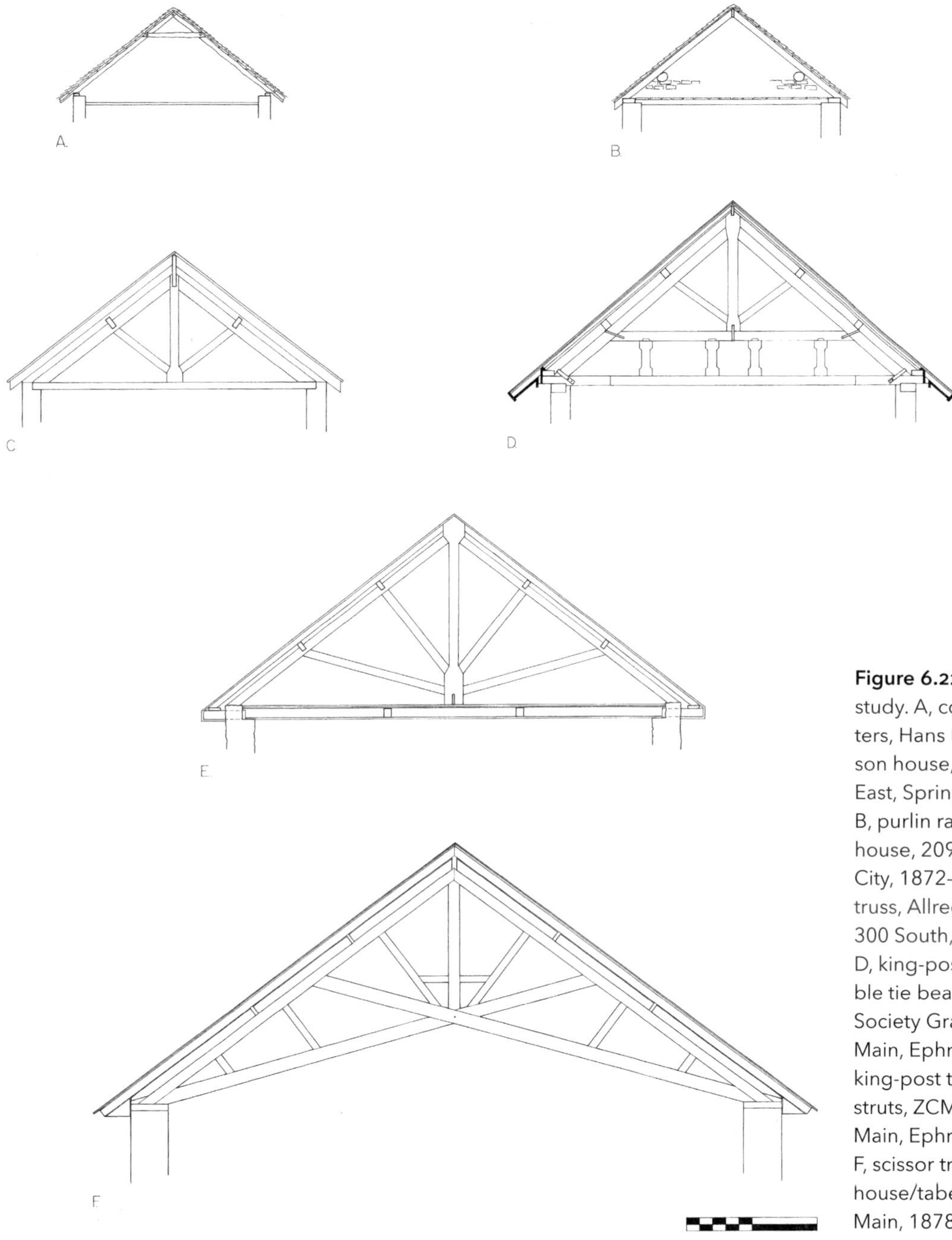

Figure 6.22. Roof construction study. A, collared common rafters, Hans Peter Christopherson house, 200 North 100 East, Spring City, circa 1865; B, purlin rafters, Orson Hyde house, 209 South Main, Spring City, 1872–76; C, king-post truss, Allred School, 63 West 300 South, Spring City, 1876; D, king-post truss with double tie beams, Female Relief Society Granary, 90 North Main, Ephraim, 1870–75; E, king-post truss with double struts, ZCMI store, 96 North Main, Ephraim, 1871–72; and F, scissor truss, Manti meetinghouse/tabernacle, 91 South Main, 1878–89.

George Peacock, reported that in late December 1868 he went to Salt Lake City and "purchased a stock of goods for the Manti Mercantile Company."[79] Peacock also noted that "the store was open [by January 1869], 600 dollars worth of goods were sold [the] first day."[80] The business grew and during the late 1870s expanded into a fashionable two-story building built just north of the original store.

Across the street resided the opposition stores (Figure 6.24). On the

Figure 6.23. Cooperation: the east side of Manti's Main Street, from Union to 100 North, 1888. From right to left: the original ZCMI store, 1868–69; the second cooperative, the Manti Co-operative Mercantile Institution, circa 1880; and two unknown privately owned and operated stores. George Edward Anderson Photographs, MSS P-1, L. Tom Perry Special Collections, Brigham Young University.

Figure 6.24. Opposition: the west side of Manti's Main Street, from Union to 100 North, anonymous photograph, circa 1885. From left to right: the Edward Fox store, 1874; unknown store; Luther Tuttle's mercantile store, circa 1880; unknown store; the John Padris house (set back and abandoned), circa 1860s; unknown store; and the Female Relief Society store/hall, 1882. Reprinted by permission of Utah State Historical Society; all rights reserved.

corner was a large gabled hall store that belonged to Edward Fox. Jens Weibye records its building date as April 1874: "[At this time] Edward W. Fox commenced his opposition Store here in Manti with Soren Christoffersen his clerk."[81] Next door was Luther Tuttle's store, constructed in 1880, although this building reflected the new concern for architectural specificity—a wooden flat false front was attached to the stone hall plan to yield both an urban sensibility and convenient surface space for signage.[82]

We have already met Messrs. Fox and Tuttle. They were responsible for building the first Manti co-op store and served on its board of directors for many years. They were also church members in good standing; Fox even let the LDS Young Men's Mutual Improvement Association, a church auxiliary organization, use the upper room of his westside opposition store for its meetings.[83] Despite such generosity some leaders wanted him punished. Apostle Hyde, speaking in Manti in 1876, told the membership that "he wants those cut off from the Church there are building [the] Oposition Store here in Manti."[84] Presumably he was referring to Fox, for soon after this Weibye noted that "the Co-op Store in Manti bought E. W. Foxes Store, and he stop to keep Store any longer."[85] Fox's enterprise appears to have been targeted for closure, and the bad feelings continued, with Fox in 1887 asking to be "cut off from the church."[86]

Oddly, next-door neighbor Luther Tuttle escaped a similar fate, though there is no indication how he did it. Perhaps by 1880, when his new opposition store was finished, the frenzy for cooperation had blown over and no one cared. The architectural evidence seems to suggest such an explanation. The new Manti Co-operative Mercantile Institution and Tuttle's store appear remarkably similar, much as did the early hall-type stores favored by the first co-op builders (Figure 6.25). Architectural historian Richard Longstreth calls the new designs "two-part commercial blocks" because the flat square plane on the front is divided into two separate levels: downstairs is the retail commercial space, fronted by an array of display windows and a prominent front door; upstairs are smaller, symmetrically arranged windows, denoting the presence of meeting rooms and offices.[87] The use of such building types in Manti signals the acceptance of a mainstream style of commercial architecture, one consistent with downtown districts in other parts of the country, becoming yet another step in the move toward a normative, secular city.

In appraising the successes and failures of cooperation, it is necessary to draw the line between self-sufficiency, which was valued, and spartan denial, which was not. On one hand, said a speaker at the 1877 Stake Conference in Ephraim, "Let the garments we wear be the work of our own hands; let us

Figure 6.25. Co-ops, opposition stores, and the importance of signs: A, the second Manti co-op; B, Luther Tuttle's store, both circa 1880.

cease scattering our means to our enemies."[88] But at the same meeting, Orson Hyde posed the real question: "What will we do when Babylon [America] falls, we can not buy any merchandise then nor sell our grain."[89] Buying and selling was never the real problem; it was just whom one did it with that mattered. And even this qualification did not last for long, since the cooperative movement was relatively short lived in all but the most fervently idealistic communities.

Community Centers

Of all the elements in the City of Zion landscape, the buildings along Main Street are probably the most difficult to read and understand. This may be because they are unfamiliar (they have not been studied to any extent before) or perhaps they lack the import of the religious buildings or the charm of the houses. I do not know. It is clear, however, that main street and its buildings figured prominently in the lives of the early Latter-day Saints, in effect becoming, once the temple was extracted, the center of town, both literally and symbolically. Here is where people gathered to attend church, pay tithing, buy food, shop for merchandise of all kinds, participate in town meetings and local politics, and be entertained. And here too was a place that epitomized the increasingly secular nature of the town.

Urban theorist Kevin Lynch talks about how a successful city is a "legible" one, in which meanings are readily apparent to its users.[90] Such legibility comes in the form of explicit signs, which in the Sanpete towns were primarily architectural: building type rather than actual signage denoted meaning (and function). The curious thing about Mormon towns is that early on they appear to lack clarity, the street presenting an undifferentiated array of hall-type buildings whose individual meanings are seemingly subservient to a larger idea of living in a sacred world. But this homogeneity does not last. After about 1870 the architectural sameness is replaced by a more complex differentiations of types—Main Street becomes home to a more readily distinguishable set of churches, tithing offices, stores (whether they be co-ops or ops), and civic buildings. Again, hidden in the change is the larger restructuring of the landscape along sacred (temple) and secular (town) lines, whose message is one of millennial deferral. This shift is most apparent in the meetinghouses that were always there but that came into their own only in the final quarter of the century.

7 MEETINGHOUSES
THE SEARCH FOR MORMON IDENTITY

> Last Sabbath [we] repaired to Fort Ephraim, where in the large meetinghouse, we found some twelve hundred people gathered from all parts of the valley. After meeting we rolled back to Manti, where another meeting was held, at which Presidents Young and Kimball spoke with much power and spirit, gladdening the hearts of a large congregation, counseling them to finish their Council House and then build a large meetinghouse and to make other improvements.
>
> —Deseret News, *May 16, 1863*

ONE CHALLENGE FACING ZION MAKERS lay in creating a distinctive Mormon style in religious architecture. Such a style was needed if this upstart religion, proclaiming itself the restoration of Christ's true church to earth in the Last Days, was not only going to distinguish itself from established churches but also provide its members with a set of visual images around which to fashion a cohesive group identity. Simply put, a new religion could not use the same old buildings—it had to have its own. Temples provided part of the answer. No other American church had them, and while it would take time for the temple idea to develop fully, by the Nauvoo period, if not sooner, these monumental buildings had become recognizable signs of Mormon identity. A church with temples was something that rarely came along.[1]

Buildings for regular Sunday worship posed another kind of problem, however. Most U.S. religions built churches, the usual name for these buildings, and by the middle years of the nineteenth century one building in particular, a rectangular box with an engaged front tower and steeple had been nearly universally accepted as the type for Christian churches of all denominations (Figure 7.1). Thus, the Latter-day Saints were forced either to invent a new and radically other kind of building, similar to what they were doing with the temple, or somehow modify the archetypal form, adding their own touches. Taking this latter course would produce a different building—a variation on the standard church type—a safer course, since it would ally them stylistically with the Christian mainstream.[2]

Figure 7.1. First Congregational Church, Lyme, Connecticut, 1816–17. Photograph from 2001.

Making things more difficult still was the fact that the whole process started late. Initially, temples had served both congregational and ritual functions, making the need for a specific house of worship unnecessary. By the end of the Nauvoo period, however, the script had changed. Shortly before his death, Joseph Smith announced that in the future the temple would be reserved for "meetings of councils and quorums, and the administration of ordinances and blessings and preaching to smaller congregations," while regular worship would take place in an elliptical "canvas" tabernacle he planned to build beside the temple.[3] The martyrdom and subsequent exodus prevented either from transpiring, but by the time the Latter-day Saints headed west it was clear they would need a congregational building of their own, in addition to the now sanctified ritual space of the temple.

As in other aspects of western Zion making, LDS meetinghouse design evolved slowly; solutions came only after a great deal of experimentation. This chapter traces the development of the Mormon meetinghouse in the West, again looking at choices and outcomes in an attempt to better understand not only the buildings but also their historical implications.

The Uses of Style

That an exceptionalist agenda existed within the LDS leadership is suggested by Smith's early use of the word "tabernacle" rather than "church." For the Saints, the latter word referred to the institution—the Church—while the former, as Smith's choice reveals, was used to establish lineage with God's biblical sanctuary, described in Exodus as a tabernacle, an elongated tent, consisting of a series of wooden frames covered by goat's hair and tanned rams' skins, having an "outer covering of fine leather," and sided with rich tapestries.[4] The portability of a tent/tabernacle enabled the Hebrew God to dwell among the Israelites as they journeyed out of Egypt back to Canaan. By the time the Latter-day Saints reached the Great Basin, a mobile tabernacle was unnecessary since their own exodus had ended. The biblical analogy lived on, however, contributing not only to the design of the Utah temples but also two of their most unique productions, the first (or "old") and second ("new") Salt Lake tabernacles.

The first church meetings in Salt Lake City were held in a large open-air arbor, called the bowery. This gathering space was supplemented in 1849 with a spacious wooden building conceived as a temporary structure to be used only until a permanent tabernacle was constructed. Built between 1851 and 1852 (Figure 7.2), the first tabernacle was designed by church architect Truman O. Angell. It was adobe, measured 64 by 126 feet, and had large trusses spanning an open interior space built to accommodate in excess of twenty-five

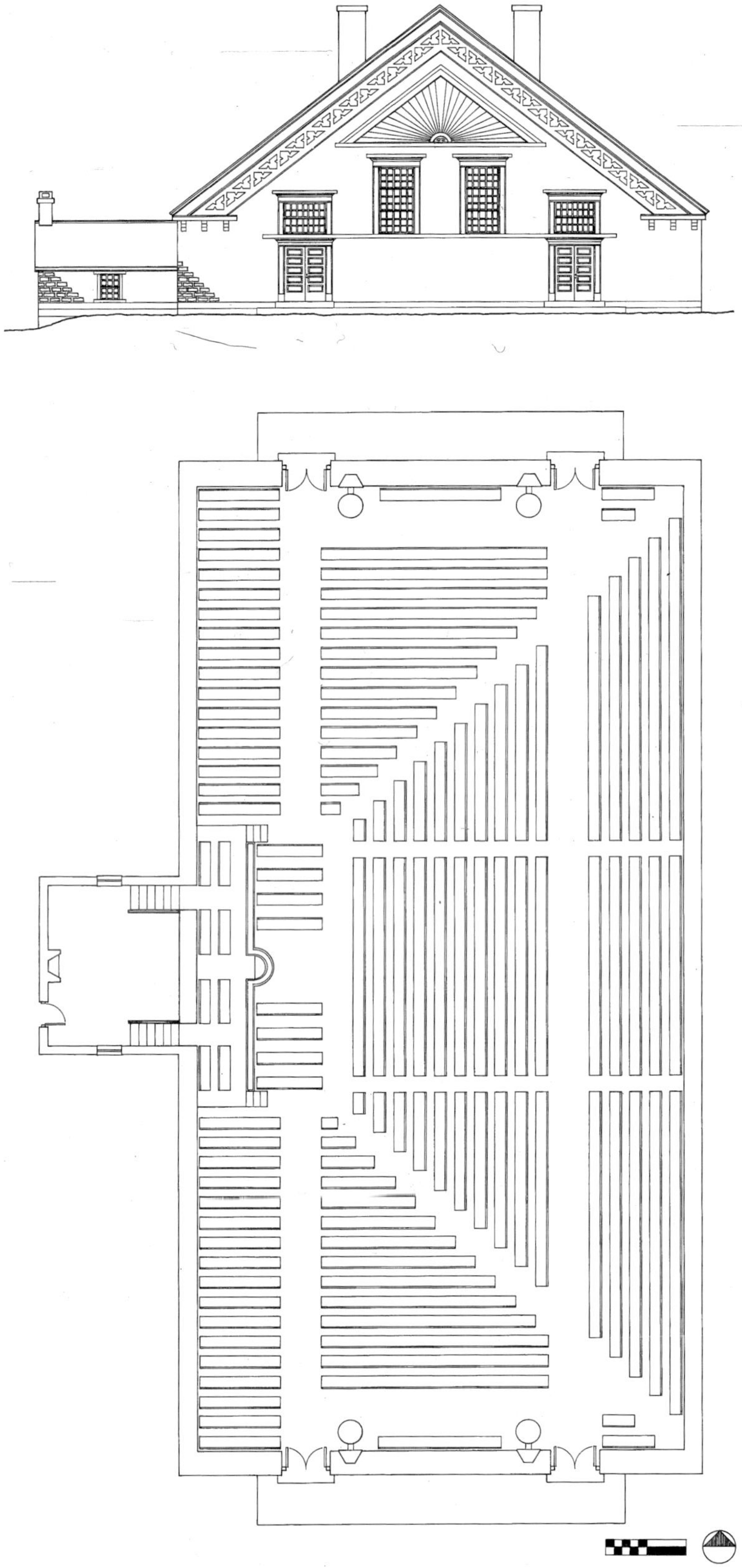

Figure 7.2. Reconstruction drawing of the south elevation and plan of the Old Tabernacle, Temple Square, Salt Lake City, 1851–52.

hundred people. Angell dropped the building several feet below grade, a partially subterranean arrangement that may have stemmed from a desire to cut costs (fewer adobes were needed) or make the immense building easier to heat and cool (the ground helped insulate the foundation) in the harsh western climate. Whatever the actual case (Angell never said), it did result in giving the tabernacle a low-slung profile that contributed to a more tent-like appearance, something that may have been desirable to the pioneer Zion makers. Lacy scroll-cut bargeboards along the long raking eaves, symmetrically spaced doors and windows, and a large triangular rising sun emblem under a pointed arch softened the effect of the short stubby walls, but not much.[5] Some liked it; others did not. One visitor even remarked that it made "no pretense evidently to any of the known order[s] of architecture,"[6] and that probably was the intention all along, an indication of Angell's genius. Such innovation came at a price, however, for the architect mused: "I have always been since my manhood a hard working Carpenter and Joiner with my own hands, but it is a trifle to labour with one's own hands to the labour of the mind, while one tires the extremities the other wearies the man in his whole system."[7]

On the inside, Angell eschewed the courts and trappings of the biblical tabernacle and employed instead an older New England meetinghouse plan. Two doors in the broad front gable opened into an expansive hall. The rostrum—the raised speakers' platform and pulpit—as is customary in eastern meetinghouses, stood transversely on the long west side of the building rather than at the end of the long nave, as in most churches. Benches faced the rostrum in a semicircular fashion and were reached from the back and sides.[8] Initially the congregation was segregated according to gender; men entered from the south, women from the north, and there was a curtain divider down the middle.[9] This practice lasted only a few years and may have been borrowed from the Quakers, who abjured mixing the sexes during meetings on the grounds that it proved a distraction for all.[10]

Angell's adobe tabernacle soon gave way to what is known as the New or Great Tabernacle of the mid-1860s, a stunning piece of architectural originality. The design was probably Brigham Young's, working in consort with architect William Folsom (who originally envisioned a broad pitched roof) and builder Henry Grow (Angell resurfaced and helped lay out the interior). Nowhere does Young explain the inspiration for the dome, but it bears an unmistakable resemblance to Joseph Smith's concept for the Nauvoo tabernacle, with ellipses at each end rather than one, and shingles (350,000 of them!) instead of canvas. The dome is supported by a series of elaborate bridge trusses resting on stone pillars, again making reference to Moses's tabernacle—here, quite literally, is God's tent in the Great Basin desert of Salt Lake City (Figure 7.3). The Saints went even further, viewing the Great Tabernacle as a

Figure 7.3. Anonymous photograph of the New Tabernacle under construction in the 1860s, Temple Square, Salt Lake City. It was completed in 1867. Reprinted by permission of Utah State Historical Society; all rights reserved.

metaphor for Zion itself, with the expansive canopy representing the enveloping church and the stone pillars the various supporting congregations, the stakes of Zion. All in all, the building is remarkable both for its courageous originality and symbolic power. With it, the Latter-day Saints struck out on a path of architectural and cultural otherness, unwilling at this point to settle for simple difference. Internally, the plan was more conventional, following the axial arrangement of aisles and benches leading to and facing a rostrum placed at the narrow end of the building. It hardly mattered, however, for the radical effect of the dome, both inside and out, remained undeniable.[11]

The two large tabernacles on Salt Lake City's Temple Square were intended for church-wide or multiward gatherings. Individual wards, of course, required less space and got smaller buildings, sometimes called "council houses" or "assembly rooms," though the most common name was "meetinghouse." These were more prosaic buildings and up until about 1870 followed the gable-front design dictum, being of the hall type and usually displaying either Federal or Greek exterior trim. The Thirteenth Ward Assembly Rooms—Salt Lake City was initially divided into nineteen separate wards—is one of the most elaborate of these early hall-type meetinghouses (Figure 7.4). Planning for it started in 1854, and seven years later it was dedicated, costing ten thousand dollars at a subscription rate of twenty-five dollars per share. The triangular pediment with plain tympanum gave the building a degree of sophistication (the Thirteenth was one of the most affluent Salt Lake City wards), as did the Tuscan pilasters, hooded moldings, and half-round blind arches. In plan, it had an aisled nave with rostrum and pulpit placed on the

Figure 7.4. Thirteenth Ward Assembly Rooms, Salt Lake City, 1854–67. Reprinted by permission of Utah State Historical Society; all rights reserved.

narrow end. A side wing was added in 1867 to house a school, although it continued the classical detailing found on the main block.[12]

Most ward meetinghouses, both in the capital city and the outlying towns, were less pretentious. The Seventh Ward Meetinghouse is typical of this large group. Started in 1862 and finished in 1877, it adheres to the meeting hall prescription, having a gable front, a standard double-aisle axial plan, and end rostrum. Its exterior is Greek, with a boxed cornice, cornice returns, dentiled frieze, and a low-pitched classical roof. The compass windows are distinctive (Figure 7.5).[13]

Beginning in the late 1860s and lasting into the early 1880s, the direction of meetinghouse design changed dramatically. The process started in St. George, the principal colony in the southern part of the Mormon empire (on today's Utah–Arizona border). Life for the colonists was arduous: little or no rain fell; and when it did come it ran off the red cliffs in torrents, washing out irrigation systems along with what hope the pioneers had. The colony was hovering on the verge of collapse when Brigham Young came to the rescue with tithing money for two seminal public works projects, the tabernacle and the temple.[14]

Talk of the tabernacle began as early as 1862, though work did not get under way until 1863 and the building was not dedicated until 1876. Its design came directly from Salt Lake City. Early on, after Brigham Young announced his intention to build a tabernacle in St. George, the local leader, Erastus Snow, wrote the president, saying, "We would like your suggestions on the size and style of the Meeting House, as well as the material you would chose." Snow went further: "But we have not determined whether to adopt a flat ceiling; a full arch, like [the] Salt Lake City Tabernacle; an arch through

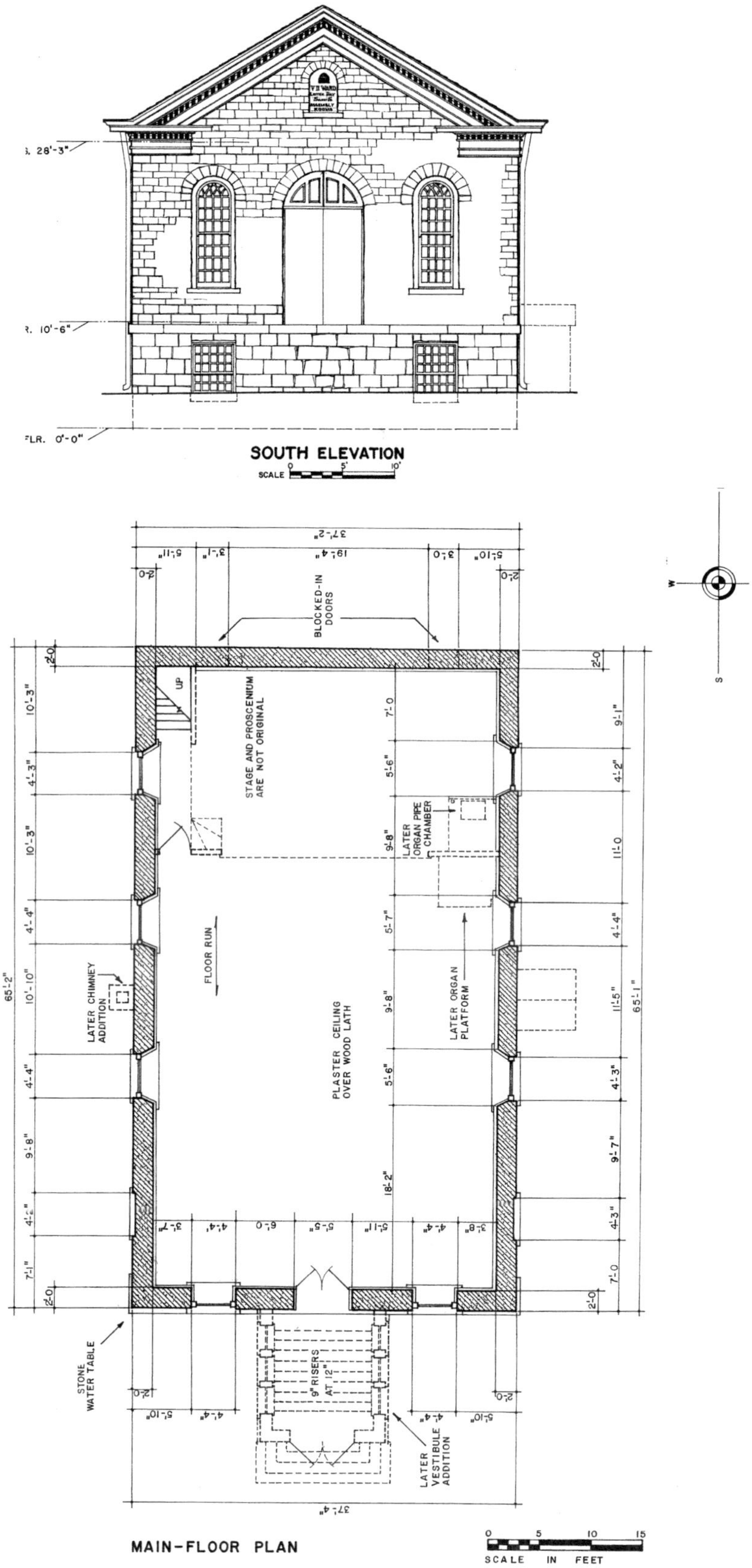

Figure 7.5. Seventh Ward Meetinghouse, south elevation and main-floor plan, 116 West 500 South, Salt Lake City, 1862–77. Historic American Buildings Survey, HABS U-22, 1967.

the center, and the building to have galleries after the old Gentile style; a circular building having a dome; or some other style."[15]

Snow's epistle elicited no immediate response, but when the president came south the following spring he informed the Dixie-ites that their building should be "100 ft. by 50 ft., with a spire 150 ft. high; and that one end of the building be so constructed that when it shall be deemed necessary the house may be conveniently enlarged."[16] Work began in June, though Snow wrote requesting additional clarification for the tower and "whether it should rest upon the walls of an outer court cut off from the main building, or added to it on the end" and asking "if you feel so inclined we would like you to send us a working draft [drawing] of your intention]."[17] Young appointed architect William Folsom to draft a plan (the tower would be placed on the end) and installed St. George resident Miles Romney as chief carpenter. Initial progress on the building was impeded by a lack of food for the workers, but by 1868 tithing support from outside increased and the project began to move forward until completion in 1876 (Figure 7.6).[18]

The St. George Tabernacle, with its tower and "spire," marks a significant turning point in LDS meetinghouse architecture. With it, Young effectively abandoned the biblical prototype he had used in the Salt Lake City

Figure 7.6. The St. George Tabernacle, 1863–1876, as it appeared in 1978.

tabernacles in favor of a more conservative approach.[19] The St. George Tabernacle was the first to connect the group stylistically to the religious mainstream, an opening move in what would, in terms of meetinghouse design, be a strategic return to conventional practice. It was also the first large public works project outside Salt Lake City, a demonstration of the LDS First Presidency's willingness to step in and actively manage the regional economy. And finally it served as yet another sign of the City of Zion's growing bifurcation. As we saw in chapter 6, by the late 1860s and early 1870s the City of Zion landscape was beginning its makeover from an architecturally all-inclusive and homogeneous sacrality to one that was discontinuous and differentiated. Whereas before the entire landscape (including the meetinghouses) was considered sacred, now only specifically designated points within it (the temples) enjoyed that status. Desacralized, meetinghouses were free to assume more normative shapes, the towered church a clearly recognizable place of worship set among the everyday clutter of the now secular town.

The architectural changes taking place in St. George resonated throughout the Mormon region and were particularly evident in the Sanpete Valley. Typologically, the change in meetinghouse architecture can be described as the move from true meetinghouses (transverse axis plan), to meeting halls (gable front with aisled plans), to churches (towered boxes with aisled plans). The Saints called all three meetinghouses or later, when they got larger, tabernacles, but the point here is that even if the name remained the same, the buildings themselves changed markedly. This shift in architectural style has rarely been noticed, but it reveals deeper transformations within LDS culture and figures prominently in the argument advanced in this book.

Meetinghouses

As Sanpete towns sprang up, so did spaces for worship. At first, meetings took place in small multipurpose buildings, hastily constructed of log and adobe. On a visit to Manti in August 1850, a church scribe noted: "Pres. B Young and party attended a picnic party or feast, in the school house in the Sanpete fort, a sawed log building twenty by twenty six feet built for school purposes and public worship."[20] In Fountain Green the first meetinghouse was just that, a "genuine pioneer cabin, with a fire place in the south end, the walls measuring 7 feet to the square, and the house covered [roofed] with clap boards and dirt."[21] The one in Moroni was similarly of log and "use[d] for the treble purpose of dancing, theatre, and meetings."[22] The settlers in Mount Pleasant in 1860 built a "log house, for meeting and school purposes," and a bowery "100 by 80 [feet], well put up and fenced around with willows and poles, leaving entrances by gates."[23]

Ephraim's first meetinghouse offers a useful portrait of one early impermanent structure that provided space not only for worship but also for public meetings and other kinds of community activities. The following description comes from the diary of Amanda B. Cox, a daughter of patriarch Orville Sutherland Cox: "One of the first buildings [constructed inside Fort Ephraim] was that of a church and school-house combined. This was built by the brethren uniting, some digging the post-holes, some going after the posts and others making the adobes. The house was made by putting cedar posts in the ground with forked tops to hold the poles used as rafters. The adobes were built in between the posts making the walls for the house. The roof was covered with dirt. This house was used for all meetings, religious and political, and for school" (Figure 7.7).[24] To the side of Ephraim's little meetinghouse also was "a commodious bowery . . . used for public meetings in the summer months."[25]

Historians like to call these early meetinghouses "impermanent" to indicate that the settlers considered them only temporary solutions to their congregational needs, but the word took on a special meaning for the citizens of Moroni, who had built in the early 1860s a "respectable adobe building." During a "heavy rain which occurred on a certain night about three years later, the dirt roof was soaked through and the house tumbled down. When the people got up in the morning they wondered what had become of their meetinghouse which, however, after due search was found in the shape of a huge mud pie with some pieces of timber sticking up through it."[26] Hastily

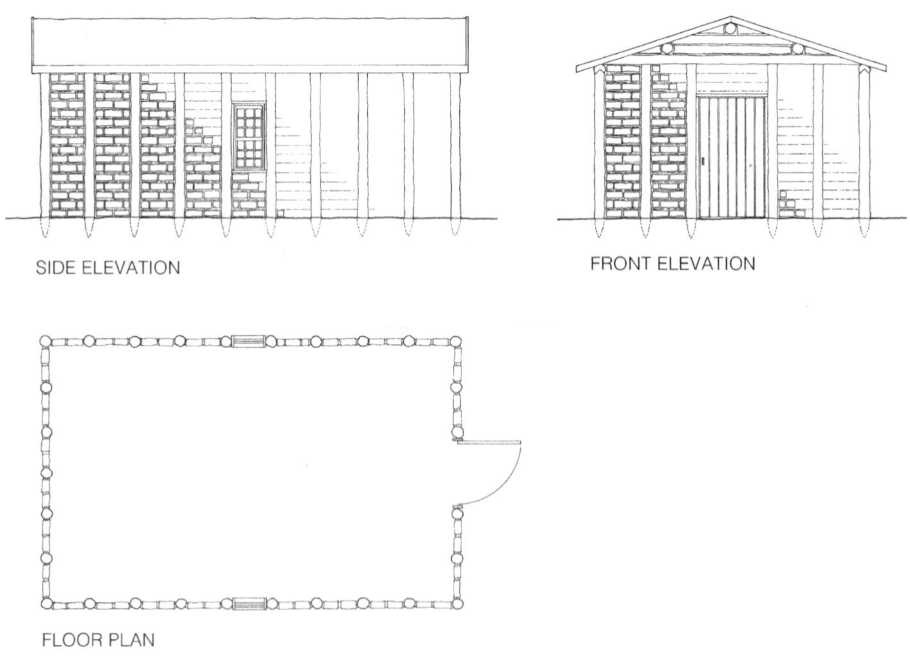

Figure 7.7. Reconstruction drawing of the first meetinghouse at Fort Ephraim, possibly late 1850s. The building consists of earthfast vertical studs infilled with adobe brick.

built brush-covered boweries also had their drawbacks. From the pages of the *Deseret News* came this: "The congregation assembled in the meetinghouse, the bowery being unfit to meet in, in consequence of the rain that had fallen."[27]

The most substantial of the early meetinghouses was the Council House in Manti. Plans were under way for the building as early as 1850, and the intention from the outset was for it to accommodate public meetings, worship, theatrical productions, and dances. Local church leaders met in the fall of that year "for the purpose of taking in consideration the best plan to be adopted in laying up or building the walls of the Council House." It was decided that nine hundred dollars [of church tithing funds] should be set aside for building the "walls of the Council House," which originally went up in what is the northern sector of town, on a site near the quarry hill.[28] A traveler with Brigham Young in November 1851 recounted that "this settlement was begun late in the fall of 1849 and has a large two story council house built of limestone."[29] Several years later, when the building was damaged by lightning, the brethren dismantled what was left, including the building stone plus the doors and windows, and hauled it to a site on what at the time was called the "Temple Block," in the center of town. Here it was re-erected. Rebuilding the Council House took place between 1855 and 1857. In February 1855, Christian Munk, a Danish carpenter, wrote: "We began work on the house which was erected for labor tithing and I worked 16 days on that building."[30] By November 1856, however, the building was still unfinished, since ward minutes mention that it still needed a stove and window glass.[31]

The Council House was demolished in 1920 (to make way for a Carnegie library), but from contemporary descriptions, oral histories, and one extant photo it is possible to reconstruct with some accuracy its appearance and plan (Figure 7.8). It was literally a big (forty-by-eighteen-foot) house that faced east, with its long side running parallel to the street, like most of the houses in town. Two stories high, it was constructed of the local oolite limestone and had large undivided rooms on both levels. The upstairs room, used mainly for dances, private gatherings, and performances, was accessed through an outside staircase. The downstairs room became home to both the city council and Sunday services. The rostrum, including a speaker's stand and benches for the bishop and other church officials, stood on the west wall, directly opposite the east front door. The house-like appearance and transverse plan are unusual in Mormon settlements but are not without precedent.

The Manti Council House is a good western example of a traditional New England meetinghouse, one that had passed from currency in the Northeast by the 1760s though still represented by many older buildings still standing throughout the region. Manti's leading citizens were New Englanders themselves and undoubtedly knew such buildings from their earlier lives. In

Figure 7.8. Reconstruction drawing of the east elevation, the second-floor plan, and the first-floor plan of the Council House, Temple Block, Manti, 1851; rebuilt 1855–57.

EAST ELEVATION

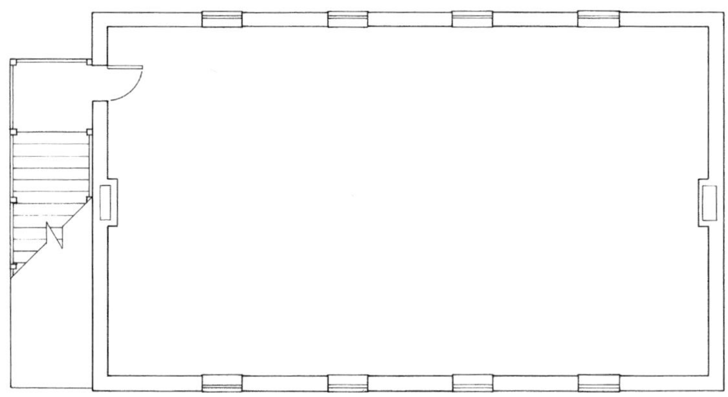

SECOND-FLOOR PLAN

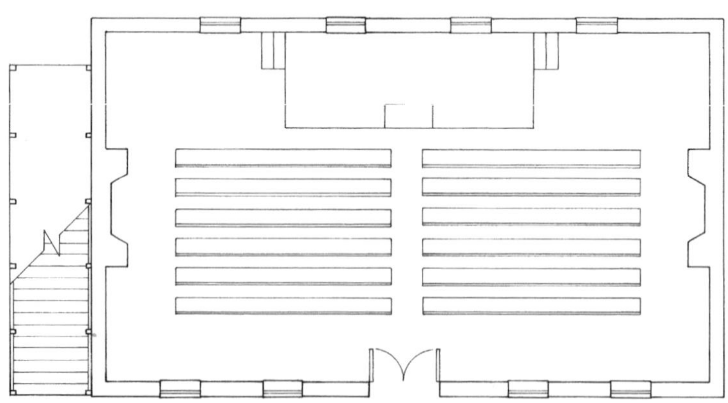

FIRST-FLOOR PLAN

searching for a workable meetinghouse design, they simply settled on this anachronistic form. The transverse plan had been used for several meetinghouses on the trek west, for the Old Tabernacle on Temple Square, and in other colonies, such as Parowan in south-central Utah (Figure 7.9).[32]

Nearly every group in town used the Council House. In 1857 Peter Olsen Hansen wrote: "The Sanpete Scientific Literary Society met at my residents *[sic]*," but the next session was "to meet again 2 weeks from [this] date [in] the upper room of the Council House."[33] George Peacock mentions in 1864 that there were "vocal and instrumental concerts at Council House."[34] The town's Thespian Society in 1860 performed *All Is Not Gold That Glitters* and *Kiss in the Dark*.[35] On January 31, 1860, a Mr. Graves of the Provo Agricultural Society delivered a "lecture in the Council House on Agriculture Home Manufacture."[36] Also, the omnipresent Jens Weibye noted that he "attended a Party upstairs in the council house, where I and family were, with about 50 No. more, and we rejoiced together."[37] Again from Weibye's daybook from

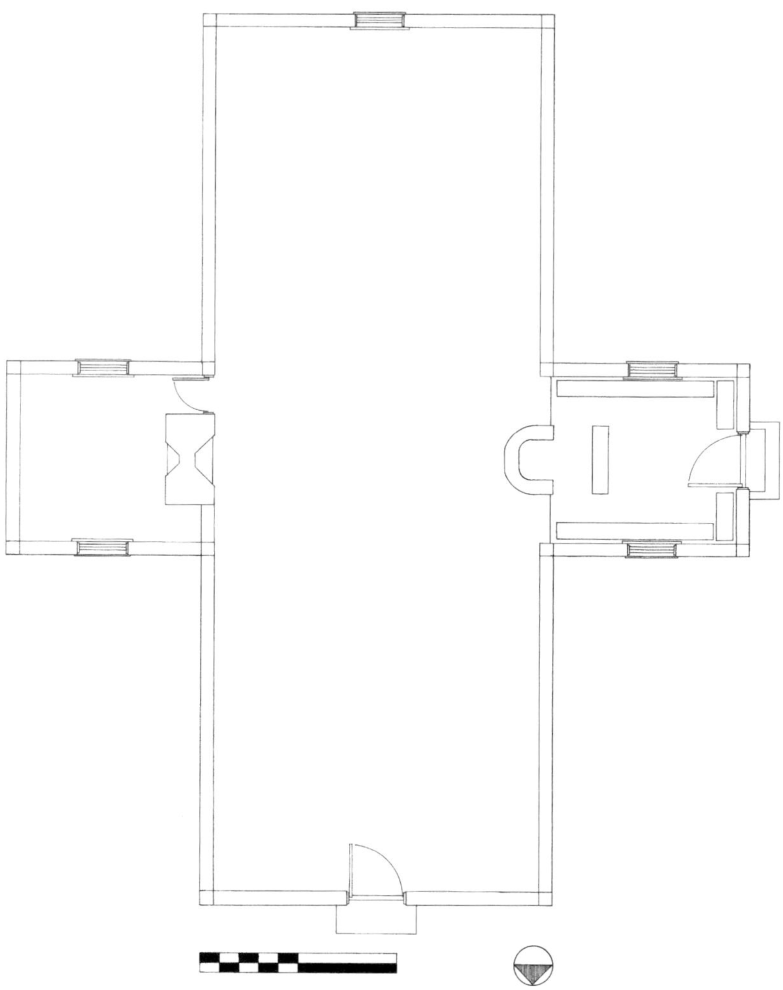

Figure 7.9. Transverse-plan meetinghouse, Parowan, Utah, circa 1860s (after Alan Barnett).

New Year's Eve of 1876: "Bp Maiben invited the Saints of Manti to meet in the Council House, we met here and had Musik by the Brass Band, Sing Choir, and Sunday Schoole Choir."[38]

Built as a public works project with tithing funds, the Council House served as the main religious building in Manti for more than twenty-five years. The design was never repeated in the valley. Instead, another and more pervasive one took hold and became the dominant form during the next phase of meetinghouse development.

Meeting Halls

Meetinghouse construction continued as the Sanpete towns grew. During the 1850s and 1860s, the trend in Mormon meetinghouse design was toward the "meeting hall." These buildings were gable-front rectangles with double-aisle "church" plans where the door faced the pulpit along the narrow dimension of the building. The gables, sometimes pedimented but most often left plain, gave the meetinghouses a look very much like early commercial and public buildings. The motivation for these rather severe and stylistically undifferentiated buildings may have come from Salt Lake City, where, as we have seen, the original tabernacle and ward meetinghouses were built in this manner. The attempt with these meeting hall–type meetinghouses may have been to strike a posture of cultural difference—to adopt a building for the Mormons that did not clearly belong in the church category.

The meeting hall design was used for all the earliest permanent meetinghouses, beginning in the 1860s. Ephraim had one of the first. Construction began in the spring of 1859, and by November 1860 the building was finished enough for Brigham Young, on one of his visits, to speak in it. A newspaper at the time reported that the president, "accompanied by many from Manti, returned to Fort Ephraim where a large stone meeting house, 60 and 44 feet, had been enclosed and the floor laid. This was the only meeting house south of Provo which comfortably convened those who were eager to hear and see the Presidency of the Church."[39] The building stood in the center of town on the main street and was fully operational in 1864.

In Spring City a small log meetinghouse had been erected after resettlement in 1859, which also served as a schoolhouse and dance hall. This building gave way in 1863–64 to a larger one made of adobe, with Henning Olsen, a Dane, as superintendent of construction (Figure 7.10).[40] Measuring thirty by fifty feet, the Spring City meetinghouse was located on Main Street and faced east. It had two large doors placed in the center of the front wall that opened onto one large room. There was a double-aisle plan with a rostrum on the west end that contained the pulpit and chairs for church officials.

The Fairview meetinghouse was similar to Spring City's except that it was stone and took longer to build (Figure 7.11); the work started in 1862 but finished with some difficulty about ten years later. The original intention was to have the building constructed with nontithed donated labor. Yet in the summer of 1862, when Bishop James Jones called on the people to turn out "to work on the meetinghouse,"[41] his call appears to have fallen on deaf ears, for no mention is made of the project in the Ward Minutes until nearly half a year later, when early in 1863 he felt compelled to speak again "on the business of the meeting house" to show "the importance of having the work pushed ahead."[42] His lecture worked this time, and in April of that year ward minutes report "brother [Price] is now about ready to commence laying rocks and raise the walls."[43] But then construction slowed, and at a June meeting the bishop again "spoke about the meeting house and said he had made up his mind to quit work on the house until the people got the spirit of building,

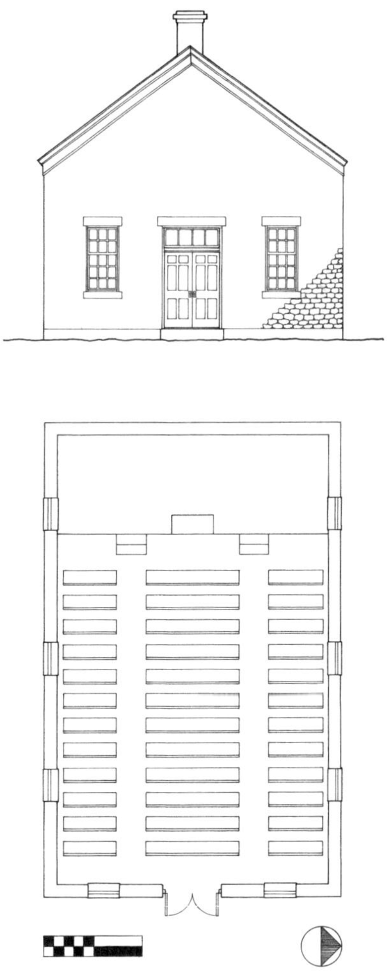

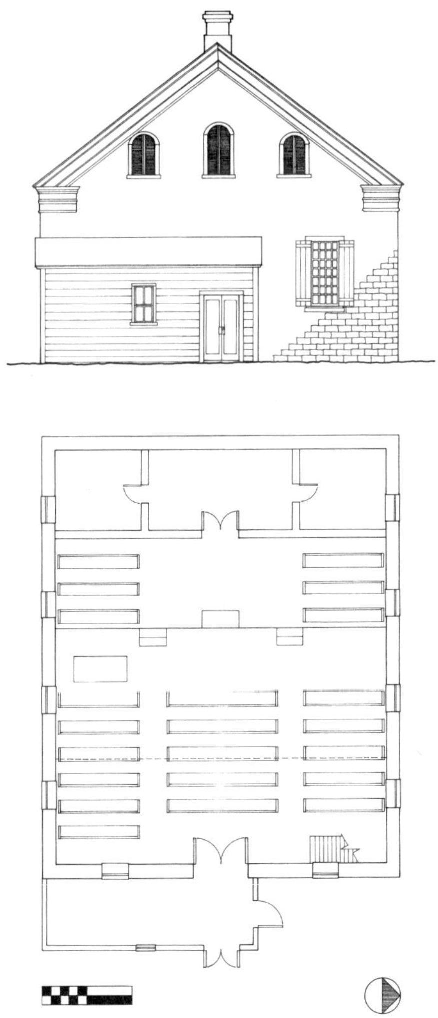

Figure 7.10 ***(left).*** Reconstruction drawing of the east elevation and plan of the Spring City Meetinghouse, 1863–64 (drawing by Craig Paulsen and James Gosney).

Figure 7.11 ***(right).*** Reconstruction drawing of the east elevation and plan of the Fairview Meetinghouse, 1862–72. The wooden vestibule is an addition, probably from the 1880s.

and said the walls might just as well had been up now if the right interest had been manifested."[44]

The problem in getting the people out to work may have resided with Jones; for several years there had been dissension in Fairview over what some felt was the bishop's unfair distribution of land (to family and friends).[45] Yet clearly other obstacles were present, not the least of which was apathy. Apostle Orson Hyde, as the highest-ranking church official in the valley, was called from his home in Spring City to help stir up interest, and his exhortations are revealing. Hyde's principal argument for getting the meetinghouse completed was delivered in a meeting on June 18, 1863. It may surprise some that Hyde played not to their spiritual devotion but to their pocketbooks and fears concerning blessings, saying first that "its [the meetinghouse's] erection will increase the value of property in general,"[46] and a few months later, "build your Meetinghouse, and you shall not want for bread, nor your children cry for it in times of famin."[47] The economics of the deal apparently made some sense, and when Hyde returned in March 1864 he could say that "he felt pleased to see the people here had made a start toward building a new meetinghouse, [for he] said, the rich would come here and the building of such a house would increase the value of real estate here more than the cost of the house would be."[48]

One potential distraction was removed when Jones resigned as bishop, but still the meetinghouse languished. His replacement, Andrew Petersen, announced an intention to "finish the new meeting house," but he too ran into problems. One involved the need to pay skilled laborers for their time, and late in 1865 Bishop Petersen received authorization from Brigham Young to "use tithing labor on the completing [of the] Meeting House."[49] This tactic worked, though not immediately, for it took Petersen another seven years, until June 1872, to get the job done. One Fairview resident, Amasa Tucker, wrote the church newspaper in Salt Lake City to say that the building "is the best house for public worship in the county; and has been completed under [as] unfavorable circumstances as any house [of its kind] in the Territory."[50] Tucker referred to ongoing trouble with the local Sanpitch Indians, but they were probably only one of the problems.

A similar fate befell the people of Mount Pleasant, who built two hall-type meetinghouses in the pioneer period. The first has already been introduced, a small adobe building called the "social hall," which was completed without delay with the help of tithed labor in the winter of 1862 and considered a "priliminary meeting house."[51] A year later Brigham Young visited and suggested a new meetinghouse of sufficient size for the expanding community. In a letter dated July 1863, Young told local bishop William Seely not only that it would be appropriate to use labor tithing for road building but also that "you are also at liberty to use labor tithing in building a meeting house in your place, to be say 35 x 50 feet in the clear, and some 20 to 22 feet between joists."[52]

Young's offer was ignored until late 1864, when local leaders decided that a new meetinghouse should be built and that the "work be contracted to one man who has to finish the house till the turn of the key."[53] Not to be hasty, however, they waited until January the following year to again declare their intention to erect a meetinghouse, resolving that it would be built of "dobies," its cost would be covered by a "poll tax of 10 dollars for all over 18 years old," the "dollars and c[ents were] to be Tithing dollars," and whatever remaining money was needed would be added "by Taxes (on property)."[54] This time a committee was given responsibility for supervising the project, and a month later a contract was let to two men, James Hansen and Ole Rosenlof, "for the sume of 14000 dollars to be complete by May 1,1866."[55] Apostle and chief real estate appraiser Orson Hyde visited Mount Pleasant and said "he was glad that [the town] had advanced so far with our meetinghouse as to have the contract made, it would not only be for our benefit in spiritual things but it would raise the value of the property more than would cost its erection." Almost as an afterthought, Hyde added that he "would like to see the surrounding block planted with ornamental trees."[56]

Work commenced. The foundation and part of the walls were laid, but in July 1865 Young visited the settlement and declared the building "to[o] small." The president wanted the plan changed and "enlargened," so construction halted and the building, such as it was, stood unattended for several years.[57] By 1869, however, they were back at it. "After some consideration," the ward minutes say, "it was determined to build [the meetinghouse] on the foundation which was built for the purpose of a meeting house a few years ago." The building, contrary it seems to Young's desires, was finished as originally planned.

Dedicated in the fall of 1871, the Mount Pleasant meetinghouse resembled both the Fairview and Spring City buildings (Figure 7.12). It was composed of a single rectangular hall, 42 x 60 feet, with three windows on each side and two windows flanking a doorway on the principal west elevation. A full triangular pediment graced both gable ends of the building. The double-aisle plan was supplemented later in the century by a gallery that stood on the west end; a stairway leading up to it was located just to the left as one entered. The bell tower is not original to the building, but was in place by 1892. The tower may have come in response to the popularity of a new type of meetinghouse that was becoming increasingly popular in the valley during the 1870s.

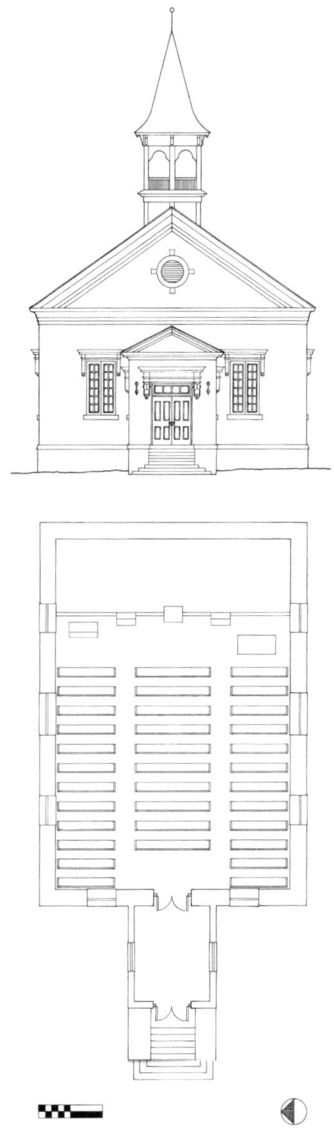

Figure 7.12. Reconstruction drawing of the west elevation and plan of the Mount Pleasant Meetinghouse, 1864–71. The cupola dates from around 1892. Drawing by Alan Barnett and James Gosney.

Churches

The final phase in the history of the nineteenth-century Sanpete meetinghouse began in the 1870s with the construction of a new building in Ephraim. The city did not actually need a new meetinghouse (it had a bowery and a rock meeting hall), but depressed economic circumstances dictated a stimulus package in the form of a substantial public works project. Through the late 1850s and 1860s, grasshopper infestations devastated the Sanpete countryside, with Ephraim being especially hard hit. Peter Madsen wrote, "We had to [sell] Oxens, wagons, clothings, for to get wheat both for bread and seed for next year."[58] As for meetinghouse construction, it seems there was nothing better to do, as Carl Dorius explained in a letter to the *Deseret News* in June 1870: "Here in Ephraim the [grass]hoppers have pretty much relieved us from our usually busy harvest work, but we are determined to have something to do any how. The plan devised by our wise and enterprising bishop [Canute Peterson] is this: the people of Ephraim are going to tear down their old meeting house and build a more substantial one in its place, thus giving employment to the poor, and beautifying the city by this and other public and private improvements recommended."[59]

The tithing-financed stimulus work started quickly. By April 1871, Dorius reported to the paper that "the work on our meeting house is progressing and in a few weeks the walls will be ready for the carpenters to put the roof on."[60] More than a year and a half later, in November 1872, the building was indeed "put under roof" but "as yet it was not finished . . . to such an extent that meetings could be held in it."[61] By 1874, however, it was pronounced complete at a cost of about thirteen thousand dollars. Still, as one contributor in the *Deseret News* observed, the steeple was "not yet erected" (it never really was), the "interior is not yet finished," and the "gallery, supported by suitable pillars, and surrounding the interior, is in [the] course of erection."[62] As late as 1881, Carl Dorius could write that "our meeting house was nearly finished inside, and we were given much praise for the labour." This was eleven years after the building was started.

Like the St. George Tabernacle, the new Ephraim Meetinghouse (later after the town was divided into two wards in 1877 it would be called by most a tabernacle) was noteworthy for its departure from the meeting hall style. The architect was Edward Jones, an immigrant convert from Wales who is listed in the 1870 census as a "surveyor."[63] In architectural matters, Jones may have had assistance from Salt Lake City. In an August 30, 1870, letter to the *Deseret News,* A. M. Musser pointed out: "Bishop C. Peterson, from Ephraim, brought with him [to Nephi] for the inspection and criticism of our master builder, Prest. Young, the projection on paper, of a fine sandstone [actually limestone] meeting house they propose to immediately erect at [Ephraim]."[64] Musser did not say whether Young simply approved Jones's plan, suggested improvements, or substituted his own. Whatever happened, Peterson returned to Ephraim ready to commence work on what would be the second church-type meetinghouse built in Zion (Figure 7.13).

Measuring forty-five by eighty-five feet, the Ephraim Tabernacle retained the basic rectangular shape and the double-aisled plan of its predecessor, but it also had several new features. One was the tower at the east end. A cupola with spire was planned, but left unbuilt until the early twentieth century. The tower clearly identified the building as religious space—a church—and the multifunctional quality of the older buildings to a great extent ended. Activities other than Sunday service took place, but no theater productions or dances were held here. Other aspects of the Ephraim building deserve mention. Notable are its Greek cornice returns, compass transoms, semicircular tower arch, and pronounced quoins. On the inside, double aisles lead to the sacrament table and elevated rostrum with its symmetrical pulpit, seats for ward leaders and featured speakers, and choir. A large mural by C. C. A. Christensen, an accomplished local painter, depicts Joseph Smith's First Vision (Figure 7.14).[65]

Perhaps the most interesting feature of the Ephraim building was its ambiguous orientation. On one hand, there was the towered east elevation that contained the main door. People entered through a set of double doors, moved through a vestibule into the nave, and filed to their seats via one of the two aisles. And on the other hand, there were prominent doors located on both south and north sides that opened onto a transverse cross aisle, which divided the building in half sideways. Oral history informants maintain that these side doors, although providing easy access to the interior, were opened only for special occasions, mainly funerals when the casket was placed in the large open aisle.[66] The arrangement, however, was not without antecedents. Such buildings are found throughout New England, where they are considered an important transitional stage in the evolution there during the eighteenth century from transverse-axis meetinghouses to aisled-nave towered churches (Figure 7.15). As with many innovations, the introduction of the pandenominational church type was met with uneven enthusiasm. More conservative congregations held on to the old idea, the side-door meetinghouse, while at the same time adopting the new towered church form, combining the two into a single form much like the Saints did in Ephraim.[67] Certainly Young and other LDS Church leaders had knowledge of these buildings and may have suggested the design. Or Jones could have come up with it on his

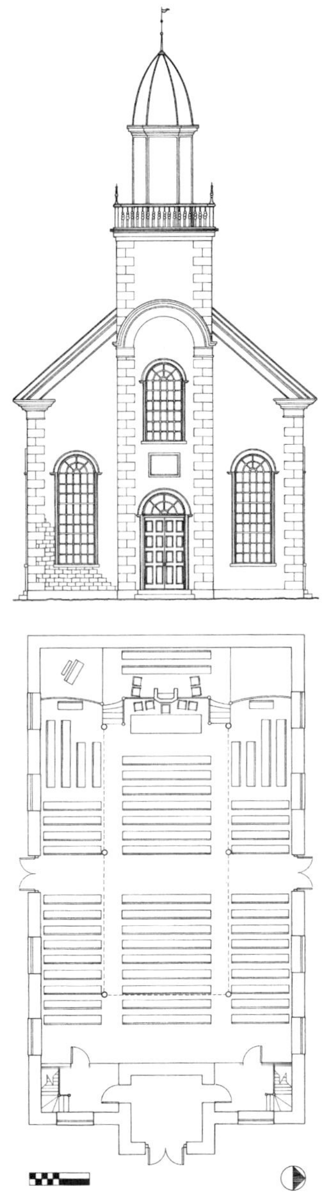

Figure 7.13. Reconstruction drawing of the east elevation and plan of the Ephraim Tabernacle, 1870–81. The building was demolished in the 1950s.

Figure 7.14. A photograph of the Ephraim Tabernacle's interior from around 1890, showing the sacrament table, raised speakers' platform, and pulpit. The "First Vision" painting behind the rostrum was by C. C. A. Christensen, a Danish immigrant and one of the most accomplished of Utah's early artists. Reprinted by permission of Utah State Historical Society; all rights reserved.

Figure 7.15. The combination meetinghouse/church type in New England: Congregational Church, Wethersfield, Connecticut, 1761–64. Note the presence of both front and side entrance doors. Photograph courtesy of Robert Blair St. George.

own, since the Ephraim meetinghouse, along with those built subsequently in Manti and Moroni, are the only examples of this specific meetinghouse design in the Mormon region.[68]

In Manti, the Council House, also called the meetinghouse, continued in use. In 1875, Jens Weibye observed that the people decided to "rebuild the old meetinghouse," work that was completed by the end of the year; Weibye noted: "I and family attended the first Complimentary dance in our Old Meetinghouse, after it is now repaired." The building still served multiple purposes; Weibye recorded that he attended a theater performance here, "the first play this season."[69] That the town was outgrowing the Council House, however, is evident in Weibye's statement from late January 1876: "We commenced to have Sunday School upstairs in the Meetinghouse, as well as below, because there is so many Children now attends Sunday School, also Many Big Boys."[70]

Plans had been under way for a new and more legitimate meetinghouse ever since the early 1860s. In Manti, work on the building proceeded, predictably, in fits and starts, a record of futility set down in the journal of Hans Jensen Hals. In 1862, he noted, "we dug several hundred loads of Stone and drove to the temple block, for a new tabernacle, which was to stand right in front of my house, but the work was discontinued"; 1869: "Brother [Orson] Hyde permitted the beginning of a new meeting house here in town"; 1870: "just a little work was done on the meeting house"; 1873: "after brother O Hyde's counsel we began to build a new meeting house"; 1877: "we began again to work on our new meeting house in the spring"; 1881: "we built the tabernacle, plastered, put in doors and windows[,] did carpentry work"; and finally, 1882: began our "meetings in the tabernacle New Year's Eve, and were happy to get the tabernacle completed enough so that we could get use out of it. We saw the necessity of having our house built."[71]

Hals's broken-record narrative echoes throughout the journals of other Manti residents. George Peacock, for instance, mentioned meeting in the bowery in July 1865, and that several days later, when it rained, a meeting presided over by Brigham Young was held in the "Council House."[72] Then in December 1869, he wrote that in Manti they "commenced labor on the new meeting house."[73] Again, from Peacock's diary on September 13, 1870: "The corner stones of a new meeting house laid. Ceremonies conducted by O. Hyde."[74] Eventually, the new meetinghouse was finished, but one wonders what happened to get people serious about its completion.

The turning point seems to have come, remarkably, late in 1875. Orson Hyde, on January 31 of that year, preached in the Council House and counseled the Saints "to build eather a new Meetinghouse or hall to meet in that will hold the People [of the town]."[75] His remarks prompted a "mass meeting of the Brethren held for the porpose of Building a House, after council of Prs. Hyde."[76] Here "it was resolved," the indefatigable Jens Weibye wrote, "to build a Meeting-house; and to build it in the Southeast corner of the Temple-block, after Prs. B. Youngs wish many years ago."[77] The old committee was fired and a new set of directors installed, with Henry Parson named supervisor of construction. Weibye was appointed clerk amid this initial burst of energy. The brethren started digging the foundation immediately, on February 8, 1875, and the work advanced rapidly at first, so much so that the foundation was in by March 8, when the cornerstones "above the ground" could be laid. To inspire the workers further, on April 25, "in the afternoon Meeting it was agreed to level a Tax of 2 percent upon the People of Manti to help to build our new Meetinghouse, 1/3 to be paid June 1, second third to be paid Sept 1st and last third to be paid Novbr 1 1875."[78]

Despite the tax levy (which may or may not have been collected), work again faltered. The building committee attempted to get things moving: early in 1876, Bishop J. B. Maiben called a mass meeting, telling the Saints that since they had agreed in a former meeting "to build a new Tabernacle on Freewill Distribution according to means," they should proceed.[79] The bishop's sentiments were seconded by the leading men in town, but it would be six months before the committee would meet again, and by then there was a need to obtain "subscriptions to liquidate the amt of indebtedness" incurred on various building projects, including the meetinghouse.[80]

Early in 1877, yet another committee for the "new Tabernacle" was appointed, and its members solemnly resolved that "the Latter day Saints in Manti City will make Voluntary donations in proportion to their means and ability" and that the newly appointed "Executive Committee [will] have the power to Collect and appropriate the Voluntary donations of the Latter day Saints in Manti toward the Erection of a new Tabernacle, and make the requisite contracts and transact all business necessary thereto until the completion of the Same."[81] Bishop Maiben was appointed general superintendent, Richard Hall head mason, Henry Parson to oversee the carpenters, Hans Jensen to procure lime, James Crawford to manage the quarrying and supply of rocks, Luther Tuttle to obtain all necessary lumber, and Maiben, Crawford, and William Andersen to provide oversight on payment of wages. Donations were crucial to the success of the project, since the committee realized it would have to pay skilled craftsmen for their time—Hall wanted $2.50 a day, assistant mason Christian Berntsen $2.00, with the wage subcommittee appointed specially to "make agreement . . . about their prices."[82]

The Manti meetinghouse (after 1877 usually called the tabernacle) is remarkably similar to the one in Ephraim (Figure 7.16). Some of the details differ—it is generally Gothic rather than Greek, and has pointed instead of compass tracery in its round-arch openings, projecting gabled pavilions on the sides, and a circular window in the tower—but the plan, with its side door and cross-aisle configuration, is for all intents and purposes the same (Figure 7.17). The connection between the two buildings remains a mystery. In Manti the architect apparently was William K. Barton, a man of many talents—though architecture does not appear to have been one of them. In the 1860 census he is listed as a "distiller" of whiskey, and in 1870, a "house painter." By 1880, he has become a "farmer" with a wife and eleven children. His role in the building's design, however, is revealed in the February 1877 building committee minutes: some of the brethren "spoke in favor of building the Tabernacle as best we can, without cutting the corner Stones, but afterwards Plaster it, or put a hard finish on it, the main thing is to have a Tabernacle where [we] can meet from time to time."[83] The discussion continued: "James Crawford and Jens Hansen said that there [is] great apposition to the costly cut corners for our Tabernacle, that Wm. K. Barton has proposed on the Tabernacle draft [plan]."[84] William Andersen agreed, saying, "It would

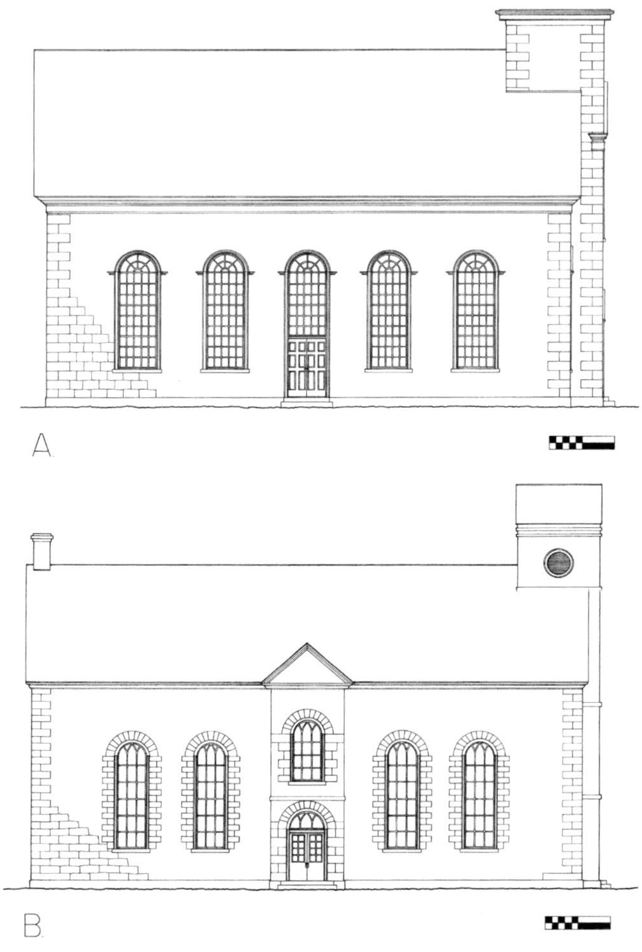

Figure 7.16 ***(left).*** The south elevations of (A) Ephraim and (B) Manti Tabernacles.

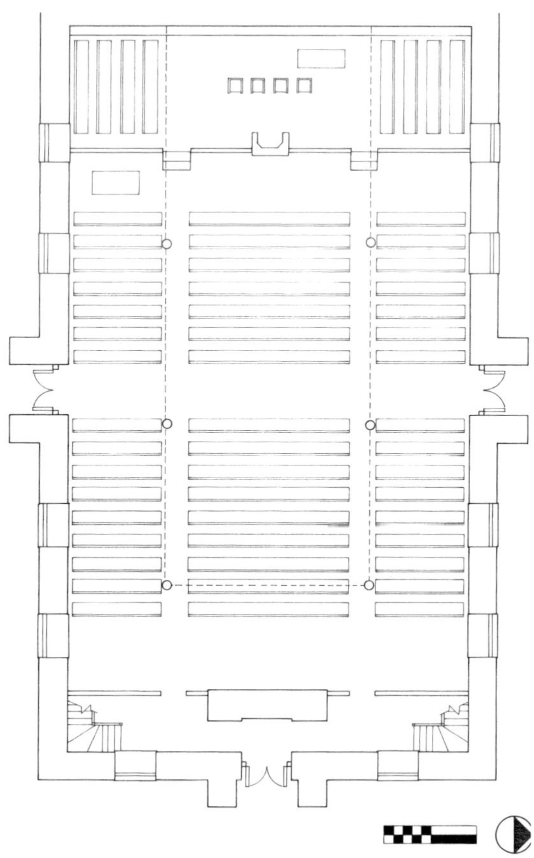

Figure 7.17 ***(right).*** Original ground-level floor plan of the Manti Tabernacle.

be well to put up our new Tabernacle rough and then plaster it." Barton defended his plan, maintaining he was "in favor [of] having nice cut corners." In the end a compromise was reached: "It was desided to put up the Corners after [Barton's] proposed plan, corse the east front, but not corse the sides and West end, all united."[85] Barton in this instance prevailed.

Many have speculated that temple architect William Folsom contributed to the tabernacle design. This does not seem the case. Folsom did not arrive in Manti to begin his work on the temple until 1878, and during a building committee meeting that year he stood up to speak in "favor of [the] new Tabernacle," adding that "he him self would do some for it, he could see the necessity of us having a larger House to hold our meetings in, [than] what we have at the present."[86] What he contributed is difficult to know, though we do know that Barton's original design had been submitted prior to Folsom's involvement. Since it looked so much like the one in Ephraim, there is a possibility that the untrained Barton could have copied Edward Jones's earlier plan. It is hard to say. In April 1877, building committee members Andrew Maiben, Henry Parson, and Hans Jensen journeyed north to get dry lumber and "see [the] Ephraim Meetinghouse Gallerie, and see how large it is."[87] What else they learned, and how many other trips they (and Barton for that matter) made, remains an intriguing though here unanswerable question. Clearly, given the parallels between the two buildings, there was some connection.

With the design in place, the Manti Saints appeared serious about finally getting the building under way. They cleared the "Temple Block of the new Tabernacle" of an old "halfbuilt house," which stood on the northwest corner, and got wood for the limekiln, tools for the masons, dry lumber for the window frames, and even passed a motion to "get a Boy from each Ward to learn Stone-cutting."[88] They also bribed a mason to relocate from his home in Ephraim, voting to bring "Bro. Morten Axelsen" to serve as chief mason Richard Hall's assistant. The arrangement with Axelsen is interesting: "John Crawford and Jens Hansen was elected a Committee to see Father Saml Mackey and try to get a City Lot of him as donation for our Tabernacle and let Bro. Morten Axelsen have that in pay for Laboring on our Tabernacle."[89] Mackey agreed but wanted one hundred dollars for the lot, although the committee had set a price of seventy-five dollars for Axelsen's labor. In the end, the mason accepted the lesser amount but did get the committee to throw in a stove for his new house.[90] It was not long before Hall, Axelsen, and another assistant, Christian Berntsen, got scaffolding up "both inside and out" and the stone walls began to rise. By May 1877 Weibye could report that "two Westry [Vestry] Doorframes is sat, in the West End of the [building]."[91]

Donations started to come in. William Maylett gave a cow (valued at eighteen dollars) to pay for Jens Jensen's labor as tender to the masons, and when a lull occurred, businessman Luther Tuttle paid "$10 to the Tabernacle for to keep it [the building] going."[92] With temple construction commencing, competition for limited labor and resources was acute; for instance, the teams and wagons needed to haul rock from the quarry were unavailable, being engaged at the temple site. The committee found itself looking for men to replace their own workers who had been called for temple duty, noting the need to secure a man "to labor on the Temple for [carpenter] H. Parsons, when he Labor on the Tabernacle."[93] Doing everything possible to keep the work going, the committee even made arrangements in the summer of 1877 to make sure that mason Hall's and Berntsen's "Hay and Grain is cut and hauled in time," so these men can work full-time on the tabernacle.[94]

The situation deteriorated to the point that Manti's leaders had to decide if they could continue the meetinghouse at all. At a mass meeting of the Priesthood in March 1878, South Ward Bishop Hans Jensen said he "wanted the Temple built and also the Tabernacle because we need it, and we need some better regulation in regard to building it." North Ward Bishop William T. Reid supported Jensen, saying he too wanted "to continue to build our new Tabernacle." After the speeches, Bishop Jensen motioned that "we amidiatly take hold of the building of our new Tabernacle, all United about the motion." President Maiben then motioned that the bishops of the two wards and their counselors "call upon the Saints in their Wards for a donation for the Tabernacle, eather in cash, Grain, or Labor, also other kind what will be useful."[95] The spirit was there, but not the action, causing Maiben to raise the same questions in September, when he pointedly asked the Saints "if they want to continue to build our new Tabernacle."[96] The answer was yes, but troubles continued about getting enough rafters (they had lumber enough for 80 and needed 240) and rock (twenty loads were ready at the quarry but no one was available to haul them).

Through 1878 and early 1879 most of the committee's time and energy were directed toward fund-raising; they still made progress, albeit slowly. Perhaps as a show of support, the "Manti Brass-Band assembled up in the tower of our new Tabernacle, and played a few tunes for us," and everyone "rejoiced that the Northeast Corner is now up to the Square 30 feet, and have a determination to continue to have the House built this year, or as soon as possible."[97] As late as May 1879, Weibye admitted that despite the advances the people were still attending "Fast meeting in the old Meetinghouse."[98] They would do so for another three years.

In 1883 visiting apostle Erastus Snow, speaking in Mount Pleasant, chastised the Manti Saints, who he said "commenced to build a [meeting]house before they knew what they wanted or had faith enough to [reach] out and lay a plan big enough."[99] Snow's barb was well aimed, for the Manti meetinghouse/

tabernacle, effectively started in 1862, was not ready for use until 1882, and then it still lacked a spire (Figure 7.18). This final touch came 26 years later, in 1908 (Figure 7.19), making the duration of the building project about 46 years (1862–1908)!

The Saints in Moroni also built a large towered meetinghouse that mimicked in plan its predecessors in Ephraim and Manti (Figure 7.20). After their first adobe building melted in the rain, Moroni residents rebuilt it, with its height raised. However, in a December 1865 letter to the *Deseret News,* Bishop George W. Bradley said the Saints in his town were "preparing for pushing the erection of their new rock meeting-house next summer; and when finished they expect it will be second to none in the Territory."[100] Not surprisingly perhaps, the subject of the rock meetinghouse was dropped for more than ten years, when in January 1878, one ward member, Charles Kemp, speaking in meeting, advised the "Saints to do right and . . . Build a Meeting House."[101] The next week, Bishop John Irons agreed, saying that "we indeed ought to build a Meeting House." At the same gathering, a committee was appointed consisting of Irons, George Bradley, Peter Olsen, Nathan Faux, and James Yorgenson "to see the size and what kind of Material the House should be built of."[102] Some rock was immediately hauled for the building, but activity was sporadic for nearly a full year. The next December, Bishop Irons again had to ask the Saints to "get the rock out in the quary for the Meeting House."[103]

By March 1879 the committee had hired a stonemason, but work stagnated. In May, George Bradley, the town patriarch, called a business meeting "concerning the Meeting House," where he said "he wanted the people to be United but he wanted them to speake and settle on something what the

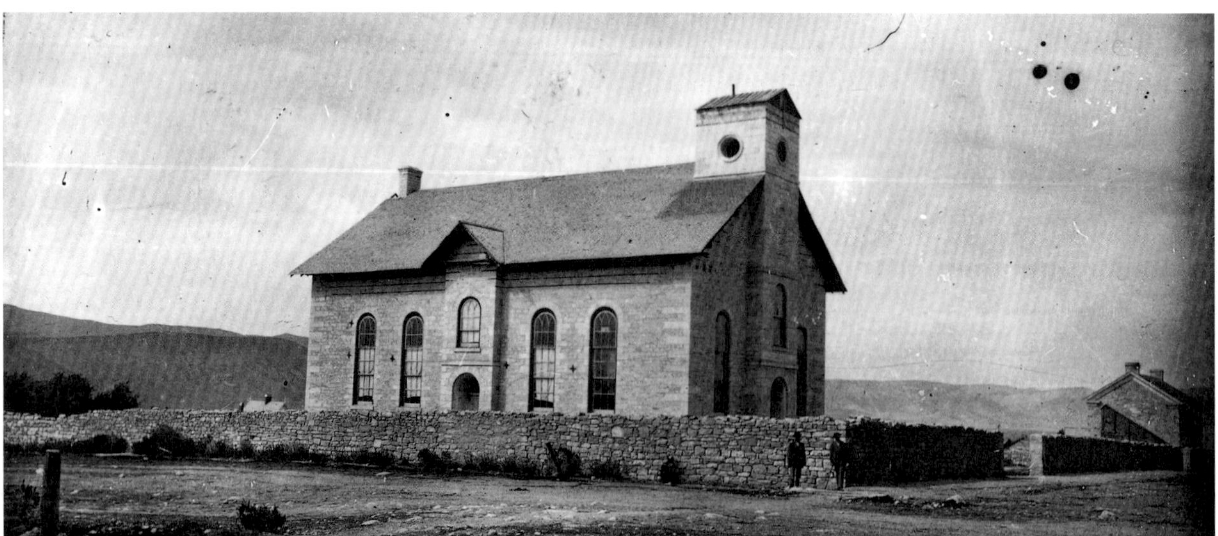

Figure 7.18. The Manti Tabernacle is still without its steeple in this photograph, circa 1888, titled "Manti Meetinghouse." George Edward Anderson Photographs, MSS P-1, L. Tom Perry Special Collections, Brigham Young University.

Figure 7.19 ***(left).*** Finally completed: the Manti Tabernacle after 1908. Reprinted by permission of Utah State Historical Society; all rights reserved.

Figure 7.20 ***(right).*** The Moroni Tabernacle, 1878–89. Reprinted by permission of Utah State Historical Society; all rights reserved.

house should be built [like] and then stick to it by our works." At this point, temple architect William Folsom rose and announced that the new church president, John Taylor, had told him "to take hold of and [superintend] the Building of the Meeting House for this Place." The Moroni brethren voiced their approval of the action, whereupon it was "mot[ioned] and carried that Bro Fulsom [act] as architect and general director of the building."[104]

Folsom's building adhered to the "Sanpete Style" developed by Jones and Barton. The overall character, however, is more eclectic, combining heavy neoclassical elements such as a boxed cornice, cornice returns, pedimented window headers, and an odd elliptical shouldered pediment over the front door. Picturesque qualities include pointed-arched Gothic arched windows over the tower door, pronounced quoins, and a telescoping octagonal roofed spire. Folsom deemphasizes the side doors by finishing them the same as the windows.[105]

Despite Folsom's presence (and prestige), the building went up slowly. In June 1880, Nathan Faux of the building committee, asked in Sunday meeting if "the people wanted to go on with the [meetinghouse]."[106] And in September of that year it was "mot[ioned] and carried that we have a Meeting House," that "we build the Meeting House of Brick," "that we release the Old committee on the Meeting house," and form a new one.[107] Where the idea for using brick came from is unknown, because the original intent, and the course followed, was to construct the building of stone. Not surprisingly, perhaps, another nine years was needed to finish the building; it was formally dedicated for use in August 1889.[108]

The Style of Use

The lack of commitment to meetinghouse construction is one of the most surprising aspects of the Zion making in the Sanpete Valley. Things worsened so much in Manti that Bishop J. B. Maiben asked whether "this people really wanted a meetinghouse."[109] They may not have, at least at the time, and for several reasons. One involved the limitations of both voluntary and tithe-based cooperation. Whether donating money and/or time, or working off their tithing obligations, there was only so much people could and would do for public and church projects. They also had to house and feed their families.

Peter Madsen, a Danish immigrant, wrote of his experience getting established in Ephraim: "Now I was commeth in a new School here was many things to learn, how to be farmer in a new land, everything was different from the land I came from, here we have to cut the brush of[f] first, and then try to plowe with Oxen, and a simple ploug to[o], and prepare for to watered the grain and make water ditches from the Creek, there was so much to do so I had to work hard all the time."[110] He also admitted "I did not labor for my self alone but had to help build Meeting hous, and make Canyon roads and different kind of work, and lived in those first year and not have any money, we exchanged work or payed in produce."[111]

Given the many demands on people's time and energy, priorities had to be set. Judging from the buildings (and the amount of time spent constructing them), meetinghouses appear to have been low on the list. Why? For starters, very few were actually using them. Throughout the Mormon West during the pioneering period, attendance at Sunday meeting was unexpectedly low. No official figures exist for the Sanpete Valley, but all we have to do is read the ward minutes from a town like Manti. September 1, 1850: "Bishop Lowery made some remarks upon the non attendance of members at meeting."[112] April 27, 1857: "Meeting opened with singing; prayer by James Wareham; after Prest [Welcome] Chapman spoke on attending meeting etc., some were in their Fields instead of at meeting. He would make such things give way for a Sabbath."[113] August 22, 1858: President Chapman "made some remarks on none *[sic]* attendance to meeting; the people growing in Coldness."[114] September 5, 1858: President Chapman "alluded to the slackness of Saints in attending Meeting then coldness etc. they thought they could get along without teaching and counsel and the cause of so much sickness in our midst was our neglect of duty etc. and lacking 'the faith once delivered to the Saints' there was a falling away among the people referred to covenants of Reformation; many had broken them."[115] April 17, 1859: Chapman complains that "some Brethern sat round outside the House when there was room inside."[116] April 24, 1859: Chapman notes "none attendance to meeting."[117] March 22, 1867:

"Elder Wareham made some few remarks in conclusion on nonattendance to Meeting."[118] Even as late as May 1885 Jens Weibye observed "we will not have any more Ward meetings here in the North Ward til next fall, because the People will not come to Meeting."[119] They were farming instead of going to meeting, so the meetings were canceled.

It was the same in the other towns, and Fairview offers a colorful example. Bishop James Jones on September 16, 1860, said, "It was the duty of him and his counselors to look after the wellfare of the Saints, felt sorry to see so few out to meeting. Said it was right for the people to attend their meetings, as to get a salvation should be uppermost in our hearts, encouraged the Teachers to be wide awake to their duties, and that the brethren should not haul hay on the Sabbath, as it would not be tolerated."[120] The next Sunday, Jones preached again, saying he "saw some in the field at work but felt himself [the need] to be [at] meeting and remember the Sabbath Day, and recomended others do the same."[121] More deaf ears, apparently, for in November Jones remarked "about so many of the brethren and sisters there stayes away from meetings and the braking of the Sabbath."[122] And the following Sunday, the bishop said, "He wanted the people to stop working on the Sabbath Day and attend their meetings, or they be disfellowshipped from the church."[123] And in 1862, Bishop Jones "said he and his counselors had been placed here to serve the people and his studies was how to build up the Kingdom of our God on the earth, said he was notified to be at Salt Lake City next Saturday, and had told the President of the Teachers Quorum to warn the people to come out to meeting to day and still there are not one fourth of them present."[124]

Things were different when Brigham Young came to town. In February 1863 Young arrived in Mount Pleasant, which at the time only had its small social hall/meetinghouse, and was greeted by a "large [concourse] of citizens"; "meeting was imidiately called to order outside of the meeting house as the congregation was so large that the house could not hold it by far."[125] Or in 1868, on another of Young's trips, this time in Manti, "the meetinghouse and a bowery built at its side for the accommodation of the people were crowded with an attentive congregation."[126] But these visits were the exception. If the ward minutes are any indication, the buildings—small as they were—were almost empty.

Does nonattendance at Sunday meeting indicate a lack of faith or rampant apostasy? Not likely. The Saints in the Sanpete towns, like those throughout the region, remained devoted to their church and its ideals. But that dedication did not necessarily mean going to church. Historian Jan Shipps has correctly observed that beginning in 1847 and lasting into the early 1880s most Latter-day Saints defined themselves as Mormons and expressed their faith individually through the very personal experience of Zion making, which included everything from participating in the trek from Nauvoo to laying out towns, constructing infrastructure, setting up businesses, establishing farms, and building temples. The move to the Great Basin was, in Shipps's view, a "recapitulation" of the Exodus story, a time of trial and redemption. Those Saints who found themselves in the Canaan Land of Utah Territory had passed the ultimate test of faith. They did not need to show up at church to demonstrate their orthodoxy. Just being part of the Zion-making experience was sufficient.[127]

This pattern began to change after about 1880 as a new generation came up in Utah, one without a migration story, and one without the task of Zion building directly before it. For these church members, regular attendance at Sunday services became a requisite part of being Mormon, an overt display of faith. The change is evident in the Sanpete church records. At the Stake Conference in 1880, President Canute Peterson opened by saying that he was "pleased to see so many of the Saints assembled."[128] Or listen to a traveler's account published in the *Deseret News* in January 1885: "I attended the Sunday Schools of Manti, was surprised to see how crowded they were. All ages were there eager in the pursuit of truth and lasting knowledge."[129]

As the importance of regular worship rose in people's estimation, so too did the buildings where such activity took place. Occupying a piece of the ever more secular Main Street, meetinghouses took on a new significance. Not only did people need them, but they also needed them to be easily recognizable as church buildings, so they got towers (and eventually steeples), but the main thing was that they now got built. Even with time and materials scarce, it had always been possible for the Saints to construct meetinghouses. All it took was interest.

Towers of Memory

If it seems that we are reading too much into these buildings, it is worthwhile to recall Brigham Young's comments on the design of the Provo Tabernacle. Provo is located about fifty miles south of Salt Lake City (and a little over eighty miles north of Manti). Started in 1856 and finished in 1867, the Provo Tabernacle predated the St. George Tabernacle in its use of a tower, but appears more an anomaly than a break with existing practice—no other meetinghouses before St. George had towers, but after St. George, they were the norm. Unlike the Sanpete buildings, the design for the Provo Tabernacle came from church headquarters in Salt Lake City and its style, according to Young, was intended to preserve among the Saints "a reminiscence of a Presbyterian meetinghouse, [so] that the children of the Saints might see in what kind of an edifice many of their fathers worshipped before they heard the Gospel."[130]

Young clearly knew the didactic value of buildings. However, especially when we consider that he had just finished working on the design for the Old Tabernacle in Salt Lake City (a towerless and distinctly *other* building), we must ask why such a "reminiscence" would be valuable, especially for a group trying to leave behind, as he often said, the "tradition of their fathers." The president never provided an answer, but it may be that his words revealed yet again the internal strife church members felt between otherness and difference (or even sameness), and the ongoing tension between radical and normative agendas. The Provo Tabernacle, like the steepled one in St. George, and the three main meetinghouses/tabernacles built in the Sanpete Valley—in Ephraim, Manti, and Moroni—clearly said something about Zion and its relation to the American core culture. These buildings were artifacts of memory, reminders of church designs the Latter-day Saints had previously known. After experimenting with the nonconformist hall-type meetinghouses found in most communities, including Salt Lake City, the move to towers and steeples (however long they took to complete) reflects a continuing theme in Mormon history, namely, the vacillation of the group between distinctively Mormon and more normative American forms for congregational structures—now called ward meetinghouses and stake centers. Such symbolic latitude was made possible by the consistency of message found in temple architecture, the subject of the final chapter.

8 MANSION ON THE HILL

THE TEMPLE AS RITUAL SPACE

> [The] preparatory work of converting a mountain into suitable temple grounds, involving as it does immense expense, will be fully compensated when the Temple shall be completed; for a more fitting place for the House of the Lord could hardly be conceived of standing alone and towering, as that edifice will, above all the works of man around.
>
> —Deseret News, *November 22, 1879*

> Now here is wisdom, and the mind of the Lord—let the house be built, not after the manner of the world, for I give not unto you that you shall live after the manner of the world.
>
> —Doctrine and Covenants of the Church of Jesus Christ of Latter-day Saints, *95:13*

IN OCTOBER 1877, following the death of Brigham Young, John Taylor assumed the office of acting LDS Church president (he would not be officially appointed until 1880). One of Taylor's first official undertakings was to notify William H. Folsom of his appointment "by the Council of the Apostles, to act as the Architect in the erection of the Manti Temple and to take on the general Superintendency of the business connected with the building thereof."[1] Folsom's résumé was impressive—his work in the capital city had included the Salt Lake Theatre (1862), the new Salt Lake Tabernacle (1867), and Brigham Young's Gardo House (1875)—and many today think his Manti temple, with its elegant French cupolas and imaginative Janus-like orientation (it faces east while appearing to face west), is the finest of LDS buildings, past and present.[2] For all its eminence, however, one can also argue that it is the building's "ordinariness," to use Dell Upton's term for the way a building fits into the everyday world around it, that makes it so important in the story of Zion making.[3]

By the time Folsom took charge in Manti, temple design had evolved considerably. Unlike the architects who preceded him, men who were breaking new ground with practically every pen stroke, Folsom could draw inspiration from a growing body of accepted practice. Slowly, through a series of experiments in Kirtland, Independence, Nauvoo, and then in Salt Lake City and

Figure 8.1. Workmen complete the east tower of the Manti Temple. Photograph by George Edward Anderson, circa 1888. George Edward Anderson Photographs, MSS P-1, L. Tom Perry Special Collections, Brigham Young University.

St. George, church leaders, especially Brigham Young (who personally oversaw all aspects of temple design and construction), had settled on a temple *location*: it would stand outside of town; a basic *form*: towers at each end would symbolize the dual Mormon priesthoods; and a *program*: secret ritual and not congregational worship would be its chief purpose (Figure 8.1). This new typology was adopted for the two temples begun in 1877, one at Manti and the other at Logan in the northern part of the Utah Territory, *and* in the final iteration of the Salt Lake City Temple, started in the 1850s but not completed until 1893, making it the first started but last finished of the nineteenth-century temples.

This chapter uses Manti to look at three aspects of temple architecture. First, the slow but steady progression toward a sequestered sacred space is chronicled in a brief (and necessarily cursory) survey of LDS temple history. A second section covers details of the Manti Temple's construction, emphasizing the philosophy of public works that propelled it forward. The third and final part looks at the temple ritual as a microcosm of LDS worldview as it was embedded in the larger landscape—Zion writ small, so to speak. Temples were collective symbols, marking the LDS Church's unique place in

America's Christian community. At the same time, they served the spiritual needs of individual Saints who through their temple work sought the ultimate blessing of celestial exaltation.

Latter-day Temples

Mormons believed that temple building was divinely ordained. The first mention of it came in a December 1830 revelation in which Jesus Christ appeared to Joseph Smith and warned his newly anointed prophet that He would "suddenly come to my temple."[4] More detailed was a message from a January 1831 visitation: "[Be it known] that my covenant people may be gathered in one in that day when I shall come to my temple. And this I do for the salvation of my people."[5] Additional information concerning temple building would be forthcoming, but the significance of these early revelations is noteworthy. On one hand, they placed the Saints firmly within the biblical story, connecting them to the temple builders of the Old Testament and particularly to King Solomon, who built the first temple in Jerusalem in the tenth century BCE. They also effectively divorced Smith and his followers from Christian denominations that did not possess temples, and this number included all others, from the Catholics to the sundry Protestant sects. What's in a name? A great deal it seems, especially when it comes to churches.[6]

Talk of temples was one thing, of course, but actual construction something altogether different. As with other aspects of the Mormon landscape, the problems faced by LDS temple designers involved knowing what such a building should look like and how it should be used. They could have replicated Solomon's Temple, which had been destroyed by the Babylonians in 586 BCE but was well known to Bible readers, being described at some length in 1 Kings 6–7 and 2 Chronicles 2–4. From these texts Mormon architects would have been aware of its size (twenty cubits wide and seventy cubits long), its three-part plan (porch, a main hall, and an inner shrine, later called the Holy of Holies), its orientation (facing east), general shape (with an entrance flanked by two pillars), and use (ritual not worship). They would also have understood its role as "House of the Lord" (where God resided among his people), *axis mundi* (the symbolic link between heaven and earth), and sacred sanctuary (to which only the duly initiated—priests and other holy men—could enter).[7]

Some of these elements found their way into Mormon temple design, but in the temple's general appearance, plan, and use, the Saints broke with biblical precedent: Smith's latter-day temple would be, to use one of architect Mies van de Rohe's favorite lines, a building "of its own time."[8] LDS theologian James Talmage explained it this way: "Regarding the plan of building and the structural design of temples, we find no close similarity, far less of aught approaching identity, in these holy houses as erected in different dispensations [eras]; on the contrary we may affirm that direct revelation of temple plans is required for each distinctive period for the Priesthood's administration, that is to say for every dispensation of Divine authority. While the general purpose of temples is the same in all times, the special suitability of these edifices is determined by the needs of the dispensation to which they severally belong."[9] In short, everything is relative, even a temple, and flexibility, as emphasized in the previous discussion of continuing revelation, a seminal LDS virtue.

Mormon temples are best considered in the same light as LDS theology, that is, as a new typology fashioned out of several strains of existing practice, traceable to Old and New Testament texts, coupled with specifically Mormon concepts derived from modern revelation. Thus, from the Hebrew temple came the idea of the building as a Holy of Holies, a space set off from the profane world for sanctified ceremonies by an ordained priesthood. From Christian tradition, at least during the early stages of temple development, came a need for open congregational spaces, meeting rooms for prayer and administering the sacrament. Contemporary revelation sparked the idea for a baptismal font, an orientation based on the duality of the restored priesthoods, a series of ceremonial endowment rooms, and a court for instruction and edification. The temple, then, helped tie the Latter-day Saints not only to an Old Testament past but also to a millennial future,[10] an insight that reminds us of another Mormon virtue: look forward, not back.

Ohio and Missouri

The first temple was constructed at Kirtland, Ohio. A sister building was planned for Independence, in Jackson County, Missouri, the site revealed to Smith as the place for gathering Zion in anticipation of the Second Coming. In contemplating the style of the temple (the two buildings would presumably be the same), the prophet was told by God: "Let it be built after the manner which I shall show unto three of you."[11] True to His word, God sent a depiction of the building in a vision witnessed by Smith along with his counselors, Sidney Rigdon and Frederick Williams, the latter recalling: "We went upon our knees, called on the Lord, and the building appeared within viewing distance."[12] It was left to Williams, a physician, to translate what the group saw into workable plans, one set for Kirtland and the other for Independence.[13]

Conflict with the Gentiles in Missouri prevented the Saints there from doing anything more than dedicating a cornerstone before being forced to evacuate the temple site. Work on the Kirtland building, however, commenced during the summer of 1833 under the direction of Smith and superintendent Artemus Millet, a Canadian stonemason. Millet's chief task lay in translating the revealed plan into stone, mortar, and wood.[14] The basics undoubtedly came from Smith, but Millet, working with other craftsmen, filled in the details for such prescriptions as "the pulpits are to be finished with panel wood, *in the best workmanlike manner;* and the building to be constructed of stone and brick of the best quality" (emphases added).[15]

Finished in 1836, the Kirtland Temple stands as the essence of design eclecticism, drawing from a number of both current and more traditional fashions (Figure 8.2). Elwin Robison, in what is certainly the best study of a Mormon building, described it as a "mixture of Georgian, Federal, Greek Revival, and Gothic elements. Although the dominant roof pediment and tower make it primarily Greek Revival in style, the temple has the tall, boxy proportions of an enlarged Federal house, not a classical Greek temple."[16] Georgian features include central tripartite Palladian windows, smooth plastered exterior, pronounced quoins, and roof dormers, while the Gothic is represented by the pointed arched windows found on the front, rear, and side elevations. Robison concedes, correctly, that such eclecticism was common in Ohio's Western Reserve during the 1830s, a time of changing fashions and frontier exigencies. He notes that the use of Gothic windows on non-Gothic churches is indicative of a shared architectural language, for such windows "were a cultural symbol for a church in the same way that small cupolas were the cultural symbol of a town hall or public structure in the late-eighteenth and early-nineteenth centuries."[17]

Figure 8.2. The first Mormon temple, Kirtland, Ohio, 1833–36. Reprinted by permission of Utah State Historical Society; all rights reserved.

For all its pretensions to otherness, from its outside appearances the Kirtland temple remains very much an American church, its normality betrayed by a rectangular shape and prominent bell tower. Moving inside, however, the story changes dramatically. Rather than having the standard church plan—a single story with a long aisled nave ending in a raised pulpit—it has two floors, four pulpits, and a series of curtains for partitioning sections of each "court," the name revealed to Smith for the meeting rooms on each floor. Naming such rooms "courts" gave a nod to Solomonic practice, though the Hebrew temple spaces were aligned end to end and not stacked on top of one another, as in Kirtland. Again, we see a merging of traditions. The lower court functioned like a typical church, being used for preaching, prayer, and taking the sacrament, while the upper court, reserved for priesthood instruction and administration, was uniquely Mormon. Curtains, referred to as "vails" and operated with elaborate systems of ropes and pulleys, allowed the courts to be divided into smaller rooms for more meetings and also to provide privacy during washings and anointings.[18]

Of particular interest are the four pulpits, one placed on each end of both the upper and lower courts (Figure 8.3). The pulpits are arranged in three ascending tiers of three pulpits each. This complex plan reflects the organization of the church's male members into two priesthoods, each divided into three offices according to their authority and prescribed duties. A key component of the Mormon restoration involved reinstating the biblical priesthoods of Aaron and Melchizedek. The lesser of the two, the Aaronic, was composed of those who administered to the everyday workings of the tabernacle, including guarding and transporting it, but who "must not approach either the utensils of the sanctuary or the altar."[19] Priests "on the order of Melchizedek" possessed the power and authority to enter the Holy of Holies and administer the sacred rituals.[20] In LDS practice, the three offices of the Aaronic priesthood are deacons, teachers, and priests in reverse order of importance; those of the Melchizedek are elders, seventies, and high priests. Following biblical precedent, the former attend to the routine aspects of worship, particularly the passing of the sacrament, while the latter have greater duties both in leadership positions and in the sacred temple ceremonies.[21]

In one of the most innovative aspects of the Kirtland Temple design, pulpits for the two priesthoods were placed in both upper and lower courts, the Aaronic to the east and the Melchizedek to the west. Pews were constructed so they could be shifted to face either end, depending on which priesthood presided. The three levels of pulpits corresponded to the three offices within each priesthood, though at Kirtland the prophet and his two counselors occupied the top tier of Melchizedek pulpits. A special curtain, again referencing

Figure 8.3. Longitudinal and transverse sections of the Kirtland Temple. Note the double pulpits and distinctive double court (ground level and second-story meeting rooms) with attic design. Historic American Buildings Survey, HABS Ohio, 43-Kirt.

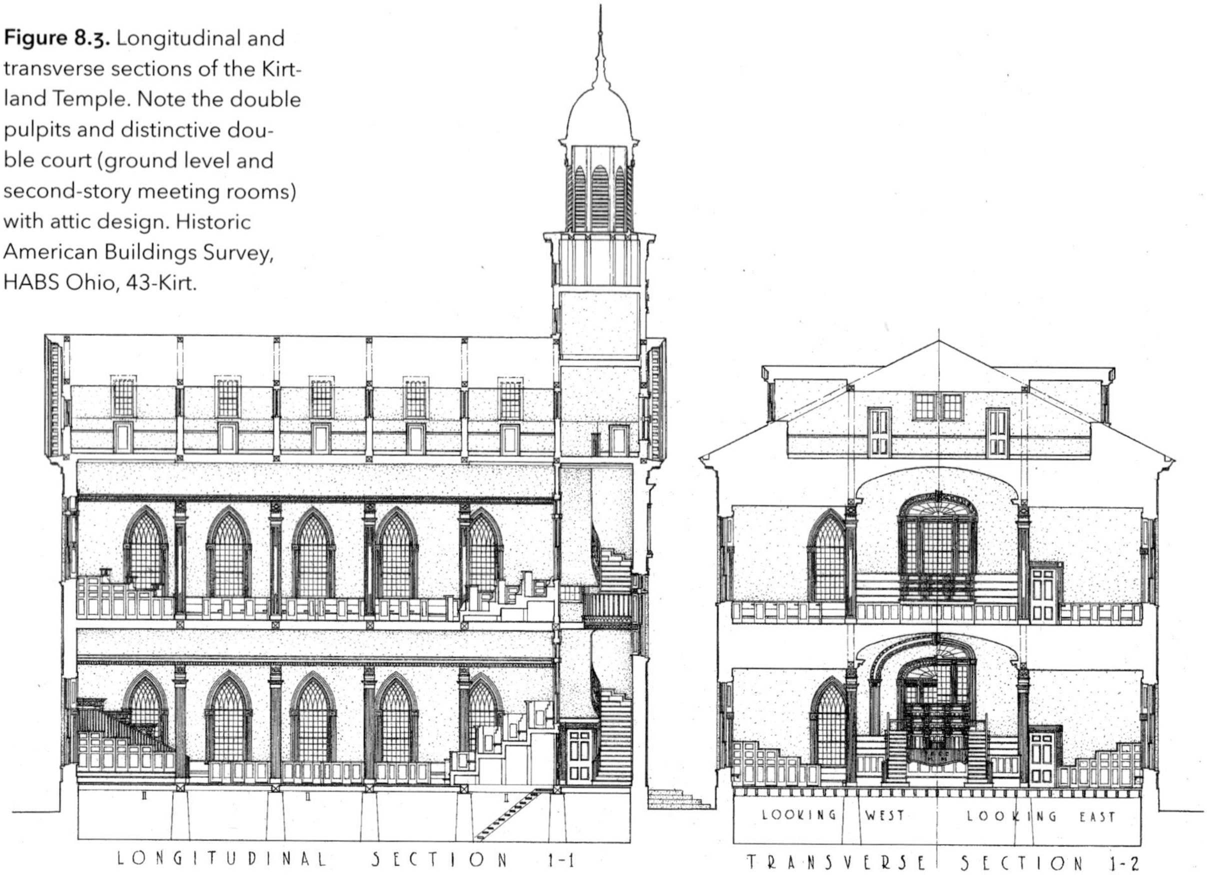

Solomon's Holy of Holies, could be dropped around the pulpits, creating a sacred sanctuary for receiving instruction from heaven.[22]

Not long after the building was completed, serious financial difficulties forced the Ohio Saints to depart for Missouri. The temple was rented, first as a school and then as a church, and finally sold in 1860 to the Reorganized Church of Jesus Christ of Latter Day Saints, a branch of Mormonism formed after the death of Joseph Smith.[23]

Illinois

After setbacks in Ohio and Missouri, Mormon temple building began anew in Illinois. Just a year after the founding of Nauvoo in 1839, Joseph Smith announced that "the time has now come, when it is necessary to erect a house of prayer, a house of order, a house for the worship of our God, where the ordinances can be attended to agreeably to His divine will."[24] Within months of this proclamation, church officials purchased a four-acre site for the building on a hill overlooking the Mississippi River. Work began early in 1841, once again under the direction of Smith. William Weeks, an architect and builder from Massachusetts, prepared the plans and supervised construction. The building's design undoubtedly emanated from the client–architect relationship that developed between the two men, with the prophet again providing the programmatic requirements and Weeks the workable solutions. The dialogue produced a building remarkable for its ability to meet both the practical and symbolic needs of the fledgling church.[25]

The Nauvoo Temple resembled the one at Kirtland in its basic shape and plan; it was a church-type structure consisting of a two-and-a-half-story rectangular block with a roof tower on the west front end (Figure 8.4). In keeping with church leaders' increasing preoccupation with refinement, the simplicity of the Kirtland temple design gave way to a more academically correct expression of current neoclassical fashion. Not only did Weeks bring the building proportions into proper alignment (tower height to building width and length), but he also enhanced the overall effect by dividing the elevations into discrete bays in a 5:8 ratio (five bays on the front and eight on the sides). The bays were marked off by a series of pilasters supporting an elaborate classical cornice. Particularly interesting is the detailing of the pilasters and entablature; instead of following specific Roman or Greek prototypes, Smith and Weeks created a "Mormon Order" rooted in LDS theology: on the frieze were stars, representing the lesser or telestial heavenly realm;

Figure 8.4. Nauvoo Temple elevation, circa 1842 or 1843. William Weeks, architect. Courtesy of the Church History Library.

the pilaster bases were decorated with moonstones, referring to the terrestrial level; and finally the capitals, shaped into the sunstones of the celestial kingdom. These stylistic eccentricities subtly branded the edifice a Mormon building, as did in its own way the domed cupola. Christian churches on the whole had pointed Gothic spires; a classically inspired tower, like the one devised by Weeks, suggests yet another deviation from orthodox practice.[26]

At Kirtland, the principal innovations had been the double courts (upper and lower), the dual orientation of the courts, and the presence of multiple pulpits. The Nauvoo Temple preserved these features (Figure 8.5) while adding others associated with a set of newly instituted liturgical ceremonies, or ordinances. Ordinances, in LDS practice, are synonymous with works, the performance of which is integral to a church member's advancement through salvation toward exaltation. Echoing Brigham Young's early statement about not caring "half so much" about faith as he did works, Mormon theologian James Talmage, in *The House of the Lord,* explains that in addition to faith a person has to provide "evidence of this spiritual sanctification by some outward ordinance."[27] It was at Nauvoo that the four principal sacred temple ordinances, long prophesied, were revealed and implemented—baptism, higher baptism (receiving the Holy Ghost), endowment, and sealing. Each would find a place in the temple, though in the case of the last two this would happen only after construction was well under way. It was also at Nauvoo that the practice of ordinances performed vicariously for the dead was instituted. The idea was that those who had died prior to the Mormon restoration had been denied the opportunity of achieving exalted heavenly status, and thus

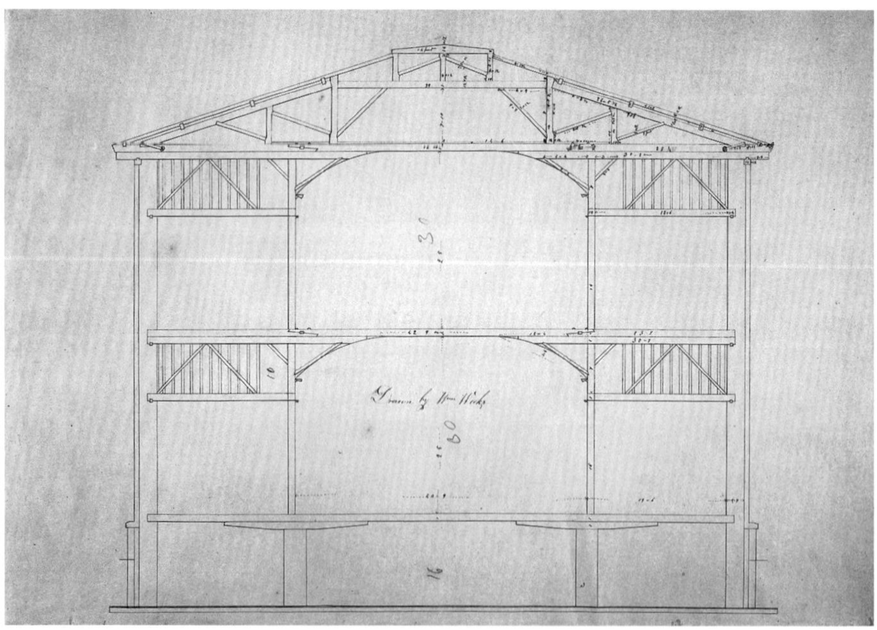

Figure 8.5. Transverse section of the Nauvoo Temple showing the double court with attic configuration. Courtesy of the Church History Library.

temple work on behalf of the dead became an extra incentive to complete the new temple.[28]

The introduction of the ordinance ceremonies (for both the living and the dead) affected the design of the Nauvoo temple in two main areas. The first was the inclusion of a basement for baptism and higher baptism. Mormons practice baptism by immersion, a symbolic act whereby members pass through a "gateway" or "portal" to Christ. Previously, this ritual had taken place in the open (at Nauvoo the Mississippi River was conveniently nearby), but now it was further sanctified by moving it indoors into a large font supported by twelve oxen. The oxen derived from Solomon's Temple (1 Kings 7:23) and represented one of the few direct connections between the Mormon and Hebrew dispensations.[29] Here in the basement church members also participated in a second ordinance, referred to as a "higher baptism," which involved receiving the "Gift of the Holy Ghost" through the laying on or "imposition" of hands by authorized priesthood officials.[30]

The second innovation came in the form of specific spaces reserved for carrying out the endowment and sealing ordinances. These rituals had not been revealed when the temple was started in 1841 and were not included in the original design. After 1842, however, a series of revelations clarified for Smith the nature of heaven and the role of individual agency in the redemption process. It had been ordained that "the privileges and glories of heaven are graded to suit the various capacities of the blessed,"[31] but new was the knowledge that "rituals conducted on earth, in specially designed places, were prerequisite for specific effects to be possible in heaven."[32] What this meant, quite simply, was that while heaven was hierarchically structured, or "graded," with celestial glory being the highest, followed by the terrestrial and telestial levels, one's place in this heavenly hierarchy was determined by works (ordinances) performed on earth, in temples. Baptism (and higher baptism) might lead to salvation and the lower degrees of glory, but the higher celestial kingdom was available only to those who participated in the new endowment and sealing ordinances.[33]

The introduction of these ordinances caused Weeks to find a place in the building for ceremonial rooms. He chose the attic, a decision that required removing the original pedimented front and replacing it with a rectangular pavilion that provided better access to the uppermost story. The endowment ceremony consisted of a symbolic recapitulation of the LDS origin story, with initiates physically retracing the events of human existence, beginning with the Creation of the world, then, in order, the idyll of the Garden, the transgression and Fall from grace, the Redemption and subsequent apostasy, and finally the Restoration of the true Gospel. For the endowment, a series of rooms were created with canvas partitions that represented the various stages of being (Figure 8.6). After ascending a staircase in the tower base, endowment participants prepared for the ritual in "initiatory" rooms to either side of the main door. From there, they moved in sequence from the Creation Room, to the Garden Room, to the Telestial (also known as the World) Room, the Terrestrial Room, finally passing through a veil into the ultimate destination, the Celestial Room. In each room, recitals and rituals accompanied by instructions "endowed" members with the information or "keys" needed to successfully negotiate the afterlife, giving the faithful a method for advancing through the three grades of heaven.[34]

Also included in the new design was a sealing room, the inner sanctum or Holy of Holies of the temple. At Nauvoo, this room was located at the back of the attic, just off the Celestial Room. The main purpose of this room was the performance of the sacred temple marriage ordinance wherein a man and woman are "sealed" together for "time and eternity," thus perpetuating temporal family relationships beyond the grave. Temple marriage is yet another

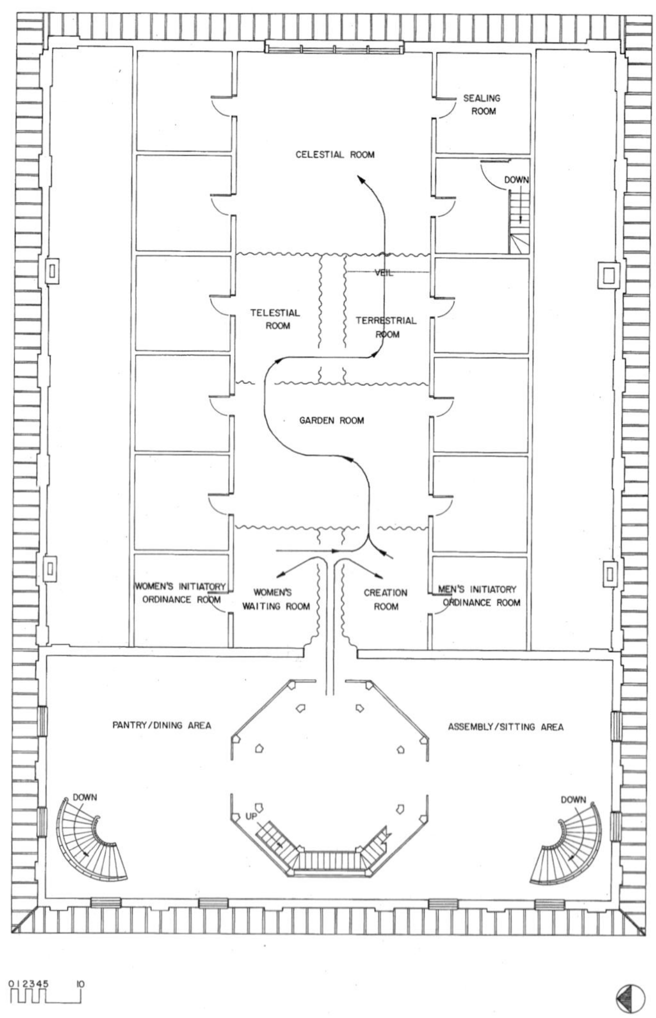

Figure 8.6. Reconstruction of the attic ritual spaces in the Nauvoo Temple (after Don Colvin, *Nauvoo Temple*).

precondition for the exaltation of the celestial kingdom. Men cannot enter the final stage of glory without a wife; and women can ascend only through their husbands.[35]

It was thus at Nauvoo that the LDS temple acquired its status as sacred sanctuary. Conceived in the manner of its predecessor at Kirtland, the Nauvoo temple morphed over time into a distinctive ritual space, the first true LDS temple. The monumental building was finished just before the Saints were expelled from Nauvoo in 1846 and destroyed not long after by fire. The precedent had been set, however. In the West, Mormon temples would continue to evolve, but in keeping with the advances made at Nauvoo, all would be reserved for carrying out the sacred ordinances.

Utah

Four temples were built in Utah during the nineteenth century. In many ways the history of this period of temple building is best described by the old adage "one step forward and one step back," since movement toward the full expression of a ritually oriented building type proceeded rather haphazardly. One of Brigham Young's first acts when the Saints reached the Valley of the Great Salt Lake in the summer of 1847 was to designate and dedicate a site for a temple. Construction did not begin immediately—there was too much else to do in getting the city under way. By 1851, however, the temple project was approved during General Conference and Truman Angell Sr. appointed architect (Young's first choice, William Weeks, had left the church by this time). Two years later crews began excavating the foundation, although further work was delayed, first by the ongoing conflict with the U.S. government over Mormon political sovereignty (an army was dispatched to Utah Territory in 1857–58 but war was averted) and then by Young's decision to divert money and other vital church resources toward erecting temples in the outlying communities of St. George (1871–77), Logan (1877–83), and Manti (1877–88). Eventually it would take almost forty years to complete the "Great Temple" in Salt Lake City. Though it was not ready for use until 1893, the building rightly earned its sobriquet, for in both size and richness of detail it outdistanced all that had come before (or since for that matter).[36]

The snail-like progress on the building was probably a godsend in terms of the building's ultimate outcome, since Angell's original plan, submitted in 1854, failed to incorporate many of the lessons learned in Nauvoo, particularly in regard to the ceremonial rooms. From all accounts, Angell worked with Young in much the same way his predecessors, Artemus Millet and William Weeks, had with Joseph Smith. For example, in 1853 Young witnessed the building in a vision and provided sketches to Angell showing the presence of six towers, three on each end. Angell, working with a young English-trained architect named William Ward, translated the sketches into a series of elevation drawings (Figure 8.7). The double-ended exterior projected on the outside of the building the two-priesthood twin pulpit plan introduced at Kirtland and followed at Nauvoo. The three towers on the east are said to symbolize the church president and his two counselors, while those on the west the church's presiding bishop and his two counselors. Young was also responsible for introducing the castellated battlements and spires, undoubtedly referencing the great Gothic cathedrals he had visited during proselytizing missions in England.[37]

Despite advances made on the building's exterior, its interior proved less promising. Angell proposed, and Young accepted, a two-story with basement "double court" design similar to that used at Kirtland and Nauvoo. The ceremonial rooms hastily inserted into the attic of the Illinois building Angell placed awkwardly in the basement. His argument for keeping the two tiers of large assembly courts rested on his belief that this was the arrangement divinely delivered to Joseph Smith and could not be altered.[38] Angell's stance is curious, given the church's pressing need for a ceremonial building (stripped of its original congregational functions). He could easily have invoked the doctrine of continuing revelation, which as we have seen, sanctioned such changes. Even odder is the fact that although he refused to redesign the temple, he anticipated the modern ritual spaces in the design for a surrogate temple called the Endowment House, a building commissioned by Young to allow the performance of the endowment ordinances while the temple was under construction.

Figure 8.7. Architect William Ward's rendering of the Salt Lake Temple, 1856. Reprinted by permission of Utah State Historical Society; all rights reserved.

Figure 8.8. Endowment House, Temple Square, Salt Lake City, 1855, Truman Angell, architect. Reprinted by permission of Utah State Historical Society; all rights reserved.

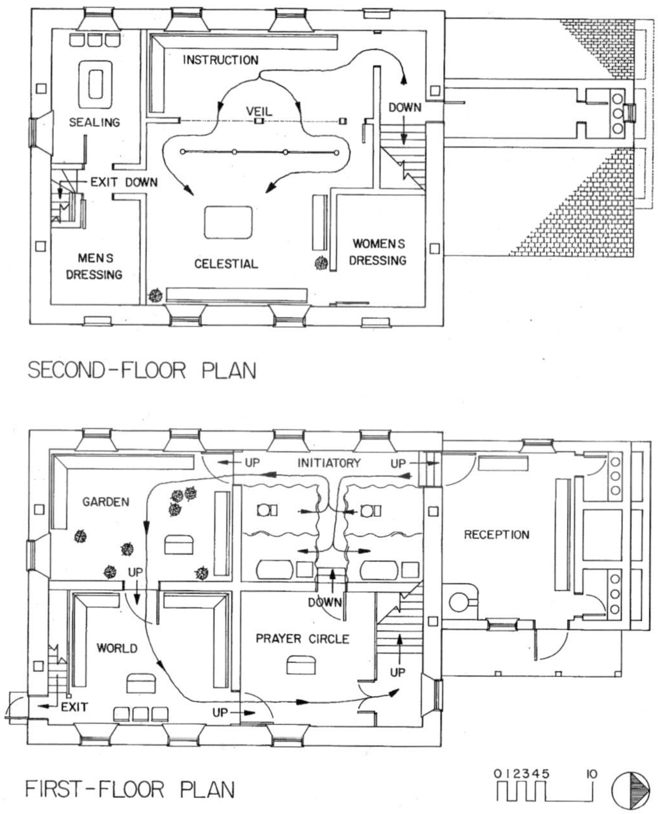

Figure 8.9. Endowment House plan (after Lisle G. Brown, "Temple Pro Tempore").

The Endowment House (Figures 8.8 and 8.9) stood on the northwest corner of Temple Square and has been reconstructed in detail by Lisle Brown in a fine study whose title begins with the Latin phrase "Temple Pro Tempore" (temple for the time being).[39] Designed by Angell and completed in 1855, the building was essentially a large Georgian-type house adapted to accommodate the endowment ceremony introduced at Nauvoo. Angell placed an annex to the north for entering and signing in. Next came a set of initiatory rooms for dressing, washing, and anointing. There was no Creation Room. Rather, next in line came the Garden Room, which was adorned with potted plants and murals depicting scenes from the Garden of Eden. The remaining rooms on the first floor were the World (Telestial) Room, devoid of decor and whose heavily curtained windows helped convey the idea of the "Dark and Lonely World," and the Prayer Circle Room, which was new to the sequence. On the second story were found, first, the rather subdued (by Garden Room standards) Instruction (Terrestrial) Room, then the Celestial Room, and finally the sealing room, or Holy of Holies. The most distinctive features on this floor were the veil separating the Instruction and Celestial Rooms through which initiates symbolically passed from salvation to exaltation, and the furnishings of the Celestial Room, which were minimal but nevertheless were, in the words of one observer, "supposed to be heaven." In 1856 a baptistry was added to the western side of the building.[40]

Almost without knowing it, Angell created in the Endowment House the interior of the modern Mormon temple. Brown lists a number of its innovations that were later incorporated into the accepted typology: first, "the physical arrangement of progressively ascending ordinance rooms, using stairs to emphasize the upward ascent," a feature intended to "imply to those progressing through the endowment ceremony that as they moved from room to room they were being raised up and were coming closer to Father in Heaven."[41] Second, "in the Endowment House the participants physically participated in the endowment in an ascending circular pattern," an innovation "not part of the conceptual interior of temples envisioned by Joseph Smith."[42] Third, the potted plants and murals in the Garden Room created an allegorical representation of the endowment story, a feature used in all subsequent temples.[43] And finally, the Endowment House "also contained the first sealing room specifically designed for marriages." Before, marriages had been performed in a variety of venues, most commonly the homes or offices of church leaders."[44]

If a step forward was taken in the Endowment House, the next turned back. Young asked Angell to design a temple for St. George in the style of the one at Nauvoo. The architect complied, presenting the president with a building that drew little upon either the exterior innovations of the Salt Lake Temple or the highly successful interior of the Endowment House. Built between 1871 and 1877, the St. George Temple, like Nauvoo's, had but a single tower (Figure 8.10). The walls and tower originally utilized the Gothic battlements employed in Salt Lake, though the cupola was oddly classical, especially in the use of a domed roof. On the inside, the plan was nearly identical to Nauvoo's and included a basement plus two large assembly courts (Figure

Figure 8.10. St. George Temple, 1871–77. Reprinted by permission of Utah State Historical Society; all rights reserved.

Figure 8.11. Transverse section showing the older double court with attic design for the St. George Temple. Courtesy of the Church History Library.

8.11). The chief difference between the two was that in St. George the endowment rooms, although still marked off with canvas partitions, were located in the basement (also proposed for Salt Lake) rather than the attic.[45] Despite its imaginative siting (recall that this temple was the first located outside the town center), the building in other regards appears an anachronism waiting for a twentieth-century remodeling that would bring it into alignment with accepted practice.[46]

The final two nineteenth-century temples were built in Logan and Manti (Figures 8.12 and 8.13). While the decision to build in St. George was tied to the precarious nature of the Dixie colony, the Cache Valley (Logan) and

Figure 8.12. Logan Temple, 1877–83. Reprinted by permission of Utah State Historical Society; all rights reserved.

Figure 8.13. Manti Temple, 1877–88. Reprinted by permission of Utah State Historical Society; all rights reserved.

Sanpete Valley (Manti) communities were never so vulnerable. Still, the infusion of public works capital that accompanied temple building boosted both economies and undoubtedly made the peripheral Kingdom stronger. Both temples were started in 1877, Logan under the supervision of Truman Angell Jr. and Manti under William Folsom. Little evidence survives concerning the design process behind these buildings, but architectural historian Laurel Andrew concludes that "the similarity in proportions and dimensions between [the two buildings], the octagonal auxiliary [corner] towers, and the return to the double-ended form suggest that Angell and Folsom may have been working in concert."[47]

Of the two buildings, Andrew finds Folsom's the more successful because of its elegant French mansard cupolas, which are not dominated by the massive castellation of the walls (like Angell's smaller classical ones), and further lend it a domestic sensibility (such roofs are often associated with public or high-end residential architecture) consistent with the building's function as House of the Lord. She also applauds Folsom's genius in dealing with what was an extremely difficult building site. Utah temples face east in anticipation of the Resurrection, but the foothill locations for both the Logan and the Manti buildings lay on the eastern sides of their respective valleys, so essentially they have their backs turned to the towns beneath them. At Logan, Angell failed to adequately address this problem; his towers are identical and the building's orientation ambiguous. Folsom, on the other hand, made his eastern tower taller (a finial on its cupola also denotes its superiority), while at the same time using the slope angle to soften the effect. In Andrew's words, "The building appears to be facing west toward the valley, not towards the mountain; the slightly greater height of the eastern end merely picks up the downward slope of the hill and continues it to the western end, where it is assumed by the terraces."[48]

On the inside, however, Angell seems to have held the upper hand. The two temples had been started under Young's watchful eye, and from all indications he intended them to follow the by now "traditional" temple plan used at Kirtland, Nauvoo, and St. George, and in the original design for Salt Lake. Out of loyalty to both Smith and Young, Truman Angell Sr. felt obliged to honor this tradition. Angell Jr. rebelled, going over his father's head by submitting after Young's death an alternative plan to the new church president, John Taylor.[49] What the younger Angell was proposing was hardly radical: he simply wanted to substitute a slightly modified version of the Endowment House plan for the now functionally obsolete double court—he proposed turning the lower court into a series of circularly arranged endowment rooms while keeping the upper one. Angell Sr. objected, saying this was not what Young had wanted. But Taylor approved the new plan and had it implemented at both Logan (finished in 1884) and Manti (finished in 1888). Architect Don Carlos Young adopted Angell Jr.'s plan for the Salt Lake Temple as well (completed in 1893).[50]

Public Works

Stories abound regarding the "communal" nature of temple construction. In the Sanpete Valley, they probably started with Brigham Young, who issued instructions that the Manti Temple could be built in a truly cooperative fashion, proclaiming dramatically in 1877, "We intend building this Temple for our selves and we are abundantly able to do it herefor no man need come here to work expecting wages for his services, the neighboring Settlements will send their men and they can be changed whenever and as often as desirable and they can get Credit on Labor Tithing or on Donation account for their services and we expect them to work till this Temple is completed without asking for wages. It is not in keeping with the Character of the Saints to make the building of Temples a matter of merchandise."[51]

Maybe not merchandise, but at the same time the temples would never have been completed if left solely to collective acts of spiritual devotion—the proverbial "girding up of loins." Temple walls rose through the dedication and sacrifice of the membership, but in reality these buildings were highly complex structures, requiring the attention of a great number of skilled workers, many of whom had to be paid for their time to keep them on the job full-time. Tithed labor, with a worker devoting one day in ten, may have been sufficient for some of the preliminary work, but once actual construction began a trained and reliable labor force was essential (Figure 8.14). Church leaders could marshal the troops, as Orson Hyde did when he told the Sanpete Saints "he wanted a constant stream of labor and means to flow toward the Temple,"[52] but at the same time, these troops had to be compensated and for this the church had to raise funds. "Let the Bishops," Young announced, "call the people of their Wards together and ascertain from them how much each one is willing to subscribe in Labor and means, monthly, quarterly, or annually, towards the erection of a Temple at Manti, Sanpete County."[53]

Temple building in the nineteenth century took the form of a massive public works project—an early kind of economic stimulus package. Tithing was directed in the form of cash, produce, or credit at the local cooperative store toward temple construction, thereby achieving the church's Zion-making purposes while also injecting money into local communities. As we have seen, such an infusion of capital saved St. George, and during the years of temple construction the residents of Manti enjoyed a period of unrivaled prosperity, with local businesses and those of the county as a whole profiting

Figure 8.14. Manti Temple workers, 1880s. George Edward Anderson Photographs, MSS P-1, L. Tom Perry Special Collections, Brigham Young University.

greatly. Timber had to be cut and transported, trees sawed into lumber, rock quarried and hauled, walls plastered and painted, moldings milled, planed, and installed—all these and many other tasks associated with erecting the Manti temple put the Sanpete population to work as never before (or after). This does nothing to diminish the role of faith. It remained an important part of the equation. At the same time we cannot ignore the willingness of church leaders to bankroll Zion making (and community growth in general) by putting the Saints to work on public works projects like the temples.[54]

Construction on the Manti Temple commenced April 24, 1877, when "Architect and Sup[erintenden]t W. H. Folsom arrived in company with Jesse W. Fox, Surveyor General, and Truman O. Angell, Church Architect for the purpose of laying out the Manti Temple Site. Bro[ther] Edward L. Parry, Master Mason, arrived from St. George [where he had supervised the rockwork on the St. George Temple] in company with Pres[iden]t Young and party."[55] The building site was formally dedicated the next day, a ceremony performed by President Brigham Young and his counselors, John W. Young and D. H. Wells, "in the presence of many hundreds of People from Manti, and other Settlements."[56] Young wanted the work to start immediately, and on the Monday following the dedication Jens Weibye recorded that over "80 Brethren" turned out and began "clearing the site with 4 span horses, 6 yok oxen, some ploughs, scrapers, peks, spades, and showels."[57]

Site preparation took nearly two years, and not until early in 1879 was the cornerstone for the foundation laid and dedicated.[58] By the next spring the building was taking shape (Figure 8.15), but progress was impeded by the superintendent's growing need for skilled craftsmen. Up to this point, common laborers, mostly volunteers, had been equal to the task of flattening the hilltop and digging the foundation trench. But "from now [on]," as Folsom told local bishops, "more skilled labor will be required on the Temple ground."[59] This meant finding and hiring craftsmen like masons, plasterers, painters, joiners, and carpenters on a permanent basis, which required additional funds. The superintendent therefore could praise the Saints in the Sanpete Temple District "for their readiness in carrying on the Temple work," while at the same time being forced to scour the territory for both good help and the means to support them.[60]

The main source of temple funds was tithing channeled into Manti both from Salt Lake City and the Southern Temple District, which included Washington, Kane, Iron, Piute, Beaver, Millard, Sevier, and Juab Counties as well

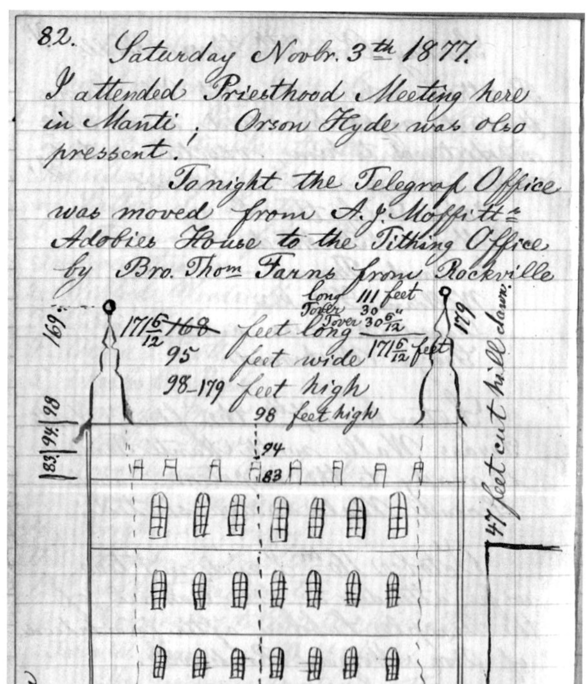

Figure 8.15. Sketch of the Manti Temple, November 3, 1877, Jens Weibye. Weibye copied a drawing that he had seen in the *Deseret News* for October 9, 1877. That the drawing does not include the mansard roof cupolas suggests that Folsom's original design may have resembled the one Truman Angell Jr. developed for the Logan Temple. Courtesy of the Church History Library.

as Sanpete (see Table 8.1). Folsom told a meeting of the priesthood in Manti in November 1877, "It is the intention of the [building] committee to pay the men laboring on the Temple out of the donations to the Temple, hence he wished that all the means donated to the Temple should be sent to Manti."[61] These would be calculated according to set "tithing prices"[62] and paid out

Table 8.1. Revenue received at the Manti Temple Office in donations, April 30, 1880

Sanpete Stake	$1,381.61	
Ephraim	$18,790.29	
Manti N[orth] W[ard]		$8,998.34
Manti S[outh] W[ard]		$7,993.63
Manti R[elief] S[ociety]		$306.67
Manti total	$17,298.64	
Mount Pleasant	$9,752.48	
Spring City	$5,654.05	
Fountain Green	$4,836.35	
Fairview	$5,402.32	
Moroni	$6013.96	
Gunnison	$4,288.52	
Wales	$2,655.86	
Fayette	$386.57	
Mayfield	$2,184.97	
Chester	$885.64	
Castle Valley	$221.15	
Freedom	$123.75	
Pettyville	$226.20	
Thistle Valley	$215.00	
total [Sanpete]		*$80,317.36*
Juab Stake	$1,079.15	
Nephi	$3,749.91	
Levan	$823.24	
Mona	$497.95	
total [Juab]		*$6,150.25*
Total		*$86,467.61*
Sevier Stake (Richfield, etc.)	$13,825.67	
Millard Stake (Fillmore, etc.)	$8,928.08	
Beaver Stake (Beaver, etc.)	$8,595.18	
Parowan Stake (Parowan, etc.)	$6,969.05	
Panguitch Stake (etc.)	$2,090.14	
Kanab Stake	$3,369.91	
St. George Stake	$11,789.11	
Trustee in Trust [Brigham Young]	$36,784.33	
Grand total of		*$179,766.38*

Source: Weibye, Day Book 6, 51–53, Church History Library. The original ledger, which contains mathematical errors, is reproduced here.

on a sliding scale according to the work performed. In April 1877 temple-building committee clerk Jens Weibye reported the following wage schedule: "That the price to be allowed common Laborers should be from $1.25 to 2.00 per Day. Men with team[s] from 2.50 to 3.50 per day; Quarrymen, 2.00 to 3.00; Stone Masons 2.50 to 3.50; Carpenters 2.50–3.50; E. L. Parry 5.00; W.S. Snow 3.75; and N. L. Christensen 3.75 . . . payable at Tithing Office prices. [And further] that Labor Tithing and Offerings should be deducted from all wages paid."[63]

Shortages remained. One problem was the failure of the Saints to prove good on their tithing obligations. Apostle Wilford Woodruff, speaking to the May 16, 1880, Stake Conference in Ephraim, said, "If the Saints paid their tithing punctually there would be no need to call for means to build Temples as there would be an abundance for that purpose."[64] And when both tithing and donations did not arrive, special assessments were tried. Orson Hyde reminded the Saints in 1877 that "sacrifices that are made without being felt will not bring the same reward as those that are," so to make it hurt a little more, he added that the "authorities wanted 50 cents per month from each family for the temple."[65] And there would be more: in 1881, Stake president Canute Peterson "said the Temple was in need of funds. That there was a special call for $400.00 which would be distributed among the different wards."[66] And even more: Jens Weibye describes how at a meeting during the spring of 1885 Stake president Canute Peterson came to speak to the Scandinavian meeting in Manti and told those in attendance, "Every family [will] have to pay $25.00 a Year in Temple donation, and then we expect to get our Manti Temple ready in the fall of 1886."[67]

Folsom remembered to acknowledge the people for their generosity, thanking everyone at Stake Conference in 1883 "for the[ir] prompness in responding to the call for means to purchase the roofing. The money being on hand at the date required."[68] He was also careful to point out that "it is not the wish, in the erection of the Temple, to be oppressive to the people, but what is accomplished to be the result of their voluntary donations."[69]

Canute Peterson in 1881 said it was the bishops' duty "to stir up the people to pay their tithing and temple donations."[70] One way to do this was to appeal to their faith. For example, Wilford Woodruff stated in August 1881 that "if we could have the privilege of looking behind the veil we would not need any sermons on Temple building; we would be so eager to rear them understanding the great necessity of this work. Just think there are 50 generations waiting for us to do work for them."[71] Another was to issue reminders of the blessings gained from such actions. An epistle from Salt Lake City spelled it out clearly: "The Lord increased their [the Mormons'] substance, provided ways of deliverance from their enemies, and bestowed gifts and knowledge upon them which are beyond all earthly price. So it will be now if we will arise in the majesty and strength of our calling as the people of God, and build these Temples with willing hearts and liberal hands, the Lord will pour out His Blessings upon us to an extent we have never heretofore known."[72] To be sure such blessings were distributed fairly, however, architect Folsom in February 1878 asked Peterson to check on the donations from the wards: "and a record of the names of the Donors should be accurately kept by the Bishops, so that when requested at the end of the year or completion of the Temple, we may be enabled to give every individual their proper credit."[73]

Making amounts given known in public was also a way of shaming members into doing their duty. According to Weibye, the practice was to call the people together, "and at these meetings the amount each person shall subscribe should be placed opposite his or her name, so that what can be depended upon may be known in writing. Each Bishop can then make a statement over his own signature to the President's Office of the amount of Labor and means that his Ward shall furnish in the aggregate and that he will be responsible for."[74]

Still another way to inspire donations was to appeal to people's pocketbooks, as Orson Hyde (he said the same thing about meetinghouses, you may remember) did when he spoke at a Stake Conference at Ephraim in 1877 of the temple's effect on property values: "The building of the Temples is a blessing financially, enhancing the value of property more than the cost of building."[75] To punctuate his message, Hyde attached a figure: "when the Temple and Meeting House are finished property in Manti will be worth 4 times as much as present."[76]

Folsom was a clever architect, but he was perhaps more adept at keeping the coffers full enough to keep the project going for the eleven years needed to complete the building. We read his letters and find him telling "those working on the Temple [that they] should come prepared with tools, provisions, etc., so as to take the responsibility of their support from the shoulders of the [superintendent]";[77] explaining to the bishop of Nephi that "we shall be pleased to have the brethren you name labor on the temple if you can possibly furnish the means to pay them. Bro. Allen is an excellent mechanic and we find him very useful, we allow him $4.00 per day at Tithing prices";[78] and writing Bishop John Murdock of Beaver: "Dear Bishop: Brother John S. Jones has a credit for labor on the Manti Temple to present date of $198.30. . . . We find him quite a useful man and would like [to keep] his services, if you can arrange to pay for him. We have no funds at this office and we are entirely [dependent] upon the donations of the different [towns] to furnish the requisite labor and material to carry on the work."[79] It is difficult to think Folsom had any time to actually work on the building. One way the Sanpete towns did help was by constructing housing for their workers. Weibye included in his daybook a sketch of the row of small houses built by the various towns at the foot of temple hill to accommodate their own workers (Figure 8.16).

And there were always troublemakers. In a Manti meeting, Folsom "said he wished all those who were engaged upon the Temple to work with a good spirit and to avoid grumbling."[80] But they grumbled anyway, and some of it was directed toward him. Talk even circulated that Folsom's large salary put a particular drain on donated contributions. President John Taylor refuted this allegation at the Stake Conference in Ephraim in 1878, saying he "had heard that there were rumors among the people that Bro[ther] Folsom received such high wages and that these were paid out of the donations to the Temple. He would say that such was not the case. Folsom, and Bro Parry were paid by the Church."[81]

Construction ebbed and flowed according to the available funding. At the Stake Conference in 1881 Folsom said that "there had been less means received this quarter than during any other quarter since the Temple was commenced, still much labor had been done. The policy of the Authorities was

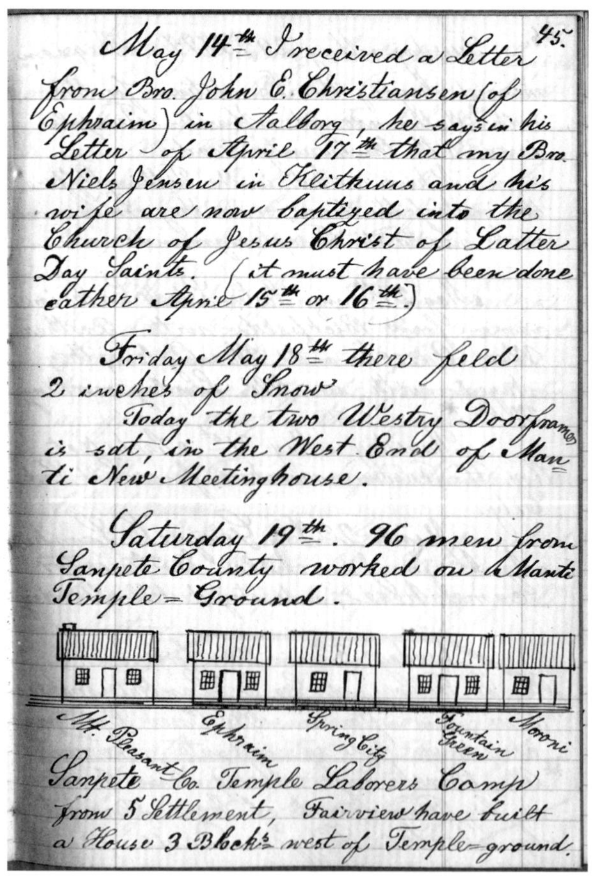
45.

May 14th I received a Letter from Bro. John E. Christiansen (of Ephraim) in Aalborg he says in his Letter of April 17th that my Bro. Niels Jensen in Kleitkuus and his wife are now baptized into the Church of Jesus Christ of Latter Day Saints. (it must have been done eather April 15th or 16th.)

Friday May 18th there feld 2 inches of Snow

Today the two Westry Doorframes is sat, in the West End of Manti New Meetinghouse.

Saturday 19th. 96 men from Sanpete County worked on the Manti Temple-Ground.

Sanpete Co. Temple Laborers Camp from 5 Settlement, Fairview have built a House 3 Block's west of Temple-ground.

Figure 8.16. Sketches of temple workers' houses from Jens Weibye's daybook, May 14, 1877. Courtesy of the Church History Library.

not to run into debt."[82] They did not, although the building, including finish work and furnishings, reportedly cost roughly $900,000, of which over a third was raised in the Sanpete Valley.[83]

Pilgrim's Progress

No element in the Sanpete Valley landscape holds as much meaning as the monumental temple at Manti (Figure 8.17). Much has been written about its great beauty, its significance as a sign of the pioneers' dedication and sacrifice, and how it serves as a sanctified place for individual Saints to carry out the temple work so vital to their salvation and exaltation. More too could be said about how it reflects such things as Mormonism's need to distinguish itself architecturally from other Christian denominations, the restoration to earth of ancient biblical practices and priesthoods, the role tithing-funded public works projects played in the Zion-making project, and the separation of the landscape into sacred and secular spheres as the enthusiasm for millenarian expectations waned after 1870.[84] One meaning is often overlooked, however, and this is the way the building and the endowment rooms in particular served as cultural agents, representing on a micro scale the message of "works righteousness" found in the landscape as a whole.

Figure 8.17. Manti Temple under construction, October 8, 1885. George Edward Anderson Photographs, MSS P-1, L. Tom Perry Special Collections, Brigham Young University.

As outlined earlier, Mormons are expected to work in their own behalf to ensure their position in the afterlife. Integral to this endeavor is the doctrine of "works" or "works righteousness," which links works to visible signs of grace called blessings. Accordingly, a person's works, whether public, personal, or spiritual, are rewarded through blessings on earth, which in turn are believed to ensure similar rewards in heaven. Earthly blessings come in a variety of forms, but the most obvious are material in nature, consisting of such things as success in business or having a fine house and an abundance of land. The temple endowment ceremony reinforces this theological construction through the process of allegory, using the arrangement and style of the lecture rooms to symbolically represent the LDS worldview in miniature. The "work hard and you shall be rewarded ethos" is one of the underlying lessons of the endowment.

The Sanpete Valley landscape is a progressive one: the Saints were repeatedly admonished by their leaders to improve their condition, to make their cities and houses beautiful, and prepare the earth in anticipation of Christ's Second Coming. It was a goal-oriented agenda, with the membership assigned tasks with specific intended results. Early on, works were often conceived and presented as group efforts, but increasingly, especially as millennial expectations faded, they became more the domain of individual Saints. This is particularly true of the endowment ceremony, which is highly personal—an intimate communing with the divine—yet progressing toward a predetermined destination. In the temple the faithful participate in a metaphorical journey, a Pilgrim's Progress (Figure 8.18), moving *onward* from room to room and from a state of sin to the joy of redemption, and *upward,* ascending toward the heavenly glory of the celestial kingdom (Figure 8.19).[85]

The architectural style of the endowment rooms helped set the tone of advance not only by creating discrete stages of the journey (each room was given its own special identity through the use of particular interior finishes) but also by emphasizing gradation (a hierarchy of importance established again through the use of embellishment) from beginning to end. It was a subtle but effective mechanism for getting the message across that works lead to a higher, exalted state not only in heaven but also on earth, since blessings

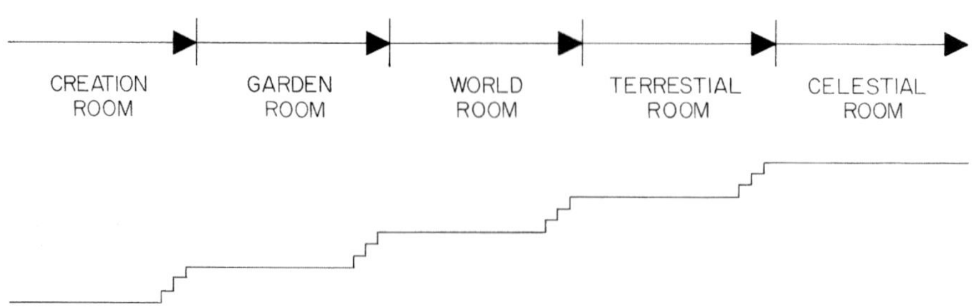

Figure 8.18. Pilgrim's Progress: a diagrammatic representation of the onward and upward movement found in the LDS temple ritual.

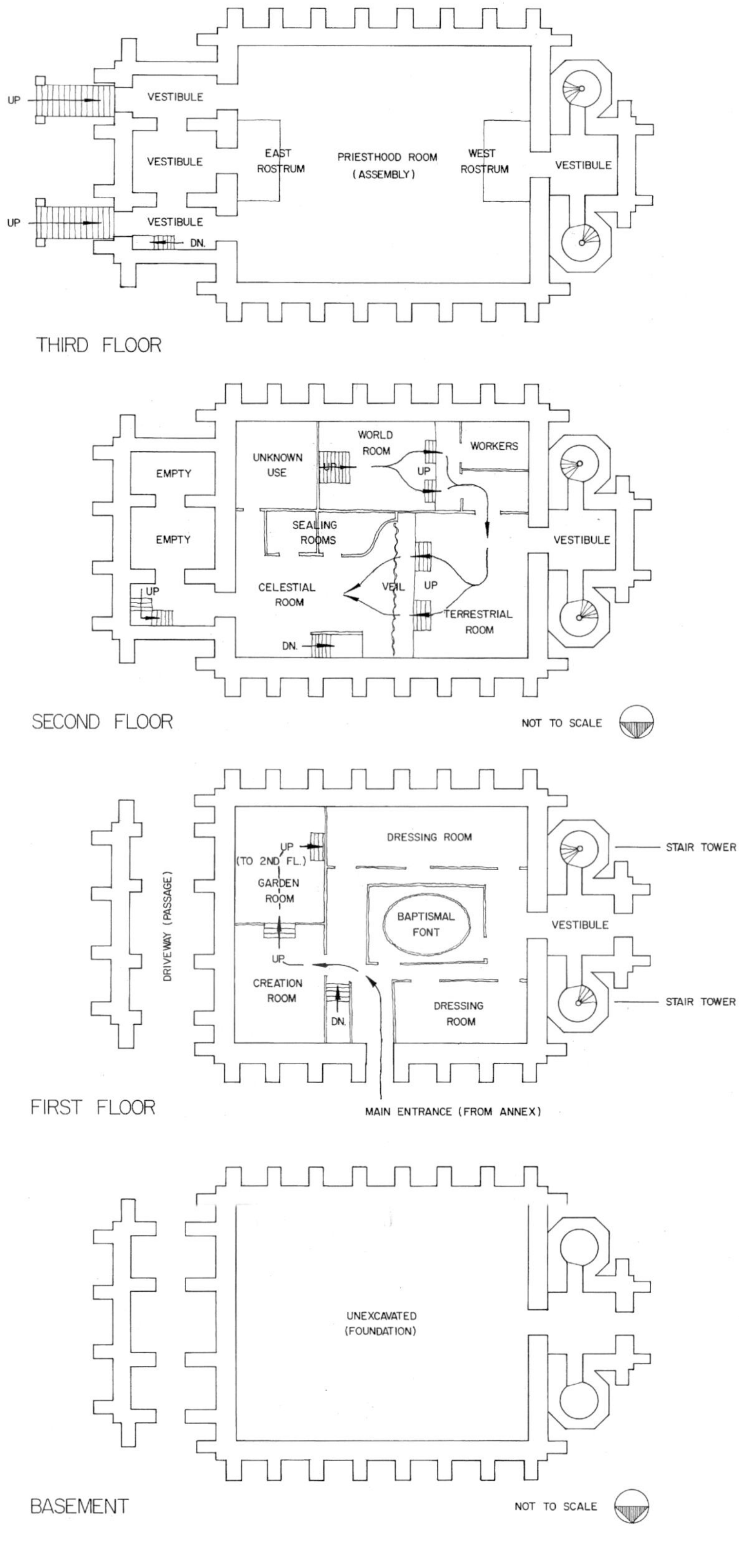

Figure 8.19. Floor-plan drawings reconstructing the interior of the Manti Temple, circa 1890.

are received equally in both realms. Decorating the endowment rooms had been initiated in the Endowment House, had continued at St. George, and was accepted practice by the time the Logan and Manti temples were commenced.[86] The styles of interior finishes for the endowment rooms break up into two categories, the first dominated by murals and the second by architectural features.

In the Manti Temple, the three mural rooms are the Creation, Garden, and World (Telestial) Rooms (Figure 8.20). In these spaces wall paintings are the most visible elements, though moldings, casings, and stair balusters are also present and add to the overall effect. More than anything the murals are intended to convey a sense of verisimilitude by making patrons feel they are actually present at the Creation, or standing in the Garden, or witnesses to the unfolding of world history. In a straightforward, literal manner, murals in the Creation Room depict the earth coming into being: clouds swirl around nebulous planets, volcanoes erupt, and lightning strikes, and there is a hint of the primitive world taking shape. A simple architrave surrounds the door, with no baseboards or crown molding, and the newels at the bottom of the stairs lack distinction—they are the kind found in most local homes.[87]

Things improve slightly in the Garden Room. Obviously, the murals here show the world in its Edenic state. Lush hues of green and blue bring the plants to life, animals roam at will, and the overall tone is one of peace and tranquillity. The architectural features take a step up: the two large false windows have round heads and fan tracery in their upper lights; the casings and baseboards are heavily molded; the altar has recessed panels and a plain cornice; and the turned newel and stair balusters are indicative of the kind found in the more refined houses in the valley. They are not as elegant, however, as the ones found in the next or World (Telestial) Room. Here all the appointments again display a noticeably higher quality. There is a balcony on one side where the altar stands. A railing of turned balusters runs along its front, supported by six turned posts. Balusters and posts are more curvaceous and intricate than those in the Garden Room, and the front panels on the altar also finer, having round arched heads and built-up casings. Curiously, the door casings are rather simple, like those in the Creation Room. A mural planned for this room was not executed in the nineteenth century. In other temples, World Room murals (and in the one painted here in the 1940s) portray major events in human history after the Fall, including the crucifixion, the Great Apostasy, war and pestilence, and finally the restoration of the True Church.[88]

Significant changes occur in the next two rooms, for the explicit imagery of murals is abandoned in favor of more implicit but equally powerful meanings presented through elaborate architectural detailing (Figure 8.21). Logically perhaps, one finds in the Terrestrial Room the penultimate level

CREATION ROOM

GARDEN ROOM

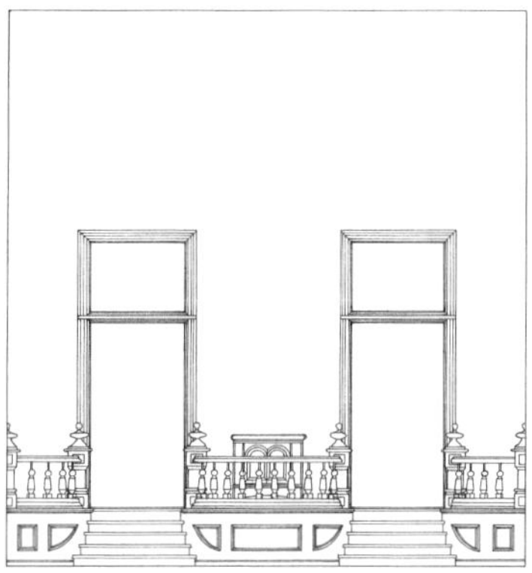

WORLD (TELESTIAL) ROOM

Figure 8.20. Interior elevations of the Manti Temple's mural rooms: Creation Room, Garden Room, and Telestial Room (originally unpainted).

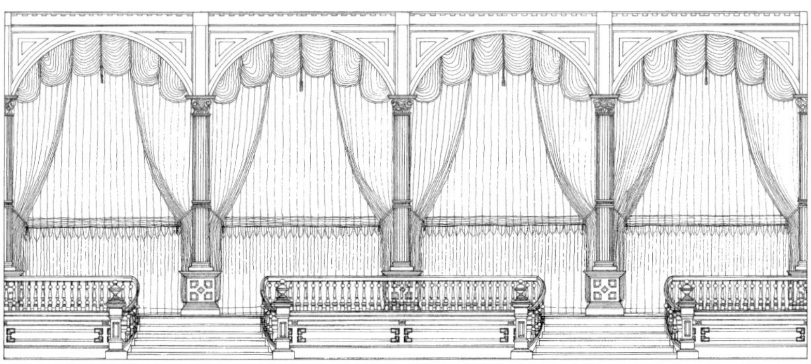

TERRESTIAL ROOM

CELESTIAL ROOM

Figure 8.21. Interior elevations of the Manti Temple rooms with architectural finishes.

of heavenly attainment, a level of finishes, features, and furnishings higher than those of the previous rooms, but a step below those gracing the Celestial Room. Of note in the Terrestrial Room are the carpets, fluted columns, arched ceilings, elaborate paneled altar, and balcony railing typical of a fine house or public building. The principal element, however, is the Veil, a drapery that stands behind the balcony. These curtains are of the finest materials available and direct attention back to the purpose of the room, which is to usher patrons into the glory of the Celestial Room.[89] The impact of the crossing into the presence of God is confirmed by the architecture of this final room. Again there is an arched ceiling, but here the moldings and pendants are of the highest quality, clearly differentiated from those witnessed earlier in the Terrestrial Room. The carpet is deeply piled and luxurious, as are the chairs and sofas. The overall fashion is French baroque, a mode of classicism popular at the time and characterized by opulence and richness of texture. The House of the Lord could have no finer apartment than the Celestial Room.[90]

The graded sequence found in the endowment rooms is purposeful. Church members quite literally ascend not only into the presence of God but also to their own personal Kingdom of God. The splendor of the Celestial Room is yet another reminder of the rewards that await those who have through their works reached the ultimate blessing of exaltation. The objective of life on earth is eternal glory in the afterlife, and the Celestial Room, ever since its advent in the Nauvoo temple and its expression in Salt Lake City's Endowment House, was "supposed to be heaven." If so, the journey was well worth the effort.[91]

As we have seen, the story told in the temple is the same one found in the City of Zion landscape. In this regard, the old adage about "earth mirroring heaven" is on target. The "works righteousness" message was apparent to all Zion makers; all they had to do was look around them at the social world they had created. Individual agency permeated everything about it: towns, city lots, houses, shops, and meetinghouses, as well as the temple, exemplified the role individuals played in shaping their own destinies. Works begat blessings, signs of God's favor, and because one's standing on earth foretold one's future in heaven, the achievement and display of wealth as signs of grace (and exaltation) were greatly encouraged.

This arrangement was no more evident than in a set of houses constructed by church leaders in Salt Lake City during the 1870s. Although they were beyond the capabilities of settlers in outlying colonies like those in the Sanpete Valley, these houses would have been known to all who visited the capital city, and such visits were, despite the distances, quite common—people coming to do their ordinance work in the Endowment House, for instance, purchase merchandise, or visit relatives. For the Sanpete colonists who by this time had an idea of what the House of the Lord looked like—it had a French roof (Figure 8.22)—the new houses built by Brigham Young, one of his counselors, George Q. Cannon, and leading businessmen Feramorz Little and William Jennings would have been quite understandable, for they were all built in the newest fashion, the French Second Empire Baroque.[92]

Style works rather insidiously, forming unconscious alliances between what may be considered unlikely partners.[93] This seems the case with the temples and the French mansions of Salt Lake City. The most famous of these elegant residences was the Gardo House (Figure 8.23), commissioned by Young in 1873 and designed by William Folsom. In addition to its pretentious name (it derived from one of Young's favorite novels), the house easily outshone all others in the city. Young wanted a house that demonstrated taste and refinement (to properly entertain guests and visiting dignitaries) and he got it: the French fashion was the rage in the East, and employing it on the western frontier emphatically conveyed both qualities. On the outside it was distinguished by its mansard roof, roof dormers, hooded window heads, bay windows, verandas, bracketed cornice, and intricacy of classical detailing rivaled only by the houses of his friends and colleagues, Cannon, Fox, and Jennings.[94]

Figure 8.22 *(left)*. Architect William Folsom achieved a domestic scale for the east elevation of the Manti Temple by digging it into the sloping hillside. From this angle, the building has the feeling of being quite literally the "house" of the Lord. Photograph from 1995.

Figure 8.23 *(below)*. Brigham Young's Gardo House, 70 East South Temple, Salt Lake City, 1873–77. Reprinted by permission of Utah State Historical Society; all rights reserved.

French styling set the Gardo House off from the typical houses in the city, denoting Young's leadership position in the church community. At the same time, particularly in its mansard roof and lavish interior finish, it formed a tight bond with the Manti Temple (and later with the Salt Lake Temple). It was immense, with forty-five rooms, and its finish commensurate with its size. It had a spiral staircase, rich paneling, classical trim, wall murals, mirrors, and Empire-fashion furniture imported from Europe (Figure 8.24).[95] This richness of detail is found in only one other space in the City of Zion landscape, and this was the Celestial Room of the Manti Temple, also designed by Folsom. Whether the temple copied the house, or the house the temple is not important. What is significant is the way the two conjoin to promote the "works" doctrine.

Visiting the Celestial Room or the Gardo House parlor, the average Saint could see the elegant furnishings, lush carpets, dense wall murals, enriched entablatures, and cut-class chandeliers and thereby experience vicariously the refined life of the leadership, the men who communed with God. Worldly wealth and earthly accumulation were clearly not things to be rejected or avoided. Rather, the message in the buildings—again the temple and the house—is that that those who prosper on earth stand in God's favor. The progressive stages in the ritual led from literal to abstract symbolization: from murals depicting the Creation, the Garden, and the Fall, to architectural representations of grandeur, the exalted state enjoyed by the Chosen both on earth and in heaven. In this way, baroque classicism connected the

Figure 8.24. The opulence of the Gardo House interior revealed in this nineteenth-century photograph was equaled only by the rich finishes used in the temple's Celestial Room. Reprinted by permission of Utah State Historical Society; all rights reserved.

French houses with the temple endowment, displaying the good life that all aspired to achieve.

The House of the Lord after all could be nothing less than the finest mansion in the territory, and this identity was further enhanced by the building's monumental size and positioning on the hill above town. As we know, early temples had been located in the center of town, occupying the expected place for a church. But they were soon to sit at a contemplative distance from the mundane, profane world. The hilltop location in Manti and Logan provided the temples with a social distance usually only available to the wealthy, and in this sense, the temple truly became a mansion on the hill. It was a house that would adequately serve the Son of God during the millennium, and it was a useful reminder to the Saints of the existing social order on earth.

CONCLUSION
THE ENDURING ZION

> Are we living in a Manner that we will have nothing to regret in the future, our surroundings look prosperous, but are we increasing in faith and good works, or are we giving away to the Spirit of the World?
>
> —*Apostle Franklin D. Richards, Fairview, June 21, 1875*

In a thoughtful essay, critic Edward Rothstein poses the question of just how much can be expected in the name of utopian idealism. The very idea of utopia speaks of perfection—making and living in a perfect world. But how can imperfect people achieve such an elevated condition? "The closer one looks," Rothstein writes,

> the more ambiguity there is. Moreover, what is in question is not only utopia's virtue but also the procedures required to reach it. Utopia stands outside of history. It is the city on the hill, society's dream image. But it can be reached only by breaking the continuity of history. Any attempt to create a utopia is necessarily revolutionary. The manners, morals, and convictions of the past have to be cast aside. The realization of a utopia requires destruction.[1]

And such destruction is rare. Human nature works against it (self-interest being a rather formidable foe), but cultural momentum figures in as well. The best way to think about it may be to assume that people, due to the circumstances of their upbringing and education, are *disposed* toward certain kinds of behaviors. These actions become so physically and mentally ingrained as to become habitual and self-perpetuating because, first, outcomes of contradictory actions are unknown and thus avoided; and second, under duress, the species displays a remarkable willingness to fall back on customary practice. In the case of the City of Zion, we see a social world conceived in utopian terms, but achieving it meant breaking with Western bourgeois tradition, and this was something of which the Latter-day Saints, no matter where they came from, were not capable. Instead, they held tenaciously to long-standing traditions and expectations, reshaping them to satisfy the peculiarities of the Zion-making project.[2]

The human landscape of Mormonism tells this story well. So much talk surrounds the Zion-making project that cutting through the rhetorical haze is not easy, but it still seems best, if our goal is to know better what the City of Zion was like, that in addition to the words we take into account things, and make the physical evidence part of our study (Figure C.1). A wide-angle view, the kind we take when we do landscape history, is best too, since taken separately any one component could be misleading. If we pay attention only to temples, for example, the impression might be that the place was radically *other,* whereas if we restrict ourselves to houses, the conclusion might be the opposite, that the familiar ruled. In either case we would be missing the crucial point, and this is that Zion had some of both, and it was the reconciliation of these positions, group and individual, sacred and secular, other and different, that made the Mormon sacred universe work. It was a slow process, and one that began almost immediately with the founding of the church in 1830. We might say it centered on the Latter-day Saints' finding a way "to be in the world."

The influence that American capitalist consumer culture had on the City of Zion must not be ignored. And it was not something that happened suddenly, with the coming of the railroad. Rather, we see its impact early, a continuous pressure on the Saints and the decisions they made in building up their Kingdom of God (Figure C.2). As we have seen, in selecting town sites the desire for more land and better opportunity meant as much as working within a church-directed settlement plan. Compact village-type towns undoubtedly fostered a degree of social cohesion, but hierarchies of lot size and location ensured that class distinctions would also be emphasized. Houses

Figure C.1. The Mormon landscape. A section drawing of the Sanpete Valley showing the principal elements in the Mormon cultural landscape.

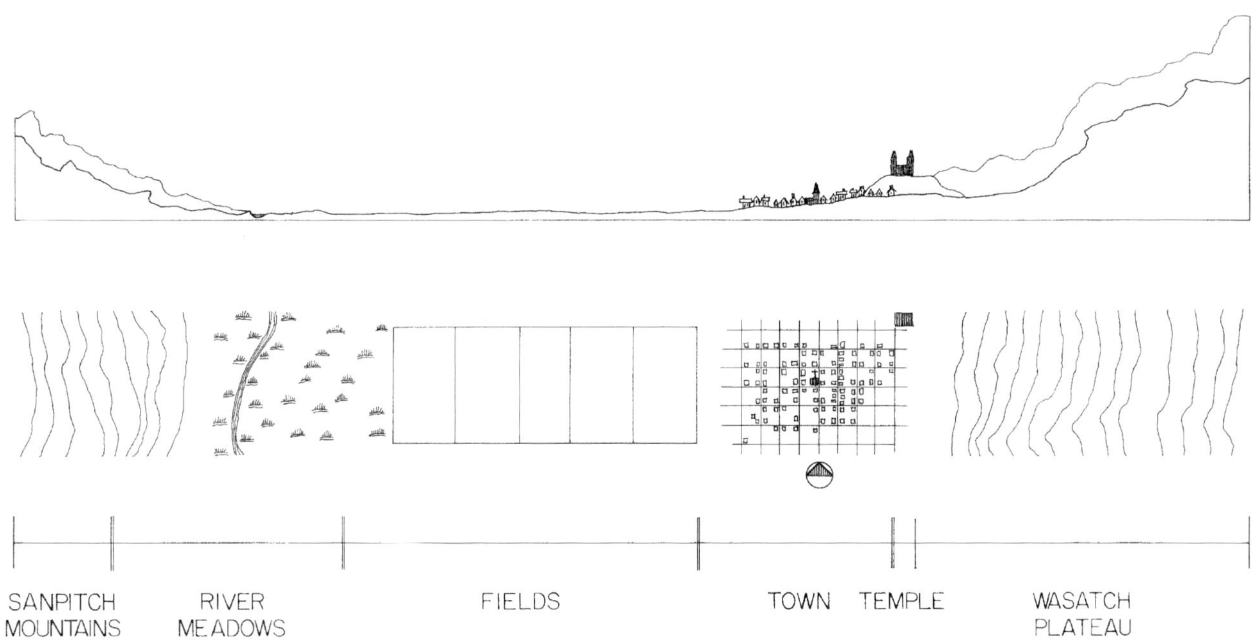

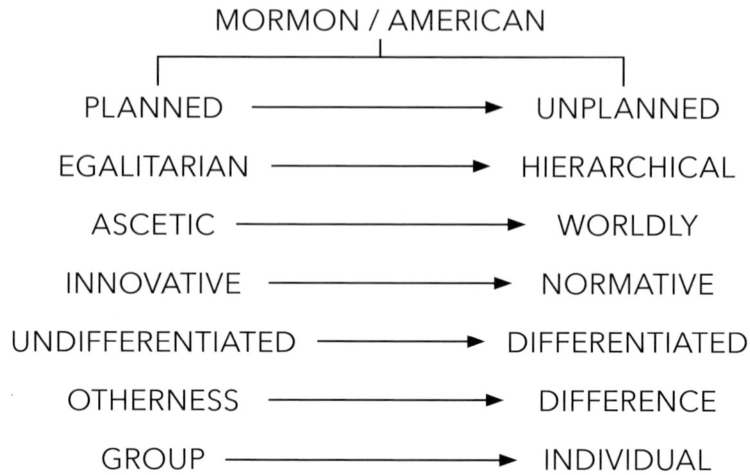

Figure C.2. The decisions facing Sanpete Valley planners and designers listed as series of oppositions, with arrows indicating the tendencies within Mormon society toward particular values.

were similarly ranked according to a family's social and economic standing, and those who could afford them built large and fashionable dwellings in the style of the world. In polygamous housing and the architecture of the Relief Society buildings, older patterns of patriarchal authority were perpetuated within the new marriage system. Various entities—some public, others private, some religious, others secular—claimed space on Main Street, a diversity of interests that demanded architectural differentiation. A distinctive Mormon style in meetinghouses and tabernacles appeared but was compromised rather quickly by less aggressive mainstream tendencies. And finally, the temples, often viewed as monuments to Mormon group identity and purpose, were on their way to becoming places where individual church members went to do their own and their ancestors' "temple work."

This is not utopia, at least in conventional terms. Historian Grant Underwood names Mormons "moderate millenarians," noting, "LDS attitudes and behavior in the nineteenth century seem less countercultural, and communitarianism and theocracy more superficial, than has often been assumed. Indeed, it may be that the oft-romanticized theocratic communalism of the Saints was doomed from the start precisely because Mormons had always been too American at heart."[3] It would seem so. One wonders in fact what would have happened if Joseph Smith or Brigham Young had insisted on enforcing the United Order? As it was they asked a great deal—calling families to settle new lands, sending men on missions, keeping track of their tithing payments—but never perhaps crossing the line. Rothstein suggests that utopias are bound to fail simply because they make it too hard for people to belong.[4] One particularly fascinating aspect of early Mormonism was its ability to facilitate church membership by deleting measures such as those aimed at social and economic leveling. Church leaders, it appears, knew when to back off.

Could it be, too, that the Mormon idea of utopia in time came to be different from the standard anticapitalist, communitarian tome introduced during the church's first years? Earthly perfection, after all, is a relative term and it seems not unreasonable to say that as the egalitarianism of the first or theoretical Zion waned, a more "moderate" (to follow Underwood's terminology) view waxed, bringing along a new set of what we might still call *utopian* values. In place of the revolutionary zeal of the early church, a less demanding ethos emerged, albeit slowly as we have seen. The turmoil that characterized the theoretical Zion was replaced over time by institutional steadiness, the product of the various competing energies within the society seeking and finding equilibrium. Life in the Mormon City would settle into a set of routines, some obvious and predictably American, others less so and uniquely LDS, but all informed by religious commitment and belief. I believe that it is this later prescription, the culture of the Gospel of Works, that we need to understand, since it was chiefly responsible for the City of Zion that was actually built during its final three phases.[5]

At the outset, I portrayed landscape production as a process whereby the built environment is constructed as a set of observable and readily understood signs that organize the social world in relation to a set of underlying cultural values and ideals. The former is visible in the landscape (in such things as building size, location, type, and style) while the latter is contained in a series of mythologies (cultural narratives or stories) that explain and validate the perceived social order. I further contended that during the nineteenth century, three stories were pivotal in producing the social world of Mormonism: millennialism, the doctrine of continuing revelation, and the Gospel of Works. Millennialism established a fundamental calling for the church; the earth lay in a state of apostasy, and it was the duty of the Latter-day Saints to gather out of Babylon and prepare the earth for the Second Coming and the subsequent Apocalypse. This was a story told with some urgency in the early days, but one that with the passing of time lost its power—the world in fact did not end in 1890, as many Saints thought. That millennialism was diminishing even earlier is witnessed by the reorganizing of the landscape after about 1870 from a City of Zion to a Mormon City mentality. The job of preparing the earth for the immediacy of the End Times gave way to settling in and bracing for a protracted stay. Life could go on as usual in the secular city, while the restoration could continue almost unnoticed in the sacred temples.[6]

The second story, the doctrine of continuing revelation, made such transformations possible. As noted earlier, Mormons believe that God continues to intervene in human life and thus change can be expected. Such flexibility can be observed in a willingness of the Saints to accept the various incarnations of Zion, each with dramatically different liturgical and social agendas.

The story can probably account too for the patience it took to work through the various iterations of the temple. With no blueprints, much was done in a trial-and-error fashion. But it was a mentality of accommodation that could allow the church to quietly move past its millennial fervor, almost like passing from adolescence to adulthood. Membership took it in stride; with so much for individual Saints to do in the temple, the old story receded from view.

And finally there is the Gospel of Works, which basically maintains that grace comes through good works, and these works will be rewarded by blessings on earth, often in terms of material advancement. The works ideology surfaced early in the church's history: Brigham Young, speaking in 1843 at Nauvoo, said, "If I had a wife and ten children, I would give all my money to build the Temple and the Nauvoo House, and would trust to God for their support. Yet I will be richer for it; for God would prosper me in business."[7] And it endured in Utah. Witness Edwin Whiting, speaking of the need to work on the Manti meetinghouse, reminding the Saints that "works were ahead of preaching" and that "the most liberal man [in terms of donations] would become richest in this worlds Goods."[8]

One of the things the landscape makes clear is the importance of earthly blessings, be they prosperous towns, well-watered lots, large houses, or the temple with its lavish baroque interiors. Again, these were all signs—"evidences"—that *one's works were working*. Heaven and earth are not dissimilar: both are graded and the Saints must work on earth to progress to the highest levels of heaven. In 1857 Manti bishop Warren Snow, after exhorting the Saints to leave earthly things for heavenly ones, "added some further instructions touching the nature of the Saints' heaven and its being on the earth with fine houses and beautiful gardens etc."[9] Finding heaven on earth, whether in the form of a fine house or in lavish finishes of the temple's Celestial Room, anticipated the exaltation one could expect in the afterlife. The landscape was a perfect metaphor, a didactic exercise in the meaning of existence.

A New Zion

It has become customary to think of Mormonism as a restoration movement, the restoring to earth in the Last Days of biblical Christianity. Theologically, we have seen that it was as much an invention as a restoration, the creative melding of Old and New Testament concepts with New World revelation. In terms of the Mormon social world, the one visible in the Sanpete Valley landscape, the term may have more applicability, however. This is not to say that the City of Zion replicated ancient practices. It did not, though some biblical undertones can be discerned. Rather, the evidence of the landscape points to a source closer to home, and this was republican America, the world many believed lost to the excesses of Jacksonian democracy.[10]

Republicanism is more than a political construct, though representative government is one part of it—albeit the part that Mormons seem to have rejected. More profoundly, republicanism is an ideology, a coherent set of beliefs about the way the world should work.[11] Some of these beliefs, such as limited government and agrarianism, are well known, but also important are three concepts that appear to have had the greatest effect on early Mormon leaders and the social world they made. The first is a steadfast belief in the *public good* (individuals contributing to the general welfare of the community); the second, *moral virtue* (a code for individual conduct centering on honesty, temperance, frugality, and industry); and the third, *equality* (of opportunity but not wealth). These qualities are embedded in the City of Zion landscape and its principal mythology, the Gospel of Works. John Patten of Manti, in 1861 said as much when he "referred to Mormonism and its evidences that he [Patten] was a True Republican in principle and that there was no real conflicting between Republicanism and Mormonism."[12]

The Public Good

The most important republican principle was a belief in the public good. Feeling that the welfare of the society was essential to both political and economic stability, each member of the community should be inclined to devote time and energy to promoting the common purpose of the group. Mormons accomplished this largely through tithing. In Zion, all households were expected to contribute 10 percent of their income to the church, which during much of the nineteenth century at least, was synonymous with the community. Since church and state were conjoined, tithed money, produce, and labor went into building and maintaining the social fabric. When the Mormons spoke of cooperation, it seems they meant paying attention at some level to the public good.

This connection was explicitly expressed in a letter James C. Brown of Manti wrote in 1868 to the *Deseret News.* In describing the opening of the local cooperative store, Brown noted that "steps have been taken by the people of Manti to form themselves into a co-operative body, and I expect in a few weeks we will have a large store established that will have for its motto 'Pro Bono Publico [for the public good].'"[13] Apostle Orson Hyde chose to think of Zion as a ship. Visiting Manti in 1860, he "again spoke on Public Interest; compared it to a Ship in a Storm all were anxious to relieve the Ship. One man works not but finds his gold on his person and when the Ship goes down and his gold sinks him but not so with the man that looks to public interest he works at the pumps and lets wife children and God take care of themselves he saves the Ship Zion."[14]

Public works were on people's minds and made manifest in the material world all around them. Writing in 1868, Jens Weibye observed, "It was proposed that we in Manti do Public work every Saturday from now til Dec 1st, except 3, 4, or 5 weeks in the Harvest Time."[15] Or John Kirkman, writing from Moroni in 1871 to the *Deseret News:* "Nothing can prevent a community from living, increasing and prospering whose members, of both sexes, are industrious and preserving, not only for the individual benefits arising from that course, but also for the general good of the whole."[16] Peter Olsen Hansen, an immigrant carpenter and farmer from Manti, kept a detailed diary, and excerpts from 1859 reveal the two sides of the coin, working for himself and working for the community. April 1: "Worked these 3 days for Bro. Barton at stone mason work. $2 day"; April 2: "Worked on tithing whole day"; April 4–7: "Worked for Br. Barton building stone fence"; April 19: "Work for one of the fence committee"; April 24: "Build on Jns. Squires fence"; April 26: "Worked for the community ½ day. Afternoon on Squires fence"; July 19, 20, 21, 22: "Have worked 4¼ day tithing."[17]

One corollary of the public works concept found in Mormonism is that if people had more in terms of time and money, they could contribute more to the group through tithing. Weibye's tithing records from Manti in 1881 are instructive of the sliding scale of tithing payments: "20 persons in Manti paid tithing over 50$ each, 21 paid over 75$, and 18 paid over 100$."[18] Among the eighteen who paid over $100 were George Albrecht, N. S. Beach, William A. Cox, N. L. Christensen, Jens Hansen, Robert Johnson, Ebbe Jessen, J. B. Maiben, Jens Olsen, J. C. A. Weibye, L. C. Hansen, Hans Jensen, and Jacob Keller. After listing these names, Weibye adds, "329 Persons have paid Tithing in Manti 1881 to the amount of $10,438.70 and out of this 329 18 persons have paid over 1/5 of the amount namely $2,334.93."[19] Five years later, in 1885, Weibye figured that "429 have paid Tithing in 1885 whereof 78 have paid over $50.00 Each and 18 of the 78 have paid over $100.00 Each. $27.00 average per Capita. 32 Men have not paid any Tithing."[20] For the public good the Saints invested in the co-ops (which, by the way, often paid dividends through the 1870s), built good houses, worked their farms, and sold their surplus to the miners in Nevada. There were no internal contradictions in their motives: they were building a Kingdom of God and would be judged, ultimately, according to their works, both as individuals and as a community.

Moral Virtue

A second republican principle involved personal conduct. A good citizen was honest, temperate, frugal, and industrious, qualities found desirable by the Mormons, who were instructed to remain faithful to the tenets of their religion, live free of sin, be honest in their business dealings—and be diligent in improving the material Zion. Apostle Amasa Lyman of Salt Lake City visited Mount Pleasant in 1865 and laid out most of the republican traits: "The Saints ought to be progressing continually, in every thing that is good; wisdom and knowledge, it is a curse instead of a blessing to be ignorant. In living our religion we are not only required to pray and go to meeting, but to build up Zion in every respect, building meeting houses, Schoolhouses, fix our roads and bridges. If we see a chance to make a dollar out of our neighbor we ought not to embrace it because in so doing we are cheating him."[21] Similarly, presiding bishop Warren Snow of Manti likewise told the people that in business, "if a man was dishonest with his brethren he was dishonest with his God,"[22] and President Welcome Chapman continued, saying that "our temporal affairs were in the hands of God; we need not be afraid, if honest with each other."[23]

In attempting to promote the virtuous life, it is not surprising that the first city ordinance in Manti outlawed blasphemy. There were attempts at prohibition, since alcohol consumption, and whiskey in particular, was considered a problem. Orson Hyde preached in Manti, giving good counsel "about Electing City Officer[s] there [who] do not drink Liquer, and do our best to stop whisky selling in Manti."[24] Weibye wrote in 1882 that W. K. Barton (one of the designers of the Manti meetinghouse) started a store that sold ice cream, lemonade, and soda water, but soon, "a sign was put up to sell Wines and Liquor." Weibye also identified "Mr. Oscar F. Cooledge" as a man who "has been selling Liquor for some time from his house."[25] Weibye's daybook entry for the October 29, 1882, includes the news that "Prest. John B. Maiben, Bp. Hans Jensen, and Bp. Wm. T. Reid spoke very much against Whisky and other strong drinks, and want us to sign a Petitin to the City Council, praying for them to stop giving License to sell whisky."[26]

Drunkenness got in the way of industry, which was a prime virtue for both republicans and Mormons. Hard work (and the blessings it engendered) was highly valued, and idleness was a sin. Manti's James Wareham sounded a common note in 1855: "Complainers were idlers."[27] Edwin Whiting of that city "referred to counsel about improvement of property this had been neglected. . . . We should try to beautify the City and build houses of Rock and not of Adobies; we should also attend to culture the Mind. A Lazy man could not advance much; our main objective was to build up the Kingdom."[28] Manti

on the basis of their own productivity—the more a family prospered the more it was assured of salvation and exaltation; and the more it could contribute to the building up of the Kingdom. The theocracy gradually crumbled under the weight of actions by the federal government, but the republican foundation upon which the Mormon social world rested survived, hardened perhaps by the mythological mortar found in the Gospel of Works. Call it what you will—the *Mormon landscape* seems about right, since it was and continues to be just that, a place created and lived in by members of the Church of Jesus Christ of Latter-day Saints—only do not confuse it with the utopian landscape prophesied in the 1830s. At the same time, it was never drawn back into the normative fold—it was not a typical American landscape, or rather, an "Americanized" landscape. The best way to think of the material world of early Mormonism is as an eclectic blend of new and old, of the sacred and the secular, the temple and the house. Making it required no wholesale destruction; instead, the dream of Zion as the *city on the hill* gave way to the realities of *Zion in the world,* a place where the Latter-day Saints could be both Mormons and Americans. It is a landscape of faith and works. It is an American landscape, with a difference.

ACKNOWLEDGMENTS

A STUDY THAT SPANS A CAREER accrues a great number of debts, so many that it would be impossible to name all those who helped along the way. In fact, at times the whole project collapses into a life dream: telling Ann about a day of fieldwork that included sitting around a piano drinking wine with two former opera singers, one of whom was naked; chatting with Glen Nielsen about how they blew up the old Ephraim meetinghouse because it wouldn't fall down like everyone in town said it would; hanging off a twenty-foot-high truss while measuring a barn with Dell in 10-degree weather, just before the owner demolished it; Randy telling me the church archive people thought I was a German tourist because I often worked in shorts and sunglasses; evenings walking the streets of Spring City with Craig, smoking cigars and remembering the old-timers who told us about the old days and the old buildings; and so many more memories and stories tied up in these pages. All I can do is say "thank you" to everyone, and I apologize to any and all whom I have missed and release those whom I have named from any responsibility. In the end, this project (and its accomplishments and faults) is mine alone.

It all started in a class at Indiana University taught by Henry Glassie. Along with the book he wrote on old Virginia houses, his course changed my life in a way he can never imagine. Now, forty years later, Henry remains very much a part of this book, a form of recognition, tribute, and friendship. Henry moved on, but Jan Shipps picked up the pieces and made me smarter about not just Mormons but their buildings, too. Jan hung on to the bitter end, and without her I would probably still be measuring houses and wondering what it all meant. My friends in Bloomington, Blanton Owen, Gary Stanton, and Steve, Ona, and Dov Siporin, gave graduate school the appearance of fun.

After I decided to work in the Sanpete Valley, a job as a Utah State Historical Society surveyor helped pay for the first round of fieldwork. I thank Kent Powell for his interest in what a folklorist could bring to historic preservation survey (he thought it odd that I wanted to draw floor plans), and to

John McCormick and Barbara Murphy for getting laid off at the same time as I did. Dave Madsen, Stan Layton, Bruce Hawkins, and Bonnie Rogers were there, too, and (closer to the present) Roger Roper, Alan Barnett, and Cory Jensen. Alan and Cory were former students who ended up with jobs in history. Good work, boys.

Living for a year in Manti, I found myself showing up regularly at the Spring City home of my high school friends Craig and M'lisa Paulsen. Often I visited at lunchtime, and my arrival usually prompted their daughter Ana to announce "Tom's home." Indeed, their home felt like my own, and still does. I must say too that no one knows old Utah buildings like Craig, who as a restoration contractor worked on most of the houses in this book. I hope his heaven is built of oolite limestone. Other Sanpeters who helped me greatly are county recorder Reed Hatch and his son Cory; Al and Iona Antrei, Jane Braitewaite, Don and Ruth Simmons, Pearl Miller, Kaye Watson, Shannon Miller, Glen and Virginia Nielson., and Kathleen Peterson. Hundreds of others also opened their doors and let me measure to my heart's content. If you want to restore your faith in humanity, do architectural fieldwork.

At the University of Utah's Graduate School of Architecture, I am indebted to both Robert Bliss and the late Carl Inoway, who as deans gave a folklorist the chance to pose as an architectural historian. Carl is gone now, but I think of him often, as I do Peter Goss, who is still around, a colleague and friend for more than thirty-five years. Peter made room for me at the school, and for this I'll always be obliged. Others there who befriended me include Bob Hermansen, Tony Serrato-Combe, Anne Mooney, Mira Locher, and Brenda Sheer. And all those students whose names escape me, except for the ones who actually liked history: Julie Osborne, Eric Tuttle, Jack Brady, Kathryn Anderson, Jim Agutter, and Matt Wallace, to name a few. I especially recognize Bob Goldberg, a colleague from the history department, and Steve Tatum, from English. The three of us share a love (and appreciation) for western history that is not common at the University of Utah, where most are afraid of appearing provincial. Bob read the manuscript and had it dialed. Thanks, Bob, and (although it grieves me to say it) let the New Yorks win sometimes.

Poring through the voluminous holdings of the Church of Jesus Christ of Latter-day Saints History Library would have been impossible without the aid of a number of excellent archivists and historians. First and foremost was Randy Dixon, who guided me toward important documents, helped me understand what I was reading, and read the manuscript for errors only he could spot. I hope that Randy's book will soon be finished, too. Photography curator Bill Slaughter made me laugh about not getting permission to use the one image I wanted. Steve Sorenson, Ron Barney, Steve Olsen, Ron Watt, Kirk

Henrichsen, Alan Morrell, Emily Utt, and Linda Haslam made this Gentile boy feel welcome and believed that what I was doing was worthwhile. This goes for a number of my LDS friends, too, including Ben Bennion, Lynn Baldwin, Don Showalter, and Rees Peterson. Don clued me in to blessings, and Lynn served as my "bishop" throughout, always providing good counsel. Ben had the hardest job: he read the rough manuscript several times and made good use of his red pen.

Funding for the archival research came from the National Endowment for the Humanities. A Helen Lee and Emil Lassen Fund Fellowship gave me time in Denmark to study the origins of immigrant houses. A Faculty Fellowship from the University of Utah's Tanner Humanities Center funded sabbatical leave for writing the first draft. Money for preparation of the illustrations came from a University of Utah Faculty Research Committee grant and a Delmont Oswald Fellowship from the Utah Humanities Council. A University of Utah Research Committee Grant supported design and publication.

My world changed dramatically in 1981 when I discovered the Vernacular Architecture Forum, a professional organization devoted to the study of ordinary buildings and landscapes. For those of us who study things others ignore, it is indescribably important to have friends and colleagues with whom to share ideas, discoveries, and fieldwork stories. VAF is a surrogate home institution for many of us and the source of many of my best friends. I need to single out Dell Upton, whose support at rough times pushed me on, and readers will see his influence throughout this book. Dell's standards are high and a constant inspiration. Other VAFers who provided help and encouragement include Edward Chappell, Susan Buck, Carl Lounsbury, Cary Carson, Willie Graham, Paul Groth, Bill Littman, Robert St. George, Jerry Pocius, Chris Wilson, Betsy Cromley, Anna Andrzejewski, Bernie Herman, Kim Hoagland, Betty Bird, and Virginia Barrett Price. Barbara Carson and Orlando Ridout V are two that went too soon.

In addition to my friends from work, there were others who didn't care much about old buildings but liked to play old-time fiddle music, fly-fish, ski tour, and bicycle up mountains, and they also made these years a joy. They include Dwight Butler, Hal Cannon, Leonard Coulson, Mitch Cocorinis, Jim Cox, Meg Glaser, Skip Gorman, Jamie Greene, John and Vickie Hoagland, Ron Kane, Duncan and Mopsey Kennedy, Bob King, Pat Lambrose, Sarah Sabiston, Tom Sauber, Patrick Sauber, John Sparano, and John Taufer. Thanks to all of you.

My family has been here with me, too. My late mother and father, Bob and Beth Carter, were always supportive. I feel my mother's ambitions for me on every page. Ann Kadesch Carter, my wife through much of the early work, I cannot thank enough. Ann lived with me in the old rock house in Manti when everything froze. Our children, Will and Beth, contributed by having productive lives of their own. Anne Brackin Oliver gave me a final boost of energy and a reason to get it done. Finally.

A nod also goes to the University of Minnesota Press. Abigail Van Slyck, coeditor of the Architecture, Landscape, and American Culture series, made me feel wanted. I greatly appreciate her guidance and trust. Gretchen Buggeln's pointed but friendly critique also made the final product so much better.

Humbly, I thank you all.

NOTES

Note on Illustrations

1. Thomas Carter, "Folk Architecture in the Mormon West: The Historical Implications of Old Houses," lecture at Fife Folklore Conference, Utah State University, Logan, Utah, June 1977.

2. Lord Raglan, *The Temple and the House* (New York: W. W. Norton, 1964).

Introduction

1. Manti Temple Historical Record, vol. 1, 1873–1934, 4, Church History Library, Church of Jesus Christ of Latter-day Saints, Salt Lake City, Utah, hereafter cited as Church History Library.

2. See C. Mark Hamilton, *Nineteenth-Century Mormon Architecture and City Planning* (New York: Oxford University Press, 1995); and John W. Reps, *Cities of the American West: A History of Frontier Urban Planning* (Princeton, N.J.: Princeton University Press, 1979).

3. The standard source is D. W. Meinig, "The Mormon Culture Region: Strategies and Patterns in the Geography of the American West," *Annals of the Association of American Geographers* 55 (June 1965): 191–220. Specific landscape traits are enumerated in Richard Francaviglia, "The Mormon Landscape: Definition of an Image in the American West," *Proceedings of the Association of American Geographers* 2 (1970): 59–61; and Richard Francaviglia, *The Mormon Landscape: Existence, Creation, and Perception of a Unique Image in the American West* (New York: AMC Press, 1978).

4. A landscape approach to architectural inquiry is gaining in popularity. For a rationale, see Dell Upton, "Architectural History of Landscape History?," *Journal of Architectural Education* 44:4 (August 1991): 195–99; and Pierce Lewis, "Common Landscapes as Historic Documents," in *History from Things: Essays on Material Culture,* ed. Steven Lubar and W. David Kingery (Washington, D.C.: Smithsonian Institution Press, 1993), 115–39.

5. References to building up Zion are legion in Smith's revelations. This one was received in April 1829 and is contained in the LDS book of revelations, *Doctrine and Covenants of the Church of Jesus Christ of Latter-day Saints* (Salt Lake City: Church of Jesus Christ of Latter-day Saints, 1974), 6:6.

6. In the 1830s, Joseph Smith noted down thirteen "articles of faith," later canonized in *The Pearl of Great Price: A Selection from the Revelations, Translations, and Narrations of Joseph Smith* (Salt Lake City: Church of Jesus Christ of Latter-day Saints, 1974), 59. See also David J. Whittaker, "The 'Articles of Faith' in Early Mormon Literature and Thought," in *New Views of Mormon History: Essays in Honor of Leonard J. Arrington,* ed. Davis Bitton and Maureen Ursenbach Beecher (Salt Lake City: University of Utah Press, 1987), 63–92.

7. Orson Pratt, *Journal of Discourses* (Los Angeles: Gartner, 1956), 16:78.

8. Hans Jensen Hals, Reminiscences and Diary, 1868–1910, 6, Church History Library.

9. Reps, "Cities of Zion: Origins of the Mormon West," in *Cities of the American West,* 287–311.

10. Formal variation in western LDS settlements is treated in Richard H. Jackson, "The Mormon Village: Genesis and Antecedents of the City of Zion Plan," *BYU Studies* 17 (Winter 1977): 223–40.

11. Mircea Eliade, *The Sacred and the Profane: The Nature of Religion,* trans. William R. Trask (New York: Harcourt Brace Jovanovich, 1959), 34.

12. The conceptual side of the equation is expertly handled in Steve L. Olsen, *The Mormon Ideology of Place: Cosmic Symbolism of the City of Zion, 1830–1846.* Dissertations in Latter-day Saints Studies (Provo, Utah: Joseph Fielding Smith Institute for Latter-day Saint History, 2002).

13. Definitions of "landscape" are found in Matthew Johnson, *Ideas of Landscape* (Oxford: Blackwell, 2007), 1–17; and Don Mitchell, *Cultural Geography: A Critical Introduction* (Oxford: Blackwell, 2000), 101–15. See also D. W. Meinig, ed., *The Interpretation of Ordinary Landscapes: Geographical Essays* (New York: Oxford University Press, 1979), 1–7; Lewis, "Common Landscapes as Historic Documents," 115–17; and Paul Groth, "Frameworks for Cultural Landscape Study," in *Understanding Ordinary Landscapes,* ed. Paul Groth and Todd W. Bressi (New Haven, Conn.: Yale University Press, 1997), 1–21.

14. George Lakoff and Mark Johnson, *Metaphors We Live By* (Chicago: University of Chicago Press, 1980), 36. See also Don Mitchell, "Metaphors We Live By," in *Cultural Geography,* 120–44; and Christopher Tilly, *Metaphor and Material Culture* (Oxford: Blackwell, 1999), 1–76.

15. Upton, "Architectural History or Landscape History?," 198; Dell Upton, "Form and User: Style, Mode, Fashion, and the Artifact," in *Living in a Material World: Canadian and American Approaches to Material Culture,* ed. Gerald L. Pocius, Social and Economic Papers No. 19 (St. John's, Newfoundland: Institute of Social and Economic Research, Memorial University of Newfoundland, 1991), 156–69; Dell Upton, "Another City: The Urban Cultural Landscape in the Early Republic," in *Everyday Life in the Early Republic,* ed. Catherine E. Hutchins (Winterthur, Del.: Henry Francis du Pont Winterthur Museum, 1994), 61–117; and Dell Upton, *Another City: Urban Life and Urban Spaces in the New American Republic* (New Haven, Conn.: Yale University Press, 2008), 1–15. Help here also came from Peter Berger and Thomas Luckmann, *The Social Construction of Reality: A Treatise in the Sociology of Knowledge* (Garden City, N.Y.: Anchor Books, 1967); Henri Lefebvre, *The Production of Space,* trans. Donald Nicholson-Smith (Oxford: Blackwell, 1991); M. Gottdiener, *The Social Production of Urban Space,* 2nd ed. (Austin: University of Texas Press, 1985); Dan Sperber, *Rethinking Symbolism,* Cambridge Studies in Social Anthropology (Cambridge: Cambridge University Press, 1974); and Anthony P. Cohen, *The Symbolic Construction of Community* (London: Routledge, 1985).

16. Jules Prown, "Mind in Matter: An Introduction to Material Culture Theory and Method," in *Material Life in America, 1600–1800,* ed. Robert Blair St. George (Boston: Northeastern University Press, 1988), 23.

17. Henry Glassie, "Structure and Function: Folklore and the Artifact," *Semiotica* 7:4 (1973): 313–49; Henry Glassie, *Folk Housing in Middle Virginia: A Structural Analysis of Historic Artifacts* (Knoxville: University of Tennessee Press, 1975); and Henry Glassie, *Material Culture* (Bloomington: Indiana University Press, 1999). See also Terence Hawkes, *Structuralism and Semiotics,* 2nd ed. (London: Routledge, 1977); John Storey, *An Introduction to Cultural Theory and Popular Culture,* 2nd ed. (Athens: University of Georgia Press, 1998); Peter Burke, *History and Social Theory* (Ithaca, N.Y.: Cornell University Press, 1992), and Richard Jenkins, *Pierre Bourdieu,* rev. ed. (London: Routledge, 1992).

18. Upton, "Form and User," 161–62; and Bernard L. Herman, "The Architectural and

Social Topography of Early Nineteenth-Century Portsmouth, New Hampshire," in *Gender, Class, and Shelter: Perspectives in Vernacular Architecture, V*, ed. Elizabeth Collins Cromley and Carter L. Hudgins (Knoxville: University of Tennessee Press, 1995), 225–42. See also Marcel Dansesi and Paul Perron, "The Signifying Order," in *Analyzing Cultures: An Introduction and Handbook* (Bloomington: Indiana University Press, 1999), 67–101.

19. Upton, "Form and User," 159; Upton, "Another City," 62–65; and Robert Hughes, *Myths America Lives By* (Urbana: University of Illinois Press, 2004), 1–17.

20. John Gager, *Kingdom and Community: The Social World of Early Christianity* (Englewood Cliffs, N.J.: Prentice-Hall, 1975), 10. See also Kenelm Burridge, *New Heaven, New Earth: A Study of Millenarian Activities* (New York: Schocken Books, 1976); R. Laurence Moore, "To Become a People: The Mormon Scenario," in *Religious Outsiders and the Making of Americans* (New York: Oxford University Press, 1986), 25–47; and Dick Hebdige, *Subculture: The Meaning of Style* (London: Routledge, 1979).

21. Brigham Young, *Journal of Discourses*, 5:4. The literature on the relationship between Mormon and American culture is extensive. See Moore, *Religious Outsiders and the Making of Americans;* Thomas O'Dea, *The Mormons* (Chicago: University of Chicago Press, 1957); John L. Sorenson, "Mormon World View and American Culture," *Dialogue* 8 (1973): 17–29; Klaus Hansen, *Mormonism and the American Experience* (Chicago: University of Chicago Press, 1981); Thomas G. Alexander and James B. Allen, *Mormons and Gentiles: A History of Salt Lake City* (Boulder, Colo.: Pruett, 1984); Marvin Hill, *Quest for Refuge: The Mormon Flight from American Pluralism* (Salt Lake City: Signature Books, 1989); Armand L. Mauss, *The Angel and the Beehive: The Mormon Struggle with Assimilation* (Urbana: University of Illinois Press, 1994); and Lee Trepanier and Lynita K. Newswander, *LDS in the USA: Mormonism and the Making of American Culture* (Waco, Tex.: Baylor University Press, 2012).

22. Explanation forms in history are treated in Gene Wise, *American Historical Explanations: A Strategy for Grounded Inquiry* (Minneapolis: University of Minnesota Press, 1980), ix–xx. The essential text in this school of Mormon historiography lends it its name; see Gustive O. Larson, *The "Americanization" of Utah for Statehood* (San Marino, Calif.: Huntington Library, 1971). For additional perspective see Moore, *Religious Outsiders and the Making of Americans*, 42–45; and Jan Shipps, "Difference and Otherness: Mormonism and the American Religious Mainstream," in *Sojourner in the Promised Land: Forty Years among the Mormons* (Urbana: University of Illinois Press, 2000), 307–9.

23. Leonard J. Arrington, *Great Basin Kingdom: An Economic History of the Latter-day Saints* (1958; repr., Lincoln: University of Nebraska Press, 1966), 409.

24. Ibid.

25. Ibid., 4.

26. See Moore, *Religious Outsiders and the Making of Americans.*

27. Shipps, "Difference and Otherness," 315. See also Tamise Van Pelt, "Otherness," *Postmodern Culture* 10:2 (2000): 1–34.

28. Useful in understanding the nature of republican thinking is Joyce Appleby, *Capitalism and a New Social Order: The Republican Vision of the 1790s* (New York: New York University Press, 1984), 1–23.

29. Fairview Ward General Minutes, 279. Church History Library.

1. Faith and Works

1. Still an excellent source on the religious history of Upstate New York in the early nineteenth century is Whitney Cross, *The Burned Over District: The Social and Intellectual History of Enthusiastic Religion in Western New York, 1800–1850* (New York: Harper and Row, 1950). See in particular 138–50.

2. Quoted in Leonard J. Arrington and Davis Bitton, *The Mormon Experience: A History*

of the Latter-day Saints (New York: Alfred A. Knopf, 1979), 7. See also Fawn Brodie, *No Man Knows My History: The Life of Joseph Smith,* 2nd ed. (New York: Alfred A. Knopf, 1976); and Richard L. Bushman, *Joseph Smith: Rough Stone Rolling* (New York: Alfred A. Knopf, 2005).

3. See Jan Shipps, *Mormonism: The Story of a New Religious Tradition* (Urbana: University of Illinois Press, 1985), 29; and Shipps, *Sojourner in the Promised Land,* 313–14.

4. *Doctrine and Covenants of the Church of Jesus Christ of Latter-day Saints,* 14:6, 45:66, and 97:21.

5. Grant Underwood, *The Millenarian World of Early Mormonism* (Urbana: University of Illinois Press, 1999), 42–57.

6. Ibid., 11–41.

7. George Q. Cannon, *Journal of Discourses,* 26:40.

8. Shipps, *Mormonism,* 41–85.

9. Ibid., 67–85; and Douglas J. Davies, *An Introduction to Mormonism* (Cambridge: Cambridge University Press, 2003).

10. Brigham Young, *Journal of Discourses,* 5:4. Emphasis added.

11. Arrington and Bitton, *The Mormon Experience,* 37.

12. Useful general treatments of Mormon history are Arrington, *Great Basin Kingdom;* Arrington and Bitton, *The Mormon Experience;* James B. Allen and Glen L. Leonard, *The Story of the Latter-day Saints* (Salt Lake City: Deseret Book, 1976); and Matthew Bowman, *The Mormon People: The Making of an American Faith* (New York: Random House, 2012).

13. Allen and Leonard, *The Story of the Latter-day Saints,* 62.

14. Quoted in Craig S. Campbell, *Images of the New Jerusalem: Later Day Saint Faction Interpretations of Independence, Missouri* (Knoxville: University of Tennessee Press, 2004), 36.

15. For the Missouri years, see Warren Jennings, "The City in the Garden: Social Conflict in Jackson County, Missouri," in *The Restoration Movement: Essays in Mormon History,* ed. F. Mark McKiernan, Alma R. Blair, and Paul M. Edwards (Lawrence, Kans.: Coronado Press, 1973), 99–119; F. Mark McKiernan, "Mormonism on the Defensive: Far West, 1838–1839," in *The Restoration Movement,* 121–40; Arrington and Bitton, *The Mormon Experience,* 44–64; Campbell, *Images of the New Jerusalem,* 23–89; and Bowman, "Little Zions, 1831–1839," in *The Mormon People,* 32–62.

16. Quoted in Robert Bruce Flanders, *Nauvoo: Kingdom on the Mississippi* (Urbana: University of Illinois Press, 1965), 29.

17. Glen M. Leonard, *Nauvoo: A Place of Peace, a People of Promise* (Salt Lake City: Deseret Book; Provo: Brigham Young University Press, 2002). This is the definitive study of this period of Zion making—an excellent study that includes a good deal of landscape history.

18. Strictly speaking the Latter-day Saints practiced polygyny, which refers specifically to a man taking multiple wives. Having more than one spouse, male or female, is called polygamy. The Latter-day Saints commonly used the latter term, and I have followed their lead. Other names for it were "living the principle," "celestial marriage," and "patriarchal marriage." See Richard S. Van Wagoner, *Mormon Polygamy: A History* (Salt Lake City: Signature Books, 1986); Lawrence Foster, *Religion and Sexuality: Three American Communal Experiments of the Nineteenth Century* (New York: Oxford University Press, 1981); and Shipps, *Mormonism,* 60–62.

19. B. Carmon Hardy, "The Persistence of Mormon Plural Marriage," *Dialogue* 44:4 (Winter 2011): 43–105. See also Shipps, *Mormonism,* 41–85; Davies, *Introduction to Mormonism,* 91–115; and John L. Brooke, "The Keys to the Kingdom," in *The Refiner's Fire: The Making of Mormon Cosmology, 1644–1844* (Cambridge: Cambridge University Press, 1994), 235–61.

20. Glen M. Leonard, "Foes Within: The Church of the Seceders," in *Nauvoo: A Place of Peace, a People of Promise,* 341–79.

21. See John G. Turner, *Brigham Young: Pioneer Prophet* (Cambridge, Mass.: Harvard University Press, 2012), 110–43.

22. *Doctrine and Covenants,* 64:24.

23. Underwood, *The Millenarian World of Early Mormonism,* 24–41.

24. See P. A. M. Taylor, *Expectations Westward: The Mormons and the Emigration of their British Converts in the Nineteenth-Century* (Ithaca, N.Y.: Cornell University Press, 1966).

25. William Mulder, *Homeward to Zion: The Mormon Migration from Scandinavia* (Minneapolis: University of Minnesota Press, 1957), 102–12.

26. Quoted in Olsen, *The Mormon Ideology of Place,* 25.

27. See Leonard J. Arrington, Feramorz Y. Fox, and Dean L. May, *Building the City of God: Community and Cooperation among the Mormons* (Salt Lake City: Deseret Book, 1976), 38–39.

28. Arrington and Bitton, *The Mormon Experience,* 34.

29. Arrington, *Great Basin Kingdom,* 4.

30. Davies, *An Introduction to Mormonism,* 6.

31. Ibid., 102–15.

32. Ibid., 79–83. See also Samuel Morris Brown, *In Heaven as It Is on Earth: Joseph Smith and the Early Mormon Conquest of Death* (New York: Oxford University Press, 2012), 203–78.

33. Davies, *An Introduction to Mormonism,* 81.

34. Jan Shipps, "In the Presence of the Past: Continuity and Change in Twentieth-Century Mormonism," in *After 150 Years: The Latter-day Saints in Sesquicentennial Perspective,* Charles Redd Monographs in Western History 13, ed. Thomas Alexander and Jessie Embry (Provo: Charles Redd Center, 1983), 11–12.

35. Eliade, "Sacred Space and Making the World Sacred," in *The Sacred and the Profane,* 20–65; and Jonathan Z. Smith, "In Search of Place," in *To Take Place: Toward Theory in Ritual* (Chicago: University of Chicago Press, 1987), 1–23.

36. The core of this idea is contained in Shipps, *Mormonism,* 109–29.

37. Olsen, *The Mormon Ideology of Place,* 19–41, 21.

38. See Robert Bruce Flanders, "A Dwelling for Man and a Dwelling for God," in *Nauvoo,* 179–210.

39. Shipps, *Mormonism,* 124–25.

40. Lowell C. Bennion, "Plural Marriage, 1841–1904," in *Mapping Mormonism: An Atlas of Latter-day Saint History,* ed. Brandon S. Plewe (Provo: Brigham Young University Press, 2012), 122–25. Bennion estimates that in 1870, a peak year for the practice, between 25 and 30 percent of Utah's population was polygamous (123).

41. See Shipps, "The Millennial Vision Transformed," in *Mormonism,* 131–49.

42. James E. Talmage, *A Study of the Articles of Faith: Being a Consideration of the Principal Doctrines of the Church of Jesus Christ of Latter-day Saints,* 49th ed. (Salt Lake City: Church of Jesus Christ of Latter-day Saints, 1968), 89–90.

43. Ibid., 96.

44. Manti Ward General Minutes, April 28, 1853, 169, Church History Library.

45. Davies, *An Introduction to Mormonism,* 165.

46. *Manti Herald and Sanpete Advertiser,* May 4, 1867, Church History Library.

47. Perry Miller, *The New England Mind: The Seventeenth Century* (1939; repr., Cambridge, Mass.: Belkap Press, 1954), 17.

48. Davies, *An Introduction to Mormonism,* 159–60; and Stephen Innes, *Creating the Commonwealth: The Economic Culture of Puritan New England* (New York: Norton, 1995), 107–59. See also Francis J. Bremer, *The Puritan Experiment: New England Society from Bradford to Edwards* (Hanover, N.H.: University Press of New England, 1995); and Max Weber, *The Protestant Ethic and the Spirit of Capitalism* (New York: Charles Scribner's Sons, 1958).

49. Manti Ward General Minutes, August 25, 1861, n.p., Church History Library. See also Davies, *An Introduction to Mormonism,* 159–67.

50. Brigham Young, Great Salt Lake City, May 6, 1855, *Journal of Discourses,* 3:153. Emphasis added.

51. Manti Ward General Minutes, May 18, 1851, Church History Library.

52. Manti Ward General Minutes, August 3, 1860, n.p., Church History Library.

53. Manti Ward General Minutes, December 15, 1850, Church History Library.

54. Fairview Ward General Minutes, 166, Church History Library.

55. Fairview Ward General Minutes, 167, Church History Library.

56. Manuscript History of the Sanpete Stake, entry for 1853, n.p., Church History Library.

57. Manti Ward General Minutes, February 16, 1851, 22, Church History Library.

58. Manti Ward General Minutes, August 11, 1861, n.p., Church History Library.

59. Fairview Ward General Minutes, 194, Church History Library.

60. Manti Ward General Minutes, November 9, 1852, 111, Church History Library.

61. Fairview Ward General Minutes, 171–72, Church History Library.

62. Fairview Ward General Minutes, 238, Church History Library.

63. The democratic impulses unleashed by the American Revolution are outlined in Gordon S. Wood, *The Radicalism of the American Revolution* (New York: Vintage Books, 1993), and Charles Sellers, *The Market Revolution: Jacksonian America, 1815–1846* (New York: Oxford University Press, 2009).

64. For a detailed discussion of Mormons and consumption, see "The Genteel Tradition" in chapter 4.

65. Manti Ward General Minutes, April 20, 1854, n.p., Church History Library.

66. Fairview Ward General Minutes, July 24, 1864, 307, Church History Library.

2. The Settlement Matrix

1. Mormon western settlement policy is outlined in Arrington, *Great Basin Kingdom,* 39–44; Bowman, *The Mormon People,* 96–123; Campbell, *Establishing Zion,* 57–91; and Wayne L. Walquist, "Settlement Processes in the Mormon Core Area, 1847–1890" (PhD diss., University of Nebraska, 1974).

2. Adelia B. Sidwell, quoted in Gary B. Peterson and Lowell C. Bennion, *Sanpete Scenes: A Guide to Utah's Heart* (Eureka, Utah: Basin/Plateau Press, 1987), 8.

3. See Albert C. T. Antrei and Allen D. Roberts, *A History of Sanpete County* (Salt Lake City: Utah State Historical Society, 1999), 2–17.

4. Reps, *Cities of the American West,* ix–xi.

5. The Sanpete Valley, along with the rest of the Mormon-settled Great Basin, became part of the United States as a result of an American victory in the Mexican War (1846–48). The system of distributing land in the West followed a familiar pattern: once the land was ceded to the United States (by the various Indian tribes or Mexico), it would be surveyed into sections and sold at an established rate to prospective developers or settlers. In this way, "the federal government would, in effect, serve as a real estate agent instead of a landlord." See Richard White, *"It's Your Misfortune and None of My Own": A History of the American West* (Norman: University of Oklahoma Press, 1991), 138. The federal survey did not reach Utah until the 1860s, prior to which time the Saints were "squatters on the public land" with the LDS Church supervising the survey and serving as land agent. See Lowry Nelson, *The Mormon Village: A Pattern and Technique of Land Settlement* (Salt Lake City: University of Utah Press, 1952), 139–40.

6. Many have looked for the origins of the Mormon village in New England, where so

many of the LDS Church leaders (and town planners) grew up. Recent scholarship, however, quite clearly shows that clusters of independent family farms rather than nucleated villages dominated the landscape of that region. See Joseph S. Wood, *The New England Village* (Baltimore: The Johns Hopkins University Press, 1997).

7. Quoted in Reps, *Cities of the American West,* 290.

8. Lowery Nelson, *The Mormon Village,* 25–53. See also John Demos, *A Little Common Wealth: Family Life in Plymouth Colony* (New York: Oxford University Press, 1970); David Flaherty, *Privacy in Colonial New England* (Charlottesville: University of Virginia Press, 1967); and Anna Andrzejewski, *Building Power: Architecture and Surveillance in Victorian America* (Knoxville: University of Tennessee Press, 2008).

9. *Journal of Discourses,* 15:364.

10. Reps, *Cities of the American West,* 288–290; Richard H. Jackson, "The City of Zion Plat," in Plewe, *Mapping Mormonism,* 44–45.

11. Hamilton, *Nineteenth-Century Mormon Architecture and Town Planning,* 17–19.

12. Richard H. Jackson, "The Mormon Village: Genesis and Antecedents of the City of Zion Plan," *BYU Studies* 17 (Winter 1977): 235–36.

13. Reps, *Cities of the American West,* 289.

14. Ibid., 290.

15. See Brian Q. Cannon, "Settling the Salt Lake Valley," in Plewe, *Mapping Mormonism,* 84–85.

16. Spiro Kostof, *The City Shaped: Urban Patterns and Meanings through History* (Boston: Little, Brown, 1991), 43–69.

17. John Reps, *The Making of Urban America: A History of City Planning in the United States* (Princeton, N.J.: Princeton University Press, 1965), 115–57; and Wood, *The New England Village,* 9–70.

18. Reps, *The Making of Urban America,* 439–74; and Dolores Hayden, *Seven America Utopias: The Architecture of Communitarian Socialism, 1790–1975* (Cambridge, Mass.: MIT Press, 1976).

19. Kostof, *The City Shaped,* 43–69; and Reps, *The Making of Urban America,* 5–19.

20. Reps, *The Making of Urban America,* 157–74.

21. Richard L. Bushman, *The Refinement of America: Persons, Houses, Cities* (New York: Vintage Books, 1993), 140–69.

22. *Journal of Discourses,* 12:288.

23. Bushman, *The Refinement of America,* 143.

24. Jules D. Prown, "Style as Evidence," *Winterthur Portfolio* 15:3 (Autumn 1980), 198. See also Thomas Carter and Elizabeth Collins Cromley, *Invitation to Vernacular Architecture: A Guide to the Study of Ordinary Buildings and Landscapes* (Knoxville: University of Tennessee Press, 2005), 54–57.

25. My use of the style concept comes from Upton, "Form and User," 159–68; and Dell Upton, *Holy Things and Profane: Anglican Parish Churches in Colonial Virginia* (New York: Architectural History Foundation; Cambridge, Mass.: MIT Press, 1986), 101–10.

26. Bushman, *The Refinement of America,* xviii (emphasis added).

27. Nelson, *The Mormon Village,* 36.

28. Reps, *The Making of Urban America,* 439–74. It is noteworthy that other utopian-minded religious groups, such as the Harmonists under George Rapp (Harmony, Pennsylvania; New Harmony, Indiana; and Economy, Pennsylvania), the Separatists of Joseph Bimeler (Zoar, Ohio), and Christian Metz's Inspirationists (Amana, Ohio), also merged the village with the grid to create communities that emphasized, like the Mormons, values of piety, unity, and cooperation.

29. See Keith W. Perkins and Mark L. Staker, "Kirtland, Ohio, 1831–1838," in Plewe,

Mapping Mormonism, 30–31; Max H. Parkin, "The Settlement of Zion, 1831–1833," in Plewe, *Mapping Mormonism,* 32–35; Alexander L. Baugh, "Settling Northern Missouri," in Plewe, *Mapping Mormonism,* 48–49; and Campbell, *Images of a New Jerusalem,* 42–43.

30. Olsen, *The Mormon Ideology of Place,* 63; Reps, *Cities of the American West,* 291–96; and Hamilton, *Nineteenth-Century Mormon Architecture and Town Planning,* 20–21.

31. Quoted in Flanders, *Nauvoo,* 180.

32. See Leonard, *Nauvoo,* 81; Flanders, *Nauvoo,* 179–210; Olsen, *The Mormon Ideology of Place,* 74, 76; Reps, *Cities of the American West,* 296–302; and Donald Q. Cannon and Brandon S. Plewe, "Building Nauvoo," in Plewe, *Mapping Mormonism,* 56–57.

33. Quoted in Reps, *The Making of Urban America,* 160.

34. I am indebted to Brad Westwood for making me aware both of Young's "anti-urbanism" and the influence Philadelphia had on his thinking. See Brad Westwood, "The Influence of Philadelphia's City Plan on Brigham Young's Original Plan for Salt Lake City" (paper presented at the Annual Conference of the Society of Architectural Historians, Cincinnati, April 1990), and "The First Uttered Plan for Salt Lake City (by Brigham Young in 1847)" (paper presented at the Annual Conference of the Mormon History Association, Provo, Utah, May 2004). See also Dell Upton, "What the Mormon Cultural Landscape Can Teach Us," *Journal of Mormon History* 31:2 (Summer 2005): 13–14; and Reps, *The Making of Urban America:* "For many of the towns that were built later during the westward march of urbanization Philadelphia served as the model. The regular pattern of streets and one or more public squares were features that became widely imitated" (174).

35. Quoted in William Mulder and A. Russell Mortensen, eds., *Among the Mormons: Historic Accounts by Contemporary Observers* (1958; repr., Salt Lake City: Western Epics, 1994), 308.

36. *Half Hours in the Wide West: Over Mountains, Rivers, and Prairies* (London: Wm. Isbister, 1883), 282–85.

37. Reps, *Cities of the American West,* 303–11.

38. Arrington, *Great Basin Kingdom,* 88–95; Campbell, *Establishing Zion,* 57–91; Bowman, *The Mormon People,* 96–123; and Richard H. Jackson, "Intermountain Colonization," in Plewe, *Mapping Mormonism,* 96–97.

39. Albert C. T. Antrei and Allen Roberts, *A History of Sanpete County* (Salt Lake City: Utah State Historical Society, 1999), 24.

40. See ibid., 61–83; Clifford Duncan, "The Northern Ute of Utah," in *A History of Utah's American Indians* (Salt Lake City: Utah Division of Indian Affairs and the Utah Division of State History, 2000), 167–224; and Virginia McConnell Simmons, *The Ute Indians of Utah, Colorado, and New Mexico* (Boulder: University Press of Colorado, 2000).

41. For the basic history of the valley I have relied on Antrei and Roberts, *A History of Sanpete County;* W. H. Lever, *History of Sanpete and Emery Counties* (Ogden, Utah: W. H. Lever, 1898); Albert C. Antrei, ed., *The Other Forty-Niners: A Topical History of Sanpete County Utah* (Salt Lake City: Western Epics, 1982); and Gary B. Peterson and Lowell C. Bennion, *Sanpete Scenes: A Guide to Utah's Heart* (Eureka, Utah: Basin Plateau Press, 1987).

42. Adelia B. Sidwell, Reminiscences of Early Manti, 2, Church History Library.

43. Ibid., 7.

44. George Peacock. Journal and Reminiscences, 1851 November–1861 April, n.p., Church History Library.

45. Andrew Jenson, Manuscript History of the Sanpete Stake, entry for 1850, n.p., Church History Library.

46. Grace Maggie Candland, "David Candland: His Life and Work," typescript, 42, Church History Library.

47. Andrew Jenson, Manuscript History of the Sanpete Stake, entry for 1854, n.p., Church History Library.

48. Manuscript History of the Moroni Ward, entry for 1869, n.p., Church History Library.

49. Christian Nielson, Diary, 42, Church History Library.

50. Reuben Newton Allred (Redick Allred's son), Autobiographical Sketch and Diary, 1898–1903, 40, Church History Library.

51. Ibid., 45.

52. Reps, *Cities of the American West,* 323–24, 326.

53. Centennial Committee, ed., *Song of a Century: A Centennial History and Memory Book of Manti* (Provo, Utah: DP Community Press, 1949), 37.

54. Lever, *History of Sanpete and Emery Counties,* 77.

55. Nelson, *The Mormon Village,* 138.

56. U.S. Census Bureau, Tenth Census, Agriculture, 1880: Production of Agriculture in Manti City, 6/1/1880, James Peacock recorder.

57. Arrington, *Great Basin Kingdom,* 28–31; Arrington and Bitton, *The Mormon Experience,* 206–19; Bowman, *The Mormon People,* 255–56; and Davies, *An Introduction to Mormonism,* 172–73. In 1857 the Manti City Council divided the city into four "wards," but these referred to political/school and not ecclesiastical districts. See Manti City Council Minutes, November 22, 1857.

58. Mount Pleasant Ward Minutes, 1858–1868, 106, Church History Archives.

59. Lever, *History of Sanpete and Emery Counties,* 78.

60. Manti City Council Minutes, 1850–1870, November 19, 1852, Church History Library.

61. Ibid., February 24, 1854.

62. Manti Ward General Minutes, November 12, 1852, 117, Church History Library.

63. Manti City Council Minutes, December 11, 1851, Church History Library.

64. Ibid., November 20, 1851.

65. Ibid.

66. Ibid., November 22, 1851.

67. Ibid., December 9, 1852.

68. Ibid., no month or day, 1858.

69. Ibid., September 5, 1857.

70. Ibid., November 22, 1851.

71. *Sanpitcher,* vol 1, no. 7, April 1867, Church History Library. This newspaper ran for several years with David Candland as the editor.

72. Manti City Council Minutes, February 6, 1852, Church History Library.

73. Ibid., March 15, 1855.

74. Ibid., January 8, 1861.

75. Antrei and Roberts, *A History of Sanpete County,* 98–99.

76. Manti City Council Minutes, May 23, 1853, Church History Library.

77. Fairview Ward General Minutes, 167, Church History Library.

78. Ibid., 156.

79. Daniel H. Wells, writing to Edwin D. Woolley, *Deseret News,* April 29, 1852, Manuscript History of the Manti Ward, 1849–, n.p.

80. *Manti Herald and Sanpete Advertiser,* vol. 1, no. 13 (May 4, 1867), 1, Church History Library.

81. Michael Scott Raber, "Religious Polity and Local Production: The Origins of a Mormon Town" (PhD diss., Yale University, 1978), 149.

82. Ibid., 151–57; and Upton, "What the Mormon Cultural Landscape Can Teach Us," 24–27.

83. *Our Yesterdays: A History of Ephraim, Utah, 1854–1979* (Ephraim, Utah: Ephraim City Corporation, 1981), 7.

84. Lever, *History of Sanpete and Emery Counties,* 282.

85. Augusta Dorius Stevens, Autobiography, 1922, 7, Church History Library.

86. Antrei and Roberts, *A History of Sanpete County,* 365.

87. Manuscript History of the Ephraim Ward, n.p., Church History Library.

88. Amanda B. Cox [Sidwell], Collection [n.d.], 3, Church History Library; and Lever, *History of Sanpete and Emery Counties,* 282.

89. Manuscript History of the Ephraim Ward, 1854, n.p., Church History Library.

90. *Our Yesterdays,* 18–19.

91. Manuscript History of the Ephraim Ward, 1859, n.p., Church History Library.

92. Amanda B. Cox [Sidwell]. Collection [n.d.]. Ms., LDS Church Archives, 3.

93. Raber, "Mormon Polity," 152.

94. Ibid., 150–151.

95. Kaye Watson, ed., *Life under the Horseshoe: A History of Spring City* (Salt Lake City: Publisher's Press, 1987), 9.

96. *Journal of Discourses* 1, July 31, 1853, 165.

97. Raber, "Mormon Polity," 153.

98. Manuscript History of the Spring City Ward, 1852, n.p., Church History Library.

99. Ibid., 1853, n.p.

100. Ibid., 1863, n.p.

101. Manuscript History of the Mt. Pleasant Ward, "History," n.p., Church History Library.

102. See Manuscript History of the Mt. Pleasant Ward, 1858, n.p.; and Mt. Pleasant Ward Minutes, 1858–1868, 1, Church History Library.

103. Quoted in Hilda Madsen Longsdorf, *Mount Pleasant, 1859–1939* (1939; repr., Provo, Utah: Community Press, 1989), 51.

104. Fairview Ward General Minutes, 116, Church History Library.

105. Ibid., 141.

106. Manuscript History of the Wales Ward, 1856, n.p., Church History Library.

107. *These Our Fathers: A Centennial History of Sanpete County, 1849–1947* (Springville, Utah: Art City Publishing Company, 1947), 196.

108. Manuscript History of the Moroni Ward, 1862, n.p., Church History Library.

109. Manuscript History of the Fountain Green Ward, 1859, n.p., Church History Library.

110. Manuscript History of the Moroni Ward, 1858, n.p., Church History Library.

111. Candland, "David Candland," 46.

112. Ibid.

113. Ibid.

114. Manuscript History of the Chester Ward, undated entry, n.p., Church History Library.

115. Ibid., 1930, n.p.

116. Ibid., undated entry, n.p.

117. Allred, Autobiographical Sketch and Diary, 52.

118. Ibid., 53.

119. Ibid.

120. Ibid., 54.

121. See Thomas Carter and Carl Fleischhauer, *The Grouse Creek Cultural Survey: Integrating Folklife and Historic Preservation Field Research* (Washington, D.C.: Library of Congress, 1988), 24–26; Paul L. Anderson, "An Idaho Variation on the City of Zion," in *Chesterfield: Mormon Outpost in Idaho*, ed. Lavina Fielding Anderson (Bancroft, Idaho: Chesterfield Foundation, 1982), 70–78; and National Register of Historic Places—Inventory Form, Mormon

Row Historic District, Grand Teton National Park, Wyoming State Historic Preservation Office, 1997.

122. Manuscript History of the Sanpete Stake, 1867, n.p., Church History Library.

123. Larry M. Logue, *A Sermon in the Desert: Belief and Behavior in Early St. George, Utah* (Urbana: University of Illinois Press, 1988), 1–16.

124. Ibid., 10.

125. Edward L. Parry, March 21, 1874, in James D. Bleak Diaries, Gd. 1, MS 1691, H. B. Lee Library Special Collections, Brigham Young University.

126. See Lowell C. Bennion, *A Bird's Eye View of Erastus Snow's St. George, Utah* (St. George, Utah: Dixie State College, 2006), 16; Garth R. Liston, "The St. George Temple Site," in "The Geographical Analysis of Mormon Temple Sites in Utah" (master's thesis, Brigham Young University, 1992), 45–64; and Laurel B. Andrew, *The Early Temples of the Mormons: The Architecture of the Millennial Kingdom in the American West* (Albany: State University of New York Press, 1978), 163.

127. Andrew, *The Early Temples of the Mormons,* 176.

128. Jens C. A. Weibye, Day Book 3, 185–86, Church History Library.

129. Ibid., 186–87.

130. Manti Temple Historical Record, 1873–1934, 1:2, Church History Library.

3. According to Need

1. Manti Ward General Minutes, February 16, 1851, Church History Library.

2. *Journal of Discourses,* 12:153.

3. See Underwood, *The Millenarian World of Early Mormonism,* 103–4.

4. Peter L. Berger, *The Capitalist Revolution: Fifty Propositions about Prosperity, Equality, and Liberty* (New York: Basic Books, 1986), 15–31; and Stephen Macedo, "Capitalism, Citizenship, and Community," in *Capitalism,* ed. Ellen Frankel Paul, Fred D. Miller Jr., Jeffery Paul, and John Ahrens (Oxford: Basil Blackwell, 1989), 113–39.

5. Quoted in Steven Olsen, *The Mormon Ideology of Place,* 25.

6. Ibid., 31.

7. See Arrington, Fox, and May, *Building the City of God,* 15–17.

8. Arrington, *Great Basin Kingdom,* 11; and Arrington, Fox, and May, *Building the City of God,* 31–32.

9. Arrington, Fox, and May, *Building the City of God,* 33–34.

10. Arrington, *Great Basin Kingdom,* 15; Arrington, Fox, and May, *Building the City of God,* 37–40; Hayden, *Seven American Utopias,* 107; and Underwood, *The Millenarian World of Early Mormonism,* 103. For a specific example from the Sanpete Valley, see Michael S. Raber, "Family Life and Rural Society in Spring City, Utah: The Basis of Order in a Changing Agrarian Landscape," in *Community Development in the American West: Past and Present Nineteenth and Twentieth Century Frontiers,* ed. Jessie L Embry and Howard A. Christy (Provo, Utah: Charles Redd Center for Western Studies, 1985), 135–62.

11. Orson Pratt, *Journal of Discourses,* November 1, 1868, 12:318–19.

12. Manti Ward General Minutes, September 14, 1851, Church History Library.

13. Fairview Ward General Minutes, July 24, 1864, 306, Church History Library.

14. Fairview Ward General Minutes, 288.

15. Manti Ward Historical Record Book E 1857–59, LDS Church Archives, January 15, 1859, Church History Library.

16. Manti Ward General Minutes, LDS Church Archives, December 15, 1850, 16.

17. My favorite is Dean May, "Brigham Young and the Bishops: The United Order in the City," in *New Views of Mormon History: Essays in Honor of Leonard J. Arrington,* ed. Davis

Bitton and Maureen Ursenbach Beecher (Salt Lake City: University of Utah Press, 1987), 115–37.

18. See Mark Leone, "Archaeology as the Science of Technology: Mormon Town Plans and Fences," in *Research and Theory in Current Archaeology,* ed. Charles Redman (New York: John Wiley and Sons, 1973), 141.

19. Arrington, *Great Basin Kingdom,* 51.

20. Reps, *Cities of the American West,* 306, and Milton R. Hunter, *Brigham Young the Colonizer* (Salt Lake City: Deseret News Press, 1940), 136–38. Some indication of the unevenness of Salt Lake City's social topography is found in Ronald W. Walker, " 'Going to Meeting' in Salt Lake City's Thirteenth Ward, 1849–1881: A Microanalysis," in Bitton and Beecher, *New Views of Mormon History,* 139–40.

21. Title searches were completed for all Manti city lots between 1869, when the federal survey was conducted, and 1890, the concluding year for this study. Once property owners were identified, federal census records provided "place of birth" and "value of personal estate" data.

22. This statement is based on the large number of transactions contained in title searches.

23. *Manti Herald and Sanpete Advertiser,* vol. 1, no. 13, May 4, 1867, 1, Church History Library.

24. Fairview Ward General Minutes, May 21, 1865, 9, Church History Library.

25. Anders Thomsen, Diaries, 2, Church History Library.

26. Manuscript History of the Mt. Pleasant Ward, 1858 entry, n.p., Church History Library.

27. Ibid., 1859 entry, n.p.

28. Manuscript History of the Spring City Ward, 1859 entry, n.p., Church History Library.

29. Spring City Ward General Minutes, vol. 11, January 4, 1869, n.p., Church History Library.

30. Fairview Ward General Minutes, 116, Church History Library.

31. Ibid., 125.

32. Ibid., 126–27.

33. Ibid., 299.

34. Ibid., 302.

35. Joseph Hansen, Diaries, 15, Church History Library.

36. Manuscript History of the Sanpete Stake, entry for 1857, n.p., Church History Library.

37. Ibid., entry for 1867, n.p. See also Richard L Jensen, "Mother Tongue: Use of Non-English Languages in the Church of Jesus Christ of Latter-day Saints, 1850–1983," in Bitton and Beecher, *New Views of Mormon History,* 273–303.

38. Dean May, "The Making of Saints: The Mormon Town as a Setting for the Study of Cultural Change," *Utah Historical Quarterly* 45:1 (Winter 1977): 75–92.

39. Mormon water policies are outlined in Arrington, *Great Basin Kingdom,* 52–54; Raber, "Religious Polity," 193–94; and Raber, "Family Life," 139. Mormon water policies within the West are treated in Donald Worster, "The Kingdom, the Power, and the Water," in *Great Basin Kingdom Revisited: Contemporary Perspectives,* ed. Thomas G. Alexander (Logan: Utah State University Press, 1991), 21–38.

40. F. C. Robinson, letter to the *Deseret News,* 12 (June 10, 1863), 400, Church History Library.

41. Manuscript History of the Fairview Ward, 1860 entry, n.p., Church History Library.

42. Fairview Ward General Minutes, 156, Church History Library.

43. Sanpete Stake General Minutes, January 5, 1878, 23, Church History Library.

44. Manti Ward General Minutes, May 12, 1851, n.p., Church History Library.

45. Manti Ward Historical Record Book E, February 6, 1859, Church History Library.

46. Weibye, Day Book 4, 156, Church History Library.

47. Weibye, Day Book 5, 11, Church History Library.

48. Spring City Ward General Minutes, vol. 2, November 10, 1869, n.p., Church History Library.

49. Manti Ward General Minutes, November 12, 1852, 117, Church History Library.

50. History of the Manti Ward, 1852 entry, n.p., Church History Library.

51. Mount Pleasant Ward Minutes, 1858–1868, 39, Church History Library.

52. Ibid., 53.

53. Fairview Ward General Minutes, 193, Church History Library.

54. Ibid., September 1, 1863, n.p., Church History Library.

55. Spring City Ward General Minutes, vol. 2, January 20, 1869, n.p., Church History Library.

56. Fairview Ward General Minutes, April 17, 1864, 295, Church History Library.

57. Severine Jensen House and Lot, 276 North 300 East (Site 199), Spring City Historic District, National Register of Historic Places–Inventory Form, 1979. Utah State Historic Preservation Office, Salt Lake City.

58. Ibid., 209 South Main Street (Site 67).

59. Ibid., 19 East 100 North (Site 169).

60. Ibid., Osborne house and lot, 398 North Main Street (Site 214); and Petersen house and lot, 287 East 500 North (Site 275).

61. Ibid., Iver Petersen house and lot, 309 North Main Street (Site 216); and the Nielsen house and half-lot, 190 West 300 South (Site 74/demolished).

62. Home ownership rates among the Sanpete Saints are difficult to determine. In Spring City, for example, the county tax assessment rolls for 1880 include valuations for 182 men. Of these, 43 did not own city lots. Were these men all renters? Probably not. It appears that several were sons of city lot owners and therefore lived with their fathers' families. A few others had houses outside the city limits and so, while considered residents of the city, did not actually own lots in town. An intriguing exploration of this topic is found in J. R. Kearl and Clayne Pope, "Choices, Rents, and Luck: Economic Mobility of Nineteenth-Century Utah Households," in *Long-Term Factors in American Economic Growth,* ed. Stanley L Engerman and Robert E. Gallman (University of Chicago Press, 1986), 215–60.

63. Keith Bennett and Thomas Carter, "Houses with Two Fronts: The Evolution of Domestic Architectural Design in a Mormon Community," *Journal of Mormon History* 15 (1989), 47–58.

64. Weibye, Day Book 2, entry for July 31, 1867, n.p., Church History Library.

65. See Leone, "Archaeology as the Science of Technology," 142–49; and Thomas C Hubka, "The Front Yard," in *Big House, Little House, Back House, Barn: The Connected Farm Buildings of New England* (Hanover, N.H.: University Press of New England, 1984), 73–77.

66. *Deseret News,* 17, March 25, 1868, 56, Church History Library.

67. Autobiography of Emerett Funk Musig, n.p., Church History Library.

68. The gendered nature of a farmstead is treated in Hubka, *Big House, Little House, Back House, Barn,* 147–51.

69. This section of barns is extracted from Thomas Carter and Roger Roper, *Of Work and Romance: Discovering Utah Barns,* Western Regional Architecture Program Publication No. 9 (Salt Lake City: Graduate School of Architecture, University of Utah, 1999). A useful summary of American barn history is found in John Michael Vlach, *Barns* (New York: W.W. Norton; Washington, D.C.: Library of Congress, 2003), 9–31.

70. See Blanton Owen, "Dry Creek: Central Nevada's Damele Ranch," in *Images of an American Land: Vernacular Architecture in the Western United States,* ed. Thomas Carter

(Albuquerque: University of New Mexico Press, 1997), 91–110; David R. Lee and Hector H. Lee, "Thatched Cowsheds of the Mormon Country," *Western Folklore* 40:2 (April 1981): 171–87; Carter and Roper, *Of Work and Romance,* 6–9; and Vlach, *Barns,* 293–95, 311–12, 349–50.

71. Carter and Roper, *Of Work and Romance,* 10–11.

72. Ibid., 12–13; Henry Glassie, *Pattern in the Material Folk Culture of the Eastern United States* (Philadelphia: University of Pennsylvania Press, 1968), 89–90, 133–41; Thomas Durant Visser, *Field Guide to New England Barns and Farm Buildings* (Hanover, N.H.: University Press of New England, 1997), 61–66; and Vlach, *Barns*, 39–41, 86–89, 172–77, 306–7.

73. Carter and Roper, *Of Work and Romance,* 15–16; Thomas Carter, "North European Horizontal Log Construction in the Sanpete-Sevier Valleys," *Utah Historical Quarterly* 52:1 (Winter 1984): 61–62.

74. Richard V. Francaviglia, "Western American Barns: Architectural Forms and Climatic Considerations," *Yearbook of the Association of Pacific Coast Geographers* 34 (1972): 153–60; Carter and Roper, *Of Work and Romance,* 17–22; Vlach, *Barns,* 329–33.

75. Carter, "North European Horizontal-Log Construction," 50–71; Vlach, *Barns,* 336–38.

76. Michael Kammen, *People of Paradox: An Inquiry Concerning the Origins of American Civilization* (New York: Vintage Books, 1973), 269–70.

77. Ibid., 269.

4. Frontier Fashion

1. *Journal of Discourses,* 2:284, May 27, 1855.

2. Ibid., 8:220, June 13, 1860.

3. Manti Ward General Minutes, July 11, 1852, 82–83, Church History Library.

4. Ibid., February 24, 1856, Church History Library.

5. Thomas Carter, "Folk Design in Utah Architecture, 1847–1890" in Carter, *Images of an American Land,* 41–60; and Thomas Carter and Peter Goss, *Utah's Historic Architecture: A Guide* (Salt Lake City: University of Utah Press, 1985).

6. *Journal of Discourses,* 8:297, June 12, 1860.

7. Fairview Ward General Minutes, May 15, 1864, 301.

8. Much of this centered on the quest for economic self-sufficiency and the promotion of home manufactures, both of which depended on the Saints' abstaining from buying Gentile goods and being swayed by the latest eastern fashions. See Arrington, *Great Basin Kingdom,* 1231–32.

9. Young's pronouncements against consumption were often aimed at reducing the Saints' reliance on outside manufacturers; see Arrington, Fox, and May, *Building the City of God,* 79–110.

10. See Robert Bocock, *Consumption* (London: Routledge, 1993); Dell Upton, *Architecture in the United States* (New York: Oxford University Press, 1998), 33–36; and Mary Douglas and Baron Isherwood, *The World of Goods: Towards an Anthropology of Consumption* (1979; London: Routledge, 2001), 36–47.

11. Spiro Kostof, *A History of Architecture: Settings and Rituals* (New York: Oxford, 1985), 547–69; Hugh Honour, *Neo-Classicism* (New York: Penguin Books, 1968), 17–42; and William F. Pierson Jr., *American Buildings and Their Architects: The Colonial and Neoclassical Styles* (Garden City, N.Y.: Doubleday, 1970), 61–156.

12. Henry Glassie, "Folk Art," in *Folklore and Folklife: An Introduction,* ed. Richard M. Dorson (Chicago: University of Chicago Press, 1972), 253–80; and Glassie, *Folk Housing in Middle Virginia,* 170–75.

13. Pierson, *American Buildings and Their Architects,* 111; and Henry Glassie, "Eighteenth-Century Cultural Process in Delaware Valley Folk Building," *Winterthur Portfolio* 7 (1972), 29–57.

14. Captain Joseph Tillinghast House, Providence, Rhode Island, Historic American Buildings Survey, National Park Service, HABS RI, 4-Prov.

15. Dell Upton, "Pattern Books and Professionalism: Aspects of the Transformation of Domestic Architecture in American, 1800–1860," *Winterthur Portfolio* 19:2/3 (Autumn 1984): 128–36. See also W. Barksdale Maynard, *Architecture in the United States: 1800–1850* (New Haven, Conn.: Yale University Press, 2002); Harold Kirker, *The Architecture of Charles Bulfinch* (Cambridge, Mass.: Harvard University Press, 1969); and Talbot Hamblin, *Greek Revival Architecture in America* (New York: Oxford University Press, 1944). For the Hitchings House, see the Francis Hitchings House, Lockport, Niagara, N.Y., Historic American Buildings Survey, National Park Service, HABS NY, 32-Lock.

16. See Richard N. Campen, *Architecture in the Western Reserve, 1800–1900* (Cleveland: Press of Case Western Reserve University, 1971), 210–18; John Drury, *Historic Midwest Houses* (Minneapolis: University of Minnesota Press, 1947); and Richard N. Holzapfel and T. Jeffery Cottle, *Old Mormon Nauvoo, 1839–1846: Historic Photographs and Guide* (Provo, Utah: Grandin Book Company, 1990), 76–80.

17. W. Randall Dixon, "The Beehive and Lionhouses," in *Brigham Young's Homes,* ed. Colleen Whitley (Logan: Utah State University Press, 2002), 124–28.

18. Fred B. Kniffen, "Folk Housing: Key to Diffusion," in *Common Places: Readings in American Vernacular Architecture,* ed. Dell Upton and John Michael Vlach (Athens: University of Georgia Press, 1986), 6–10.

19. A review of the early literature on Mormon housing is found in Thomas Carter, "Building Zion: Folk Architecture in the Mormon Settlements of Utah's Sanpete Valley, 1849–1890" (PhD diss., Indiana University, 1984), 5–9.

20. Henry Glassie, "Architectural Technology," in *Material Culture,* 244.

21. Carter, "Folk Design," 44–47; and Thomas Carter, "North European Horizontal Log Construction in the Sanpete-Sevier Valleys," *Utah Historical Quarterly* 52:1 (Winter 1984), 50–71.

22. See Harley J. McKee, *Introduction to Early American Masonry* (New York: National Trust for Historic Preservation, 1973), 41–59.

23. Ibid., 9–39. See also Carl J. Christensen, *Sanpete Oolite Limestone as a Building Material,* Bulletin no. 140 of the Utah Engineering Experiment Station (Salt Lake City: University of Utah, 1967).

24. Leon S. Pitman, "A Survey of Nineteenth-Century Folk Housing in the Mormon Culture Region" (PhD diss., Louisiana State University, 1973), 21–55; and Richard H. Jackson, "The Use of Adobe in the Mormon Culture Region," *Journal of Cultural Geography* 1:1 (Fall/Winter 1980): 82–95.

25. Pitman, "A Survey of Nineteenth-Century Folk Housing in the Mormon Culture Region," 41–47; see also David Murphy, "Building in Clay on the Central Plains," in *Perspectives in Vernacular Architecture III,* ed. Thomas Carter and Bernard Herman (Columbia: University of Missouri Press, 1989), 74–85.

26. Monika Minnhagen, *Bondens bostad: En stuidie roande boningslangans form, funktion, och forandring i sydostra Skåne* (Lund: Folklivsarkivet I Lund, 1973), 40–41; Grith Lerche, "Timber Framed Buildings in Denmark," *Vernacular Architecture* 4 (1973), 14.

27. Thomas Carter, "Cultural Veneer: Decorative Plastering in Utah's Sanpete Valley," *Utah Historical Quarterly* 49:1 (Winter 1981): 68–77.

28. Manuscript History of the Moroni Ward, entry for 1866, n.p.

29. *Desert News,* vol. 17, November 4, 1868, 312.

30. Fairview Ward General Minutes, 269.

31. *Deseret News,* vol. 17, March 25, 1868, 56.

32. Philip and Lizabeth Hurst, Letters, 1873–1901, September 10, 1873, n.p., Church History Library.

33. Sanpete Stake General Minutes, February 15 and 16, 1879, 38.

34. Fairview Ward General Minutes, 251–52.

35. Carl Christian Nikolai Dorius, Diary, 1860 May–April 1893, 286, Church History Library.

36. Marguerite L. Jensen, History of Christian A. Larsen, manuscript, 1952, 6, Church History Library.

37. Sara Jane Hurst Jones, "A Brief History of Emma Jane Hurst Tucker," manuscript, ca. 1979, 2, Church History Library.

38. Lever, *History of Sanpete and Emery Counties,* 283.

39. Joseph Hansen, Diaries, manuscript, 14, Church History Library.

40. Dean L. May, "The Making of Saints: The Mormon Town as a Setting for the Study of Cultural Change" *Utah Historical Quarterly* 45:1 (Winter 1977): 75–92.

41. Pitman, "A Survey of Nineteenth-Century Folk Housing in the Mormon Culture Region," 5.

42. Ibid., 203.

43. Bjarne Stoklund, "Houses and Culture in the North Atlantic Isles: Three Models of Interpretation," *Ethnologia Scandinavica* (1980): 122.

44. For southern I-houses, see Glassie, *Pattern in the Material Folk Culture of the Eastern United States,* 66–69; James Patrick, *Architecture in Tennessee* (Knoxville: University of Tennessee Press, 1981); and Howard Wight Marshall, *Folk Architecture in Little Dixie: A Regional Culture in Missouri* (Columbia: University of Missouri Press, 1981). The Allreds' history is taken from National Register of Historic Places—Inventory Form, Spring City Historic District (Site 71), Utah State Historic Preservation Office, 1979.

45. National Register of Historic Places—Inventory Form, Utah State Historic Preservation Office, 1978.

46. Glassie, *Pattern in the Material Folk Culture of the Eastern United States,* 129, 132–33; Carter, "Building Zion," 165–82; and Carter and Goss, *Utah's Historic Architecture,* 33–36.

47. M. W Barley, *The English Farmhouse and Cottage* (London: Routledge and Kegan Paul, 1961); Eric Mercer, *English Vernacular Houses* (London: Her Majesty's Stationery Office, 1975); R. W. Brunskill, *Illustrated Handbook of Vernacular Architecture* (London: Faber and Faber, 1971).

48. U.S. Census Bureau, "Population Schedules of the Ninth Census of the United States, 1870," Mount Pleasant, Utah.

49. Thomas Carter, "Danes," in *American's Architectural Roots: Ethnic Groups That Built America,* ed. Dell Upton (Washington, D.C.: Preservation Press, 1986), 118–23; and Carter and Goss, *Utah's Historic Architecture,* 24–25; and Carter, "Building Zion," 221–41.

50. U.S. Census Bureau, "Population Schedules of the Eighth Census of the United States, 1860," Manti, Utah; and "Ninth Census, 1870," Manti, Utah.

51. Carter, "Building Zion," 183–95; Carter and Goss, *Utah's Historic Architecture,* 18–20.

52. Carter, "Folk Design," 51–58.

53. Design eclecticism is treated in Thomas Carter, " 'The Best of Its Kind and Grade': Rebuilding the Sanpete Valley, 1890–1910," *Utah Historical Quarterly* 54:1 (Winter 1986): 98–99; and Carter and Goss, *Utah's Historic Architecture,* 110, 127–30. For the history of the Hans Peter Olsen family house, see National Register of Historic Places—Inventory Form, Utah State Historic Preservation Office, 1987.

54. Glassie, *Folk Housing in Middle Virginia,* 176–93; and Carter, "Building Zion," 291–300.

55. Gabrielle M. Lanier and Bernard L. Herman, *Everyday Architecture of the Mid-Atlantic: Looking at Buildings and Landscapes* (Baltimore: The Johns Hopkins University Press, 1997), 11.

56. See Glassie, *Folk Housing in Middle Virginia,* 117–22; Cary Carson, "Architecture as Social History," in *The Chesapeake House: Architectural Investigations by Colonial Williamsburg,*

ed. Cary Carson and Carl R. Lounsbury (Chapel Hill: University of North Carolina Press, 2013), 12–28; and Mark Wenger, "Town House and Country House," in Carson and Lounsbury, *The Chesapeake House,* 120–55.

57. Dell Upton, "Vernacular Domestic Architecture in Eighteenth-Century Virginia," *Winterthur Portfolio* 17:2/3 (Summer/Autumn 1982): 107–9.

58. Alvira Coolidge Cox, Correspondence, manuscript, 1862–1908, n.p., Church History Library.

59. Room names and uses come from extensive interviews with older Sanpete Valley residents in the spring of 1978, supplemented by specific conversations with Sarah Beck (born 1899), Spring City, November 8, 1987; and Calvin Mickelsen (born 1897), Manti, July 2, 1988. My questions centered on how these people remembered the houses being used by their grandparents.

60. National Register of Historic Places—Inventory Form, Spring City Historic District (Site 296), Utah State Historic Preservation Office, 1979.

61. Carter, "Folk Design," 50; Carter, "Building Zion," 139–64.

62. Lisbet Balslev Jorgensen, "Arbejderboligen," in *Danmarks Arkitektur: Enfamiliehustet* (Copenhagen: Gyldendal, 1985), 64–78.

63. National Register of Historic Places—Inventory Form, Spring City Historic District (Site 232), Utah State Historic Preservation Office, 1979.

64. Richard Francaviglia, "Mormon Central-Hall Houses in the American West," *Annals of the Association of American Geographers* 6 (1971): 65–71.

65. National Register of Historic Places—Inventory Form, Utah State Historic Preservation Office, 1976; and Lever, *History of Sanpete and Emery Counties,* 413–14.

66. Lever, *History of Sanpete and Emery Counties,* 193–94.

67. On the picturesque, see Upton, "Pattern Books and Professionalism," 120–27; see also David Schuyler, *Apostle of Taste: Andrew Jackson Downing, 1815–1852* (Baltimore: The Johns Hopkins University Press, 1996), 38–42; and Jane B. Davies, "Alexander J. Davis: Creative American Architect," in *Alexander Jackson Davis: American Architect, 1803–1892* (New York: Rizzoli, 1992), 8–21.

68. *Journal of Discourses,* 24:167, May 19, 1883, at Manti.

69. Upton, "Pattern Books and Professionalism," 142–49; and Thomas Carter, "Traditional Design in an Industrial Age: Vernacular Domestic Architecture in Victorian Utah," *Journal of American Folklore* 104:414 (Fall 1991): 425–33; and Carter and Goss, *Utah's Historic Architecture,* 37–43.

70. Peter L. Goss, "The Architectural History of Utah," *Utah Historical Quarterly* 43:3 (Summer 1975): 220; Carter and Goss, *Utah's Historic Architecture,* 108–9.

71. Jens Christian Larsen Breinholt, "The Life of J. C. L. Breinholt, 1891–1898," Typescript, 26, Church History Library.

72. National Register of Historic Places—Inventory Form, Utah State Historic Preservation Office, 1980.

73. National Register of Historic Places—Inventory Form, Utah State Historic Preservation Office, 1977.

74. Historic American Buildings Survey, HABS U-64, 1968.

75. U.S. Bureau of the Census, "Population Schedules of the Ninth Census of the United States, 1870," Ephraim, Utah.

76. National Register of Historic Places—Inventory Form, Spring City Historic District (Site 109), Utah State Historic Preservation Office.

77. Christian Olsen Hansen Diaries [ca. 1850–72], manuscript, October 5, 1860, Church History Library.

78. Peterson Family Papers, Letter dated Ephraim July 31, 1867, n.p., Church History Library.

79. Peter Madsen, Autobiography, 30, Church History Library.

80. Lever, *History of Sanpete and Emery Counties,* 529; Lula Llewellyn Whiting, "Biography of Rees [R.] Llewellyn," manuscript, Utah State Historical Society Collection, 1960.

81. See Gail Winkler and Roger Moss, *Victorian Interior Decoration: American Interiors 1830–1900* (New York: Henry Holt, 1986).

82. Marilyn Conover Barker, *The Legacy of Mormon Furniture* (Salt Lake City: Gibbs Smith, 1995), 137–41.

83. Carter and Cromley, *Invitation to Vernacular Architecture,* 58.

84. Greg Umbach, "Learning to Shop in Zion: The Consumer Revolution in Great Basin Mormon Culture, 1847–1910," *Journal of Society History* 38:1 (2004): 29–61. My thanks to Laurie Bryant for pointing out this article.

5. Polygamy and Patriarchy

1. Lowell C. Bennion, "Plural Marriage," in Plewe, *Mapping Mormonism,* 122–25; Lowell C. Bennion, "Mapping the Extent of Plural Marriage in St. George, 1861–1880," *BYU Studies Quarterly* 51:1 (2012): 27–68; Lowell C. Bennion and Thomas Carter, "Touring Polygamous Utah with Elizabeth W. Kane, Winter 1872–1873," in *Colonel Thomas L. Kane and the Mormons, 1846–1883,* ed. David J. Whittaker (Provo: BYU Studies, 2010), 164–65, 183–85; Kathryn M. Daynes, *More Wives Than One: Transformation of the Mormon Marriage System, 1840–1910* (Urbana: University of Illinois Press, 2001), 98–102; and R. Carmen Hardy, "The Persistence of Mormon Plural Marriage," *Dialogue: A Journal of Mormon Thought* 44:4 (Winter 2011): 43–105.

2. Many multiple-wife households existed in Nauvoo by 1846, but since polygamy was still an underground and clandestine doctrine, no precedents were established for what followed in Utah.

3. See Jeffery Ogden Johnson, "Determining and Defining 'Wife': The Brigham Young Households," in Whitley, *Brigham Young's Homes,* 1–12; W. Randall Dixon, "The Beehive and Lion Houses," in Whitley, *Brigham Young's Homes,* 128–31. For a map of Brigham Young's Salt Lake City houses, see Bennion, "Plural Marriage," 125.

4. Thomas Carter, "Living the Principle: Mormon Polygamous Housing in Nineteenth-Century Utah," *Winterthur Portfolio* 35:4 (Winter 2000): 223–51.

5. Ibid., 244; and U.S. Bureau of the Census, "Population Schedules," 1870.

6. See Lowell C. Bennion, Alan L. Morrell, and Thomas Carter, *Polygamy in Lorenzo Snow's Brigham City: An Architectural Tour* (Salt Lake City: College of Architecture and Planning, University of Utah, 2005), 181–82; and Bennion and Carter, "Touring Polygamous Utah," 17–32.

7. Jessie L. Embry, *Mormon Polygamous Families: Life in the Principle* (Salt Lake City: University of Utah Press, 1987), xvi.

8. Dixon, "The Lion House," 128–31.

9. Lawrence Foster, *Religion and Sexuality: Three American Communal Experiments of the Nineteenth Century* (New York: Oxford University Press, 1981), 199–211; and Bowman, *The Mormon People,* 125–29.

10. See Carter, "Living the Principle," 225–31.

11. Frederick Walter Cox Family History, manuscript, [n.d.], 7, Church History Library.

12. Ibid., 8.

13. Ibid., 11.

14. Norma Wanlass, "Of the Old Cox House," manuscript, [n.d.], 1, Utah State Historical Society.

15. Frederick Walter Cox Family History, manuscript, [n.d.], 10, Church History Library.

16. Manti Ward General Minutes, January 19, 1861.
17. Wanlass, "Of the Old Cox House," 2.
18. Carter, "Living the Principle," 243–44.
19. U.S. Bureau of the Census, "Population Schedules," Manti, 1870.
20. *Deseret News,* June 18, 1879, 320.
21. This portrait of the apostle is based on Myrtle Stevens Hyde, *Orson Hyde: The Olive Branch of Israel* (Salt Lake City: Agreka Books, 2000).
22. Ibid., 272–75.
23. Mary Ann Price Hyde, Reminiscence, manuscript [ca. 1880], 3, Church History Library.
24. Ibid., 4.
25. Manuscript History of the Spring City Ward, entries for 1863, n.p., Church History Library.
26. Hyde, *Orson Hyde,* 454.
27. Jens C. A. Weibye, Day Book 4, 177, Church History Library.
28. Mormon attitudes toward divorce were quite lenient, and there appears to have been no great stigma attached to failure in marriage, monogamous or polygamous. For an exhaustive treatment of marriage in Manti, see Daynes, *More Wives Than One,* 141–70; Foster, *Religion and Sexuality,* 216–20.
29. Hyde, *Orson Hyde,* 477.
30. "Population Schedules," Spring City, 1880; and Kaye Watson, *Life Under the Horseshoe: A History of Spring City* (Spring City, Utah: Spring City Corporation, 1987), 271.
31. Reuben Allred, Autobiography and Diary, manuscript [n.d], 40, Church History Library.
32. Ibid., p. 61.
33. Lever, *History of Sanpete and Emery Counties,* 118–20; and "Population Schedules," Manti, 1860, 1870, and 1880.
34. This history of the Guymon family is based on a term paper by Stephanie Smith, University of Utah, April 4, 2000. See Lever, *History of Sanpete and Emery Counties,* 523–24.
35. Jens Christian Andersen Weibye, Day Book 1, 35–36, Church History Library.
36. Jens Christian Andersen Weibye, Day Book 2, April 26 and 27, 1867, n.p., Church History Library.
37. Ibid., June 1867.
38. Ibid., July 25 and 26, 1867.
39. Ibid., September 1867.
40. Ibid., November 5, 1867.
41. Ibid., October 23, 1868.
42. Ibid., October 11, 1868.
43. Ibid., March 9, 1869.
44. Ibid., March 31 and April 5, 1869.
45. Ibid., May 7, 1869.
46. Ibid., June 9, 1869.
47. Ibid., June 30, 1869.
48. Ibid., July 31, 1869.
49. Ibid., July 31, 1869.
50. Ibid., August 27 and 28.
51. Ibid., September 24, 1869.
52. Ibid., October 30, 1869.
53. Ibid., April 22, 1870.
54. Ibid., April 25, 1870.
55. Ibid., June 28 and 30, 1970.

56. Ibid., August 5, 1870.
57. Ibid., August 23, 1870.
58. Ibid., August 25, 1870.
59. Ibid., October 21, 1870.
60. Ibid., December 3, 1870.
61. Jens Christian Andersen Weibye, Day Book 3, 24, Church History Library.
62. Jens Christian Andersen Weibye, Day Book 4, 75, Church History Library.
63. Weibye, Day Book, 3, 190.
64. Weibye, Day Book 4, 62.
65. Ibid., 63.
66. Weibye, Day Book 4, 73.
67. Ibid., 165.
68. Ibid., 4, 179.
69. Ibid., 179.
70. Jens Christian Andersen Weibye, Day Book 5, 31, Church History Library.
71. Ibid., 65–66.
72. Ibid., 83.
73. Ibid., 86.
74. Ibid., 122.
75. Ibid., 181.
76. Ibid., 185.
77. Ibid., 196.
78. Ibid., 196.
79. Ibid., 184.
80. Ibid., 189.
81. Ibid., 189.
82. Ibid., 191.
83. Ibid., 194.
84. Ibid., 194 .
85. Ibid., 198.
86. Jens Christian Andersen Weibye, Day Book 6, 12–13, Church History Library.
87. Ibid., 65.
88. Ibid., 70.
89. Ibid., 77.
90. U.S. Bureau of the Census, "Population Schedules," Manti, 1880.
91. Weibye, Day Book 6, 99.
92. Ibid., 100–101.
93. Ibid., 112.
94. Jens Christian Andersen Weibye, Day Book 7, 14, Church History Library.
95. Ibid., 64.
96. Ibid., 86.
97. Ibid., 159.
98. Jens Christian Andersen Weibye, Day Book 8, 68, Church History Library.
99. Ibid., 117–18.
100. Ibid., 147.
101. Ibid., 135.
102. Lawrence Foster, *Women, Family, and Utopia: Communal Experiments of the Shakers, the Onedia Community, and the Mormons* (Albany, N.Y.: Syracuse University Press, 1991), 202.
103. Arrington and Bitton, *The Mormon Experience,* 229.
104. Foster, *Religion and Sexuality,* 211–16; Foster, *Women, Family, and Utopia,* 190–95; and Bowman, *The Mormon People,* 124–51.

105. Carter, "Living the Principle," 239–51.

106. Ibid., 239–51.

107. Augusta Dorius Stevens, Autobiography, manuscript, 1922, 7–8, Church History Library.

108. Peter Madsen, Autobiography, manuscript, 28, Church History Library.

109. Redick Newton Allred, Autobiographical Sketch and Diary, 1898–1903, Book 1, n.p., August 30, 1852, Church History Library.

110. Sara Jane Hurst Jones, "A Brief History of Emma Jane Hurst Tucker," manuscript, ca. 1979, 2, Church History Library.

111. Augusta Dorius Stevens, Autobiography, manuscript, 1922, 8 and 11. Church History Library.

112. Elizabeth Crawford Munk, "Memories of the Old Council House of Manti," manuscript, 3, Utah State Historical Society.

113. See Hamilton, *Nineteenth-Century Mormon Architecture and City Planning,* 97–98; and Carolyn Butler Palmer, "Building Autonomy: A History of the Fifteenth Ward Hall of the Mormon Women's Relief Society," *Buildings and Landscapes* 20:1 (Spring 2013): 69–94. I am also indebted to Palmer's 1993 University of Utah master's thesis, "The Architecture of Women in Mormon Society: The Relief Society of Sanpete County."

114. Mary Ryan, "The Power of Women's Networks: A Case Study of Female Moral Reform in Antebellum America," *Feminist Studies* 5:1 (Spring 1979): 66–85; Carroll Smith-Rosenberg, "The Female World of Love and Ritual: Relations between Women in Nineteenth-Century America," in *The American Family in Social-Historical Perspective,* ed. Michael Gordon (New York: St. Martin's Press, 1983), 418–20; and Suzanne Lebsock, *The Free Women of Petersburg: Status and Culture in a Southern Town, 1874–1860* (New York: W. W. Norton, 1984), 195–236.

115. Jill Mulvay Derr, Janath Russell Cannon, and Maureen Ursenbach Beecher, *Women of Covenant: The Story of Relief Society* (Salt Lake City: Deseret Book, 1991); Jill Mulvay Derr, " 'Strength in Our Union': The Making of Mormon Sisterhood," in *Sisters in Spirit: Mormon Women in Historical and Cultural Perspective,* ed. Maureen Ursenbach Beecher and Lavina Fielding Anderson (Urbana: University of Illinois Press, 1987), 153–207; and Cheryl Lynn May, "Charitable Sisters," in *Mormon Sisters: Women in Early Utah,* ed. Claudia Bushman (Salt Lake City: Olympus Publishing, 1976), 224–39.

116. Manuscript History of the Manti Ward, 1849, n.p.; Weibye, Day Book 2, May 7, 1868.

117. Weibye, Day Book 3, 157.

118. Spring City Ward Relief Society Minutes, 16, Church History Library.

119. Ibid., 15–16.

120. Ephraim Ward Relief Society Minutes, vol. 1, n.p., Church History Library.

121. Manti Ward Relief Society Minutes, entries for 1878, n.p., Church History Library.

122. Ephraim Ward Relief Society Minutes, entry for December 14, 1881.

123. Ibid., entries for 1881.

124. Manti Ward Relief Society Minutes, 1871, n.p.

125. Ibid., 1877, n.p.

126. Ibid., August 16, 1879, 35.

127. Ephraim Ward Relief Society Minutes, 1881, n.p.

128. Manuscript History of the Manti Ward, n.p.

129. Weibye, Day Book 7, 33.

130. Weibye, Day Book 4, 57.

131. Manti Ward Relief Society Minutes, 55–59.

132. Spring City Ward Relief Society Minutes, 15.

133. Ibid., 18.

134. Ibid., 166.
135. Ibid., 19.
136. Ibid., April 2, 1873.
137. Ibid., 60.
138. Ibid., 21–22.
139. Ephraim Ward Relief Society Minutes, 1869, n.p.
140. Ibid., December 2, 1869, n.p.
141. Spring City Ward Relief Society Minutes, 128.
142. Ibid., 61.
143. Ephraim Ward Relief Society Minutes, 1881 entries, n.p.
144. *Our Yesterdays: Ephraim's First One Hundred Years* (Ephraim, Utah: Ephraim City Corporation, 1981), 32.
145. Spring City Ward Relief Society Minutes, 97.
146. National Register of Historic Places—Inventory Form, Spring City Historic District (Site 32), 1979.
147. Spring City Ward Relief Society Minutes, 19.
148. Ibid., 16.
149. Ibid., 6.
150. Ibid., 14.
151. Spring City Land Records, Book A, County Recorder's Office, Manti.
152. Spring City Ward Relief Society Minutes, 28.
153. Ibid., 38.
154. Ibid., 73.
155. Ibid., 74.
156. Ibid., 78.
157. Ibid., 100.

6. Business as Usual

1. Manuscript History of the Fairview Ward, entries for 1900, n.p., Church History Library.

2. This discussion is based loosely on Eliade, *The Sacred and the Profane,* 20–65; Kostof, *The City Shaped,* 271–75; and Kim Dovey, *Framing Places: Mediating Power in Built Form* (London: Routledge, 1999), 9–16.

3. See C. Mark Hamilton, "The Salt Lake Temple: A Symbolic Statement of Mormon Doctrine," in *The Mormon People: Their Character and Traditions,* ed. Thomas G. Alexander (Provo: Brigham Young University Press, 1980), 106–7.

4. "Geographical competence" is treated in Yi-Fu Tuan, *Space and Place: The Perspective of Experience* (Minneapolis: University of Minnesota Press, 2001), 67–84.

5. Diane Shaw, *City Building on the Eastern Frontier: Sorting the New Nineteenth-Century City* (Baltimore: The Johns Hopkins University Press, 2004), 19–40. The map of Salt Lake City's social topography is based on the unpublished research of W. Randall Dixon, Salt Lake City historian. See also Walker, " 'Going to Meeting' in Salt Lake City's Thirteenth Ward, 1849–1881," 139–40.

6. Weibye, Day Book 2, January 2, 1871.

7. U.S. Bureau of the Census, "Population Schedules," Manti 1870.

8. Hamilton, *Nineteenth-Century Mormon Architecture and City Planning,* 98–100; and Ronald O. Barney and W. Randall Dixon, "Church Headquarters," in Plewe, *Mapping Mormonism,* 114.

9. Survey Files, Utah State Historic Preservation Office.

10. Weibye, Day Book 4, 62.

11. Ibid., 64.
12. Ibid.,141.
13. Weibye, Day Book 8, 50–51.
14. Ending in-kind tithing is discussed in Arrington, *Great Basin Kingdom,* 409. Photographs of several tithing offices, including the new Victorian type, are found in Hamilton, *Nineteenth-Century Mormon Architecture and City Planning,* 99–101.
15. Weibye, Day Book 4, 67.
16. Spring City Ward General Minutes. February 26, 1888, 24, Church History Library. See also Watson, *Life Under the Horseshoe,* 44.
17. Spring City Ward General Minutes, 26–27.
18. National Register of Historic Places—Inventory Form, Utah State Historic Preservation Office, 1979.
19. *Our Yesterdays,* 38; and Watson, *Life Under the Horseshoe,* 49.
20. *Our Yesterdays,* 37–38.
21. Weibye, Day Book 5, 107.
22. Weibye, Daybook 6, 148.
23. Hamilton, *Nineteenth-Century Mormon Architecture and City Planning,* 127–35.
24. Manuscript History of the Mount Pleasant Ward, entry for 1862, n.p., Church History Library.
25. Hilda Madsen Longsdorf, *Mount Pleasant, 1859–1939* (1939; repr., Provo, Utah: Community Press, 1989), 82–83.
26. Manuscript History of the Fountain Green Ward, n.p., Church History Library.
27. Manuscript History of the Moroni Ward, entry for 1865, n.p., Church History Library.
28. *These Our Fathers,* 181–85.
29. *Our Yesterdays,* 89, 94–95.
30. Watson, *Life Under the Horseshoe,* 59.
31. George Peacock, Journal and Reminiscences, 1851 November–1861 April, manuscript, entries for 1853, n.p., Church History Library.
32. Ibid., March 9, 1857.
33. George Peacock, Journal and Reminiscences, 1851–1875, manuscript, 75, Church History Library.
34. Manuscript History of the Moroni Ward, entries for 1873, n.p., Church History Library.
35. Peacock, Journal and Reminiscences, 1851–1875, 77.
36. Ibid., 78.
37. Weibye, Day Book 3, 154.
38. For a background on American courthouse design and construction, see Martha J. McNamara, *From Tavern to Courthouse: Architecture and Ritual in American Law, 1658–1860* (Baltimore: The Johns Hopkins University Press, 2004), 81–102; and Carl R. Lounsbury, *The Courthouses of Early Virginia* (Charlottesville: University of Virginia Press, 2005).
39. See *Song of a Century: A Centennial History and Memory Book of Manti, 1849–1949,* 2nd ed. (Provo, Utah: Daughters of the Utah Pioneers, 1978), 153. The history of the courthouse contained in this book differs from Peacock's and Lowry's: "In 1864, a court house was constructed in Manti 18x20 feet of adobe and plastered on the outside and inside, at a cost of $850.00. This served until 1873 when $800.00 was appropriated for the construction of an additional room to be built of stone. Another room and a porch was added in 1878 at a cost of $700.00. In 1885 a vault was built of rock 12 by 18 by 8 feet with a cement floor for the safe-keeping of county records. In 1894, $2,000.00 was appropriated to remodel the court house, a court room and assessor's office being added to the second floor."
40. Manuscript History of the Ephraim Ward, entries for 1873, n.p.

41. Centennial Book Committee, eds., *Ephraim's First One Hundred Years* (Ephraim, Utah: Ephraim City Corporation, 1981), 22.

42. Carter and Goss, *Utah's Historic Architecture,* 97, 101, and 106.

43. National Register of Historic Places Inventory—Nomination Form, Utah State Historical Society, January 1985.

44. Ibid., no page.

45. Arrington and Bitton, *The Mormon Experience,* 211–12.

46. *Song of a Century,* 118.

47. Manuscript History of the Ephraim Ward, entries for 1863, n.p., Church History Library.

48. *Our Yesterdays,* 39–40.

49. Manuscript History of the Mount Pleasant Ward, entries for 1876, n.p., Church History Library.

50. The land where the Allred School stands was initially owned by the Women's Relief Society, which sold it to the school district in 1878. There is little evidence that the Sisters constructed the building or used it as a hall. Some have speculated that Apostle Orson Hyde could have performed temple endowments here, though again the connection seems circumstantial; see Allen Roberts, "The 'Other' Endowment House: Unraveling a Mystery," *Sunstone* 3:5 (July–August 1978), 9–10; and Watson, *Life Under the Horseshoe,* 75.

51. Manuscript History of the Manti Ward, April 14, 1874, n.p., Church History Library.

52. *Song of a Century,* 118.

53. Manti Ward General Minutes, June 10, 1855, n.p., Church History Library.

54. Ibid.

55. *Our Yesterdays,* 10.

56. *Manti Herald and Sanpete Advertiser,* vol. 1, no. 6., March 23, 1867, Church History Library.

57. Ibid., vol. 1, no. 7, March 20, 1867.

58. Names and dates for this portion of Main Street are taken from Longsdorf, *Mount Pleasant,* and the Sanpete County Land Records, County Recorder's Office.

59. Sanpete Quarterly Conference Minutes, Manti, entry for May 19, 1883, n.p., Church History Library.

60. Ibid., entry for May 20, 1883, n.p.

61. Bowman, *The Mormon People,* 169–70.

62. Manti Ward Historical Record Book E, August 2, 1857, n.p., Church History Library.

63. Weibye, Day Book 2, entry for February 9, 1868.

64. See Arrington, Fox, and May, *Building the City of God,* 79–110.

65. Weibye, Day Book 2, entry for January 3, 1870.

66. Sanpete Stake General Minutes, February 14, 1880, 54.

67. Manuscript History of the Moroni Ward, entry for 1868, n.p.

68. Ibid.

69. Manuscript History of the Spring City Ward, entries for 1873, n.p., Church History Library.

70. Manuscript History of the Fairview Ward, entries for 1869, n.p., Church History Library.

71. Manuscript History of the Ephraim Ward, entries for 1872, n.p., Church History Library.

72. Ibid., entries for 1872, n.p.

73. National Register of Historic Places—Inventory Form, Utah State Historic Preservation Office, 1971.

74. Sanpete Stake General Minutes, November 22, 1877, 11, Church History Library.

75. Ibid., August 17, 1878, 32.

76. Marguerite L. Jensen, History of Christian A. Larsen, manuscript, 1952, 6, Church History Library.

77. *Our Yesterdays,* 40.

78. *Deseret News,* vol. 17, March 18, 1868, 45.

79. George Peacock, Journals and Reminiscences, 1851–1875, entries of December 21, 22, and 23, 1868, Church History Library.

80. Ibid., January 3, 1869.

81. Weibye, Day Book 3, 126.

82. See Kingston Heath, "False-Front Architecture on Montana's Urban Frontier," in Carter, *Images of an American Land,* 21–39; and Lever, *History of Sanpete and Emery Counties,* 193–94.

83. Weibye, Day Book 5, 156.

84. Weibye, Day Book 4, 196.

85. Weibye, Day Book 3, 143.

86. Weibye, Day Book 8, 129.

87. Richard Longstreth, *The Buildings of Main Street: A Guide to American Commercial Architecture* (Washington, D.C.: Preservation Press, 1987); and Carter and Goss, *Utah's Historic Architecture,* 59–73.

88. Sanpete Stake General Minutes, November 18, 1877, 10, Church History Library.

89. Ibid., 12.

90. Kevin Lynch, *The Image of the City* (Cambridge, Mass.: MIT Press, 1960), 2–3.

7. Meetinghouses

1. Davies, *An Introduction to Mormonism,* 199–201.

2. Carl Lounsbury, "God in the Details: The Transformation of Ecclesiastical Architecture in Early Nineteenth-Century America," *Perspectives in Vernacular Architecture* 13:1 (2006): 1–21; Louis P. Nelson, *The Beauty of Holiness: Anglicanism and Architecture in Colonial South Carolina* (Chapel Hill: University of North Carolina Press, 2008), 350–53; and Gretchen Buggeln, *Temples of Grace: The Material Transformation of Connecticut's Churches, 1790–1840* (Hanover, N.H.: University Press of New England, 2003), 173–76.

3. *Journal History,* June 8, 1845.

4. Exodus 25:1–27:21 (New Revised Standard Version).

5. Ron Walker, "The Salt Lake Tabernacle in the Nineteenth Century: A Glimpse of Early Mormonism," *Journal of Mormon History* 32:3 (Fall 2005): 201–3.

6. Ibid., 200.

7. Quoted in Scott C. Esplin, ed., *The Tabernacle: An Old and Wonderful Friend* (Provo, Utah: Religious Studies Center, Brigham Young University, 2007), 113.

8. Peter Benes, *Meetinghouses of Early New England* (Amherst: University of Massachusetts Press, 2012).

9. Walker, "The Salt Lake Tabernacle," 234. See also Elwin C. Robison, *The First Mormon Temple: Design, Construction, and Historic Context of the Kirtland Temple* (Provo, Utah: Brigham Young University Press, 1997), 95.

10. Catherine C. Lavoie, "Quaker Beliefs and Practices and Eighteenth-Century Development of the Friends Meeting House in the Delaware Valley," in *Quaker Aesthetics: Reflections on a Quaker Ethic in American Design and Consumption,* ed. Emma Jones Lapsansky and Anne A. Verplanck (Philadelphia: University of Pennsylvania Press, 2003), 156–87.

11. Elwin C. Robison, *Gathering as One: The History of the Mormon Tabernacle in Salt Lake City* (Provo, Utah: BYU Studies, 2013).

12. Walker, " 'Going to Meeting' in Salt Lake City's Thirteenth Ward, 1849–1881," 14.

13. Seventh Ward Chapel, Historic American Buildings Survey, U-22, SALCT, 5, 1967. See also Hamilton, *Nineteenth-Century Mormon Architecture and City Planning,* 53–92.

14. Larry Logue, *A Sermon in the Desert: Belief and Behavior in Early St. George, Utah* (Urbana: University of Illinois Press, 1988), 9–10.

15. Quoted in Michael N. Landon, " 'A Shrine to the Whole Church': The History of the St. George Tabernacle," *Mormon Historical Studies* 12:1 (Spring 2011): 127.

16. Ibid.

17. Ibid., 128.

18. Logue, *A Sermon in the Desert,* 82; and Hamilton, *Nineteenth-Century Mormon Architecture and City Planning,* 63–64.

19. It will become apparent as this chapter proceeds that some ambiguity existed within the LDS community concerning nomenclature for these congregational buildings. In Salt Lake City, a clear distinction was made between the larger "tabernacles" and smaller ward "meetinghouses." In the colonies, however, which until the late 1870s and early 1880s usually consisted of a single ward, the two terms appear interchangeable; it is only later that a degree of consistency emerges as the outlying towns grow large enough to support both tabernacles and ward meetinghouses.

20. *Journal History,* August 7, 1850, n.p., Church History Library.

21. Manuscript History of the Fountain Green Ward, entries for 1860, n.p., Church History Library.

22. Manuscript History of the Moroni Ward, entries for 1860, n.p., Church History Library.

23. *Deseret News,* vol. 14, July 26, 1865, 338.

24. Amanda B. Cox [Sidwell], Collection [n.d.], manuscript, 2–3, Church History Library.

25. Manuscript History of the Ephraim Ward, entries for 1857, n.p., Church History Library.

26. Manuscript History of the Moroni Ward, entries for 1859, n.p., Church History Library.

27. *Deseret News,* vol. 14, July 26, 1865, 339.

28. Manti Ward General Minutes, March 6, 1851, n.p., Church History Library.

29. Andrew Jenson, Manuscript History of the Sanpete Stake, November 3, 1851, n.p., Church History Library.

30. Christian Nielsen Munk, Journal, 11, Church History Library.

31. Manti Ward General Minutes, November 16, 1856, n.p., Church History Library..

32. Alan B. Barnett, " 'We Must Do Right and Be Guided by the Priesthood': A Study of the Parowan Meetinghouse and Its Role in the Mormon Community" (master's thesis, University of Utah, 1994), 4.

33. Peter Olsen Hansen, Diaries [ca. 1850]–1872, manuscript, n.p., Church History Library.

34. George Peacock, Journals and Reminiscences, 1851–1875, December 27, 1864, 25. Church History Library.

35. Manti Ward General Minutes, January 22, 1860, n.p., Church History Library.

36. Ibid., January 31, 1860, n.p.

37. Weibye, Day Book 2, entry for February 19 and 20, 1868, n.p., Church History Library.

38. Weibye, Day Book 4, 77, Church History Library.

39. Manuscript History of the Ephraim Ward, entries for 1860, n.p., Church History Library.

40. Manuscript History of the Spring City Ward, entries for 1859, n.p., Church History Library.

41. Fairview Ward General Minutes, June 15, 1862, 237–38, Church History Library.
42. Ibid., March 19, 1863, 264.
43. Ibid., April 19, 1863, 267.
44. Ibid., June 21, 1863, 271.
45. Ibid., 248–306.
46. Ibid., June 28, 1863, 273.
47. Ibid., November 1, 1863, 280.
48. Ibid., March 4, 1864, 291.
49. Ibid., May 28, 1865, 9.
50. Manuscript History of the Fairview Ward, entries for 1869, n.p., Church History Library.
51. Mount Pleasant Ward Minutes, 1858–1868, manuscript, 40, Church History Library.
52. Ibid., 53.
53. Ibid., 59.
54. Ibid., 60.
55. Ibid., 91.
56. Ibid.
57. Ibid., 96.
58. Peter Madsen, Autobiography, 1855, 26, Church History Library.
59. Manuscript History of the Ephraim Ward, entries for 1870, n.p., Church History Library.
60. Ibid., entries for 1871, n.p.
61. Ibid., entries for 1872, n.p.
62. Ibid., entries for 1874, n.p.
63. Manuscript History of the Sanpete Stake, entry for 1871, n.p., Church History Library.
64. *Journal History,* August 30, 1870, 1, Church History Library.
65. Richard L. Jensen and Richard G. Oman, *C. C. A. Christensen, 1831–1912: Mormon Immigrant Artist* (Salt Lake City: Church of Jesus Christ of Latter-day Saints, 1984), 24.
66. Interview with Glen and Virginia Nielson, Ephraim, Utah. September 13, 1990. Mr. Nielsen was the bishop of Ephraim when the tabernacle was demolished in 1955.
67. See Edmund W. Sinnott, *Meetinghouse and Church in Early New England* (New York: McGraw-Hill, 1963); Peter Benes and Phillip D. Zimmerman, *New England Meeting House and Church, 1630–1850* (Boston: Boston University and Currier Gallery of Art, 1979); and Buggeln, *Temples of Grace,* 89–91.
68. See Hamilton, *Nineteenth-Century Mormon Architecture and City Planning,* 65–75.
69. Weibye, Day Book 4, 72–73, Church History Library.
70. Ibid., 140.
71. Hans Jensen Hals, Reminiscences and Diary, 1867–1910, manuscript, Church History Library. Quotes are from pages 8 (1862), 90 (1869), 91 (1870), 95 (1873), 97 (1877), 101 (1881), and 192 (1882).
72. George Peacock, Journals and Reminiscences, 1851–1875, July 14 and 16, 1865, 32, Church History Library.
73. Ibid., December 15, 1869, 63.
74. Ibid., 68.
75. Weibye, Day Book 3, 166, Church History Library.
76. Ibid., 167.
77. Ibid., 168.
78. Ibid., 175.
79. Manti Tabernacle Committee Council Minutes, 2, Church History Library.
80. Ibid.
81. Ibid., 6.

82. Ibid., 24.
83. Ibid., 23–24.
84. Ibid., 24–25.
85. Ibid., 25.
86. Ibid., 19.
87. Ibid., 29.
88. Ibid., 29–30.
89. Ibid., 29.
90. Ibid., 31 and 37.
91. Weibye, Day Book 5, 45, Church History Library.
92. Manti Tabernacle Committee Council Minutes, 30, Church History Library.
93. Ibid., 32–33.
94. Ibid., 8.
95. Ibid., 19–20.
96. Ibid., 36.
97. Weibye, Day Book 5, 111–12, Church History Library.
98. Ibid., 180.
99. Sanpete Quarterly Conference Minutes, August 18, 1879, n.p., Church History Library.
100. Manuscript History of the Moroni Ward, entries for 1865, n.p., Church History Library.
101. Moroni Ward General Minutes, January 6, 1878, 44, Church History Library.
102. Ibid., January 12, 1878, 44.
103. Ibid., December 8, 1878, 60.
104. Ibid., May 4, 1879, 66.
105. Hamilton, *Nineteenth-Century Mormon Architecture and City Planning,* 67–68.
106. Moroni Ward General Minutes, June 8, 1879, 68, Church History Library.
107. Ibid., September 5, 1880, 96.
108. *These Our Fathers,* 186–87.
109. Manti Tabernacle Committee Council Minutes, October 14, 1878, 38, Church History Library.
110. Peter Madsen, Autobiography, 1898–1909, manuscript, 26, Church History Library.
111. Ibid., p. 27.
112. Manti Ward General Minutes, September 1, 1850, n.p., Church History Library.
113. Manti Ward Historical Record, Book E, 1857–1859, April 27, 1857, n.p., Church History Library.
114. Ibid., August 22, 1858, n.p.
115. Ibid., September 5, 1858, n.p.
116. Ibid., April 17, 1859, n.p.
117. Ibid., April 24, 1859, n.p.
118. Ibid., March 22, 1857, n.p.
119. Weibye, Day Book 8, 66, Church History Library.
120. Fairview Ward General Minutes, p. 166, no page, Church History Library.
121. Ibid., 164.
122. Ibid., 173.
123. Ibid., 174.
124. Ibid., 245.
125. Mount Pleasant Ward Minutes, 1858–1868, 47, Church History Library.
126. Manuscript History of the Manti Ward, n.p., Church History Library.
127. Jan Shipps, "In the Presence of the Past: Continuity and Change in Twentieth-Century Mormonism," in *After 150 Years: The Latter-day Saints in Sesquicentennial Perspective,*

by Thomas G. Alexander and Jessie L. Embry (Provo, Utah: Charles Redd Center for Western Studies, 1983), 1–35.

128. Sanpete Stake General Minutes, November 20 and 21, 1880, 61, Church History Library.

129. Manuscript History of the Sanpete Stake, entries for 1885, n.p., Church History Library.

130. Quoted in John H. McBride, Benjamin C. Pykles, Emily Utt, and R. William Keach II, "Rediscovering Provo's First Tabernacle with Ground-Penetrating Radar," *BYU Studies Quarterly* 51:2 (2012): 64.

8. Mansion on the Hill

1. Manti Temple, Historical Record, vol. 1, 10, Church History Library.

2. Paul L. Anderson, "William Harrison Folsom: Pioneer Architect," *Utah Historical Quarterly* 43:3 (Summer 1975): 259.

3. Upton, *Architecture in the United States,* 21–24.

4. *Doctrine and Covenants of the Church of Jesus Christ of Latter-day Saints,* 36:8.

5. Ibid., 42:36.

6. Laurel B. Andrew, *The Early Temples of the Mormons: The Architecture of the Millennial Kingdom in the American West* (Albany: State University of New York Press, 1978), 30.

7. Hershel Shanks, *Jerusalem's Temple Mount: From Solomon to the Golden Dome* (New York: Continuum, 2007), 123–62; Stanley Tigerman, *The Architecture of Exile* (New York: Rizzoli, 1988), 58–86; and William J. Hamblin and David Rolph Seely, *Solomon's Temple: Myth and History* (London: Thames and Hudson, 2007).

8. David Spaeth, *Mies van der Rohe* (New York: Rizzoli, 1985), 39.

9. James Talmage, *The House of the Lord: A Study of Holy Sanctuaries Ancient and Modern* (Salt Lake City: Bookcraft, 1962), 110.

10. Shipps, *Mormonism,* 82–83.

11. *Doctrine and Covenants of the Church of Jesus Christ of Latter-day Saints*, 95:14.

12. Quoted in Robison, *The First Mormon Temple,* 8.

13. Only the Independence drawings survive, but it seems likely that two sets were prepared, since the Kirtland building closely follows those sent to Missouri. See ibid., 8–25.

14. Ibid., 32–34; and Andrew, *The Early Temples of the Mormons,* 37–38.

15. Quoted in Andrew, *The Early Temples of the Mormons,* 33.

16. Robison, *The First Mormon Temple,* 16.

17. Ibid., 18–19.

18. Ibid., 85–96.

19. Hebrew Bible (NRSV), Numbers 17:18.

20. New Testament (NRSV), Hebrews 6–7.

21. Arrington and Bitton, *The Mormon Experience,* 206–7.

22. Robison, *The First Mormon Temple,* 16–25; Andrew, *The Early Temples of the Mormons,* 29–53; and Hamilton, *Nineteenth-Century Mormon Architecture and City Planning,* 37–40.

23. Robison, *The First Mormon Temple,* 99–109.

24. Quoted in Don F. Colvin, *Nauvoo Temple: A Story of Faith* (American Fork, Utah: Covenant Communication, 2002), 16.

25. Andrew, *The Early Temples of the Mormons,* 61–79; Hamilton, *Nineteenth-Century Mormon Architecture and City Planning,* 40–42; and Colvin, *Nauvoo Temple,* 15–40.

26. Andrew, *The Early Temples of the Mormons,* 79–96.

27. Talmage, *The House of the Lord,* 71–72.

28. Davies, *Introduction to Mormonism,* 91–115; Andrew, *The Early Temples of the Mormons,* 91–96; and Colvin, *Nauvoo Temple,* 80–126, 179–232.

29. Talmage, *The House of the Lord,* 130–31; and Andrew, *The Early Temples of the Mormons,* 80–82.

30. Talmage, *The House of the Lord,* 89–93.

31. Ibid., 95.

32. Davies, *An Introduction to Mormonism,* 198.

33. Talmage, *The House of the Lord,* 93–109.

34. Ibid., 93–103; Colvin, *Nauvoo Temple,* 220–22; and Davies, *An Introduction to Mormonism,* 211–13.

35. Talmage, *The House of the Lord,* 101–9; and Davies, *Introduction to Mormonism,* 213–14.

36. Hamilton, *Nineteenth-Century Mormon Architecture and City Planning,* 42–46; Talmage, *The House of the Lord,* 136–200; Andrew, *The Early Temples of the Mormons,* 97–162; and C. Mark Hamilton, *The Salt Lake Temple: A Monument to a People* (Salt Lake City: University Services, 1983).

37. Hamilton, *The Salt Lake Temple,* 8–45. Masonic origins are considered in Andrew, *The Early Temples of the Mormons,* 141–50. The Masonic influence on early Mormon architecture and ritual is a topic of great interest; see Matthew B. Brown, *Exploring the Connection between Mormons and Masons* (American Fork, Utah: Covenant Communications, 2009). For those wanting to make their own comparisons, see William D. Moore, *Masonic Temples: Freemasonry, Ritual Architecture, and Masculine Archetypes* (Knoxville: University of Tennessee Press, 2006).

38. Hamilton, *The Salt Lake Temple,* 54–55.

39. Lisle G. Brown, " 'Temple Pro Tempore': The Salt Lake City Endowment House," *Journal of Mormon History* 34:4 (Fall 2008): 1–68.

40. Ibid., 45.

41. Ibid., 55.

42. Ibid., 56.

43. Ibid., 62–64.

44. Ibid., 65.

45. Ibid., 56.

46. Andrew, *The Early Temples of the Mormons,* 163–74; and Hamilton, *Nineteenth-Century Mormon Architecture and City Planning,* 46–48.

47. Andrew, *Early Temples of the Mormons,* 176.

48. Ibid., 180.

49. Hamilton, *The Salt Lake Temple,* 54–57.

50. Ibid., 54–57.

51. Weibye, Day Book 6, 36, Church History Library.

52. Sanpete Stake General Minutes, February 17, 1878, 27, Church History Library.

53. Weibye, Day Book 4, 190, Church History Library.

54. Arrington, *Great Basin Kingdom,* 108–12.

55. Manti Temple Historical Record, vol. 1, 3, Church History Library.

56. Weibye, Day Book 5, 40–41, Church History Library.

57. Ibid., 43.

58. Ibid., 86.

59. Sanpete Stake General Minutes, May 7, 1879, 43, Church History Library.

60. Ibid., February 14, 1880, 55.

61. Ibid., November 3, 1877, 17.

62. Ibid., entries for 1877, 20.

63. Weibye, Day Book 6, 40–41, Church History Library.

64. Ibid., May 16, 1880, 57.

65. Ibid., November 3, 1877, 18.

66. Ibid., February 19 and 20, 1881, 67.

67. Weibye, Day Book 8, 10, Church History Library.

68. Sanpete Stake General Minutes, November 17 and 18, 1883, 92–93, Church History Library.

69. Manti Temple, Letterpress Copybooks, 1877–1959, manuscript, 61, Church History Library.

70. Sanpete State General Minutes, May 14 and 15, 1881, 71, Church History Library.

71. Ibid., August 13, 1881, 72.

72. Weibye, Day Book 4, 193, Church History Library.

73. Manti Temple, Letterpress Copybooks, 53, Church History Library.

74. Weibye, Day Book 4, 191–92, Church History Library.

75. Sanpete Stake General Minutes, November 18, 1877, 7, Church History Library.

76. Ibid., November 3, 1877, 19, Church History Library.

77. Ibid.

78. Manti Temple, Letterpress Copybooks, 62, Church History Library.

79. Ibid., 78–79.

80. Sanpete Stake General Minutes, May 20 and 21, 1882, 78.

81. Ibid., November 15 and 16, 1879, 50.

82. Ibid., August 13, 1881, 72.

83. Glen R. Stubbs, *Temple on a Hill: Manti Temple* (Rexburg, Idaho: Ricks College Press, 1988), 18.

84. Hamilton, *Nineteenth-Century Mormon Architecture and City Planning,* 51–52.

85. The best description of this journey is found in Talmage, *The House of the Lord,* 181–200.

86. Brown, " 'Temple Pro Tempore,' "54–66.

87. Manti Temple and Annex Additions and Alterations, 1982, Church History Library; Jensen and Oman, *C. C. A. Christensen,* 55–62; and Stubbs, *Temple on a Hill,* 30.

88. Manti Temple and Annex Additions and Alterations, 1982, Church History Library; Jensen and Oman, *C. C. A. Christensen,* 55–62; and Stubbs, *Temple on a Hill,* 30.

89. The room is shown in *The Manti Temple* (Manti, Utah: Manti Temple Centennial Committee, 1988), 100–101.

90. See ibid., 102–3. Images and descriptions of the Celestial Room in the Salt Lake Temple are found in Talmage, *The House of the Lord,* 189–91; and Hamilton, *The Salt Lake Temple,* 122–24.

91. The quote is from Brown, " 'Temple pro Tempore,' " 45.

92. *The Second Empire, 1852–1870: Art in France under Napoleon III* (Philadelphia: Philadelphia Museum of Art, 1978), 35–73.

93. This argument is based on Upton, *Holy Things and Profane,* 101–62.

94. Sandra Dawn Brimhall and Mark D. Curtis, "The Gardo House," in Whitley, *Brigham Young's Homes,* 173–201.

95. See ibid., 176–77.

Conclusion

1. Edward Rothstein, "Utopia and Its Discontents," in *Visions of Utopia* (New York: Oxford University Press, 2003), 8.

2. Upton, "What the Mormon Cultural Landscape Can Teach Us," 25–27; Richard Jenkins, *Pierre Bourdieu,* rev. ed. (London: Routledge, 2002), 74–84; and Pierre Bourdieu, *Outline of a Theory of Practice* (New York: Cambridge University Press, 1977), 72–95.

3. Underwood, *The Millenarian World of Early Mormonism,* 104.

4. Rothstein, "Utopia and Its Discontents."

5. See Upton, "What the Mormon Cultural Landscape Can Teach Us," 26–27; Michael

Walzer, "Puritanism as a Revolutionary Ideology," *History and Theory* 3:1 (1963–64): 59–90; and Michael Walzer, *The Revolution of the Saints: A Study in the Origins of Radical Politics* (Cambridge, Mass.: Harvard University Press, 1965).

6. Underwood, *The Millenarian World of Early Mormonism,* 139–42.

7. Quoted in Flanders, *Nauvoo,* 204.

8. Manti Ward General Minutes, January 27, 1861, n.p., Church History Library.

9. Manti Ward Historical Record Book E, 1857–59, March 22, 1857, n.p., Church History Library.

10. Arthur M. Schlesinger Jr., *The Age of Jackson* (Boston: Little, Brown, 1953); Nathan O. Hatch, *The Democratization of American Christianity* (New Haven, Conn.: Yale University Press, 1989); Sean Wilentz, *The Rise of American Democracy: Jefferson to Lincoln* (New York: W.W. Norton, 2005); and Sellers, *The Market Revolution.*

11. Gordon S. Wood, *The Creation of the American Republic, 1776–1787* (1969; repr., New York: W. W. Norton, 1972).

12. Manti Ward General Minutes, June 2, 1861, n.p., Church History Library.

13. Manuscript History of the Manti Ward, entries for 1868, n.p., Church History Library.

14. Manti Ward General Minutes, January 7, 1860, n.p., Church History Library.

15. Weibye Day Book 2, May 20, 1868, n.p., Church History Library.

16. Manuscript History of the Moroni Ward, entries for 1871, n.p., Church History Library.

17. Peter Olsen Hansen, Diaries [ca.1850]—1872, manuscript, n.p., Church History Library.

18. Weibye, Day Book 7, 15, Church History Library.

19. Ibid., 26.

20. Weibye, Day Book 8, 42, Church History Library.

21. Mount Pleasant Ward Minutes, 1858–1868, 92–93, Church History Library.

22. Manti Ward General Minutes, March 8, 1857, n.p., Church History Library.

23. Manti Ward Historical Record Book E, May 24, 1857, n.p., Church History Library.

24. Weibye, Day Book 5, 13, Church History Library.

25. Weibye, Day Book 7, 45, Church History Library.

26. Ibid., 64.

27. Manti Ward General Minutes, June 10, 1855, n.p., Church History Library.

28. Manti Ward Historical Record Book E, February 14, 1859, n.p., Church History Library.

29. Manti Ward General Minutes, March 8, 1857, n.p., Church History Library.

30. Manuscript History of the Mount Pleasant Ward, entries for 1859, n.p., Church History Library.

31. Manti Ward General Minutes, June 30, 1861, n.p., Church History Library.

32. Manti Ward General Minutes, August 11, 1861, n.p., Church History Library.

33. Manti Ward Historical Record Book E January 15, 1859, n.p., Church History Library.

34. Mount Pleasant Ward Minutes, 1858–1868, 104, Church History Library.

35. Sanpete Stake General Minutes, November 18, 1877, 10–11, Church History Library.

36. Manuscript History of the Mount Pleasant Ward, entry under "History," n.p., Church History Library.

INDEX

Acord, Nancy, 173
Adam-ondi-Ahman, 5, 33
adobe, 103, 107, 110, 218; common bond, 104
Allen, Joseph, 140, 263
Allred, David, 114; house of, 115
Allred, Elizabeth "Betsy" Parks, 110, 170
Allred, Elizabeth Brough, 110, 170, 173
Allred, Isaac, 53, 57
Allred, James A., 38, 49, 50, 51, 108; I-house of, 109, 110
Allred, Redick R., 38, 57, 164
Allred, Reuben, 47, 57–58, 148
Allred's Settlement, 50; plat of, 53; reconstruction of, 51, 52
Andersen, William, 201, 230, 231
Anderson, George Edward: photos by, 25, 62, 65, 86, 177, 197, 204, 234, 241, 259, 265
Andrew, Laurel, 257
Angell, Truman O., Sr., 99, 251, 253, 257, 258, 259; meetinghouses and, 212; Salt Lake City Tabernacle and, 122, 210, 212, 254; Young and, 252, 254
antipolygamy laws, 15
architecture: domestic, 93–94, 96; main street, 181, 182; nonresidential, 182; polygamous, 135, 138, 139, 163; Relief Society, 276; religious, 209, 217; residential, 94; temple, 241; undifferentiated/differentiated, 182
Arrington, Leonard, 9
ashlar stonework: photo of, 104
Axelsen, Morton, 158, 232
axial order, 175, 176, 177, 213, 214, 217

baptism, 4, 188, 189, 248, 249
baptismal houses, 188
barns, 87, 88–90
baroque classicism, 272–73
Barton, William K., 231–32, 235, 280, 281
Beck, Hans, 56
Beck, Sarah, 305n59
Beehive House, 97, 99, 125, 135; photo of, 100
Behunin, Isaac, 47, 48, 51, 80, 83; family lot of, 84
Benson, Ezra T., 20, 21
Berntsen, Christian, 154, 167, 230, 232, 233
Bimeler, Joseph, 295n28
Black, George, 38, 52
Black Hawk War, 46
blessings, 19–20
Book of Mormon, 1, 2, 36
Boston: plan of, 29
Bradley, George W., 75, 234; on house building, 103; Moroni and, 55
Brady, L. S.: on blessings, 19
Brady, Lindsay, 75
Braithwaite, George, 157, 167
Breinholt, Jens Christian, 123
brick, 102, 103, 104
British Mission, 7
Brown, James C., 204, 279
Brown, Lisle, 253, 254
building materials, 101–3
buildings: adobe, 218; city, 194; civic, 178, 197; commercial, 180, 183, 199–208; congregational, 314n19; didactic value of, 239; industrial, 67; inventing, 209; main street, 184–208; multipurpose, 217; religious, 29, 178, 180, 183, 210; secular, 183
Bushman, Richard, 30, 32
Butleigh Court: alterations to, 96

Campbellites (followers of Alexander Campbell), 5
Canal Creek, 47, 50, 56, 57; photo of, 78
Candland, David, 37, 56, 105; quote of, 23; shingle and sawmill of, 86
Cannon, George Q., 62, 271
capitalism, 65, 67, 68, 79, 107
celestial kingdom, 248, 249, 251, 266
celestial marriage, 6, 8, 10, 21, 134, 292n18
Celestial Room, 250, 254, 270, 272, 278, 319n90; photo of, 272
Central School, 196, 204
Chapman, Welcome, 19, 54, 236–37, 281; on house building, 93
Chase, John D., 68; on appointments, 22
Chester, 56, 165; growth of, 57, 58; map of, 57
Christensen, C. C. A., 27, 228
Christensen, Jacob, 154, 155
Christensen, N. L., 160, 262, 280
Christoffersen, Soren, 206
Christopffersen, Ane, 160
Christopherson, Hans Peter: house of, 205
churches, 189–90, 210, 226–27, 229–35
Church of Christ, 1
Church of Jesus Christ of Latter-day Saints. *See* Mormon Church
City Creek, 35, 45, 80
city halls, 178, 194–96, 195
City of Zion, 13, 25, 114, 163, 181, 278, 283; building, 4, 10, 12, 16, 21, 27, 33, 46–47, 63, 107; consumer culture and, 275; cultural drift of, 183; gender relations in, 162; landscape of, 2, 3, 8, 9, 11, 124, 133, 208, 217, 270, 272, 277, 279; meritocratic nature of, 92; plan of, 30–31, 32–33, 120; plat of, 28, 34, 46, 82; population density of, 28; revision of, 38; social world of, 274
Clawson, James: house of, 114, 115
Clay County: resettlement in, 32
co-ops, 192–93, 202, 203, 204, 207; signs of, 207
cohabitation, 139–41, 143–45, 147
collective spirit, 66, 67, 92, 108
community: boundaries, 11; corporate, 183; engagement, 121; identity of, 195; life, 41; secular, 183; work, 73
community centers, 208
Cooledge, Oscar F., 281
cooperation, 65, 67, 80, 200, 202–3, 206, 207, 208, 283; capitalism and, 68; limits of, 81; Mormon, 201; tithe-based, 236
Cox, Amanda B., 49, 218
Cox, Cordelia Morley, 139, 141
Cox, Emeline Whiting, 139, 140, 149
Cox, Emma Petersen, 141; house of, 142
Cox, Frederick Walter, Sr., 148, 168, 201, 282; house of, 139–40, 141, 142
Cox, Isaiah, 60, 75
Cox, Orville Sutherland, 140, 218
Cox, Theressa, 141
Cramer, Christopher, 160, 168
Crawford, Cecelia Sharp, 148; house of, 149
Crawford, Elizabeth Snow, 148; house of, 150
Crawford, James, 201, 230, 231
Crawford, John, 148, 232; house and lots of, 149, 150
Creation Room, 250, 254, 268, 269
crossroads urban settlement pattern, 85
cross-wing houses, 85, 122, 123, 124

Davies, Douglas, 9; on exaltation, 18
Davis, Thomas: family lot and granary of, 91
decorative painting, 131
Dehlin, Paul, 306
DeMill, Freeborn, 19
Deseret News, 81, 103, 191, 193, 204, 219; advertisement in, 52; on Candland, 86; on co-op, 202; on Ephraim, 77, 226, 282; on Female Relief Society, 168; on Fort Ephraim, 37; letters to, 78, 79; on Manti, 238, 279; on Moroni, 234, 280; on Mount Pleasant, 196–97, 205, 283; quote from, 23, 209, 240; on schools, 197; on Springtown, 51
design, 210, 242, 254; differentiation by, 124–25, 127–31; diversity of, 107–8, 110–16; options, 115
Disciples of Christ, 5
divorce, 6, 102, 143, 145, 164, 307n28
Doctrine and Covenants of the Church of Jesus Christ of Latter-day Saints: quote from, 240
Dorius, Carl, 106, 226

Eagle Emporium: Manti Branch of, 199
Eliade, Mircea, xxiii, 10–11
Ellis, J. T., 52, 81
End Times, 3–8, 16, 209, 277, 278

Endowment House, 153, 160, 252, 257, 268; described, 253–54; ordinance work in, 270; photo of, 253; plan for, 253
endowment rooms, 255, 266, 268
endowments, 248, 249, 250, 252, 253; temple, 8, 266, 273
Ephraim, 20, 37, 47, 48, 54, 73, 82, 86, 107, 128, 209, 262, 263, 264, 282; activity zones in, 180; block arrangement for, 46; building in, 49; city hall, 194; co-op store in, 202; growth of, 53, 194; map of, 49; meeting hall at, 222; meetinghouse at, 218; Methodists in, 189; model for, 39–40; population of, 77; schools in, 196; social hall in, 192; wards for, 42
Ephraim Relief Society, 167, 170–71
Ephraim Tabernacle, 167, 226, 227, 228, 230, 231, 232, 239; photo of, 228; reconstruction drawing of, 227
"Ephraim Utah Block Parade" (Anderson), 204
equality, 66, 68–69, 279, 282–83
Everyday Architecture in the Mid-Atlantic (Lanier and Herman), 116
exaltation, 6, 10, 242, 265, 270; salvation and, 9, 17, 18, 19; works and, 20

Fairview, 54; co-op store in, 202; described, 175
Fairview Meetinghouse, 223, 225; reconstruction drawing of, 223
faith: works and, 17, 19
farming, 48, 73, 81, 87, 106
Far West, 5, 33, 139
Faux, Jabez: house of, 120
Faux, Nathan, 234, 235
faux graining, 131, 132
faux painting, 131, 132
federal, 93, 97, 110, 111, 115, 143, 213, 244
Female Relief Society, 168, 171, 193, 203; granary, 205; hall, 173, 206
fences, 45; picket, 86–87, 121
First Congregational Church, 210
First Vision, 1, 227; painting of, 228
fluidity, 152–58, 160–62
flume, water, 78
Folsom, William H.: building by, 212, 216, 235, 259, 261, 263; design by, 232, 272; Manti Temple and, 240, 257, 271; salary for, 264
Fort Ephraim. *See* Ephraim
forts, 38, 39, 45, 48, 54, 107
Fountain Green, 23, 115, 129, 150, 151, 191, 217; founding of, 54, 55, 63
Fourth General Epistle of the Church, 37, 63
Fox, Edward W., 201, 204, 206; store of, 206, 207
Fox, Jesse W., 259, 271
Francaviglia, Richard, 90

Garden Room, 250, 254, 268, 269
Gardo House, 240, 271, 272; Celestial Room of, 272
General Authorities, 42, 69
genteel tradition, 32, 94–97, 99, 101–3, 105–6
Gentiles, 5, 10, 16, 45, 67, 178, 183, 189, 216; antipolygamy, 162; conflict with, 6, 7, 23, 243
Georgian style, 96, 99, 115, 125, 139, 196, 244, 253
Glassie, Henry, xxiv, 285
Gospel of Works, 22, 36, 106, 277, 278, 279, 284; cooperative society and, 67
Gothic style, 93, 122, 123, 190, 230, 244, 248, 252, 254
Gothic Revival style, 115, 148, 157, 189
graining, 131, 132
Great Basin, 8, 14, 17, 27, 60, 103, 124–25, 238
Great Salt Lake Valley, 23, 35, 251
Great Tabernacle, 212–13
Greaves, Peter, 204, 221; house of, 123, 124, 132
Greek Revival style, 93, 97, 110, 111, 115, 118, 145, 191, 193, 194, 197, 244
Green, John: house of, 94, 95
grid, 30, 41, 52
Guymon, James, 149, 150, 151; house of, 151
Guymon, Martha, 150–51
Guymon, Mary Ann Couch, 149, 150, 151
Guymon, Mary Boden, 150
Guymon, Rhoda Leach, 150, 151

Hall, Richard, 167, 230, 233; land of, 42
hall-parlor houses, 112, 117–18, 119, 145, 147, 148; floor plan and photo of, 112
halls, 206; city, 178, 194–96; described, 181–82; meeting, 217, 222–25; social, 178, 191–93, 224

Hals, Hans Jensen, 229
Hambleton-Potter mill site, 53
Hansen, Jens, 231, 232, 280
Hansen, Joseph, 76, 107
Hansen, Peter Olsen, 221, 280
Hardy, Aaron, 135
Hardy, Amy, 135
Hardy, Emma, 135
harmonists, 29, 295n28
Herman, Bernard L., xxv, 116, 287
Hitchings, Francis: house of, 97, 99
Holy Ghost, 248, 249
Holy of Holies, 242, 243, 245, 246, 250, 254
Homestead Act (1862), 56
Hougaard, John, 78, 197
House of the Lord, 242, 257, 270, 271, 273
House of the Lord, The (Talmage), 248
houses, 98; adobe, 110; baptismal, 188; building, 87, 93, 94, 103, 105–6, 107, 108, 113, 122, 148; closed-plan, 116, 117; council, 178, 180, 191, 194, 195, 204, 209, 213, 219, 220, 221, 222, 229; cross-wing, 85, 122, 123, 124; Danish-style, 112; designing/views of, 85, 115; French, 122; Georgian, 97, 101; hall-parlor, 112, 117–18, 119, 145, 147, 148; I-houses, 101, 108, 109, 110, 115, 120, 129–30, 145, 148, 149, 157, 168, 169; immigrant, 107, 111–12; inequality of, 124; log, 102; Mormon, 106–8, 110–25, 127–31, 133, 135; one-on-one, 139; open-plan, 107, 116–17, 119, 120, 122, 123; peasant-type, 112–13; polygamous, 134, 135, 136, 143, 147, 148–51, 162–73, 276; Scandinavian, 147; separate, 148–51; siting, 83, 85; temple-form, 111; three-part villas, 113, 114, 147; workers, 119, 264
Hurst, Philip, 105
Hyde, Ann Eliza Vickers, 143–44, 147
Hyde, Elizabeth Gallier, 144, 147
Hyde, Julia Reinert, 144; house of, 145
Hyde, Marinda Johnson, 143–44, 145
Hyde, Mary Ann Price, 143, 144, 147; polygamy and, 169, 170; quote of, 134; Relief Society and, 166, 169, 170, 171, 173
Hyde, Orson, 20, 22, 42, 62, 73–74, 94, 143, 148, 172, 208, 230, 281, 312n50; death of, 147; family lot of, 84; family of, 144, 145; on house building, 105–6; house of, 144, 146, 205; on industriousness, 282; labor tithing and, 81; on legitimate power, 43; meetinghouse and, 224, 229, 263; on mobility, 73; Mount Pleasant and, 225; on opposition store, 206–7; pasture of, 83; profit making and, 68; quote of, 64; Relief Society and, 166–67, 173; Spring City and, 82; tithing and, 258, 262; on water/settlers, 80; Zion and, 279
Hyde, Sophia Lyon, 144, 147

I-houses, 108, 110, 115, 120, 129–30, 145, 148, 149, 157, 168; described, 101; photo of, 109
identity: community, 95; cultural, 11, 74, 77, 93, 107, 108; group, 209; Mormon, 10, 209; secular, 183
immigrants, 7, 23, 75, 108; arrival of, 95; houses for, 107, 111–12
independence, 5, 32, 240, 317n13
individualism, 17, 67, 68, 92
inspirationists, 29, 295n28
Instruction (Terrestrial) Room, 254
Iron Mission, 150
Irons, John, 234
irrigation, 24, 79; photo of, 78
Ivie, James, 53

Jackson, George, 201
Jackson County, 5, 11, 12, 110, 149, 177; expulsion from, 32; restoration and, 14–15; sacred spaces in, 16
Jennings, William, 199, 271
Jensen, Hans, 166, 188, 232, 233, 281
Jensen, Jens Christian, 147; house of, 20, 147
Jensen, Jens Severine: house of, 114, 115; lot of, 82
Jensen, John Henry, 20
Jensen, Karen Nielson, 20
Jensen, Soren: house of, 119
John Frank Allred School, 197, 198, 205, 312n50
Jones, Dan, 19, 20–21, 68
Jones, Edward, 226, 227, 232, 235
Jones, Elijah, 74
Jones, James N., 21, 45, 54, 74, 105, 223, 237; labor tithing and, 81; resignation of, 224; on watermasters, 80

Kammen, Michael, 92
Kemp, Charles, 234
Kimball, Heber C., 69; on house building, 93; Manti and, 38; Young and, 36–37, 209
Kingdom of God, 23, 54, 270, 275; building, 78, 81, 106, 280
Kirkman, John, 280
Kirtland, 5, 14, 32, 110, 111, 143, 240, 317n13
Kirtland Temple, 243, 247, 251, 252, 257; described, 245; finishing, 244; innovations at, 248; longitudinal/transverse sections of, 246; photo of, 244; pulpit plan for, 252
Kjar, J. Christian, 156, 160
Kjar, Magrethe Weibye, 156, 160
Klingensmith, Philip: on blessings, 20
Kofford, Paul, 125; house of, 127–28

land, 68–69, 72–78; distribution of, 41–42, 294n5; occupation of, 23; public, 72, 294n5; sales, 72, 73; speculation, 72
landscape, 31–32, 68, 123, 162, 191, 228, 241, 278, 282; American, 16, 17, 284; architectural, 120, 289n4; axial, 175, 176; City of Zion, 2, 3, 8, 9, 11, 124, 133, 208, 217, 270, 272, 277, 279; common, 23; definitions of, 290n13; End Times, 3–8; evolution of, 8–17; housing, 107, 114; Mormon, 8–17, 32, 63, 93, 242, 266, 274–75, 283–84; nonaxial, 175, 176–77; organization of, 176; polygamous, 138, 165; production of, 277; sacred, 13, 15–16, 63, 208; secular, 15–16, 17, 208; of works, 17–22
Lanier, Gabrielle, 116
Larsen, Annie, 173
Larsen, Christian A., 106, 203
Larsen, Peter, 154
Law of Consecration and Stewardship, 66, 228
Leone, Mark, 68–69
Lion House, 135, 136
Little Stone Fort, 140
Llewellyn, Ann, 129
Llewellyn, Rees R.: house of, 129–30, 131; social hall and, 191–92
Logan, 11, 200, 255, 273; layout of, 59; liquor at co-op, 200
Logan Temple, 177, 251, 255, 257, 258, 268; building, 61; dedication of, 16; illustration of, 256; photo of, 61
Longstreth, Richard, 207
Lowery, Abner, 193
Lowery, John, 19, 64, 75, 80, 81, 236; on house building, 93; Manti and, 43
Luke, William, 158, 195
Lyman, Amasa, 281
Lynch, Kevin, 208

Madsen, Peter, 128, 226, 236
Maiben, Andrew, 232, 233
Maiben, John B., 187, 188, 222, 230, 281; on meetinghouse, 236
Main Street (Manti): photo of, 206
Main Street (Mount Pleasant), 178, 200
Main Street (Spring City), 222
main streets: buildings on, 184–208; Mormon, 175, 182, 183, 238, 276
Major, Ellen, 172; house of, 65, 117–18
Major, William, 172; house of, 65, 117–18
Manti, 11, 68, 140, 204, 257, 273; activity zones in, 180; agricultural census for, 42; block arrangement for, 46; civic buildings in, 178; ethnic makeup of, 75–76, 78; fence issue in, 45; founding of, 43, 63; growth of, 46–58, 194; irrigation system in, 79; layout of, 38, 59; lots in, 71, 72, 76; lots/polygamous families in, 138; map of, 181; plan for, 41, 178, 180; plat for, 39; prominent homes/institutions in, 71; reconstruction of, 40; schools in, 196, 197–98; setback zoning ordinance in, 44; settlement of, 37, 85; store, 199
Manti Baptismal House: sketch of, 188
Manti City Council, 43, 44, 45, 297n57
Manti City Hall, 195
Manti Co-operative Mercantile Institution, 206, 207
Manti Council House, 180, 191, 194, 204, 209, 219, 220, 221–22, 229
Manti Female Relief Society Store (and Hall), 168, 169
Manti Hay Land and Forage Company, 79
Manti Herald and Sanpete Advertiser, 46, 199
Manti Mercantile Company, 205
Manti North Ward, 75, 201
Manti North Ward School, 180, 197–98
Manti Relief Society, 160, 166–67, 168

Manti South Ward Meeting House, 18
Manti South Ward Relief Society Hall, 166
Manti South Ward School, 198
Manti Tabernacle, 229, 230, 231, 239; photo of, 23, 62, 235
Manti Temple, 167, 177, 251, 255, 257, 263; architectural finishes at, 269; building, 61, 240, 241, 258, 259, 261, 262, 265–66, 268, 270–73; Celestial Room of, 272; dedication of, 16; illustration of, 256, 260; interior of, 267; mural rooms at, 268, 269; photo of, 62, 177, 241, 259, 265, 271, 283; site for, 61–62
Manti Temple Office: revenue received at, 261
Manti Tithing Office, 153, 186; photo of, 187; receivables for, 184
Manti Ward Minutes: quote from, 93
masonry: art of, 104
material culture, 22, 77, 107, 116, 275, 281
Maylett, William F., 201, 232
McMillan, Duncan, 189
meeting halls, 217, 222–25
meetinghouse blocks, 74, 83
meetinghouses, 57, 62, 67, 80, 167, 175, 177, 180, 185, 186, 189, 209, 210, 214, 216, 217–19, 221–22, 263, 270, 276; building, 224, 225, 226, 227, 229, 230, 233, 234, 235, 236, 237, 238, 239; development of, 217, 222; eastern, 212; hall-type, 213; New England, 219; photo of, 228; popular, 225; side-door, 227; tabernacles and, 314n19; transverse-plan, 221, 227
mercantile stores, 202, 205, 206, 207
Merriam, A. E., 195, 196
Methodist churches, 189
Metz, Christian, 295n28
Mexican War (1846–1848), 294n5
Mickelsen, Calvin, 305n59
Mies van de Rohe, Ludwig, 242
millennialism, 3, 4, 15, 16, 276, 277, 278
Millet, Artemus, 244, 251
Moffit, A. J., 153, 201
Molter, Peter: family lot of, 90
monogamy, 6, 134, 139, 307n28
Morley, Isaac, 47, 50, 139, 140; Manti and, 43; Sanpete Valley and, 36
Morley, James T. S., 50, 75
Morley Settlement, 139
Mormon (father of Moroni), 2
Mormon Church, 1, 284, 295n6; forms of, 21–22; survey and, 294n5
Mormonism, 4, 8–9, 15, 64, 183; capitalist system and, 65; importance of temple-based rituals, 9, 10, 17; initial formulation of, 2; material world of, 284; myths of, 17; Protestant-millenarian, 9; Republicanism and, 279; sacred world of, 16; social world of, 277
Mormons: inferiority complex of, 103, 105; mainstream society and, 205; Puritans and, 18, 19
Moroni, 2, 37, 57, 193, 218; meetinghouse, 229, 234; mercantile house, 202; photo of, 25; plan for, 55; settlement of, 54, 55, 63; social hall, 192; tithing office, 186; water for, 56
Moroni Tabernacle, 235, 239
Mount Nebo, 25
Mount Pleasant, 44, 56, 57, 73, 81, 105, 110, 111, 152, 153, 165, 185, 189; activity zones in, 180; downtown of, 178, 199; founding of, 42–43, 54; growth of, 194; population of, 54; religious zone of, 185; schools in, 196–97; settlement of, 52; social hall in, 191, 192; water from, 45
Mount Pleasant Meetinghouse, 224, 225
Mount Pleasant Tithing Yard, 185
Munk, Christian, 219
Musser, A. M., 62, 226, 227

Nauvoo, 11, 13, 14, 16, 111, 125, 134, 139, 140, 143, 165; abandoning, 7; building, 66; emergence of, 5–6; endowment ceremony at, 253; Georgian houses in, 97; lessons learned from, 33; multiple-wife households in, 306n2; patriarchal marriage in, 6–7; tabernacle in, 212
Nauvoo Expositor, 6
Nauvoo House, 14, 33, 278
Nauvoo Temple, 247, 249, 250, 251, 254, 257; building, 246, 247, 270; ordinances at, 248; pulpit plan for, 252; ritual spaces in, 250; transverse section of, 248
Nelson, Lowry: on farmland, 39–40
neoclassicism, 30, 31, 94, 95, 96, 100, 107, 112, 113, 133, 193; acceptance of, 123; Federal, 97; Mormon, 97, 99, 101; popularity of, 108

New Jerusalem, 2, 4, 5, 8, 10, 14, 27
Nielsen, Jacob, 83; family lot of, 84
Nielson, Christian, 37–38
nonaxial order, 175, 176–77, 178, 180, 183

Old Tabernacle, 221, 239; reconstruction drawing of, 211
Oldham, John: house of, 112, 118
Oldham, Sarah, 112, 118
Olsen, Andrew: house of, 132
Olsen, Christian Nielson, 127–28
Olsen, Frederick, 57, 74, 173
Olsen, Hans Peter: house of, 131, 132
Olsen, Mary: polygamy and, 169–70
Olsen, Steven, 12–13, 65
opposition stores, 206, 207
Order of Enoch, 66
ordinances, 189, 249, 251
Osborne, William, 83; family lot of, 84
Otterson, Hans, 152; house of, 113–14
outbuildings, 87, 88, 90

Padris, John: house of, 206
Parry, Edward L., 60, 259, 262, 264
Parson, Henry, 230, 232, 233
patriarchal society, 6–7, 162–63, 276
Patten, John, 42, 278, 279
Peacock, George, 193, 205, 221, 229, 282; on house building, 103
Penn, William, 30, 34, 35
Petersen, Andrew, 224; house of, 136, 137
Petersen, Iver, 83; family lot of, 84
Petersen, Marinus, 83; family lot of, 84
Petersen, S. C.: house of, 86
Peterson, Canute, 42, 73, 139, 226, 227, 238, 263; on co-op stores, 203; house of, 125, 126, 128; on merchandise/manufacturing, 105; on tithing/temple donations, 262
Petty, Albert, 52, 55
Philadelphia, 33; plan for, 29, 31, 35; urbanization and, 296n34
picket fences, 86–87, 121
Pilgrim's Progress, 266; diagrammatic representation of, 266
Pitman, Leon, 107–8
planners: decisions facing, 276
plans, 9, 35, 258; city, 30–31, 32–33, 120; closed, 116, 117; open, 107, 116–17, 119, 120, 122, 123; transverse, 221, 227
polygamy, 6, 8, 56, 141, 143, 148, 162, 276, 292n18, 306n2, 307n28; architecture of, 135, 138, 139, 163; gender roles and, 87, 162; introduction of, 6, 162–63; opposition to, 15, 134; participation in, 15, 72–73, 134, 136; preserving, 162, 163; trials of, 163, 164–65, 169–70, 173–74; women's status and, 173–74
Poulsen, Peter, 160
Poulson, Lars: granary of, 91
Pratt, Orson, 27, 67
Pratt, Parley P., 36
Presbyterians, 178, 180; churches by, 189, 190
Price, John, 54, 223
priesthood, 4, 27, 243, 245
principle, 6, 15, 134, 292n18
property, 86; owning, 64, 66, 67, 171; private, 68
Provo Agricultural Society, 221
Provo Tabernacle, 238, 239
public good, 279–80
public works, 18, 21, 60, 67, 258–65; impact of, 280
Puritans: Mormons and, 18, 19

Quinn, George, 204; store of, 196, 204
Quorum of the Twelve, 7, 42, 143

Raber, Michael, 47, 50
rafters: collared common, 205; purlin, 205
rag carpet bee, 165
railroads, 15, 16, 108, 122, 166, 183, 200
Rees, John, 54, 55
Reid, William T., 201, 233, 281
Relief Society, 165, 166–67, 168, 170, 172–73, 202, 276. *See also* Female Relief Society
Reorganized Church of Jesus Christ of Latter Day Saints, 134, 246
Reps, John, 24, 25
restoration, 2, 4, 6, 7, 15, 22, 248, 249, 265, 278
revelations, 2, 8, 242, 249, 278; doctrine of continuing, 277
Richards, Franklin D., 62; quote of, 274
Rigdon, Sidney, 243
rituals, 8, 210, 249, 250; temple, 9, 10, 17, 266
Robison, Elwin, 244
roof construction: study of, 205
Rothstein, Edward, 274, 276

St. George, 11, 59–60, 240–41, 258; architectural changes in, 217; layout of, 59; meetinghouses in, 214; photo of, 61
St. George Tabernacle, 214, 216–21, 226, 238, 239
St. George Temple, 59, 177, 251, 257, 259; building, 60, 61; dedication of, 16; designing, 254; transverse section of, 255
Salt Lake City, 11, 27, 33, 34, 37, 38, 55, 56, 75, 140; anomaly of, 17; block arrangement for, 46; building, 35–36; cultural core in, 182; function of, 178; layout of, 34, 34, 59; plan for, 35; principal activity zones in, 179; prominent homes/institutions in, 70; social topography of, 300n20, 310n5
Salt Lake City Tabernacle, 122, 212–13, 214, 216, 240
Salt Lake City Temple, 16, 59, 177, 241, 251, 272; plan for, 258; rendering of, 252
Salt Lake Council House, 178, 195
Salt Lake Theater, 178, 240
salvation, 265; exaltation and, 9, 17, 18, 19
Sandstrom, Eric, 114; house of, 115
Sanpete County co-op, 199
Sanpete County Courthouse, 178, 193, 194, 195
Sanpete Scientific Literary Society, 221
Sanpete Temple District, 260
Sanpete Valley, 1, 19, 22, 50, 62, 73, 116, 120, 121, 127, 130, 131; building materials in, 101–3; domestic architecture of, 93–94, 96; growth of, 23, 37–38, 47; history of, 58; houses in, 123–24; landscape of, 63, 266, 278, 282; photo of, 24, 25; section drawing of, 275; settlement of, 35, 36, 37, 41, 62, 75; temple construction in, 258; towns in, 36–46, 63, 69, 82, 178, 184, 237
Sanpitch Indians, 24, 224
Sanpitch River, 24, 39, 56
Scandinavian Mission, 7
schools, 180, 204, 205, 218, 312n50; building, 196–99
sealing, 248, 249, 250
Second Coming, 3, 4, 5, 16, 65, 243, 266, 277
Seely, William S., 54, 73, 224–25, 382
settlement patterns, 37; agricultural, 26; grid, 52; Mormon, 25, 26, 28, 275
settlements, 36, 63, 88
Seventh Ward Meetinghouse, 214, 215
Shipps, Jan, 4, 10, 237
Shomaker, Jezrell, 43, 75, 199
Smith, Albert, 153, 154
Smith, George A., 51, 60
Smith, Joseph, Jr., 1, 22, 27, 33, 134, 249, 251, 252, 257, 276; arrest of, 5, 7; celestial marriage and, 6; City of Zion and, 13, 28, 46–47; communitarian ethic and, 65; death of, 7, 143, 246; First Vision of, 227; Law of Consecration and Stewardship and, 66; Law of Tithing and, 66; Mormon state and, 6; Moroni and, 2; plans and, 9, 30, 177; plat by, 33, 34; revelations of, 242, 289n5; style and, 33; tabernacles and, 210, 212; temples and, 210, 242, 243–44, 245, 246
Smith, Joseph, Sr., 1
Snow, Erastus, 62, 68, 282; epistle by, 214, 216; meetinghouse and, 233
Snow, Lorenzo, 62, 282, 283
Snow, Warren S., 188, 200, 262, 278, 281, 282
social equality, 66, 68–69
social halls, 178, 191–93, 224
social molecule, 117–18, 119
social order, 22, 67, 273, 277
social structure, 27, 30, 116–17
social topography, 11, 300n20, 310n5
social world, 16, 277, 279
Solomon, King, 242, 245, 246
Solomon's Temple, 242, 249
spaces: domestic, 165; public, 29; ritual, 250; sacred, 16, 241
Spanish Fork Canyon Road: building, 81
spatial conventions, 11, 117–18, 175, 183
spirituality, 2, 21, 22, 65, 248, 258
Spring City, 38, 47, 48, 52, 73, 77, 82, 108, 114, 127; co-op store in, 202; ethnic distribution in, 77; growth of, 50; historical records of, 188; irrigation ditches in, 78; lots in, 57; Methodists in, 189; plat of, 53; reconstruction of, 51; schools in, 197; settlement of, 49–50; stewardship typology of, 84; tax assessment in, 301n62
Spring City Female Relief Society Hall, 172
Spring City meetinghouse, 222, 223, 225
Spring City Ward, 74, 188
Stake Conference, 200, 201, 207, 238, 262, 263, 264
Staker, Alma, 110, 111

Staker, Elizabeth, 110, 111
Staker, Nathan, 110
Stevens, Augusta Dorius, 47, 163, 164
stewardship, 66, 67, 228; family, 81–83, 85–88, 90–91; typology of, 84
streetscape: Sanpete Valley, 200
Study of the Articles of Faith, A (Talmage), 17
style, 33; as communicative act, 32; difference/otherness and, 32; as dramatic concept, 32; landscape, 31; uses of, 210, 212–14, 216–17, 236–38
symmetry, 95, 96, 101, 112, 114, 122, 123

tabernacles, 15, 60, 61, 167, 180, 214, 217, 222, 232, 233, 276; building, 230, 239; designing, 210; meetinghouses and, 314n19
Talmage, James, 17, 242–43, 248
Taylor, John, 62, 122, 235, 257–58; Folsom and, 264; leadership of, 240; quote of, 1, 175
telestial (level of heaven), 9, 249
Telestial Room, 250, 269
temple block, 58, 69, 219, 230, 232
Temple Square, 14, 59, 69, 143, 177, 178, 211, 213, 221, 253; photo of, 253
temples, 27, 67, 177, 183, 208, 209, 214, 278; basic form for, 241; building, 16, 61, 66, 242–43, 246, 249, 251, 258, 260, 263; as collective symbols, 241–42; fronts, 96; in Illinois, 246–51; latter-day, 242–55, 257–58; in Missouri and Ohio, 243–46; siting, 59, 61; in Utah, 251–55, 257–58
terrestrial, 9–10, 248, 249
Terrestrial Room, 250, 268–70. *See also* Instruction (Terrestrial) Room
Thatcher, Moses, 200
Thespian Society, 221
Thirteenth Ward Assembly Rooms, 213, 214
Thompson, John, 125, 127
Thomsen, Anders, 73
three-part villas, 113, 114, 147
Tillinghast, Joseph: house of, 97, 98
tithing, 66, 67, 68, 208, 214, 236, 261, 263, 311n14; in-kind, 183, 185; labor, 81, 225, 258, 262; paying, 184–85, 262, 280
Tithing Office, 54, 154, 178, 184–89, 262
towns, 85; development of, 25, 56, 87; differences in, 45–46; ethnic, 76–77; planning, 58, 95
trusses: king-post, 205; scissor, 205
Tucker, Amasa, 224
Tucker, Emma Jane, 106, 164
Tuttle, Lola: house of, 120, 121
Tuttle, Luther, 201, 204, 206, 207, 230, 232; house of, 120, 121; store of, 206; store sign of, 207

Underwood, Grant, 3, 276, 277
United Order, 36, 66, 80, 187, 199, 276
Upton, Dell, xxiv, xxv, 47, 117, 240, 287
Utes, 37, 51, 107, 147

Vance, Isaac: house of, 99, 101
Van Cott, John, 62, 201
Van Houghton, Peter, 189–90
villages, 295n6; medieval, 29; patterns of, 29; settlement of, 28
villas, three-part, 113–14, 147
Vision of Enoch, 65
Vorhees, Isaac, 153, 154

wainscotting, faux-grained, 132
Wakara (Walker), Chief, 36
Wales, 55; founding of, 54; population of, 76–77
wall stenciling, 132
Walter, Frederick, 140
Ward, William, 252
Wareham, James, 199, 237, 281
Wasatch Plateau, 23, 102
Wasatch Range, 23, 25
water: policies, 45, 300n39; rights, 78, 79–80; sources, 43–44; work and, 78–81
Weeks, William, 246, 247, 248, 249, 251
Weibye, Jens Christian Andersen, 62, 86, 136, 153, 154, 155, 157, 161, 162, 163, 189, 193, 206, 229, 232, 233, 237, 259–60, 262, 263, 264, 281; appointment of, 230; co-op and, 201; house of, 152, 155, 156, 158, 159, 160, 161; on Hyde, 144; journal of, 188, 201; on Manti Council House, 221–22; Relief Society and, 167, 168; telegram to, 184; temple sketch by, 260; tithing and, 186, 187, 280; on water, 80
Weibye, Maren Kirstine Gregersen, 153, 154, 156, 157, 162; death of, 160
Weibye, Sisilie Marie Pedersen, 152, 153, 154, 155, 156, 158, 160

Thomas Carter has been an architectural historian for almost four decades; he worked first with the Utah State Historic Preservation Office and then in the University of Utah's College of Architecture and Planning. His teaching and scholarship focus on the vernacular building traditions of the American West. Among his publications are *Utah's Historic Architecture: A Guide* (with Peter Goss), *Images of an American Land: Vernacular Architecture Studies in the Western United States*, and *Invitation to Vernacular Architecture: A Guide to the Study of Vernacular Buildings and Landscapes* (with Betsy Cromley). He is professor emeritus in the College of Architecture and Planning at the University of Utah.